AN
INTERPRETATION
OF
SHAKESPEARE

BY
HARDIN CRAIG

LUCAS BROTHERS PUBLISHERS
Columbia, Missouri

Copyright 1948
HARDIN CRAIG
Printed in U.S.A.

Reprinted by Lucas Brothers Publshers
Columbia, Missouri.

Preface

THIS book deals with the interpretation of Shakespeare. Because he lived so long ago, because he lived in a different age from ours, because the scope of his thought is so extraordinarily wide, and because his expression is often at once so condensed and so imaginative, Shakespeare needs a good deal of interpretation if he is to be understood and appreciated by modern readers. Nothing can be truly appreciated which is not understood. The author found out long ago as a teacher of Shakespeare that, if the persons he addressed, orally or in print, did not know enough for proper appreciation, there was only one thing to be done, namely, to tell them as clearly and kindly as he could what they needed to know. This book therefore, like others of his utterances about Shakespeare, contains a good deal of information.

What has just been said presupposes a rather interesting thing. It presupposes that Shakespeare's own meanings are much the most significant meanings for his plays as wholes and for passages, scenes, and characters within them. To occupy such a ground is, frankly, to attempt to see with Shakespeare's eyes and to know that those eyes were the eyes of an Elizabethan. This requires imaginative insight as well as knowledge, and these things the author of this book does not attribute to himself in any transcendent measure. He can plead only his study, his long experience, and his modest success. The book is perhaps prevailingly a piece of historical criticism.

But to seek out and to believe in original meanings and situations does not mean that we too are not alive and reasonable creatures. Shakespeare exists because he is able to please us, and when he comes to life he breathes with our breath. We read Shakespeare for what he may mean, or come to mean, to us, for the pleasure he may give us, and for the inspiration he is still capable of bringing about in our hearts and minds. This book is really about us. It attempts to attend, not only to interpretation, but to appreciation. Our age needs Shakespeare as a living part of its emotional and intellectual present.

Both these ends have been kept in mind from the beginning. The meanings of plays and of single scenes, issues of all sorts, have been explained and their qualities commented on and illustrated. There is much in this book which is here for the sake of appreciation only, and the tones and rhythms of plays have been preserved as far as the author's skill was adequate and space would permit.

There are certain things that have been written into the book. The first of these is the idea of the unity of Shakespeare. The author has striven to hear Shakespeare's voice amid the various voices of his characters, to discover his point of view (which turns out to be the point of view of humanity), and to learn his habits of thought and the architectonic quality of his art. The book is intended to be about Shakespeare, and it tries to stick to its subject.

It is also the belief of the author that Shakespeare was no mere imitator of his predecessors and contemporaries in the drama, but was an original creative artist. This belief has been written into the book. The author has tried to show how Shakespeare changed, enlarged, and re-created the drama of his age. Shakespeare was a great original thinker like Bacon. Among other things of lesser importance the author has, when confronted by difference of opinion as to both fact and interpretation, deliberately sought to support what seemed to him the most probable hypothesis. Controversial points have rarely been debated.

There are still many dark regions in Shakespeare. His more popular plays have been worked over and elucidated for centuries. It has seemed a useless thing to dwell at disproportionate length on such plays. But others of Shakespeare's plays are not at all well known. They have been considered inferior, as no doubt they are, to his greater masterpieces; but this does not mean that they are devoid of interest and significance. Most of these neglected plays are far greater than they are thought to be, and all of them have importance in building up a true image of the great dramatist. The neglect of these plays is due partly to an absurd tradition, coming perhaps from a misinterpretation of Ben Jonson, that Shakespeare was a very uneven genius, which is really not true. Confronted by this situation, the author decided that the book might be more useful and more original if it contented itself with briefer treatments of more familiar plays and took time to explore the darker regions. It turns out that these regions are not dark at all.

Another matter which has necessitated careful attention is this: There are few fields through which stalk more openly a band of vicious popular errors—wrong ideas about Shakespeare, misinterpretations of plays and characters, and misunderstandings of situations. The author has assaulted these marauders with some valiancy but no great hope of victory, for he realizes that Shakespeare belongs to the people and that they will probably continue to have the kind of Shakespeare they wish to possess.

Finally, as to the matter of doing a complete job in the treatment of Shakespeare, the thing is hopeless within the limits of a book many times longer than this. Therefore the author has not adopted a scheme of treating all the plays after a fixed pattern, but has preferred to approach each play as it seemed to him it might best and most appropriately be approached. This procedure may give the impression of lack of system, but it at least avoids a specious pretense of completeness.

As an editor of Shakespeare and a commentator on his works, the author is already on record with reference to many of the subjects considered in this book. He has exercised no care about noting quotations from himself. Nothing has been copied, but in some instances the same things in pretty much the same words have no doubt been said by the author elsewhere. In the first chapter are somewhat extensive excerpts from *The Enchanted Glass*. As to borrowings from other writers on Shakespeare, credit has been given for what the author has chosen to repeat, but he has not exercised any great care in citing works and pages, except in cases where it was thought the citation in question might be difficult to find. He has not given references for the commonplaces of fact and opinion which make up the vast body of Shakespeare scholarship.

The author wishes to make special acknowledgment of indebtedness to Professor Dwight L. Durling, Queens College, Flushing, New York, editorial adviser to The Dryden Press, whose editorial assistance has been invaluable, as have been his suggestions as to both matter and expression. He wishes also to thank Professor W. Leslie Garnett, Kent State University, Kent, Ohio, for her kindness in reading and commenting on the manuscript in its earlier form.

Shakespearean quotations are taken from the Globe text.

H. C.

Chapel Hill, North Carolina
April 1947

Table of Contents

AN INTERPRETATION

OF SHAKESPEARE

CHAPTER I

Shakespeare as an Elizabethan

A GREAT deal is definitely known about the life and dramatic career of William Shakespeare (1564-1616). Besides information derived from documents, from casual contemporary allusions, and from what might be called literary criticism, there is a considerable body of tradition, a good deal of it, however, late and unreliable. Manuscripts of some of Shakespeare's works and many documents containing personal information about him must have perished in the fire of London in 1666. However, the records of Stratford-on-Avon, where he spent his first and his last years, still remain. They give us about what we should expect. Indeed, we possess a far greater amount of actual information about Shakespeare than we do about most Elizabethans.

The dates for Shakespeare's birth, or rather his christening, and for his death are recorded in the baptismal and the burial registers of Stratford along with similar information about his brothers and sisters, his wife and children. Shakespeare was baptized on April 26, 1564, and died on April 23, 1616. A tradition says that he died on his birthday. The Episcopal Register of the diocese of Worcester records the issue of his marriage license and of the marriage bond. At Somerset House in London is to be found Shakespeare's will, dated March 25, 1616. Other records, of land that he bought and sold, lawsuits to which he was a party, tax returns, give information as to his financial resources and his activities as a citizen. Records of the theatrical company to which he belonged, especially as regards its various relations to the court, furnish much information covering Shakespeare's life as an actor and man of the theater.

The search for additional information about Shakespeare has been carried on with unparalleled zeal; and even our own generation, after more than two centuries of Shakespeare scholarship, has made considerable additions to our formal knowledge of Shakespeare's life. For example, in 1910 C. W. Wallace discovered in the Public Record Office in London papers pertaining to a suit in the court of Chancery (1612) in which Shakespeare appeared as a witness. His deposition is signed with his own hand, and his testimony reveals that he had been for some years after 1602 a lodger in the house of a Huguenot wigmaker named Mountjoy, who lived at the corner of Muggle and Silver Streets in London. More recently still Dr. Leslie Hotson discovered in the Controlment Rolls of the court of the Queen's Bench the record of a writ (29 November, 1596), issued at the petition of one William Wayte, which binds William Shakespeare, Francis Langley, and others over to keep the peace. This seems to have been a retaliatory action on Wayte's part against a similar order issued shortly before at Langley's suit against Wayte and his step-father, William Gardener, a Surrey justice of the peace whose jurisdiction covered Paris Garden and the Bankside. It is revealed by this discovery that Shakespeare had recently moved from Bishopsgate to Southwark, probably with his company, in order that they might occupy for a season Langley's newly constructed Swan theater, and that a quarrel involving Shakespeare had broken out between Langley and Gardener, whom other records show to have been an overbearing and litigious man. The players were at this time under severe attack by the authorities of the city of London, who were attempting to suppress them.

A great disaster was the evident loss or destruction of Shakespeare's personal papers. Of his correspondence only one short letter is known to exist. In it a Stratford neighbor, Richard Quyny, asks Shakespeare for the loan of thirty pounds. Shakespeare is mentioned, however, in several letters still preserved, mainly in connection with his activities as a citizen of Stratford. The Herald's College in London preserves two drafts of a grant of a coat of arms dated October 20, 1596, to Shakespeare's father, who was still living, although we may believe that the application was put forward by William Shakespeare, by that time gaining in position and wealth. Remarks about Shakespeare's plays and a few personal anecdotes about him appear in the letters and diaries of the time.

First publications of his works furnish much information about him. The First Folio (1623), edited by his fellow actors John Heminges and Henry Condell, contains, besides other laudatory verses, a poetic eulogy of Shakespeare by his celebrated contemporary, Ben Jonson, who also gives information about him in other works. The title pages and dedicatory epistles of *Venus and Adonis* (1593) and *The Rape of Lucrece* (1594) reveal Shakespeare's earlier relation to the Earl of Southampton; and the title pages of various plays issued in quarto form, before the collected edition of 1623, also the entries of plays in the Stationers' Register, furnish information as to Shakespeare's connection with printers and dramatic companies and as to approximate dates of composition of some of his plays. The practice of quoting Shakespeare and of alluding to his works began early; there is a wealth of such material. When the quotations and the allusions are definite, they constitute a valuable kind of literary knowledge. There are also various encomiums of Shakespeare by his contemporaries, outstanding among which is an enthusiastic estimate of Shakespeare as a poet and dramatist by Francis Meres in *Palladis Tamia*, or *Wit's Treasury* (1598), with mention of the poems and sonnets and of six comedies and six tragedies.

Matters of this kind are matters of fact; the quantity is large, the records are consistent, and to disregard these matters as is done by the believers in a Pseudo-Shakespeare is unfair and illogical.

It has always seemed a trifle absurd that one should have to argue that William Shakespeare, who was baptized at Trinity Church in Strat-ford-on-Avon on April 26, 1564, and died a prominent citizen of that place on April 23, 1616, was actually the author of the plays and poems universally assigned to him without question during his life and for two and one-half centuries after his death, but we do; and the task is made harder by the circumstance that there are no arguments to argue against. It is much easier to argue against argument than to argue against fanatical prejudices and assertions based on romance and manufactured mystery. Poe says that perversity is a natural human instinct; the perversity of a series of men, their joy in the singularity of opposing what everybody else believes, caused them to invent and espouse a hopeless cause.

The first things that might be brought up are the presuppositions that underlie the whole case against Shakespeare. It is assumed (1) that Shakespeare had no education. We have no right to assume that. We know that there was a standard Elizabethan grammar school maintained at Stratford during his youth. No records covering that school are known to exist, but Professor Baldwin in his book called *William Shakspere's*

Small Latine & Lesse Greeke has shown beyond peradventure that Shakespeare's works were written by a man schooled in just such an institution as the Edward VI grammar school at Stratford. (2) It is assumed that a person of ordinary birth and presumably meager education can never succeed in literature or achieve eminence, although we have in this country the instances of Abraham Lincoln and Mark Twain and many, many others. (3) It is assumed that there is no evidence covering the literary life of William Shakespeare; whereas we have the testimony of Camden, Drayton, Weever, Webster, and about 160 other contemporaries, including the best informed literary man of the day, namely, Ben Jonson. (4) It is assumed that we have little information about Shakespeare; whereas we have much more about him than we have about any of the Elizabethan dramatists except Jonson and possibly Chapman. We know almost nothing about Dekker, Middleton, Webster, and others who were regarded as equally important with Shakespeare or were more popular than he. The great fire of London of 1666 cleaned out the ordinary commercial and personal records which exist, for example, for Dryden and Samuel Johnson at a later date. The defect in records applies to a whole group. Jonson, Chapman, and Fletcher lived on into the thirties, when the world had grown more conscious of the value of the drama and the interest of literary persons. (5) It is assumed, for example, that Oxford, who died in 1604, could have written the plays of the later period. It is known that the style of *The Tempest, Cymbeline,* and *The Winter's Tale* resembles that of Beaumont and Fletcher, and that style did not make its appearance until several years after Oxford's death. Besides, the dates of a number of these plays are definitely known. Whatever we may think of J. M. Robertson as a critic, we owe him a great debt for his book, *The Baconian Heresy: A Confutation* (1913), in which he employed his skill as a man trained in the nature of evidence to scatter to the four winds the claims of the Baconians.

Most of the argument for Bacon's or Oxford's or Fulke Greville's or Darby's authorship of Shakespeare's plays rests on allusions. Suppose one has an allusion which does not support a given thesis but might be reconciled to that thesis. One such allusion does not prove it, nor would five or ten or a hundred. Yet the multiplication of these passive instances creates a sense of fact. The reason for this is that the arguer has constructed a thesis or hypothesis, and has gone out and searched for matter which can be reconciled with that hypothesis. His whole case is thus built up within itself. Such arguments have no controls, and, as Bacon says, the fact that a system of thought is consistent with itself is no proof of the truth of that system. A true hypothesis is one supported by proof independent of the presuppositions of that hypothesis.

The other common resort of the Pseudo-Shakespeareans has been to cyphers. They have been extensively used, but never fairly, never without a mathematical advantage in favor of the user, so that he will have more than a fifty-fifty chance to find what he is looking for. The most enlightening treatment of the subject I have encountered is that of Frederick Erastus Pierce, who had in his education the rare combination of higher mathematics and English literature. He shows that in these cyphers the truth has not an even chance to emerge. Given an hypothesis and an ardent observer and a sufficient freedom in the interpretation of symbols, the thing desired as a support for the hypothesis is sure to emerge.

Posterity has naturally craved more personal details about Shakespeare and has made an effort to collect them from hearsay. Thus has grown up a body of tradition, usually late in getting recorded and often inconsistent with knowledge from other differing sources. As to the validity of these details, some may be true. Whether they are true or not and however much scholars may do to discredit them, many of them are ineradicable from the popular mind. For example, the world has decided without any very convincing reasons that Shakespeare must have stolen deer. One has simply to do one's best to discriminate among traditions. The seventeenth century, which was not indifferent to Shakespeare, furnishes the best traditions. Thomas Fuller wrote a little life of Shakespeare in his *Worthies* (1662), and John Aubrey included Shakespeare in his *Lives of Eminent Men*, which was compiled 1669-1696, but not published until 1813. The Reverend John Ward, vicar of Stratford, the Reverend William Fulman, the Reverend Richard Davies, and some others collected local tales and examined some records. All of these accounts, except Aubrey's, were used by the first modern editor of Shakespeare, Nicholas Rowe, in a life prefixed to his edition of the plays (1709). There were traditions of Shakespeare still floating about unrecorded as late as the time of the great eighteenth-century editors of Shakespeare, Dr. Samuel Johnson and Edmund Malone.

Aubrey's tradition that Shakespeare was a butcher's son, and that "when he killed a calf, he would do it in a high style and make a speech," has been disposed of as a mistaken reference to a rural game called Killing the Calf. The deer-stealing tradition may be disposed of as a fiction based on the allusions to Falstaff's depredations against Justice Shallow, whose "old coat" contained a dozen white luces, in *The Merry Wives of Windsor*. If it is necessary to provide a prototype for Justice Shallow, Justice Gardener, as advocated by Dr. Hotson, is a far more probable one than Sir Thomas Lucy of Charlecote Hall. As for the horse-holding story collected by Dr. Johnson, it has nothing to commend it. Nevertheless, Shakespeare probably helped his father in the shop, possibly indulged in poaching in his youth, and almost certainly would have had to begin at the bottom when he entered the craft of acting.

The conception that Shakespeare was an educated man, according to the standards of his time, is important, because from it one gets a true idea of the nature of his works. They are not the output of an uneducated man, but works woven out of the best culture of the Renaissance. Shakespeare also shows familiarity with the manners and speech of ladies and gentlemen. Shakespeare's family was of good position and, on his mother's side, well connected. There were gentle-folk in the neighborhood of Stratford with whom, when he had retired to his native town, he is known to have had social relations. It is certainly no very wild conjecture to suppose that such associations were also open to Shakespeare in his youth.

Just when Shakespeare left his native town is a matter of doubt. He was there in 1584 and probably 1585, but we have no knowledge of his whereabouts again until 1592, when he had already become well launched on his career as actor and dramatist. What happened to Shakespeare during these seven or eight years we have as yet no means of knowing. Aubrey, following the actor William Beeston, a son of Christopher Beeston, probably an associate of Shakespeare's, makes the only statement that has even the semblance of supporting testimony. Aubrey says, in refutation of Jonson's famous charge:

> Though, as Ben Jonson says of him, that he knew but little Latin and less Greek, he understood Latin pretty well, for he had been in his younger years a schoolmaster in the country.

There is no objection to the idea that Shakespeare spent some portion of the dark years teaching school; but it seems equally probable, in the light both of the extraordinary knowledge of theater and drama which he had achieved by 1592 and of his rise in his profession by that year, that he joined a theatrical company early, perhaps before the last mention of him in Stratford, and spent these years in learning his trade.

In any case, the first allusion to Shakespeare in London is both striking and puzzling. In his deathbed confession, *A Groatsworth of Wit bought with a Million of Repentance*, written in the summer of 1592, Robert Greene attacks Shakespeare. He is advising three of his companions, Marlowe, Peele, and probably Nashe, to cease writing plays for the players:

> Base minded men all three of you, if by my miserie you be not warnd: for vnto none of you (like mee) sought those burres to cleaue: those Puppets (I meane) that spake from our mouths, those Anticks garnisht in our colours. Is it not strange, that I, to whom they all haue beene beholding: is it not like that you, to whome they all haue beene beholding, shall (were yee in that case as I am now) bee both at once of them forsaken? Yes trust them not: for there is an vpstart Crow, beautified with our feathers, that with his *Tygers hart wrapt in a Players hyde*, supposes he is as well able to bombast out a blanke verse as the best of you: and beeing an absolute *Iohannes fac totum*, is in his owne conceit the onely Shake-scene in a countrey.

This passage is clearly aimed at Shakespeare, who was a player and was obviously by that time a successful dramatist. The matter is clinched by the pun on his name and by the words, "with his Tygers hart wrapt in a Players hyde," which are a burlesque of "O tiger's heart, wrapt in a woman's hide!" which occurs in *3 Henry VI* (I, iv, 137). This magniloquent line was long supposed to have been purloined from *The True Tragedy of Richard Duke of York* (published in quarto in 1595), then regarded as a play probably by Marlowe and the source of *3 Henry VI*; but it is now pretty generally admitted that *The True Tragedy* is a stage version of *3 Henry VI* and therefore later. The line is thus seen to be an example of Shakespeare's supposed bombast chosen for parody from *3 Henry VI*, already known to Greene in the summer of 1592.

It is necessary to follow the report of this attack with its reaction. Shakespeare was offended, as apparently was Marlowe, because Greene states in his pamphlet that he had once been an atheist like Marlowe, but had repented. As to reparations, Greene was dead and out of reach; but Nashe, who had the reputation of being a bitter satirist, was suspected of having had a hand in the abuse. Nashe denied it, and Henry Chettle was brought into the affair; whereupon Chettle, in his *Kind-Harts Dreame* (1592), denied any responsibility except that which arose from his having prepared Greene's manuscript for the printer. He says by way of apology:

> The other [Shakespeare], whome at that time I did not so much spare, as since I wish I had, for that as I haue moderated the heate of liuing writers, and might haue vsde my owne discretion (especially in such a case) the Author beeing dead, that I did not, I am as sory as if the originall fault had beene my fault, because my selfe haue seene his demeanor no lesse ciuill than he exelent in the qualitie he .professes: Besides, diuers of worship haue reported his uprightnes of dealing, which argues his honesty, and his facetious grace in writting, that approoues his Art.

As appears from Greene's allusion, *3 Henry VI* was on the stage by the summer of 1592; if so, *2 Henry VI* had of course already been written. Now *2 Henry VI* is a play of primitive style and of a new species. It is a pity that we do not know what play or plays Shakespeare wrote first, because of the very nature of Shakespeare's dramatic genius. All Shakespeare commentators since Malone's time or before have represented Shakespeare merely as a promoter of Elizabethan drama as he found it. They have regarded him as an imitator of his predecessors and contemporaries, and later of Beaumont and Fletcher. For example, J. W. Mackail says in *The Approach to Shakespeare* (Oxford, 1930, p. 29):

> He [Shakespeare] was employed more and more as an adapter and reviser of plays for reproduction; retouching the work of Kyd, remodeling that of Peele and Greene, and collaborating with Marlowe.

The trouble with such statements is that there is no evidence of such general activity on Shakespeare's part. It is true that he shows the influence of these men, also that he often chose a topic for his plays that had already been treated on the stage. But the statement gives a false impression and has no basis in fact. Shakespeare, on the contrary, seems to have been an innovator from the start. It is not, for example, a foregone conclusion that Marlowe's *Edward II* antedated *2* and *3 Henry VI*; and, if Shakespeare's plays are the earlier, Shakespeare must be regarded as the pioneer in the field of the detailed and serious dramatization of history, even granting that Marlowe's play is a history play rather than a Senecan tragedy.

What sort of man then was William Shakespeare? His contemporaries speak of him as fluent, as one whose "mind and hand went together," as gifted, friendly, upright. There is almost always affection in their tone when they speak. Their favorite adjective is "gentle," an interesting word in the light of its meaning in that age. It was an epithet that meant "well born," "well bred," "polite in behavior," as well as "kind," "mild," and "modest." They called him "Gentle Will" and "Friendly Shakespeare." Our greatest poet was a gentle, friendly man in the opinions of those who knew him, and he is that sort of man in the inferences one may draw from his works. One would like to have people who read his works think of him in that way still.

Shakespeare's works are appropriate to a man of the kind he seems to have been. His genius, like that of Chaucer and Goethe, was of the normal objective kind. His works are written from the point of view of general humanity, which means that they have in them the minimum of affectation, formalism, dogmatism, egotism, and prejudice. They are about life, about people, and about recurrent human situations. His people are lovers, husbands, fathers and sons, mothers and daughters, kings, counselors and subjects, servants, inn-keepers and soldiers, beggars, tramps, and country people. They are made of ordinary human stuff, and show ordinary human needs, passions, and qualities. Even his villains are usually within the pale of our sympathies, like good men gone wrong. Shakespeare tells us, not how to meet life, but how men like us do habitually meet it. His principles are as simple as his stories and as unchangeable as life. One goes to Shakespeare, therefore, for the ultimate, which is at the same time the intelligible. His vein is to represent rather than to expound, and his representations are significant and convincing.

There is possibly no better expression of Shakespeare's universality than the great sonnet beginning:

> Let me not to the marriage of true minds
> Admit impediments.

Indeed, in trying to give expression to the Shakespearean quality, we may resort to Shakespeare himself and declare that he gave away his secret when he said,

> One touch of nature makes the whole world kin.

It is certain that Shakespeare was one man with one great mind. It is possible to know the qualities of that mind, its development, its logic, its morals, its sense of beauty, its style; and from this fact comes the greatest of all arguments for the actuality and integrity of Shakespeare. It follows that Shakespeare should be studied as a whole and not in individual and isolated works only; for, as the late Dr. F. J. Furnivall used to say, his plays are to be regarded as "successive offshoots of one great mind." It happens that this was a mind strongly marked by the culture and temper of the age of Queen Elizabeth of England.

When we say that Shakespeare was an Elizabethan, we render ourselves liable to be asked, "What of it? What difference does it make?" Before this question one grows diffident after repeated failures to answer it satisfactorily. The fact that Shakespeare was an Elizabethan does make a difference; and one may try again, although it is perhaps impossible to make the matter clear, except to those who have trained historical imaginations.

In the first place, the Elizabethans lived very differently from the people of our times. One does not claim great significance for this fact, but the fact can be proved; and, if it can, it really means that Elizabethan minds were filled with different ideas and images from those of modern minds and entertained a different set of living problems. Elizabethan houses were different from ours. Some of their houses, especially timbered town-houses, like those in Chester, and stone town-houses, like those which stood until the "blitz" in Coventry, were very fine indeed; so also many castles and country mansions were architecturally admirable by any standards. They had glass in windows, balustraded stairways, and fireplaces provided with chimneys instead of mere holes in the roof through which the smoke found its way out as best it could. The Elizabethans were great builders. But of course the luxuries I have mentioned were exceptional and were largely confined to the rich. The houses of workmen and agricultural laborers were apt to be very bad indeed, probably by no means so good as the stables in which many modern cows and horses live. The fact, however, that towns were relatively small and that life was largely rural (the population being engaged in agriculture and stock-raising) did much then, as it does now, to alleviate what we call slum conditions. Still, one fancies that the lives of the poor were pretty crowded and pretty filthy. People heated their houses and cooked their food mainly at open fires of wood in fireplaces. Houses must have been cold, and it is a strange thought that English houses are in the winter of 1946-1947 still very cold. The people habitually ate roasted flesh and drank malted drinks. Clothing seems to have been durable, but it cannot have been very sanitary, since nobody in England except the Queen had any underwear. Modern sanitation was unknown, and sewers were open, evil-smelling ditches. No wonder the Elizabethans were scourged by plagues and epidemics. No wonder so many people died in childhood, and no wonder the expectation of life was so short. Certainly the fact that death was always knocking at the door must have affected Elizabethan thought and Elizabethan character. Yet, in spite of all dangers and difficulties, the Elizabethans were, for the most part, active, cheerful country people, living rather eagerly in a fairly primitive way. Those of us who know the lives lived by pioneers, mountaineers, and remote country people in our own land will have little difficulty in comprehending the lives lived by Elizabethans. We may go so far as to say that the subjects of Queen Elizabeth had, many of them, an outlook not widely different from that of our own not very remote ancestors. There is nothing insurmountable in these barriers, and the features of normal Elizabethan physical life are largely matters of curious antiquarian interest. A good many Elizabethan words and customs, forgotten elsewhere, have lived on in our own Appalachian mountains.

When one looks into it, however, one can see that the Elizabethans did different things in their lives from what we do in ours, and many of them. Their mental content also was different, by and large, from ours. If we may judge by what they accomplished, they must have used their intelligences more than the modern man uses his; they were more full of personal aspiration; and we have, in order to understand them, the constant job of translating, not words only, but manners of life and thought also. This ability to translate, adapt, and find life in the literature of the past is necessary for our task.

I remember the interest with which I read, while I was a university student, *The Diary of Master William Silence* by the Right Honorable D. H. Madden. It becomes as apparent to all readers of Shakespeare as to the author that "Shakespeare had passed many days among scenes and pursuits which haunted his memory throughout life, storing his mind with such thoughts and images as found expression" in his plays and poems. And that, whatever else Shakespeare may have been, "he was beyond doubt a sportsman, with rare skill in the mysteries of woodcraft, loving to recall the very names of the hounds with which he was wont to hunt; a practical falconer, whose hawking-language was not book-learning; and a horseman and horse-keeper, accustomed to speak the homely language of the stable, whose knowledge of the horse and his fifty diseases was such as can be gained only by experience." What one finds in Shakespeare's works justifies Madden's opinions over the whole field of sport—including angling, bear-baiting, and the chase, or deer-hunting, with its ceremonials, as well as falconry and horsemanship.

The Elizabethans had also their own special interests as a people, and in these matters their differences from us are often striking; but again they are all matters which can be understood and not infrequently paralleled in the modern world. The Elizabethans were, for example, fond of drinking, but they had no distilled liquors, and drinking took so much time that it was an avocation. Their drinks were milder, and drinking was less dangerous as a social practice than it is now. Many men drank too much, and drinking was a sort of career in itself. Falstaff labored at it; and sack, rather than highway robbery, was his true vocation. We are familiar with his famous panegyric on sack (*1 Hen. IV*, IV, iii, 93-135). But we must also remember the heartbroken words of Cassio, who says, "O God, that men should put an enemy in their mouths to steal away their brains!"

The Elizabethans were much interested in maintaining the social order. Rebellion was the thing they regarded with most horror, and the sixteenth century throughout, although it had many rebellions, adhered firmly to the principles laid down by Sir John Cheke in *The Hurt of Sedition: How Grievous it is to a Commonwealth*. Shakespeare is firm in his convictions on this subject. Hotspur, as well as Macbeth, reveals Shakespeare's opinions. He believed also in social order, which seemed to him the chief principle that God had impressed upon the world. Ranks and classes, obedience to law and respect for superiors, were to Shakespeare expressions of God's will. It is hard for us, with our traditions of liberty and resistance to tyranny, to understand that Shakespeare is not being merely dramatic when he puts the great speech on order into the mouth of Ulysses in *Troilus and Cressida* (I, iii, 75 ff.), or when he puts the praises of the ordered life of bees into the mouth of the Archbishop of Canterbury in *Henry V* (I, ii, 183-220). Every man dressed, or was required to dress, according to his rank and occupation, and there is more than loyalty to the memory of Pompey in the reproaches uttered by the tribunes, Flavius and Marullus, in the opening scene of *Julius Caesar* when they blame the Commoners for being in the streets without their aprons (I, ii). There is to be found in Shakespeare no encouragement, as there is in American life, for a man to rise by his merits, or otherwise, above the rank and class in life to which God has assigned him.

For another thing, the Elizabethans were almost fanatically patriotic. With very poor support from their Queen and her ministers, Elizabethan soldiers fought bravely in France, in the Low Countries, and in Ireland. They actually overthrew the power of Spain in their defeat of the Invincible Armada. One sees this love of country in Shakespeare, whose history plays are perhaps the most genuinely patriotic works in English literature. Gaunt's speech about England in *Richard II* (II, i, 31-66) and the Bastard's speech in *King John* (V, vii, 110-18) are famous. There is that about these speeches which still stirs the heart. They were actually in the minds and on the tongues of English people in the dark days of 1940 and 1941.

The Elizabethan English were also deeply interested· in religion. Perhaps a greater percentage of people were earnestly seeking the salvation of their souls in England in the later sixteenth century than at any other time and place on record, unless it be Switzerland during the same epoch or New England a generation later. The Elizabethans were not Puritans as we understand the term, but they were in earnest about religion. Shakespeare's plays themselves may be fairly said to be religious. His great national hero, King Henry V, utters a devout prayer before the battle of Agincourt (IV, i, 306-22), and most of Shakespeare's villains add irreligion to their other bad qualities. The cynicism of Edmund in *King Lear*, although it is often mistaken for independence of thought, is merely atheism (I, ii, 128-44). Shakespeare is also aware of the fondness of his age for religious controversy, and, although he does not indulge in it himself, it is near the surface in *King John*, *Henry V*, and *Henry VIII*.

There are also many other ways in which Shakespeare shows that he had Elizabethan tastes and opinions. He knew country sports and the merriments of Mayday. He alluded to them often and like one who was familiar with them and liked them. He loved the wit-combats of gay high society, and his courtiers are often too witty, in this sense, to be interesting to us. In an almost unforgivable way Shakespeare made puns on all occasions, sometimes very grave occasions. But he had of course many interests that we share with him and his age, or at least understand and admire. He had, for example, a vast enthusiasm for action, and his lofty ideals were impassioned. Like his age he believed that this is a world in which something can be done, if man has only the courage and stamina and brains to try. Like his age he held the marriage bond as sacred. His husbands and wives are true to each other, and there is no more poignant aspect of *Macbeth* than the falling apart in loneliness, as the tragedy grows dark and imminent, of the sinful husband and the sinful wife (IV, v). His stress on loyalty of children to parents, servants to masters, and subjects to sovereigns is insistence on Elizabethan virtues.

That the Elizabethans accepted as fact and truth many things which we do not accept and often regard as contemptible superstitions is a matter of importance. So great is Shakespeare that it is hard for us to believe that he was ever actually in error. But he was often in error, and certain important things follow from that fact. So true is this that, in reading Elizabethan literature, it is not the truth that matters so much as what the Elizabethans thought was the truth. We need not only a history of truth but also a history of error. We are forced continually to put ourselves in Shakespeare's place and say, "What did he really think were the facts of the case?" He probably believed large quantities of miraculous natural history; as, for example, that ostriches could digest iron, that the elephant was intellectually on a par with man, and that the toad was venomous as well as ugly and yet had a precious jewel in his head. The audience would believe that Othello had certainly seen anthropophagi and men whose heads do grow beneath their shoulders. Shakespeare probably believed in the formless bear cub which was licked into shape by its dam, in the unicorn (itself a figment of the imagination) which was captured by inducing it to sink its horn into a tree, in the pelican which fed its young from the flesh of its own breast, and of course in the social, economic, and political culture of the bee.

This unnatural natural history was innocent enough, in fact had its merit in unifying man with other creatures of earth; but the ignorance of the Elizabethans with reference to the human body and the human mind was a more serious matter. They believed in the four elements, the four humors, the four qualities, and the doctrine of excess and balance. Blood, phlegm, red bile, and black bile were physiologically disparate, and yet the whole practice of medicine in that period was based upon their supposed coordination. It is actually true that the sick were far safer in their own hands or in no hands at all than in those of learned physicians, who knew so many things that were not true. Elizabethan medicine was murderous. The Elizabethans did not know that the blood circulates or that the nerves carry impulses from the brain to the body and from the body to the brain. For nerves they substituted a system of invisible fluids which they called spirits. The Elizabethans were controlled in their thinking by hypotheses of these non-existent things.

It must be said, however, that their system of psychology was for general purposes very good; so that, with a change of basis and a few corrections, Elizabethan psychology works well to this day. It is called faculty psychology, and it had been worked out, very largely by Aristotle, from clear and correct observations of human behavior. Human beings still confront the same issues and still react in human ways. There is thus a reason why we should think of Shakespeare as a good psychologist, for he certainly knew humanity, and his opportunities for knowing humanity were probably better than ours. Psychology is defined as a study of the reaction of man to his total environment, and the makers of faculty psychology had been careful observers. Men and women in the world do act pretty much as Shakespeare's men and women act, although we have a very different physiological system by which to account for behavior. Sudden jealousy, like that of Othello, does occur; and a man may strangle his wife in temporary madness. Antony, the great soldier, disgracefully left the field of battle, deserted his men, and threw an empire away because he was infatuated with Cleopatra. A man may still behave in the same mad way because he is similarly infatuated. Great and feral passions still seize upon the human heart, and you and I have no immunity and no insurance, except wisdom, humility, and prayer, that we may not run amok.

Among universally credited errors of the age I list also the broad system of superstition which we call witchcraft. Its dark practices and no doubt its practitioners were known to Shakespeare. A world with witchcraft in it is not like our world, since such a world is not only more mysterious but more disturbing and threatening.

One might observe also that life in the Renaissance seems to have been more clearly marked externally than is modern life; as if it carried with it the symbols of identification and action. Curiosity in private life seems to have been less restrained, as one observes in the Elizabethan attitude toward the unfortunate and the grotesque, the insane and the physically deformed. Clear marking, as if for recognition, seems to have been demanded. Liveries and class costumes were universal. The significance of color in dress, of hatchments and insignia, was to make things recognizable. Indeed, we possibly miss much of the political and social meaning of Elizabethan plays because we have lost this form of communication. One may be sure there were symbols of green in the staging of *Othello* and of blue in the playing of the story of Juliet, since green was a symbol of jealousy and blue of true love. Gossip and slander were common and were not controlled, as in our time, by devices of concealment and privacy. There seems, for example, to have been far greater intimacy between master and servant than there is in the modern world, that is, if we may judge from *The Comedy of Errors*, *Romeo and Juliet*, *The Taming of the Shrew*, and *Twelfth Night*. People lived in streets thick with beggars and noisy with cries and clanging bells. Such conditions would in part account for and render more natural the sentimentalized posturing, the posing presented as the natural thing, that characterizes Elizabethan drama, which tends to be prevailingly clamorous and rhetorical. The world was full of signs and symbols which, like military commands, might institute prompt and supposedly appropriate actions.

The final question is this: were the Elizabethans, aside from the more or less accidental variations mentioned above, really and ascertainably different from the men and women of this age? Different in their natures and hearts? The historical interval of time is not enough to produce any obvious variations, such as there are between the Greeks and Romans, on the one hand, and modern men, on the other. Differences of race are inconsiderable, even between Americans and Elizabethans. There can be no such differences between ourselves and the subjects of Queen Elizabeth as exist, for example, between us and the Chinese. Nevertheless, there are variations and important ones.

The Elizabethans loved their ideals and patterns of action and pursued them ardently. Because they did this, they accomplished a great deal both in art and life, but they did not understand their philosophy very well and were vague in mind about it. This vagueness in the realm of ideals and rational actions was, however, compensated for by great sharpness of outline in the realm of the perceptual and the conceptual. It must have required great vividness of conception and of imagination operating under heat to enact and enforce the statutes for the burning of heretics and papists. Burning a human being alive under conditions of solemnity and in the face of the people is an awful thing to contemplate. Those responsible were sure they were right, and yet they were as wrong and un-Christian as hell itself. This unreasoning clarity of mind does much to account for the surprising ferocity of the Renaissance, a ferocity of fanaticism and dogmatism far worse than anything recorded of the Middle Ages. Note the vindictiveness of punishments and the cruelty of judges. Consider the judicial murders of Surrey, Lopez, and Raleigh. It would be interesting to inquire to what extent religious persecutions were also political, personal, or motivated by economic rivalry; for such circumstances, as in the case of the persecutions of our times, would have increased their cruelty; but here one can only remark, on the basis of current experience, that the cruelties of that age seem characteristic of its cocksure mentality. We may ask this question: Does not a state of mind which arises from such mental habits always eventuate in crisis? When certain modern nations recently substituted a fanatical executive system for reason and true religion, they acted and reacted with mechanical promptitude to a set of slogans. If convictions are deep and imaginative conceptions unjustifiably clear, the tragedy of passion, as in the case of Othello and Macbeth, stalks upon the stage. Strong feeling, superficial thinking, and the errors which arise from overhasty generalization were the bases of tragedy, then as now; and we ask if the Renaissance, in its exaggerations (the customary resort of unreflective minds), does not provide the chief occasions for human tragedy; indeed, if Shakespeare's age is not the greatest tragic age.

If then one grants that, along with vagueness and inconsistency in ideals—the result of confused thinking, of no thinking at all, or of hasty generalization—there was in the Renaissance great clarity in individual concepts, great proclivity for action, and an almost universal doctrine of obedience to tenet, so that action assumed the form of individual impulse, mob violence, or bitter partisanship, one will certainly find plenty of things in the life of the time calculated to initiate action. If the mind of the age, collectively and individually, was like a loaded cannon, there were plenty of sparks in the age to touch it off. Remember that the Elizabethans loved proverbs, and proverbs are a sort of ready-to-wear wisdom, signals for action. At a distance the age presents the spectacle of a series of disasters and fulminations. Certainly this vividness of existence, these contrasts in daily life, account for the sudden joy and sorrow, hope and despair, love-at-first-sight and friendship converted to hate, laughter and tears, which are part of the general temper of the time and serve to differentiate it from our age. It was a time of enduring conflicts, fierce duels, impossible conspiracies, and sudden killings in the heat of passion. There was rage in the attitude toward torture and the punishment of malefactors. Faith in the power of the spoken word eventuated in fiery oratory, and loud laughter was as easy a resort as tears.

All in all, it seems that the life of Elizabethan England was, relative to our own, more fanatical, more explosive, in religion, politics, family relations, love, and friendship, and vastly more certain of itself. There are well-known stories of what men did out of pure excitability under stress of one passion or another, such as that of Sir John Davies, who broke a cudgel over Richard Martin's head while Martin was seated at the barristers' table in the hall of the Middle Temple. But perhaps we do not need Martin when we have Hotspur. No political motive would be more readily understood than vengeance and personal hatred. There are records of feuds between families and records of the chief dreads of the time, which were felt intensely—the Turks, the Spaniards, the Papists, insurrection in the populace, the gaunt and horrid spectre of the plague; the fear of the everlasting fires of Hell, of witchcraft, of robbery and murder. We know that all these things were real, tangible, and operative and that there was a widespread feeling of insecurity—a superb background against which to play a drama of feud and love like *Romeo and Juliet*, or of hate like *The Revenger's Tragedy*.

The world is still full of terrible things, and men still meet them and react to them in pretty much the same way in which the Elizabethans did; and yet perhaps there was more haste and less reason in the mentality of the Elizabethans, in spite of their supremely active intelligence, than in that of modern civilized men.

One has no right to apply too rigidly to the myriad-minded Shakespeare judgments derived from general consideration of the temper of his times; few readers of Shakespeare would, however, fail to perceive in him the intense mental activity, the vivid belief in life's possibilities, and the assertive courage of his time. One must conclude that, however much he may have transcended his age, he was nevertheless a child of the Renaissance.

CHAPTER II

The Beginnings

THE COMEDY OF ERRORS
THE TWO GENTLEMEN OF VERONA
LOVE'S LABOUR'S LOST
A MIDSUMMER-NIGHT'S DREAM
TITUS ANDRONICUS
ROMEO AND JULIET

a. Early comedies.

BY THE end of the year 1594, when after long sieges of the plague the theatrical companies were again permitted to act before London audiences, Shakespeare, then a member of the Lord Chamberlain's company, had, it is believed, written eleven plays—comedies, *Love's Labour's Lost, The Comedy of Errors, The Two Gentlemen of Verona, The Taming of the Shrew,* and *A Midsummer-Night's Dream*; histories, *1, 2,* and *3 Henry VI,* and *Richard III*; tragedies, *Titus Andronicus* and *Romeo and Juliet.* A majority of the eleven plays show evidence of having been revised after they were first written, so that we may have before us, lacking external evidence, the difficult task of dating plays from their earliest parts. Among these plays certain ones, *Love's Labour's Lost, The Comedy of Errors,* and *The Two Gentlemen of Verona,* the Henry VI plays, and *Titus Andronicus,* evidently belong to the earliest period, although their dates relative to each other are difficult to determine. *The Taming of the Shrew* might be placed with this group or with *A Midsummer-Night's Dream, Richard III,* and *Romeo and Juliet,* to form an early, but not the earliest group of Shakespeare's plays. *King John* may be almost as early as *Richard III.* It is possible that we do not possess all of the plays Shakespeare wrote before 1594, and no early play can be accurately dated. Humphrey Moseley entered in the Stationers' Register, September 9, 1653, as by "Mr. Fletcher and Shakespeare,"

The History of Cardenio, probably the same as *Cardenno* acted before King James by Shakespeare's company in 1613 and possibly known to Theobald in the eighteenth century. At the same time Moseley entered "Henry ye first & Hen. the 2d by Shakespeare and Davenport." On June 29, 1660, he entered "The History of King Stephen; Duke Humphrey, a Tragedy; Iphis and Ianthe or a marriage without a man, a Comedy; by Will. Shakespeare." Among the manuscript plays burned by John Warburton's cook were "Henry ye 1st by Will. Shakespear and Rob. Davenport; *Duke Humphrey* Will. Shakespear" and "A Play by Will. Shakespear." The existence of plays thus attributed to Shakespeare on Henry I, Stephen, and Henry II suggests that Shakespeare may have produced, along with *King John*, a series of history plays dealing with the period of the Angevin kings of England. A play, not otherwise known, called *Love's Labour's Won*, is mentioned by Meres. It is natural to suppose from its title that such a play was a companion piece to *Love's Labour's Lost* and was therefore written about the same time.

1. *The Comedy of Errors.*

The Comedy of Errors is possibly the earliest Shakespearean comedy preserved. *Gesta Grayorum* mentions the play in connection with the celebration of the annual revel at Gray's Inn on Holy Innocents Day (December 28), 1594. To this revel had been invited the members of the Inner Temple; but when the guests arrived, there were no seats for them, and a near riot occurred:

> After such sports, a Comedy of Errors (like to Plautus his *Menechmus*) was played by the players. So that night was begun and continued to the end in nothing but confusion and errors; whereupon it was ever afterwards called *The Night of Errors.*

The style of *The Comedy of Errors* and certain allusions in it to contemporary events indicate that the play is earlier than even 1594. It is the most artificial of the comedies, as indicated by an abundance of doggerel verse, speeches balanced between speakers, characters set off formally against each other, alternate rhymes, puns and quibbles. It seems also to be a play designed, like *The Taming of the Shrew*, for the public stage. It lacks those typically Renaissance social features which appear in *Love's Labour's Lost* and *The Two Gentlemen of Verona*. For Shakespeare it must have functioned as an exercise in plot management. Not only does Shakespeare catch the resilient efficiency of Plautus, but he betters Plautus. The borrowing of a scene from the *Amphitruo*, the locking of Antipholus of Ephesus out of his own house, caused Shakespeare to make a most interesting change in comic method. Plautus in his realistic world begins with truth and then involves his characters in error; Shakespeare in the mad world of Ephesus begins his episodes with error and enlightens them with flashes of truth. In another respect, which is possibly an expression of Shakespeare's own nature, *The Comedy of Errors* is most significant in what it reveals about Shakespearean comedy. Shakespeare never writes comedy of the cool, objective kind that appears in Plautus, Ben Jonson, and Molière. Shakespeare loved to play with edged tools. Somebody's life or somebody's happiness is at stake even in his comedies. After the introduction of the good Aegeon, with his moving appeal to the duke to spare his life, we never get him out of our minds. In the midst of confusion worse confounded we continue to hope that he will be saved. Shakespeare is, moreover, unwilling for Adriana to remain a shrew, but characteristically provides for her reformation; nor is he willing for Antipholus of Syracuse to remain an eligible bachelor, but provides him with a Luciana. Such things as these indicate the popular intention of *The Comedy of Errors*.

Menaechmi is pure comedy, witty and clear, much simpler than *The Comedy of Errors*, of which it is the original form. There seem to have been many Greek and Latin comedies which depicted the confusion arising from identical twins, and in modern times such comedies are known as comedies of error. Plautus's own play was well known during the Renaissance and was a favorite for reading and acting in schools. It is a realistic tale about the doings of certain commonplace people of rather low morals and is strongly marked by the conventions of Roman social life. The men appropriate what they can lay their hands on; the wife has no rights, and there is not even a suggestion, except from her own clamorous tongue, that she is entitled to any; the slave, a clever chap, is beaten; there is a parasite who has attached himself to Menaechmus the Citizen and is something of a blackmailer, and there is a courtesan of characteristic greed and conventional respectability.

The scene is in Epidamnus, and the events are quite simple. Peniculus, the parasite, is waiting in hope of his dinner when Menaechmus the Citizen enters from his own house talking back to his wife, Mulier, calling her a prattling fool and a common scold. He has just stolen her cloak, which he immediately bestows on Erotium, the courtesan, who is so much pleased that she arranges to give him and the parasite a dinner. The second act introduces Menaechmus the Traveler with his slave Messenio. This Menaechmus has been for five years in search of his twin brother stolen away when they were seven years old. He has been given the name of the lost Menaechmus and has, according to Messenio, visited the Istrians, the Spaniards, the Massilians, the Illyrians, the whole Adriatic, Magna Graecia, and the whole coast of Italy. Messenio warns his master against the Epidamnians, whose harlots and swindlers are organized to prey upon travelers. In comes Erotium, who thinks she recognizes her lover and insists on his coming in to dinner, the dinner prepared for his twin brother. In Shakespeare Antipholus of Syracuse dines with the wife and not the mistress. Here Menaechmus the Traveler, seeing a chance for a free meal and thinking himself a match for the Epidamnians, accepts the invitation of Erotium in spite of the warnings of Messenio. In the third act he enters from the house of Erotium well dined and wined and scoffs at Peniculus. He has Mulier's stolen cloak and also her chain (stolen earlier), ostensibly to have them repaired, really to keep them as his own. To deprive the parasite of a dinner was a serious matter, and Peniculus, bent on revenge, hurries off to tell Mulier of her husband's wickedness. That husband enters after prolonged delay in the law courts and is duly belabored by Mulier's tongue. He feels himself deeply wronged and entirely innocent. The error is thick in this act and is made worse by misunderstandings between the Citizen and the Courtesan.

The genius of Plautus manifests itself splendidly in the fifth act, which is masterly. It contains a long and extremely amusing scene between Menaechmus the Traveler and his brother's wife, Mulier, which is heightened by an interview with Senex, her father, and further heightened by a side-splitting examination of the angry Citizen by Medicus in order to determine his sanity. It is much better than the encounter with Dr. Pinch (in *The Comedy of Errors*), for Shakespeare's play misses the humor of the situation. It is the Traveler who in Plautus was suspected of insanity, who actually counterfeited insanity, and it is the Citizen who undergoes the examination. Finally, Messenio is clever enough to see that he and his master, without knowing it, have actually found the twin brother of whom they had been in search, and he brings about a recognition. In cool cynicism Plautus has Menaechmus the Citizen, in order to accompany his brother to Syracuse, offer for sale his whole property, including Mulier, if any buyer appears—*si quis emptor venerit*.

When *Menaechmi* comes to us in Shakespearean form, it has been greatly amplified, first of all by such romantic additions as the story of Aegeon and Aemilia, which is but a variation of the theme of *Apollonius of Tyre*, later used in *Pericles*; secondly, by the adjustment which permits a love affair between Antipholus of Syracuse and Luciana, sister-in-law to Antipholus of Ephesus. There are also many minor ways in which human sentiment is added to the cool tale that Plautus tells.

In *The Comedy of Errors* Shakespeare shows already in operation his ability to discriminate among characters of all ranks, an ability which one would think of as fundamentally dramatic. This play discriminates lightly but surely between the identical brethren, masters, and slaves. A lesser genius might have contented himself with carrying external into internal likeness. The Antipholi are not alike in their characters and dispositions in spite of certain Plautine qualities which are carried over in both. Antipholus of Ephesus is a self-willed, rather dissolute man, not, however, to a point where his standing as a citizen of Ephesus is imperiled. His commercial credit is good, and he has been a valiant soldier in the service of the Duke. Plautus frankly depicts him as a lewd and dishonest man. The character in Shakespeare is far better than its prototype, but none the less has the markings of that prototype. Antipholus of Ephesus is in general a lively character. Plautus's discrimination between the masters is much less emphatic than that of Shakespeare. Menaechmus the Traveler, in Plautus, is quite as Greek as is his brother. He craftily accepts the cloak and the chain purloined by his brother, just, to be sure, as Antipholus of Syracuse accepts the chain; but the chain in Shakespeare is not stolen goods. Antipholus of Syracuse offers to pay the goldsmith for it, and later makes no attempt to conceal the facts. Menaechmus the Traveler, suspected of insanity, feigns insanity in order to frighten his accusers, and deftly makes his escape to the boat. When he comes back on the scene he is annoyed to find his slave Messenio claiming that he has had a promise of freedom, as to be sure he has, but from the other Menaechmus. Nowhere is there any motive but simple selfishness, and both the Menaechmi are ordinary, rather shifty Greeks of the merchant class. Although Menaechmus the Traveler has journeyed widely he shows few marks of the man of the world except self-confidence and a disposition to take advantage. It is not so with Antipholus of Syracuse, who is an experienced traveler, curious about foreign lands, properly wary of the ways of strange peoples, a well-disposed man, capable of true love and honest sentiment.

It was a clever device on the part of the remaker of the plot to lay the scene in the famous city of witchcraft, Ephesus. The ancient city was noted for pagan worship, and St. Paul, who was aware of the reputation of the city, addressed to the Christians there perhaps the most magnificent of his epistles. The citizens of Ephesus seem to have utilized for profit their reputation for sorcery, and ancient Ephesus had a bad name. Antipholus of Syracuse knew well where he had landed, recognized his danger, and sought to escape. Just as Antipholus of Ephesus grows more and more indignant, so does his brother grow more and more frightened and bewildered. All in all, both characters have undergone in Shakespeare's hands changes in natural and appropriate ways.

The Dromios, possibly Shakespeare's own creations, have at least some marks of difference. Of course there is nothing important to be discovered in such light, clownish, and improbable characters; and yet the more staid and responsible traveler is given the more jocular and impudent Dromio, a sort of all-licensed fool, who apparently is flogged and expects to be flogged rather frequently. The more lively of the masters is given a rather more serious, protesting, bewildered slave.

Again, it is easy to say that Adriana is a shrew, one of the two types of women in earlier Elizabethan comedy, and that Luciana exemplifies the other type, the mild, ingenuous, sweet-tempered young woman who has no individuality. But these judgments are only relatively true. Adriana has some of the qualities of the wronged and neglected wife, as indeed had Mulier in the Plautine original, but Adriana's claims are recognized and respected; she is allowed to reform her conduct. Adriana is not unreasonable and has some individuality. Luciana is a responsible young woman and has more sense than does Bianca in *The Taming of the Shrew*. She deserves the good husband she gets in Antipholus of Syracuse. One might go so far as to say that *The Comedy of Errors* is a comedy rather than a farce, although it is usually played as a farce and although Coleridge in a famous passage describes it as a typical farce.

It is not, however, in romantic materials only that the plot of *Menaechmi* has been expanded. There has also been added an increment in kind from another play by Plautus, *Amphitruo*. In point of fact that comedy is a much bolder, more satirical, and more scandalous play than is *Menaechmi* and presents one of the most popular themes in classical drama, the birth of Hercules. Amphitruo is a soldier just returning from a glorious campaign. Jupiter, the amatory father of gods and men, has fallen in love with Alcmena, wife of Amphitruo, takes on the form of her husband, visits her, and begets Hercules. While Jupiter is in the house of Amphitruo, the owner returns and is denied admission for the astounding reason that he is already within. Jupiter is assisted by Hermes, who takes on the form of Sosia, servant of Amphitruo. Much comedy results from Sosia's conversing with his double. It is easy to see that this scene is closely paralleled in *The Comedy of Errors* (III, i, ii) and that it is the occasion of the introduction of two Dromios into that play. This clever addition has occasioned a good deal of unnecessary talk about its increasing the improbability of the plot. *Amphitruo* is a rougher, more brutal, and more brilliant comedy than *Menaechmi*. One cannot see, however, that *The Comedy of Errors* was affected in any way by the tone of *Amphitruo* except perhaps in the vulgar description which Dromio of Syracuse gives his master of Nell (or Luce) in the second scene of the third act.

Whether or not Shakespeare was responsible for these additions, romantic and classical, is a matter of doubt. One can only say that Shakespeare seems to have known W. W.'s English translation of *Menaechmi* published in 1595, that he must have become acquainted with it in manuscript, and that he possibly knew the play in the original Latin. It would have been characteristic of his genius to make the changes and like his habits to have consulted all available sources in writing his play. Many critics since Malone have thought that Shakespeare may have been rewriting a lost play called *The Historie of Error* acted at the Queen's palace of Hampton Court on New Year's Day, 1577, and possibly mentioned in the Revels Accounts in 1582 as "The History of Ferror." Such a supposition is within the bounds of likelihood, but, after all, we have only the name to judge by. It has also been suggested that the *Amphitruo* scene, except the beginning and the end (ll. 1-10, 149-88), was taken over without great change from an old play. The beginning and end of the scene are in blank verse, a thing which is a pretty definite indication of Shakespeare's hand, while the body of the scene appears in doggerel verse. This verse form occurs in other plays, and one cannot say that Shakespeare might not have used it here; but the fact that the scene is one episode from one source does lend some plausibility to the belief that it is an extraneous unit. The Aegeon plot is probably Shakespeare's, since it is written in blank verse, which Shakespeare tended from the beginning of his career to use for serious narrative. The courtship of Luciana by Antipholus of Syracuse is also probably his, since it appears in rhyme, which he used for lovers' talk, a large part of it in quatrain rhyme similarly used in *Love's Labour's Lost*. Generally speaking, there is no reason to deny to Shakespeare the composition of *The Comedy of Errors*, which is a masterpiece of construction like all his early plays. The play is very short, and Dover Wilson may be right in his conjecture that certain indoor scenes, such as the dinner of Antipholus of Ephesus with Balthazar at the Porpentine, have been lost from the text because they required the use of the inner stage. The play as we have it, though originally written for the public stage, has evidently been adapted for acting on a stage without an inner chamber.

The Comedy of Errors is extremely deft in its handling. In spite of its many interests it is clear and easy to follow just as drama, without the aid of long explanatory speeches such as Plautus usually employs in order to make his action clear. The play begins in an epical manner with the story of Aegeon. So convincing is the pathos of the old man's situation that on the strength of the speech of the Second Merchant (V, i, 119-27)—

> Anon, I'm sure, the duke himself in person
> Comes this way to the melancholy vale,
> The place of death and sorry execution,
> Behind the ditches of the abbey here. . . .
> To see a reverend Syracusian merchant, . . .
> Beheaded publicly for his offence,

T. W. Baldwin thinks that Shakespeare must have had in mind the Priory of Holywell near the Theatre where Shakespeare's earlier plays were acted. Behind this priory or abbey. was the place of execution where a number of Roman Catholic priests were put to death.

The action of the comedy proper begins with the second scene of the first act, with the arrival in Ephesus of Antipholus of Syracuse and his servant, Dromio. The master, realizing that he is in a dangerous city, sends his servant with money to be kept safe at the Centaur. He has no sooner done so than error pops in in the person of Dromio of Ephesus, and the *Menaechmi* theme has begun. Dromio of Ephesus demands that Antipholus of Syracuse come home to dinner, while the Syracusan wants to know what has been done with his money. The dialogue is composed of clear and literal speaking on Dromio's part, plausible remonstrance by Antipholus, and exasperated and exact repetition by Dromio, and ends in a beating by Antipholus. Even after Dromio of Ephesus has saved himself by flight the matter lies so uneasily on the mind of Antipholus of Syracuse that he begins to fear the witch town of Ephesus. It had suited Plautus better to play up the wicked seductions of Epidamnus (I, ii, 97-103):

> They say this town is full of cozenage, . . .
> And many such-like liberties of sin:
> If it prove so, I will be gone the sooner.

The first scene of the third act brings in the *Amphitruo* episode, and the second scene the courtship of Luciana by Antipholus of Syracuse. It also contains some doggerel verse which leads into the Grobianism of the description by Dromio of Syracuse of the frightful charms of Nell or Luce. When his master asks whereabouts in the anatomy of the fat creature lies France, Dromio's reply seems to indicate a general date for the composition of the play (ll. 126-7):

> In her forehead; armed and reverted, making war against her heir.

There is a pun on the word "hair" of course, but the allusion seems to be to the civil war in France of the Catholic League against Henry of Navarre, which lasted from August, 1589 until July, 1593. The scene returns to the *Menaechmi* story at the end (ll. 170-90), and a change will be noted. The chain, which in Plautus had been stolen by Menaechmus the Citizen from Mulier and given to Erotium, is here in process of completion and delivery by Angelo the goldsmith on order by Antipholus of Ephesus. This alteration betters the characters of both the twin masters.

The second scene of the third act opens with love speeches in quatrain rhyme by Antipholus of Syracuse as he pays court to Luciana. It is an odd situation, since Luciana thinks that Antipholus of Syracuse is her sister's husband. She protests against his apparent treachery to her sister, but seems to be somehow convinced against her will by his eloquence. Truth in the spoken word had to be believed, and, when she leaves (l. 70), it is with a surprisingly naïve speech (ll. 69-70):

> O, soft, sir! hold you still:
> I'll fetch my sister, to get her good will.

She goes straight to Adriana and reports (IV, ii), but does not obtain the good will.

The story goes on in the first scene of the fourth act, but has been greatly complicated in Shakespeare by an urgent demand on Antipholus of Ephesus for payment for the chain, which he had indeed ordered but had not received. He is accordingly arrested for debt in the London manner and sends the wrong Dromio to his home to procure gold for his ransom.

The shrew theme occupies the second scene of the fourth act. Adriana is violent, but not so much so as her predecessor, Mulier, and is herself a person of better standing. Mulier is a mere Roman wife from whom any interference with her husband's doings is a mere impertinence. The scene also shows the immediate delivery of the ransom money to the wrong Antipholus. The fourth scene supplies the suggestion of madness and, as in *Menaechmi*, relates it in the first instance to the traveler. In the next scene is the uproarious examination of Antipholus of Ephesus for insanity by Dr. Pinch, but here, both in setting and execution, Shakespeare is inferior to Plautus. The fourth scene of the fourth act is wildly confused, but it is to be noted that the twin heroes have each come into a fixed mood. Antipholus of Ephesus is a bundle of indignation, and Antipholus of Syracuse is filled with superstitious dread of Ephesus.

The fifth act is very skillful and very rapid in action. It is an assembly or recognition scene and proceeds necessarily from error into truth. As one looks it over, one sees many gleams of dramatic interest, as in the conversation between the Abbess and her daughter-in-law (V, i, 38-112), which is beautifully ironical; as also in the danger point (ll. 130 ff.) when Aegeon crosses the stage on his way to execution. He is in charge of officers and accompanied by the Duke, a most reluctant executor of the law. The style of perplexed or indignant clarity also, on which the play subsists, is nowhere better used than in the speech of Antipholus of Ephesus (ll. 214-53). All the way through the play the characters react in perfect sincerity and with automatic faithfulness, which, it will be seen, is a necessary feature of a comedy of errors. The play is like Lucian or Swift in its adherence to a point of view. The characters speak and act what they believe to be truth while the audience, knowing the secret, chuckles in superiority. The recognition itself is held off until the latest possible time, an almost improbable time, since for either twin to see his fellow would have brought the comedy down like a house of cards. In dramatic manipulation *The Comedy of Errors* is not superior to *Menaechmi*, but it is far richer and of far greater general significance. It is worth pointing these things out because they show so well the difference between Elizabethan comedy and classical comedy.

2. *The Two Gentlemen of Verona*.

The dating of *The Two Gentlemen of Verona* is a difficult matter, but the play must be an early one. The text is correct and readable and the style relatively mature, but along with these qualities are the most glaring inconsistencies. In the matter of names, *Padua* occurs for *Milan* (II, v, 1), *Verona* for *Milan* (III, i, 81 and possibly V, iv, 129). Time sequence is mixed up, and there are various inconsistencies in speech and action. One would say, for example, that Proteus ought not to tolerate Speed's talk about Julia (I, i, 102-3). It is certainly odd that Valentine and Proteus journey from Verona to Milan by ship, although Julia apparently takes the same journey in the only possible way—by land. Lucetta is the champion of Proteus in Act I, scene ii, but warns her mistress against his falsity in Act II, scene vii, which bears some resemblance to the Portia-Nerissa dialogue about the suitors in *The Merchant of Venice*. There is also an unexplained and unnecessary reference to a letter in Act IV, scene iv, lines 126-9, and, finally, the famous puzzling silence of Silvia in the last scene of the play. One expects that Julia's lovers will play parts in the play, but their rôles cannot be traced. Silvia's suitors are equally difficult. Some hint of an explanation for the latter group may be found in the two Eglamours—Julia's suitor (I, ii) and Silvia's friend (V, i). When the Duke and Proteus are discussing how they may make Silvia forget Valentine after his banishment (III, ii, 31-3), Proteus says,

> The best way is to slander Valentine
> With falsehood, cowardice and poor descent,
> Three things that women highly hold in hate.

Proteus and Thurio, two of Silvia's lovers, are certainly guilty of falsehood and cowardice respectively; and Sir Eglamour, who is perhaps of poor descent, may be the third of Silvia's lovers. This state of the case would indicate that two ladies, originally one in the source, have had one set of lovers divided between them. Dover Wilson argues that *The Two Gentlemen of Verona*, as we have it, shows evidence of drastic abridgment and adaptation. The soliloquies, he thinks, have been shortened; scenes have been telescoped and sometimes omitted; some scenes have been rewritten or patched in prose; and the Speed scenes are, he thinks, un-Shakespearean. However these things may be, and there is much evidence of confusion, the play is unmistakably early in its tone. In the performance by the Stratford players in 1938, not for some reason acceptable to contemporary dramatic critics, the comedy was interpreted as an affair of boys and girls— heroic and cowardly, formal and informal, virtuous and outrageous, with all the determined idealism and the unconscious selfishness and inconsistency of youth. In such a dramatic performance the famous quixotic line (V, iv, 83) of Valentine when he forgives his nefarious friend Proteus,

> All that was mine in Silvia I give thee,

becomes intelligible and harmless. This line so shocked Sir Arthur Quiller-Couch that he declares that it shows that there is no longer even one gentleman of Verona, but this is to take the matter too seriously. Valentine is merely playing overmagnificently the part set down in current courtly dogma of the perfect friend.

The Two Gentlemen of Verona has a significance in Shakespeare's dramatic development not always recognized. It was most fortunate that he chose that story, or group of stories, early in his career; for it engaged him in a popular body of Renaissance fiction full of social ideas, sensational, ingenious, and fascinating. The story, originally the same as that which underlies *Twelfth Night* and fragmentarily reproduced in many narratives and plays, might almost be described as the most familiar plot of Renaissance comedy. The closest analogues to *The Two Gentlemen of Verona* are the story of Felix and Felismena in Montemayor's *Diana Enamorada* and the adventures in friendship and love of Claribel and Floradine in Henry Wotton's *A Courtlie Controversy of Cupid's Cautels* (1578), a translation of five stories from Jacques d'Yver's *Le printemps d'Yver*. Probably neither Montemayor nor Jacques is an immediate source. There are two main features of the plot, the pursuit of a wayward lover by a maiden disguised as a page and the problem made familiar by Lyly's

Euphues, of the man who woos the ladylove of his sworn brother in friendship. These themes appear again and again in Renaissance drama and fiction, and one can see that Shakespeare's handling of them in *The Two Gentlemen of Verona* enabled him to develop the technique which he later employed in his great romantic comedies. The love-versus-friendship theme appears in an extraordinarily large number of Renaissance works.

As Shakespeare presents it, there is added to the fascinating story of a girl disguised as a page going in search of a wayward lover, the story of the sworn friend false in the rivalry of love. I believe that Shakespeare made this addition to the plot in order to give the story a happy ending by providing lovers for both women, as well as to exploit the love-friendship theme already popularized in England by Lyly in *Euphues.* But whether this is true or not, the most original thing he did was to center the interest of his story in the disguised woman, a thing which had never been done before in England or in Italy, except to a minor extent in the case of Dorothea in Greene's *James IV.* There is a certain new consistency in Julia's character. Shakespeare has indicated to us how she felt as a woman in man's clothes and how she bore her helplessness. It is often said that Julia is an early sketch for Viola and Imogen, and it is true that the psychology of a woman in Julia's situation is more excellently presented in Viola and triumphantly realized in Imogen; but the dramatic discovery has already been made in Julia. Similarly, the presentation of Silvia may have suggested to Shakespeare the self-contained, humorous, and efficient woman he was later to give us in Portia and Rosalind. *The Two Gentlemen of Verona* has long been regarded as the forerunner of much of Shakespeare's later work in social comedy. If so, it is also the forerunner of nearly all that the Elizabethan drama ever achieved in that form. I emphasize this by suggesting that the task of writing a play on a popular Renaissance topic started Shakespeare in one of his great lines of achievement, namely, the individualizing and humanizing of women in the drama.

3. *Love's Labour's Lost.*

Love's Labour's Lost was published in a revised state in 1598, the year in which it was mentioned by Francis Meres in *Palladis Tamia* and alluded to by Robert Tofte in *Alba.* By that time it must have been an old work, since it shows even in the revised state all the characteristics of Shakespeare's earliest style: rhyme in couplets, quatrains and sonnets, doggerel verse, and end-stopped blank verse free from light and weak endings. The play also teems with puns and conceits and is artificial and highly elaborate in plot. The characters, who are lightly but clearly delineated, are balanced off mechanically one against another. A princess and three ladies-in-waiting are wooed by a king and three attendant lords. In its sophistication as a courtly comedy it surpasses Lyly himself. In the play are the Renaissance fashion of established academies for the pursuit of learning, courtly entertainment and courtly gossip, and the language of euphuism, all so employed that it is difficult to say whether Shakespeare means to make fun of these things or whether he was working delightedly in an atmosphere and style whose extravagance he enjoyed. The play is youthful and pastoral, full of a Renaissance zest for learning and for school books and school days. In *Love's Labour's Lost* Shakespeare may be said to have discovered the temper of the courtly audience, of the gay youths with Southampton at their head who took delight in a drama which showed them pictures of themselves and their world. That it is Shakespeare's play is made clear by its foreshadowings, particularly in the attitudes of the lovers. Biron is the first of Shakespeare's critical and intellectual heroes, an early Benedict, and Rosaline the first of his witty and self-possessed heroines.

Love's Labour's Lost begins with the courtly theme—the emptiness, insincerity, and vanity of the court *vs.* the wisdom, color, and sincerity of country life, but not country life alone. Shakespeare, who had been brought up in the country, knew about the rough hands of milkmaids and the realities of holding the plow. The antagonist of courtly life in *Love's Labour's Lost* is not mere pastoralism; it is the life of contemplation, with all the merits of a pastoral existence and none of its rigors. In other words, the play opens with an attempt to establish that last word in Renaissance refinement, an academy. Ferdinand of Navarre, with his three friends and followers, Biron, Dumain, and Longaville, has made his castle into a monastic institution. It is a youthful venture, and, having no experience as to what constitutes the practical in this world, the members first make laws and then proceed to enforce an unworkable ideal.

The statutes call for an ascetic life, with which in general nobody quarrels, but in so far as it is monastic all the world knows that there are difficulties. It is Biron who calls attention, not only to the difficulty, but to a present obstacle. He will sign up and promise to study for three years, but, as for the promise not to see a woman during that term, he will study to break it and not break his troth. Since the French king's daughter is on her way to treat with the King of Navarre about Navarre's surrender of certain provinces to the French king, the resolution to abstain from women's society is to have an immediate test and apparently a severe one; the Princess is a maid of grace and complete majesty. The Princess arrives accompanied by a clever courtier named Boyet and three charming ladies-in-waiting: Rosaline, first and not least charming of Shakespeare's witty and resourceful women, Katharine, and Maria. Although the party of the Princess is not permitted to enter the palace but is to be entertained in the park, the dramatic advantage is on their side from the start. As if dealing cards, the dramatist, with formal regularity, sees to it that each lord, from the King down, is smitten with love for one of the ladies. The King falls in love with the Princess, Longaville with Maria, Dumain with Katharine, and Biron with the dark Rosaline. The courtiers stand guilty but unconvicted, and in a scene of clever and simple ingenuity they have their defections revealed to one another. This is the third scene of the fourth act, a famous and most amusing scene. It is based on the device of eavesdropping. All youthful Renaissance lovers had to have relief from their agonies, and that relief conventionally is in the composition of poetry. Biron, really as deeply involved as the rest of them, is the first to conceal himself. He overhears the gentle complaints of the King, who also hides and has the advantage of Longaville and of Dumain, who enter one after the other and reveal their love-longing. In the ensuing revelations Biron delights in his apparent victory, only to be revealed as the chief sinner of all. The betrayal of Biron is the main service of the minor plot to the major plot. The clown, Costard, has been entrusted with love letters from Armado to Jaquenetta and from Biron to Rosaline, and by a characteristic blunder transposes them in delivery. The academicians are thus all convicted of breaking their vows.

The interesting thing about the complicated issue is that Biron defends the treachery of the lovers in a really great speech (IV, iii, 314-334) which seems to give us Shakespeare's view of the whole transaction:

> Learning is but an adjunct to ourself
> And where we are our learning likewise is:
> Then when ourselves we see in ladies' eyes,
> Do we not likewise see our learning there? . . .

Other slow arts entirely keep the brain;
And therefore, finding barren practisers,
Scarce show a harvest of their heavy toil:
But love, first learned in a lady's eyes,
Lives not alone immured in the brain;
But, with the motion of all elements,
Courses as swift as thought in every power,
And gives to every power a double power,
Above their functions and their offices.
It adds a precious seeing to the eye;
A lover's eyes will gaze an eagle blind.

This seems to point to the irresistible and dynamic power of love and to its kinship with all beneficent forces. Much has been made of the speech and the quick unanimous decision which follows it on the part of the lovers to devote themselves, forsworn or not forsworn, to the immediate business of courtship; but before we make *Love's Labour's Lost* too philosophic, let us remember that the lords were very young and that the play was written to please a court, one of whose chief interests lay in the casuistical ins and outs of love and courtship. Again, a serious meaning is seen in the temporary frustration of the lovers in spite of their best efforts, a frustration due to the intervention of the hand of fate. The father of the Princess dies, and all courtship is suspended for a year. No doubt Shakespeare does mean to say that the lovers, when they are permitted to begin again, should·exercise a little more sense and meantime should take steps to acquire it. But again we have the formal element in a sort of punishment for broken vows. The King must retire for a year to a forlorn and naked hermitage, and Biron must cure his gibing spirit by spending a year in care of the speechless sick and converse with groaning wretches. He must learn another serious, perhaps cruel, side of life; yet, after all, this is pretty simple ethics.

The underplot, not without immediate reflection of the main plot, is so devoted to ridiculing current pedantry and affectation that, but for its wit, it has grown old-fashioned and hard to bring to life. There are no rich comic situations such as those in *A Comedy of Errors*, but many of the lines are unforgettable. "Remuneration! O! That's the Latin word for three farthings" remarks Costard. "He draweth out the thread of his verbosity finer than the staple of his argument" is one of the excellent pedantries of Holophernes, from whom also comes, "Priscian a little scratched, 'twill serve" and "Ah! good old Mantuan! who understandeth thee not, loves thee not." The immortal characterization of the whole group comes from Moth: "They have been at a great feast of languages, and stolen the scraps."

4. A Midsummer-Night's Dream.

A Midsummer-Night's Dream is the best of Shakespeare's early comedies. It has courtly interest, popular appeal, and a marvelous ingenuity in plot construction; there is no better managed multiple plot in the range of Elizabethan drama. This is the more remarkable because of the blending of varied elements and the creation of a dreamlike atmosphere. The plot of the wedding of Theseus and Hippolyta, the statesmanlike Theseus derived from Plutarch, forms, so to speak, the framework or border of the tapestry. The plot of the lovers, Demetrius and Helena, Lysander and Hermia, forms the central theme and is treated with such lightness of touch, such conventionality of style, such suggestion of youthfulness, that, in spite of its threatened griefs, it is not taken too seriously. The famous drama prepared by Bottom and his associates—"A tedious brief scene of young Pyramus and his love Thisbe; very tragical mirth"—is designed for the wedding of the royal personages. The fairy plot of Oberon and Titania ties the others together and serves to unify them. The king and queen of the fairies have come to Athens to attend the wedding; fairies are much interested in marriages and births. Oberon is jealous of Titania and Theseus, and rightly so; for Titania, who as a fairy has no social morals, has before this time assisted Theseus in some of his not too creditable love affairs. Titania pretends also to be jealous of Oberon and Hippolyta. Fairies get their recruits by the adoption of stray babies; therefore these jealousies are not marital but are jealousies of favor. When the disagreements of Oberon and Titania have been adjusted, they bless the marriage bed of Theseus and Hippolyta, and also of the lovers, whose difficulties they have likewise smoothed out. The weather accordingly improves.

The style of A Midsummer-Night's Dream serves like color to illuminate and separate the plots. Theseus and Hippolyta, as royalty, speak in blank verse; the lovers speak usually in rhymed couplets, which formalize their troubles; the fairies appropriately employ a lyrical measure, trochaic tetrameter, except of course Oberon when he speaks as a king; the rustic actors speak in prose, the only appropriate medium and long conventionally employed for scenes of clownage; even the play of Pyramus and Thisbe has a meter of its own, a ballad measure as absurd as the play itself.

A Midsummer-Night's Dream is thus a culmination of Shakespeare's early achievements in comedy. The play is a masterpiece in the weaving together into one story of a series of apparently unrelated plots, a method for which Shakespeare has always been famous. By his practice he refuted the classicists in drama in the matter of the unities, although the critical world down to the times of Dr. Samuel Johnson refused to see that he had done so. Dr. Johnson's enlightened common sense made him see that Shakespeare himself is the arbiter, since he never fails to attain his purpose: "as he commands us, we laugh or mourn, or sit silent with quiet expectation, in tranquility without indifference." As to variety in the picture of life, Johnson says truly enough, "That the mingled drama may convey all the instruction of tragedy or comedy cannot be denied, because it includes both in its alternations of exhibition, and approaches nearer than either to the appearance of life, by showing how great machinations and slender designs may promote or obviate one another, and the high and low cooperate in the general system by unavoidable concatenation." That Shakespeare "approximates the remote and familiarizes the wonderful" enables him to show human nature "as it acts in real exigencies." With one strong puff from his manly chest Dr. Johnson blew away the fog of criticism surrounding Shakespeare's violations of the unities of time and place; for, said he, "The truth is, that the spectators are always in their senses, and know, from the first act to the last, that the stage is only a stage, and that the players are only players." "Imitations produce pain or pleasure," he says, "not because they are mistaken for realities, but because they bring realities to the mind." Shakespeare himself was not ignorant of this principle if we may judge by the words which pass between Theseus and Hippolyta as they witness (V, i, 212-16) the "Tedious brief scene of young Pyramus and his love Thisbe; very tragical mirth." She says

> This is the silliest stuff that ever I heard,

to which Theseus replies,

> The best in this kind are but shadows; and the worst are no worse, if imagination amend them.

She rejoins truly,

> It must be your imagination then, and not theirs.

There is a unity derivable from multiplicity, an ancient and natural form of art seen to this day in early tapestries and in oriental decorative art. Such art rejects perspective and distributes its emphasis.

Another feature of *A Midsummer-Night's Dream* which challenges discussion is its possible reflection of living men and current events. The attempt to prove topical and allegorical significances in Shakespeare's plays has not on the whole met with success. In practice we have to admit with Matthew Arnold: "Others abide our question. Thou art free." But from the earliest times critics have observed a puzzling yet unmistakable allusion to Queen Elizabeth in this play—Oberon is instructing Puck on where to find the flower called love-in-idleness, whose juice has magical powers over the eyes of awakening lovers; and he says (II, i, 148-64):

> Thou rememberest
> Since once I sat upon a promontory,
> And heard a mermaid on a dolphin's back
> Uttering such dulcet and harmonius breath
> That the rude sea grew civil at her song,
> And certain stars shot madly from their spheres,
> To hear the sea-maid's music?
> *Puck.*   I remember.
> *Obe.* That very time I saw, but thou couldst not,
> Flying between the cold moon and the earth,
> Cupid all arm'd: a certain aim he took
> At a fair vestal throned by the west,
> And loosed his love-shaft smartly from his bow,
> As it should pierce a hundred thousand hearts;
> But I might see young Cupid's fiery shaft
> Quench'd in the chaste beams of the watery moon,
> And the imperial votaress passed on,
> In maiden meditation, fancy-free.

This is an allusion to some attempt (there were many such) to gain the favor of the Virgin Queen by a show of pageantry and music. What the occasion was has long been the quest of scholars. Most of them have thought the passage alludes to an assault on Elizabeth's heart by the Earl of Leicester in his "princely pleasures" at Kenilworth in 1575. A newer and on the whole a better idea is that of the late Edith Rickert, who saw in the passage and in all the events of the play an extended reference to the festivities at Elvetham in 1591, where the Earl of Hertford sought to win the Queen's favor for the so-called Hertford heir, his child by Lady Katharine Grey, tyrannously declared illegitimate by Elizabeth. In this view the "changeling child" in dispute between Titania (Elizabeth?) and Oberon (King Henry VIII?) is the disprized youth, and the play, as well as the pageant, was designed to urge the Queen to heed her father's will and restore the youth to legitimacy. This theory is supported by many convincing details and, although it has some difficulties, is the most credible of all accounts so far advanced. One effect of its acceptance would be the dating of the play, as originally written, in 1591.

b. Early tragedies.

1. *Titus Andronicus.*

Shakespeare's earliest tragedy, *Titus Andronicus* (publ. 1594), has been so disappointing to readers and critics that they have attempted to relieve him of the responsibility of writing so bloody, so revolting a play. The case for his authorship, externally considered, is nevertheless a very good one. Strange's men produced a *Titus and Vespasian* in Henslowe's theater on April 11, 1592. This is not Shakespeare's play, but may be a forerunner of it. It at least suggests that Shakespeare's company had a play on the subject in their repertory, for in *Tito Andronico*, a German version, the Lucius of Shakespeare's play appears as Vespasianus. The German *Titus* is probably one of those carried to Germany in the late sixteenth century by the English traveling players. A play, however, recorded by Henslowe as having been acted by the Lord Chamberlain's or the Lord Admiral's company on the 7th and 14th of June, 1594, may very well have been Shakespeare's. The title-page of the first quarto edition, published that year, states that the play had been played by the Earl of Derby's (i.e. Lord Strange's), the Earl of Pembroke's, and the Earl of Sussex's servants. This has caused more confusion than it warrants. It does not necessarily mean that all these companies had acted this particular play, but only that they had all acted a play on the same subject. The Elizabethans did not discriminate among versions, but among subjects. For example, it was not necessary at the time of the publication of the First Folio to enter *King John* in the Stationers' Register, since *The Troublesome Raigne* had already been entered. Indeed, there is an illustration closer at hand than that. John Danter, on February 6, 1594, entered a prose version, *A Noble Roman History of Titus Andronicus,* and was apparently at liberty to print Shakespeare's *Titus Andronicus* on the same entry. *Titus Andronicus* was claimed as Shakespeare's by the editors of the First Folio in 1623. The play was in their stock, and they were able to supply a version to the printers with one scene not previously published. Meres lists *Titus Andronicus* as one of Shakespeare's tragedies in *Palladis Tamia* in 1598.

Nor is the case, internally considered, a bad one. It is yet to be shown that the Elizabethans looked upon the play with horror and revulsion; it is not the only violent tragedy of the time, nor the only case of blood and horror in Shakespeare himself. The play is, moreover, well and powerfully written. The fact that *Titus Andronicus* is well written and well constructed is not necessarily an argument for Shakespeare's authorship, but, when it is pointed out what was done in this particular dramatization of the story, the probability is increased. From the sources of the play it is possible to see how *Titus Andronicus* differs from other versions. There are a Dutch play, *Aran en Titus*, by Jan Vos, first printed in 1641, but evidently much older; a German play, *Tito Andronico*, published in 1620; and a lost German play, acted at Linz in 1699, of which a program survives. There is also the newly discovered "*The History of Titus Andronicus, The Renowned Roman General* . . . Newly translated from the *Italian* copy printed at Rome." This is preserved only in an eighteenth-century chapbook, but is plausibly connected by Dr. J. Q. Adams with Danter's entry mentioned above. With it is the already familiar ballad, "*The Lamentable and Tragical History of Titus Andronicus* . . . To the tune of *Fortune my Foe*," a ballad drawn at least in part from Shakespeare's play and therefore to be disregarded.

Not one of these versions, although telling the same story, approaches the problem as Shakespeare approaches it. Shakespeare's first act is so constructed as to make a Senecan tragedy out of the crude story. That act begins with the momentous quarrel between Saturninus and Bassianus for the imperial diadem. Titus enters from his conquests, and he himself makes the fatal decision between the claimants. He chooses Saturninus and in this tragical blunder provides for his own ultimate downfall. Titus next exacts the sacrifice of one of Tamora's sons to the shades of his own fallen offspring, thus instituting a motive of revenge. Bassianus and Marcus carry off Lavinia, and Titus makes a fatefully wrong decision also in that matter. Finally, Saturninus chooses Tamora as his queen, without, however, forgiving the offence committed against him in the seizure of Lavinia. These are first-act matters, and the tragedy unfolds in perfect Senecan order from these causes selected or invented by Shakespeare. This expert plot management is an indication of Shakespeare's authorship.

Titus Andronicus was apparently written after June 26, 1593, the date of Peele's *Honour of the Garter*, and yet looks like an early and very careful essay in the neo-Senecan tragedy probably invented by Thomas Kyd and gloriously exemplified in *The Spanish Tragedy*. It is even possible that Kyd's lost play on the story of *Hamlet* affected Shakespeare thus early in his dramatic career. The old *Hamlet* probably belonged to Shakespeare's company, since he felt free to rewrite it later. Shakespeare may have acted in both *The Spanish Tragedy* and the old *Hamlet*. An early play of *Titus Andronicus* was carried to the continent by traveling companies of English players and in various versions is represented by a Dutch drama by Jan Vos, *Aran en Titus* (publ. 1620), and by the German versions enumerated above. These continental plays deal with the story of Titus .Andronicus, but they are not based on Shakespeare's play. They differ in just those features which serve to recast the story as a Senecan tragedy with tragic guilt and the revenge motive. They agree, moreover, among themselves in certain important variations from the Shakespearean text, although their agreements as compared with Shakespeare's play point to a common source with *Titus Andronicus*. If we could subtract these plays from Shakespeare, we might ascertain the truly interesting and important thing about the whole matter, namely, what Shakespeare did to this plot when he handled it. Procedure is rendered easier and more certain by the contribution of Dr. J. Q. Adams. The existence of a quarto version of *Titus Andronicus* dated 1594 was known to Gerard Langbaine and apparently to Malone, but no such edition was at hand until 1904 when a copy was discovered at Malmö, Sweden. This copy passed into the possession of H. C. Folger and eventually into the Folger Shakespeare Library. It was issued by Dr. Adams in facsimile in 1938. In his introduction to the volume he announced the discovery of a prose tale of Titus Andronicus reprinted from time to time following Danter's version and finally appearing as a chapbook during the eighteenth century. The presumption is that this largely fictitious prose tale is the source of the Titus Andronicus dramas. The parts invented or emphasized by Shakespeare are the rivalry of Saturninus and Bassianus for the imperial throne; the funeral of the sons of Titus; the carrying off of Lavinia by Bassianus with the slaying by Titus of his son Mutius and the events which follow from it—in other words, the entire first act. Besides these, there is the sending of young Lucius with a present of weapons in the second scene of the fourth act, and the whole of the second scene of the third act, a lyrical scene of the madness of Titus which reinforces the climax of the play. The result of these shifts and emphases is that the bloody and violent action of the plot is shoved back into the second and third acts, and one may say that Shakespeare has provided both a political and a personal setting for the tragedy. In other words, *Titus Andronicus* is theoretically—in intent and structure—a very great tragedy. Practically it is not so. The style is usually excellent and conforms in its strength and dignity to the somber theme of the tragedy. In spite of Shakespeare's masterly motivation in his re-arrangement of scenes, and in spite of excellent invention and noble rhetoric, *Titus Andronicus* remains a relatively unpleasing work. We may say that the subject is impossible, unsuited to Shakespeare's wise and gentle genius, and these things are true; but it is the change in our race and its *mores* which is to be blamed, or it may be to be congratulated, that *Titus Andronicus* has lost its charm. The play was popular in its day, and it, or some version of it, was recorded fifteen times in Henslowe's Diary. Ben Jonson, looking scornfully back at its ancient vogue, speaks in *Bartholomew Fair* (1614) to those "who swear *Ieronimo* and *Andronicus* are the best plays yet." Ravenscroft made a Restoration version of *Titus Andronicus*, acted in 1678, and the drama was revived at Drury Lane Theatre in 1717, so that it still had some popular appeal as late as that, but in the nineteenth century, when the play was revived by Ira Aldridge in London and Dublin, it is said that the actors of Aldridge's company were reluctant to appear in it. The modern objection to *Titus Andronicus* is not mere squeamishness. The play is indeed horrible with a horror that nobody but Shakespeare could have given it.

2. *Romeo and Juliet*.

Romeo and Juliet, Shakespeare's other early tragedy, is a masterpiece, romantic rather than Senecan. It may go back in its earliest form to 1591, since the Nurse says (I, iii, 23), " 'Tis since the earthquake now eleven years." This Tyrwhitt thought an allusion to the earthquake of April 6, 1580. Our version, which has been revised, was printed in 1599. Part of the success of *Romeo and Juliet* is attributable to the excellence of the story, a story so great, so human and moving in its barest outlines, that it is impossible to tell it so badly that it loses its interest. The development of Elizabethan drama may owe much to the happy choice of a few great plots, such as those of Romeo and Juliet and Dr. Faustus. *Romeo and Juliet* is based on a widely current story appearing in many versions, and always striking. It is in the *Ephesiaca* of Xenophon of Ephesus and in the *Novelle* of Massuccio of Salerno (1476). Luigi da Porto writes it in developed form (1530). Bandello tells it (1554), as does Pierre Boisteau (1559), a version appearing in Painter's *Palace of Pleasure* (1566). Arthur Brooke wrote in English hexameters his poem *Romeus and Juliet* (1562), which is Shakespeare's immediate source. The great story had grown and developed throughout its history, and, although Shakespeare made interesting changes in the narrative, they are relatively few and structurally unimportant. Shakespeare's exploitation of youthful sentiment is his principal contribution; for, as he presents it, the play expresses from the point of view of tragedy the ardors and errors of impetuous youth.

Romeo and Juliet is not of course a mere tale of a particular youth and maiden who are caught up and destroyed by the selfish and worldly quarrels of their elders. It treats the wrongs that guiltless youth forever suffers from the wickedness of the organized society into which it is born. Not only does society by its vanities, greeds, and vices spoil its youth, generation after generation, but it often takes the lives of young men and destroys their happiness and that of young people of the other sex. In a very large and general view the habits of war bring down great scourges upon us—spoil our lives, destroy our property, and take the lives of our young men, who have had nothing to do with the conditions which make it necessary for them to give their lives to save their country. This introduces a perplexing question, for which perhaps the best answer is that the sins of the fathers are being visited upon the children and that that is an inevitable law of nature. And yet it is a mistake to look upon youth in this play or in the world as merely martyred. Youth is truly dependent on age, for youth is foolish, headstrong, and over-impetuous. This is true of Romeo and Juliet, who, like all youth, rejected the ways of wisdom and policy and, in the ill-considered pursuit of their desires, met their death. When youth ceases to be over-impetuous, age will cease to be over-cautious. We must rationalize and equate these qualities and not say that youth is right and age is wrong. Youth is right from the point of view of youth, and age is right from the point of view of age. Both youth and age are children in the eye of God. We merely stress the age-old clash between youth and the venerable forms of the world into which youth is born. We may even go a little further and say that youth carries on a battle against age and that in our generation youth has won and still holds vast conquests. It is amusing to live long enough to see youth, grown middle-aged and a little gray, take up arms against succeeding youth which will certainly intrude upon it.

Romeo and Juliet is a tragedy of partisanship in state and family, although it is primarily a tragedy of love and courtship; it is also a tragedy of youth and age. Since it is made to hinge on personal honor, there enters the hand of fate. Could Romeo have lived a self-respecting man and yet refrained from slaying Tybalt? Why might not Friar John have got through to Mantua and informed the impetuous Romeo of the true state of the case? Why could not Friar Lawrence, old and infirm as he is, arrive at the tomb of the Capulets ahead of Romeo? May we in life rely on the success of any such venture? Good fortune often loiters on the way, and mischance moves with the speed of lightning.

The problem of this play as a tragedy has never been completely solved, and it may never be. Two lovely, innocent young figures, who were all that they had a right to be even in practical wisdom, are certainly caught in a net not of their own making. They would have been wiser and more prudent had they been older, but in that case they would not have been Romeo and Juliet. The existence of that tragic net stresses the fact that we cannot select our ancestors or even our parents. Our heredity controls us. We are doomed, shall we say, because of Adam's fall; but who was Adam? Was he too doomed by the dust of which he was made? Romeo and Juliet certainly were not prudent, for they tried to do a thing, a brave and beautiful thing, against the general compelling scheme on which the world is based. It was beyond their powers and unachievable by their methods. Their environment was to them an ultimate law. When we realize what their purpose is, we know that they are going to suffer. According to Hegel we are satisfied to see the law assert its ancient prerogative; we see this gladly as regards the feudist families and reluctantly as regards the two young lovers. But our rebellion in behalf of the children outweighs any satisfaction we may feel, and that is not all. The failure of these young lovers was not determined. They suffer through a set of forces by no means certain in their operation. We know these forces, for they may operate on us today. Romeo and Juliet are "star-crossed." No one can deny that; nevertheless, but for a minor failure of contrivance, human contrivance, they would have succeeded, escaped from Verona, and lived happily in a distant land.

Romeo and Juliet struggle valiantly and sweetly, and their words are words of beauty. There are a variety of telling expressions of human situation. Note these cases in which situations are brilliantly revealed. In the first scene appear Sampson and Gregory, not important characters and yet perfectly discriminated. They are both bullies equally anxious to fight. Gregory is a humorist; Sampson, quite used to missing the point of Gregory's wit, is humorless. In the same scene observe the two styles of Romeo, the sentimental style of the professed lover and the ordinary style of the man.

> Ay me! sad hours seem long.
> Was that my father that went hence so fast?

Mercutio's famous speech about Queen Mab, spoken while the youthful Montagues are on their way to the Capulet's ball (I, iv, 53-94), although utterly unrelated to the theme of the play, is so much a matter of mere background, so much an ebullition of mere youth, that it does not seem excrescent. Indeed, all the speeches of the earlier part of the play seem mere echoes of nature. When Romeo beholds Juliet (I, v) he speaks in the very voice of youthful love. He says to a servingman, "What lady is that, which doth enrich the hand of yonder knight," and then breaks out into one of the most spontaneous, the most unpremeditated utterances in all drama:

> O, she doth teach the torches to burn bright!
> It seems she hangs upon the cheek of night
> Like a rich jewel in an Ethiope's ear;
> Beauty too rich for use, for earth too dear!
> So shows a snowy dove trooping with crows,
> As yonder lady o'er her fellows shows.
> The measure done, I'll watch her place of stand,
> And, touching hers, make blessed my rude hand.
> Did my heart love till now? forswear it, sight!
> For I ne'er saw true beauty till this night.

Upon this youthful, natural, impulsive speech of innocent love crashes the terrible voice of Tybalt like the voice of doom or untoward fatal accident:

> This, by his voice, should be a Montague.
> Fetch me my rapier, boy. What dares the slave
> Come hither, cover'd with an antic face,
> To fleer and scorn at our solemnity?
> Now, by the stock and honour of my kin,
> To strike him dead I hold it not a sin.

Another speech of Romeo (II, vi, 3-8) has always seemed perfectly expressive of the fire and passion of the play and of Romeo himself. Friar Lawrence has just uttered a pious wish:

> So smile the heavens upon this holy act,
> That after hours with sorrow chide us not!

To this Romeo replies:

> Amen, amen! but come what sorrow can,
> It cannot countervail the exchange of joy
> That one short minute gives me in her sight:
> Do thou but close our hands with holy words,
> Then love-devouring death do what he dare;
> It is enough I may but call her mine.

The active, daring Renaissance itself never found a better voice. Indeed, Romeo is, along with Philip Sidney and Henry of Navarre, one of the typical men of the Renaissance. Observe, not only his haste, but his practical efficiency. How quickly does he consummate his marriage, how deftly make his escape! Note the savage certainty in his resolution to slay Tybalt (III, i, 130-4). But nowhere does the hard core of Romeo's character appear more strikingly than in the scene in Mantua. Balthasar tells him that Juliet's body sleeps in Capel's monument, and Romeo says:

> Is it even so? then I defy you, stars!

The reflection of the mood is plain in Romeo's almost pathetic pleading with Paris to avoid his impending fate (V, iii, 58-67). Paris' speech ends, "for thou must die," and Romeo's reply is:

> I must indeed; and therefore came I hither.

The ultimate judgment upon Romeo would show him as an exemplar of Shakespeare's conception of the finest Renaissance man: "for he was likely, had he been put on, To have proved most royally."

Juliet too stands out from the generality of women, has in her the qualities of a Portia or an Hermione. Shakespeare has endowed her with rare intelligence, resourcefulness, and a courage which is surpassingly excellent. Where is there such a test of courage as Juliet is subjected to when she swallows the sleeping potion (IV, iii, 14-58)? Note the wise and searching words, the bravery tempered by wisdom, and the final plunge actuated by love.

> Farewell! God knows when we shall meet again.
> I have a faint cold fear thrills through my veins,
> That almost freezes up the heat of life:
> I'll call them back again to comfort me: . . .
> O, if I wake, shall I not be distraught,
> Environed with all these hideous fears?
> And madly play with my forefathers' joints?
> And pluck the mangled Tybalt from his shroud?
> And, in this rage, with some great kinsman's bone,
> As with a club, dash out my desperate brains?
> O, look! methinks I see my cousin's ghost
> Seeking out Romeo, that did spit his body
> Upon a rapier's point: stay, Tybalt, stay!
> Romeo, I come! this do I drink to thee.

This is the ultimate of terror.

"Men fear death," says Bacon, "as children fear to go in the dark. . . . Groans and convulsions, and a discoloured face, and friends weeping, and blacks and obsequies, and the like, show death terrible . . . Revenge triumphs over death; Love slights it; Honor aspireth to it; Grief flieth to it; Fear pre-occupateth it. . . . Death hath this also; that it openeth the gate to good fame, and extinguisheth envy."

It is useless to comment at length on *Romeo and Juliet*, whose lessons are obvious and whose beauty is perennial. Perhaps the broadest significance of the play lies in the succession of the generations. Youth is forever born into a world not of its own making, and the sins of the fathers are continually visited upon the children. What had this youth and maiden to do with the ancient, stupid feud of the Montagues and Capulets? And what in general has youth had to do with the error, perplexities, injustices, and crimes which it finds in our world or in any world? Youth often destroys itself in the age-old sins and cruelties of a new and unknown life, destroys itself because of its own ignorance and willfulness. The tragedy is that age has its heart broken because it has destroyed youth.

CHAPTER III

The Beginnings (continued)

THE HENRY VI PLAYS AND RICHARD III

1. The Henry VI Plays.

THE deeper comprehension of the issues of life which even the early comedies reveal found in the history plays its natural outlet. Of these 2 *Henry VI* seems to be Shakespeare's earliest effort in the dramatization of history; at least it is the most primitive of his history plays in style and technique. It would seem to have been written as early as 1591. It is a serious, and on the whole a successful, attempt to depict the troubles of the middle years of Henry VI's reign and to give them their political and historical significance. It is the first real history play. There had been plays on historical subjects before, but they were plays only and not history. Such are Greene's *James IV*, Peele's *Edward I*, and *The Famous Victories of Henry V*, which in the use of selected and invented episodes shirked the responsibilities which Shakespeare assumed. Holinshed's account of the reign of Henry VI is dramatized by Shakespeare with a fidelity that no other dramatist had observed. It is as if Shakespeare had taken England as his hero. Even Marlowe's *Edward II*, in which play he comes nearest actual history, is further from the two principal sources than Shakespeare is from his source and is more Senecan, more dramatically artificial. Moreover, with the certainty derived from Greene that 3 *Henry VI* was on the stage by the summer of 1592, Marlowe's historical tragedy, which can hardly be earlier than that year, is probably a later play than the second, if not the third part, of *Henry VI*. The crude and powerful play which presents so vividly the passion of Suffolk and Margaret, the malice of Winchester, the rectitude and the pathos of the good Duke Humphrey, the humorous life and courageous death of Jack

Cade, and the steady climb of dogged York, appears to be the work of a pioneer.

A different aspect appears in *1 Henry VI*, which is pretty obviously based on an older play in the older style, probably a chauvinistic play glorifying the English and belittling the French, a Talbot play with a crude and cruel picture of Joan of Arc. This old play was apparently revised or rewritten in such a way as to make it much closer to Holinshed, also to make the play look forward to *2* and *3 Henry VI*. The added parts seem to be the scene in the Temple Garden where the red rose becomes the symbol of Lancaster and the white rose of York, the more kindly scenes of Joan's rise to power, the partisanship of York and Somerset which cause the defeat and death of Talbot, Suffolk's capture of Margaret, and the weak King's violation of his pledge to Armagnac's daughter. Perhaps the Talbot scenes have been rewritten. These parts are skilful, usually true to history, and rather mature in style.

Henslowe enters a "Harry the Sixt" in his *Diary* in the spring of 1592, as acted by Lord Strange's Men at the Rose theater. It is possible that this was Shakespeare's play. Whether or not the play alluded to by Nashe in *Pierce Penniless* (1592) was Shakespeare's is a matter of doubt. Nashe says,

> How would it haue ioyed braue Talbot (the terror of the French) to thinke that after he had lyne two hundred yeares in his Tombe, hee should triumphe again on the Stage, and haue his bones newe embalmed with the teares of ten thousand spectators at least (at severall times), who, in the Tragedian that represents his person, imagine that they behold him fresh bleeding.

Dr. J. Q. Adams has suggested that Shakespeare wrote *2* and *3 Henry VI* as a counter-attraction to the theatrical success of a Talbot play. In any case, Shakespeare did treat the theme; and *1 Henry VI* in its existing form, with its moving representation of Talbot's warfare and death, may well have been the play Nashe praises.

The first part of *King Henry VI* appears only in the First Folio of 1623; no quarto is known. The opinion has long been held by scholars that the play as it stands contains the work of other hands than Shakespeare's. The play presents many parallels to the works of other authors in thoughts, phrases, and dramatic devices. In about fifty cases the text recalls Greene; in about twenty, Peele; in twenty or more, Marlowe; Nashe comes in for eight or ten. There are in addition some one hundred and twenty cases of likeness in words and phrases to various other dramatists. But this is not all. The play teems with parallels to Spenser, both to the *Shepheards Calender*, which had been published (1579), and to the *Faerie Queene*, which had not. Parallels·to Kyd, Golding, Gabriel Harvey, and others have been pointed out. This vast reliance on current works has been taken as an indication that *1 Henry VI* is in part the actual work of some of these men; but on the face of it it might be said that these resemblances are too numerous and too widely scattered to render any such hypothesis very probable. It seems, in general, more probable that we have to do rather with a situation in which a great deal of dramatic language was, so to speak, common property, passing mainly by the words of actors from play to play. Indeed, a great deal of this minor borrowing may be due to the fact that Shakespeare as a young actor and dramatic enthusiast had his head full of stage talk and poured it out in an early play.

Perhaps of more importance to the argument for multiple authorship are certain very marked inconsistencies in the play, which may be due to the original plotting by one or more hands and the imperfect revision by Shakespeare. It is, for example, pretty generally agreed that there are two different interpretations of the essential character of Joan of Arc. The picture is at best disagreeable enough to modern taste and knowledge, but there seem to be two accounts at variance with each other, the one horridly conceiving of Joan as a witch and an impure woman and the other treating her more fairly. The first of these is based on Hall's *The Union of the Illustre Families of Lancaster and York* and the second on Holinshed's *Chronicles of England, Scotland and Ireland*. There are also other cases in which the play is in part based on Hall in disagreement with Holinshed, although since these authorities throughout this period often agree word for word, the matter is difficult to determine. It is unlike Shakespeare to embody in one play such glaring inconsistencies. Indeed, there is only one other case, that of *King John*, in which he did not go back to the chronicles and produce a work of sound and fairly consistent historical truth. He may in *1 Henry VI* have been following a plot whose outlines had been laid down by another dramatist. Certainly there·is nowhere in Shakespeare a historical plot which does such violence to chronology. The play covers the period from the funeral of Henry V on November 7, 1422, to the death of Talbot on July 17, 1453, and is full of anachronisms. Talbot's death is made to occur before Joan's capture in 1430, and Henry's marriage to Margaret of Anjou in 1444. Burgundy deserted the English seven years after the death of Joan; Henry VI speaks of remembering what his father said although he was but nine months old when Henry V passed away; and so on. It must be said, however, that, disregarding this chronological license, *1 Henry VI* is well enough plotted.

Because of Nashe's allusion we may be pretty sure that the play was in existence by 1592, and also because Henslowe records in his *Diary* a "new enterlude," called "harey vi," on March 3rd of that year and many times during the season. The play, according to Nashe, gave an account of the heroical death of Talbot; and this play would satisfy that demand, since it does present in moving fashion the death of the hero and his son and takes pains to dramatize the greatness of his reputation, the manliness of his character, and the baseness of the political intrigues by which he was betrayed. Certain modern authorities now think that Shakespeare was a member of Lord Pembroke's company, whereas the play of Henry VI was being played by Lord Strange's men at Henslowe's Rose; but the older and better opinion is that he belonged to the latter group of players.

This does not, however, dispose of the belief that in this play Shakespeare was rewriting an older play. The grounds for this opinion are the unusual plotting and the inconsistencies above referred to. Some critics have thought they detected differences in style in different parts of the play, but in actuality such differences are not clear. If Shakespeare did rewrite a Talbot play, he did it in connection with *2* and *3 Henry VI*, and there are two possible hypotheses. According to the first he became interested in the downfall of the house of Lancaster and made this play prefigure the ruin of that dynasty. It deals clearly and earnestly with the quarrels of the nobles of the English court, which betrayed Talbot and lost France to the English crown. We know that this was Shakespeare's conception of the matter. And there are three great disastrous issues which he would have been obliged to get under way in this play and finish in the remaining plays of the sequence, namely the downfall of Humphrey Duke of Gloucester, largely at the instigation of his enemy, Winchester; the disastrous marriage of the young King to Margaret, brought about by the base motives of Suffolk; and the rise to power of Richard Duke of York. All these themes are indeed powerfully begun, and the inauguration of them may furnish the correct account of the origin of the play.

But because *1 Henry VI* was apparently new in the spring of 1592, and because from Greene's reference we know that even *3 Henry VI* was in existence in the summer of that year, and because the plot structure of *1 Henry VI* does not indicate that the play was done freshly as an independent work, one is tempted to resort to a second hypothesis, namely, that Shakespeare had already written the second and third parts of *Henry VI* by the spring of 1592, and at that time rewrote an old play on the earlier part of the reign, concerning himself largely with making of it an introductory first member of the series of York-Lancaster plays. The play gives (II, iv) a picturesque account of the origin of the symbols of the white rose for York and the red rose for Lancaster, in the quarrel of Bedford and York in the Temple Gardens, a story for which there is no known source and which was possibly invented to serve its admirable purpose. It may be said also that, whenever one has to do in *1 Henry VI* with matters which look forward in history to the succeeding plays, one finds a steady and consistent use of Holinshed's *Chronicles* of 1587, one of Shakespeare's favorite books. It is used in the authoritative manner in which Shakespeare customarily employed it, so that one is almost forced to conclude that Shakespeare's main reason for handling this subject was to provide a basis for his own earlier work on the later years of the reign of King Henry VI.

Traces of an earlier play may perhaps be found in matter derived from Hall only, and the strong work of the reviser engaged in setting the York-Lancaster story was with matter drawn exclusively from Holinshed's *Chronicle* or occasionally from Fabyan's *Chronicle*. The main dependence on Hall is in the death of Talbot and the trial and condemnation of Joan. In view of the power of the writing one can hardly believe that Shakespeare, even if he was following Hall at second hand, did not pen the Talbot scenes for which he had so carefully provided in the selfish partisanship of Somerset and York, and it is not out of line with Shakespeare's custom to have written such poetical matters in rhyme; but he may very well have been following an old play instead of Holinshed's *Chronicle*. As to the scenes of Joan's downfall, they follow Hall and his prejudices and are not consistent with earlier parts of the play, which are based on Holinshed. To be sure, Holinshed records Joan's "conversation with wicked spirits," her repudiation by her father, and her seeking to save her life by claiming to be with child; but he saves her honor by showing that the charge against herself is false. It is in the scene (V, ii) where she is shown in talk with wicked spirits and is deceived and deserted by them, and in her vulgar and frantic defence of herself, that there seems to be dependence on Hall.

So much attention has always been paid by commentators and critics to the authorship of *1 Henry VI* that almost no attention has been paid to the question of what kind of play it is. The modern world has been so greatly alienated by the horrid picture of the gleeful and brutal martyrdom of Joan of Arc that the play has suffered in its estimation. It has been called dull and uninspired. One simply has to face the fact that the Elizabethans, including Shakespeare, regarded Joan as a witch in league with devils and therefore an evil thing. At best she is this in Holinshed. In Hall and elsewhere she is a pretender, a liar, and a strumpet, her only power coming from the juggling fiends who keep the word of promise to her ear and break it to her hope. Where, in the earlier part, the play follows Holinshed, something of the romantic charm of Joan comes through as well as her bravery and skill in battle and her wisdom in council (I, ii, 72-86, 129-35; II, i, 54-9, 72-7):

> Dauphin, I am by birth a shepherd's daughter,
> My wit untrain'd in any kind of art.
> Heaven and our Lady gracious hath it pleased
> To shine on my contemptible estate:
> Lo, whilst I waited on my tender lambs,
> And to sun's parching heat display'd my cheeks,
> God's mother deigned to appear to me
> And in a vision full of majesty
> Will'd me to leave my base vocation
> And free my country from calamity: . . .
> Expect St. Martin's summer, halcyon days,
> Since I have entered into these wars.
> Glory is like a circle in the water,
> Which never ceaseth to enlarge itself
> Till by broad spreading it disperse to nought. . . .

With such passages should be associated the fact that Shakespeare puts into Joan's mouth words of pure patriotism and no small degree of eloquence in her appeal to Burgundy in the third scene of the third act (ll. 44 ff.). Indeed, we here encounter for almost the first time the psychological principle of sudden change of opinion and mood. The truth when uttered being irresistible, the erring hearer passes first through the stage of uncertainty and then has set up within him a flow of spirits of conviction and repentance, so that his whole being is given a new set and direction. Burgundy says, merely on the strength of Joan's speech (ll. 78-84),

> I am vanquished; these haughty words of hers
> Have batter'd me like roaring cannon-shot,
> And made me almost yield upon my knees.
> Forgive me, country, and sweet countrymen,
> And, lords, accept this hearty kind embrace:
> My forces and my power of men are yours:
> So farewell, Talbot; I'll no longer trust thee.

This is followed by a most puzzling and objectionable line. Joan says:

> Done like a Frenchman: turn, and turn again!

One distrusts the habit of Shakespeare scholars who, if they find something in Shakespeare they do not like, immediately suggest that it is an interpolation; but, if there is any line which looks like a chauvinistic intrusion, this is it. There is certainly some truth and beauty in the part of Joan, so that one may see that Shakespeare was on the right track in dramatizing Holinshed, but that he did not then possess the maturity and understanding necessary to carry through a consistent depiction of her and possibly took over too readily a discordant conception by an earlier playwright.

In its political aspect *1 Henry VI* is not without consistency, vigor, and insight. Shakespeare dramatizes the ferocious partisanship, the jealousy and mutual hatred of Holinshed's nobles and shows while doing so a full realization of the ominous consequences of such behavior. Winchester is Shakespeare's worst churchman, and, lest the audience should fail to perceive it, he puts into the words of Humphrey Duke of Gloucester complete denunciation, both personal and political, and moreover has Winchester stay behind in the villain's role at the end of the first scenes of the first and the fourth acts in order to confess his evil intentions. His acts are almost worse than his intentions. There is almost nowhere a better picture than in this play of the feuds, the brawls in the streets and in the parliament house itself; as also of the official despair of the mayor of London, whose business it was to keep an orderly city (III, i, 76 ff.). Interpretation comes from honest Bedford (I, i, 44 ff.) and from the aged patriot Exeter, brother of Winchester and yet a loyal man (III, ii, 186 ff.). Certainly the main course of the wreck of the empire of King Henry V is well understood and realistically presented.

Shakespeare begins also in most picturesque fashion the career of "dogged" York. The scene in the Temple Garden with its quarrel between York, or Plantagenet as he is called, abetted by Suffolk and Warwick, against the doughty Somerset is perhaps the best known in the play (II, iv, 25-113):

> *Plan.* Since you are tongue-tied and so loath to speak,
> In dumb significants proclaim your thoughts:
> Let him that is a true-born gentleman
> And stands upon the honour of his birth,
> If he suppose that I have pleaded truth,
> From off this brier pluck a white rose with me.
> *Som.* Let him that is no coward nor no flatterer,
> And dare maintain the party of the truth,
> Pluck a red rose from off this thorn with me. . . .

The opportunity for York's ambition grows rapidly. We have the death of Mortimer pathetically presented, then the scene in the parliament house with the quarrel between Winchester and Gloucester and the fatal decision to restore Plantagenet to the dukedom of York—climax of the political action of the play. Shakespeare's irony here is strong as he depicts the horrid falsity of York and the self-seeking policy of the others (III, i, 160-76):

> *War.* Let Richard be restored to his blood;
> So shall his father's wrongs be recompensed.
> *Win.* As will the rest, so willeth Winchester.
> *King.* If Richard will be true, not that alone
> But all the whole inheritance I give
> That doth belong unto the house of York,
> From whence you spring by lineal descent. . . .
> *Plan.* And so thrive Richard as thy foes may fall!
> And as my duty springs, so perish they
> That grudge one thought against your majesty!

We see York next in the act of deserting Talbot. The very style is frivolous (IV, iii, 23-33):

> *York.* O God, that Somerset, who in proud heart
> Doth stop my cornets, were in Talbot's place!
> So should we save a valiant gentleman
> By forfeiting a traitor and a coward.
> Mad ire and wrathful fury makes me weep,

That thus we die, while remiss traitors sleep.
Lucy. O, send some succour to the distress'd lord!
York. He dies, we lose; I break my warlike word;
We mourn, France smiles; we lose, they daily get;
All 'long of this vile traitor Somerset.

Shakespeare permits this same selfish villain to curse and torment Joan at her capture and trial (V, iii, iv). The audience is surely well prepared for the disloyal schemer of *2 Henry VI.*

If the selfish treason of York is well prefigured, the lustful villainy of Suffolk is no less finely established. Some excuse for York is to be found in his ambition for his family and his rights; there is no justification for Suffolk. We see him as he coolly calculates the expediency of his political affiliation. At first he declines to follow York (II, iv, 112 ff.), but, when York has gained power, he becomes friendly enough. His capture of Margaret of Anjou, although presented in a rather attractive scene (V, iii, 45-194) is marked by the deepest treachery of the play. He cannot marry Margaret himself, but he counts securely on the frailty of his weak-willed King. According to the beliefs of the time love could be engendered in the mind of a man by beholding a picture of the beautiful one or by listening to an impassioned description of her charms. Suffolk so inflames the young king's mind that against his honor, pledged to the Earl of Armagnac's daughter, and against the advice of the loyal protector Humphrey of Gloucester, the King offers a great award of provinces by way of dower and gives Suffolk the Tristram-like commission of bringing Margaret to England, there to be Suffolk's mistress while she is the King's wife. Shakespeare seems to have been aware of the weakness of King Henry VI to the point of imbecility, and although he knew of the King's saintliness, he neither here nor later presents him in any kingly proportions.

Lord Talbot stands out magnificently, a legend in his own day, a popular hero of great appeal. Not intimately characterized, he is none the less interesting as an unsurpassed warrior, shrewd, competent, and honorable. We see him fight a drawn battle with Joan (I, v, 4-14), hear him pay honor to the brave Salisbury [when others have forgotten him (II, ii, 4-33)] and with the nonchalance of Robin Hood enter the castle of the Countess of Auvergne (II, iii), defeat her wiles by superior cunning, and refuse to take vengeance upon her. He fights a story-book war around Rouen (III, ii, 75-84). He scorns the falsity of Burgundy when that noble deserts his allies; in the King's presence he tears the garter from the leg of the cowardly Sir John Fastolfe, and stays to explain the ideals of the noble order (IV, i, 33 ff.). Finally, we see him surrounded by an overwhelming force of the enemy, deserted by his countrymen because of the private quarrel between York and Somerset, and at last dying heroically in battle. His glory is augmented by the loyal gallantry of his son. One can understand why Nashe should have said, "How would it have joyed brave Talbot (the terror of the French) to think that after he had lain two hundred years in his tomb he should triumph again on the stage, and have his bones new embalmed with the tears of ten thousand spectators."

1 Henry VI may be an unpleasant play. Indeed, there is no episode in it that does not leave a bad taste in the mouth. But it is not a weak or a dull play. It is a play of passion, feud, violence, and treachery, such perhaps as was needed to make a beginning in York and Lancaster's long jars, a period of civil war which Shakespeare's England still remembered.

The second and third parts of *Henry VI* likewise remain largely unknown even to students of Shakespeare. Part II is probably a better play and better known than is Part III, but both have the quality of faithfulness to history and both depict realistically the political and personal passions of rude men in a time of feuds, even without the controlling hand of a strong king. With the chronicles of these days before them it is no wonder that the Elizabethans dreaded sedition and believed in the necessity of dominant rulers.

It was long thought on the basis of a famous and authoritative study by Malone that 2 and *3 Henry VI* are based respectively on two quartos: *The First Part of the Contention betwixt the two famous Houses of York and Lancaster* (1594) and *The True Tragedy of Richard Duke of York* (1595), which were regarded as ¯older and less perfect forms of these plays. The plays themselves were thought of as Shakespeare's revisions of the work of other dramatists. These quartos and the Folio versions themselves are, like *1 Henry VI,* full of phrases readily paralleled in the works of Marlowe, Greene, Nashe, Spenser, Kyd, and Golding; for they too are written in the dramatic style current in English drama about the year 1590. It has since become obvious that *The First Part of* the *Contention* is merely an early version of *2 Henry VI* that has suffered some degeneration at the hands of actors on the stage. The older view regards the *Contention* as taken down from recital by actors. The same theory has been made to account for the relation between *The True Tragedy of Richard Duke of York* and *3 Henry VI*. This is too complicated and lacks support, since, aside from printers' errors, there is nothing in the *Contention* and the *True Tragedy* not easily accounted for by stage degeneration. What happened was that about 1598 Shakespeare rewrote older versions of all three plays and gave them not only the name of the king but a fuller integration with one another and with the Lancastrian plays. These versions were printed in the First Folio. Of the early versions that of *1 Henry VI* is lost.

It need not be wondered at that critics were so long deceived as to the relation of the quarto to the Folio versions of these plays or even that excellent scholars devoted so much careful effort to an attempt to prove the truth of a wrong hypothesis. It is natural, when two versions of the same work exist—one perfect, the other less so—that the shorter, less perfect version should be regarded as the earlier, and the fuller, more perfect version as the later; such is a sort of normal sequence in the work of an author. There also were the borrowing habits of actors and the current language of the stage to reinforce the suggestion of Greene's, or Peele's, or Marlowe's authorship. The erroneous idea was also current that Shakespeare was a borrower from the works of others and not a creator in his own right. But as soon as the question was looked at from another point of view, as soon as the concept of an actual stage version, made perhaps to be acted in the provinces, came to be understood, the true relations of quarto and Folio versions became apparent. Almost nobody now adheres to the older hypothesis, and one effect of the discovery has been to move the Henry VI plays back to the year 1592 and beyond.

The second part of *Henry VI* is a better play in unified construction than is *1 Henry VI* and is not without its admirers. In this play Humphrey Duke of Gloucester is a tragic figure cadent, and Richard Duke of York is a tragic figure crescent. The play has thus some resemblance in structure to the plays based on Roman history. It is none the less episodic rather than connectedly dramatic. At the beginning of the play the threads of earlier action are gathered up—Gloucester and Winchester with the new attack on Gloucester through his foolish Duchess, Suffolk and Margaret in their liaison, and especially the persistent drive of the Duke of York, ambitious to gain the crown for himself.

The contrast between *1 Henry VI* and *2 Henry VI* is very great in style and construction. The latter is far more carefully wrought. It is more formal in poetic style, more archaic in language, and it follows the chronicle with far greater fidelity. If the well established idea that Shakespeare began his career with greater artificiality be true, one is almost forced to conclude that *2 Henry VI* was written earlier than *1 Henry VI*. There are many long, pompous speeches in *2 Henry VI*, which seem designed to express the dignity as well as the passionate ferocity of the leaders of that time, qualities which are provided for in the chronicles. There is only one passage in *2 Henry VI* which seems to look back to an earlier play, and that need not be to Part 1. Gloucester says (I, i, 144-5):

> If I longer stay,
> We shall begin our ancient bickerings.

The play is in general self-explanatory.

It begins by gathering up the threads of the story as it is told in Holinshed, which are carefully twined together. There is the story of Suffolk and Margaret; also the feud between Winchester (here Cardinal Beaufort) and Humphrey Duke of Gloucester. Then follows the story of York's steady and unscrupulous advance on the crown. The play as it stands is like a Plutarchan tragedy in that Humphrey Duke of Gloucester goes down as York goes up. The earlier part deals with the successful attack on Gloucester through the folly and pride of his Duchess. It is a concerted attack by a wolf-pack of political enemies, all of whom are actuated by their own private ambitions. Indeed the play resembles *Richard III* in the quarreling of Yorkist factions after they have united to dispossess the Lancastrians. Much of this is done by Queen Margaret, particularly in the third scene of the first act and the fourth scene of the fourth act. In *2 Henry VI* the Queen and Suffolk will for their own ends destroy the good Duke (I, iii, 45 ff. and III, i, 4 ff.), Buckingham and Beaufort out of their private malice; and York, the arch-schemer of them all, will double-cross his fellow conspirators and remove the honest Humphrey from his path (III, i, 331-83). Incidentally the spectacle of these royal and noble persons plotting a common, brutal murder is now a horrid one, and in Shakespeare's time must have been even more so. Suffolk says (III, i, 261-5):

And do not stand on quillets how to slay him:
Be it by gins, by snares, by subtlety,
Sleeping or waking, 'tis no matter how,
So he be dead.

These stories, all well known, appeared in the *Mirror for Magistrates*. Among the nineteen tragedies in the edition of 1559, the eleventh is *William de la Pole, Duke of Suffolk*, the thirteenth *Jack Cade*, the fourteenth *Richard Plantagenet, Duke of York*, the fifteenth *Lord Clifford*. From the table of contents it is apparent that it had been intended to include "Good duke Humphrey Murdered, and Eleanor Cobham his wife banished," an announcement repeated in the edition of 1571. To the edition of 1578 are added elaborate stories: *Eleanor Cobham, Duchess of Gloucester* and *Humphrey Plantagenet, Duke of Gloucester*. There is a fairly close agreement in point of view between all of these stories in the *Mirror for Magistrates* and in 2 *Henry VI*. Holinshed's *Chronicles* generally agree. The material being so familiar, one need not believe that Shakespeare wrote 1 *Henry VI* before he wrote 2 *Henry VI*, especially since the style of the latter play is pretty obviously in the very earliest stage of formalism. This drama seems to be the first heir of his invention.

The first scene of the first act gives us the formal presentation of the Queen to Henry VI by the man who has married her as the King's proxy. The meeting is carried through ceremoniously, but is followed by an outburst of indignation by the nobles at the famous dower of Anjou and Maine which Suffolk has given away to obtain her. The method is epical, but it is interesting to observe the effects produced on the various persons present. Humphrey is heart-broken and ashamed; Warwick, whom Shakespeare confuses with an earlier Warwick, is personally aggrieved, since he has conquered the provinces; York with his sullen selfishness regards the dowry as a diminution of his own estate. Only Beaufort is so far sunk in personal hatred that he uses the loss of territory as an occasion for an attack on Humphrey. The aged patriot Salisbury speaks with justice in defence of Humphrey and foresees the ills which threaten the King's state (ll. 200-5).

The play is for a time taken up with the tragedy of Humphrey Duke of Gloucester and his wife Eleanor Cobham. Eleanor is warned by her husband, but she nevertheless seeks to control events through the wicked impostors John Hume and John Southwell, with the witch Margery Jordan and the conjurer Roger Bolingbroke. This is a simple case of black magic, which is recorded in Holinshed and belongs to the story of the unfortunate Duchess. Into the midst of it come two strange and unpleasant bits from the Chronicle—the story of Humphrey's detection of the imposture of the rascal Simpcox, no doubt intended to illustrate the good sense and good government of Duke Humphrey, and the strange trial by combat between the armorer Horner and his man Peter. This Shakespeare handles as an apologue in which one sees the honest armorer defeated by his foolish, cowardly man. Although Shakespeare has Horner confess his treason and has King Henry praise God for His justice, one cannot help seeing in it the triumph of wrong over right in the downfall of Gloucester and the rise of York. The revelation of Eleanor's evil practices in open court and the disgrace of Gloucester (II, i) is a masterpiece of malice. The audience knows that the sorcerers are in the pay of Gloucester's enemies, and the gloating of the Queen and Beaufort is an ugly spectacle. This is near the turning point of Gloucester's story, and one should not forget the scene (II, ii) in which York convinces Salisbury and Warwick of the justice of his claims. They become his followers out of honest convictions. The truth is that the law of primogeniture was only coming into recognition. In the fourth scene of the second act Shakespeare has presented well and with pathos the humiliation of the Duke and Duchess of Gloucester. He has realized the meaning of this scene in the dignified shame of the Duke and the bitter suffering of the Duchess. She is barefoot, covered with a white sheet, with verses pinned to her back, and she walks before the jeering populace (II, iv, 34-6):

> The ruthless flint doth cut my tender feet,
> And when I start, the envious people laugh
> And bid me be advised how I tread.

She fears for her husband, but he is strong in the faith of all good servants (ll. 59-63):

> I must offend before I be attainted;
> And had I twenty times so many foes,
> And each of them had twenty times their power,
> All these could not procure me any scathe,
> So long as I am loyal, true and crimeless.

Surely in this scene, not an especially skilful one, we have a foretaste of Shakespeare's realistic power in the presentation of simple human passion.

Humphrey's catastrophe is upon him, and in the really powerful third act he is set upon by all his enemies. He realizes his danger and brushes aside the false and trivial charges made against him (III, i, 108 ff., 142 ff.). He is a victim of the dangerous institution which permitted the accusation of high treason by his peers, an institution liable to much abuse. He has the King's good will, the King knows him innocent, and this of itself would have saved him had it not been that the saintly monarch, although always able to see the side of justice, was too weak to implement his judgment with his will. But even so, the indictment is on the way to collapse. His unscrupulous enemies have only murder left. This is arranged by Suffolk with the assistance of Beaufort and the consent of all the parties. Suffolk's guilt is obvious to the King and to Warwick, who displays the indignation of an honest man. The horror with which the King regards Suffolk is presented in penetrating style (III, ii, 39-47):

> What, doth my Lord of Suffolk comfort me?
> Came he right now to sing a raven's note,
> Whose dismal tune bereft my vital powers;
> And thinks he that the chirping of a wren,
> By crying comfort from a hollow breast,
> Can chase away the first-conceived sound?
> Hide not thy poison with such sugar'd words;
> Lay not thy hands on me; forbear, I say;
> Their touch affrights me as a serpent's sting.

And the Queen tries her feminine wiles in vain. The best that can be said of her is that she prefigures Lady Macbeth (ll. 73-120). It is only fair to credit Shakespeare with suggesting her falsity in the artificiality of her speech. Guilt settles upon her and her lover. He is banished, and part of their punishment is the stiff and unsympathetic leave-taking in which they engage; nor is Beaufort permitted to escape. It is the temper of the play that he should die in torment with every indication of impending damnation (III, iii, 8 ff.). Here too is a faint foreshadowing of the sleep-walking scene in *Macbeth*.

The tragedy of Humphrey Duke of Gloucester is thus complete except for the fate of his murderer. On the death of Suffolk Shakespeare has lavished great care, and one would say that, if anywhere, the youthful Shakespeare is here to be seen. Vengeance, conscious of itself, comes from an unexpected quarter, and Suffolk meets it with the pride of Lucifer (IV, i, 118-38):

Whit. Thou shalt have cause to fear before
I leave thee. . . .
Suf. Come, soldiers, show what cruelty ye can,
That this my death may never be forgot!
Great men oft die by vile bezonians:
A Roman sworder and banditto slave
Murder'd sweet Tully; Brutus' bastard hand
Stabb'd Julius Caesar; savage islanders
Pompey the Great; and Suffolk dies by pirates.

The play now turns to the planned revolt of York. His opportunity
comes in the first scene of the third act when he accepts the charge of
fighting the Irish rebels. According to the stiff dramaturgy of the play
he is given a great soliloquy, like those of his hopeful son in *Richard III*.
This speech, for the convenience of the dramatist, has all the qualities of
the Marlovian hero—unscrupulous plotting, towering ambition, and the
longing for a crown (ll. 331-83):

Now, York, or never, steel thy fearful thoughts,
And change misdoubt to resolution:
Be that thou hopest to be, or what thou art
Resign to death; it is not worth the enjoying:
Let pale-faced fear keep with the mean-born man,
And find no harbour in a royal heart. . . .
My brain more busy than the labouring spider
Weaves tedious snares to trap mine enemies. . . .
'Twas men I lack'd and you will give them me: . . .
Say he be taken, rack'd and tortured,
I know no pain they can inflict upon him
Will make him say I moved him to those arms.
Say that he thrive, as 'tis great like he will,
Why, then from Ireland come I with my strength
And reap the harvest which that rascal sow'd;
For Humphrey being dead, as he shall be,
And Henry put apart, the next for me.

York claims that he has set Cade on to raise a revolt in his own absence.
The story of Jack Cade was well known, and in the *Mirror for Magistrates* he is presented as a conscience-smitten rebel and a reasonable creature.
He is not a comic character. What Shakespeare has done is to keep a
certain amount of sympathy for Cade because of his bravery and frankness
and to go to Holinshed's accounts of the revolt of Wat Tyler and John

Ball in 1381. From them come the ideas of killing all the lawyers and abolishing all law, hanging the "Clarke of Chatham," and abolishing grammar schools. John Ball made a speech to the people on Blackheath advocating equality. The actual events, such as the defeat of the Staffords, the breaking open of the jails, the conference with the King, the murder of Lord Scales and Sir James Cromer, the slaying of Matthew Gough, the dispersal of Cade's followers by the promise of freedom, and the flight and death of Cade are all from the *Chronicles* and all pertain to Cade's rebellion. The literary result of Shakespeare's mixture of sources is a character of real complexity and very great interest. Indeed, it is doubtful if anything in the play gives a better foretaste of Shakespeare's power in the depiction of character. The scene of Cade's death (IV, x) is masterly. Shakespeare has seen into the heart of a hungry man and a brave one. Cade falls before the honest and powerful Alexander Iden, and his last words are not unworthy (ll. 63-80):

> O, I am slain! famine and no other hath slain me: let ten thousand devils come against me, and give me but the ten meals I have lost, and I'ld defy them all. Wither, garden; and be henceforth a burying-place to all that do dwell in this house, because the unconquered soul of Cade is fled. . . .

The fifth act is given over to the fateful advance of York, who, like his wicked son, Richard III, has determination and also guile. York temporizes, but with the support of Salisbury and Warwick finally takes the field. The Elder Clifford is slain by York, and Somerset by York's son Richard. Thus the main props of the Lancastrian cause are torn down. The act reveals the atmosphere of family feud characteristic of all the York-Lancaster plays. The battle is presented as a series of single combats, debates, forays, and flights—one of the most successful ways to dramatize a battle. Richard, who, students of history like to tell us, was only two and one-half years old at the time of the first battle of St. Albans, appears a full grown warrior much at home in the mêlée and with characteristic impertinent brutality. York is triumphant and we are ready for a true tragedy of Richard Duke of York.

In spite of Shakespeare's manifest intention to be faithful to history it is surprising how poorly his York-Lancaster plays reflect the actual history of that troubled period. If one considers the actions of his characters and analyzes them, one will see greed, treachery, and corruption; but Shakespeare has attributed the vile acts to men whose characters and motives are not explained and of whose actions there is little certainly known except in terms of personal antipathy or partisan approval. Around the whole is an atmosphere of at least some chivalry. Humphrey of Gloucester was a far worse man than Shakespeare makes him out to be. The same is true of Warwick. York was better than he is painted. Economic factors were unknown to Holinshed, and the fierce rivalry of France, Burgundy, and England is scarcely apparent. Nearly all actions are personal and voluntary, and history appears to be controlled exclusively by kings and rulers and their agents.

The case of Henry VI is peculiarly puzzling. He was a man of very weak mind and was actually at various times insane. York's first period of control was due to Henry's incapacity. History, written largely by Lancastrian sympathizers, had chosen to make of him a saint on earth and to endow him with divine favor, but, even so, he is inconsistent throughout: sometimes weak, cowardly, and foolish, and again speaking and acting with wisdom and spirit.

Edward IV is distinguished in history as a very able general, but there is very little of this except by inference in the plays. He is made willful and sensual. Of the London merchants and provincial lords who put him in power there is scarcely a trace. Edward's unscrupulous cruelty and his deliberate destruction of the nobility are not developed into visible factors, and his contest with Warwick and the Nevilles is not shown for what it was. Clarence was feeble, vacillating, and greedy, and the inferential connection between his nature and his fate is not hard to see. Richard, who plays an important part in *3 Henry VI*, is two characters. Early in the play, though a great fighter and cruel like all his clan, he seems on the whole loyal to his family and wise in comment. About halfway through the play Shakespeare makes him into a Machiavel. It is necessary therefore to read these plays as pieces of made-over history, next door to fiction; they are not as historical as is *The Last of the Barons*.

The Third Part of King Henry VI must have been written immediately after the *Second Part* and was probably planned with it. There is almost no break in the story; there are few inconsistencies between the plays; and the style is for the most part the same stiff blank verse with long speeches, mythological and historical comparisons, slight and inferior comedy, and a grave presentation of hate, prejudice, and bloodshed. It is a play of feud rather than of revolution. York's downfall comes quickly from the daggers of Clifford and the Queen at the end of the first act after the Lancastrian victory at Wakefield. The play looks forward to *Richard III* mainly in the precocity of Richard, too young to have participated in the battles of St. Albans and Towton and only nineteen at the time of Tewkesbury, with which the play ends. *3 Henry VI* is, however, a play, not so much of the downfall of Richard Duke of York, as of the rise to power of his son Edward, who became King Edward IV.

The Henry VI of the first act is not without courage and good sense, and yet is guilty of disinheriting his own son, a thoroughly inconsistent act. In point of fact he was insane, and the story is that he was incapable of recognizing his infant after it had been born. His decision provokes a tirade from Queen Margaret (I, i, 230-56), with whom for the first time the audience has some sympathy. An odd bit of the psychology of the time makes him conscience-smitten, so that he admits the weakness of his case (l. 134). There was an issue of the time which the Tudor chroniclers ignore, namely, the question of whether parliament had the right to fix the succession to the crown. Both Yorkists and Lancastrians were careful to secure parliamentary mandates, but the Tudor chroniclers are all for primogeniture.

As to the details of the action, the third scene gives us an early case of Shakespeare's pity for children in Clifford's brutal murder of Rutland. The death of York in the fourth scene was apparently intended to be a moving spectacle, and it is. Margaret's gloating over the death of Rutland, her furious tirade against York (ll. 66-108), and her crowning him with a paper crown reach the highwater mark of melodrama. York's rejoinder contains the phrase "She-wolf of France" and presents a great invective including the famous line (137):

> O tiger's heart wrapp'd in a woman's hide!

In a story so cruel on both sides one suspends sympathy and looks upon the whole matter as beyond reality.

The second act gives us the battle of Towton and the death of Clifford. In the first scene the vanquished Yorkists, with their courage, and Richard with his family loyalty are historical. Clifford's great speech in the second scene (ll. 9-42), intended to stir the manhood of the King, elicits a reply which is best understood as that of a melancholiac. The scene contains one

of those improbable rows before battle often used in Shakespeare, in line
with the ancient epic and no doubt always unnatural. The battle itself
is presented by means of the usual alarums and excursions, but in the midst
of it one finds an apologue, rather Senecan in style and almost without
interest. As an indirect description by contemplation it hardly succeeds.
King Henry sits apart on a molehill and speculates on the shepherd's life.
To him there enter at one door a son who has slain his father and at another a father who has slain his son. In the theater of the time the apologue
may have been expressive of the horror of civil war, for the dread of that
was widespread among the Elizabethans; but the crudity of it reveals how
far Shakespeare has yet to go as a dramatist. The death of Clifford, which
occurs in the fifth scene, is more moving than that of York. It is simpler,
and in it is something of the truth from the lips of dying men. Genuine
irony appears in the disappointment of the butcherly Yorkist brethren.
Death has enabled Clifford to escape their hands.

The third act offers the most careful piece of dramaturgy in the play.
Warwick, who is presented not as one thirsting for power and wealth, but
as a patriotic statesman, is sent on his famous fool's errand to negotiate
an advantageous marriage between King Edward IV and Lady Bona,
sister-in-law to Louis XI. Warwick is thwarted, not as in history by the
King's desire to discredit him and assert his own independence as a king,
but by the sensuality and willfulness of Edward. Lady Grey refuses to
sell her goods at less than the established price, and, as often happens in
the world, becomes a wife instead of a mistress. The portrait of her
throughout the play is done with charm and sympathy. Following Edward's choice of the honest widow and perhaps in some sense provoked
by it, comes Richard's first characteristic soliloquy. He gives vent to his
dark, cruel, selfish, and unnatural purpose, and takes his stand, like the
long line of villains who were to succeed him on the Shakespearean stage,
as an opportunist and a hypocrite, poised to watch the ebb and flow of
circumstance and to seize his advantage wherever it may appear. His
Machiavellianism is as crudely put as that of Barabas and Aaron (III, ii,
182-95):

> Why, I can smile, and murder whiles I smile,
> And cry "Content" to that which grieves my heart,
> And wet my cheeks with artificial tears,
> And frame my face to all occasions.

> I'll drown more sailors than the mermaid shall;
> I'll slay more gazers than the basilisk;
> I'll play the orator as well as Nestor,
> Deceive more slily than Ulysses could,
> And, like a Sinon, take another Troy.
> I can add colours to the chameleon,
> Change shapes with Proteus for advantages,
> And set the murderous Machiavel to school.

The third scene of the third act is well managed and worth study. It is deeply ironical. Just as Queen Margaret has, like Constance, seated herself on the ground and has been lifted up by Louis as a mark of his favor, Warwick enters to propose a marriage between Edward IV and the Lady Bona. Argument for righteousness is suddenly overthrown by its ancient enemy, personal advantage, and Louis yields to Warwick's plea. Then a post arrives with letters and there is a sudden change. King Edward has wedded the Lady Grey. Shakespeare now begins to show how he can manipulate the motives and passions of ruin. Warwick accepts the rôle of kingmaker, and, in the third scene of the fourth act, Edward is made a prisoner in spite, it must be said, of some bravery and incisiveness (i, 127 ff.). At the end of the act, however, Edward has escaped, returned to England, captured York, and imprisoned King Henry. In several places it looks as if Shakespeare's mind was at work on an understanding of King Henry VI. He seems to have decided that Henry was a saint on earth, too good to succeed in the struggle against great evil. Indeed, he puts a pious speech in Henry's mouth, expressive of idealistic faith (IV, viii, 38-50).

The fifth act of *3 Henry VI* presents the famous battle of Barnet, made familiar to older generations by Bulwer-Lytton in *The Last of the Barons*. The defection of Clarence, in part due to self-seeking, is made reasonable in Shakespeare by loyalty to his brother. Warwick dies heroically at a time when his arm is needed for victory. His last speeches are in the Senecan style which characterizes the play, and his relation to his brother Montague is not without pathos (V, ii, 11-26):

> Thus yields the cedar to the axe's edge,
> Whose arms gave shelter to the princely eagle,
> Under whose shade the ramping lion slept,
> Whose top-branch overpeer'd Jove's spreading tree
> And kept low shrubs from winter's powerful wind. . . .

> Lo, now my glory smear'd in dust and blood!
> My parks, my walks, my manors that I had,
> Even now forsake me, and of all my lands
> Is nothing left me but my body's length.

Some suggestion of the soldiership of Edward IV is offered in the third scene and in the fourth, which is devoted to Margaret's battle of Tewkesbury, and in the latter scene Margaret's speech in encouragement of her followers is one of the strongest in the play (ll. 1-38):

> Great lords, wise men ne'er sit and wail their loss,
> But cheerly seek how to redress their harms.
> What though the mast be now blown overboard,
> The cable broke, the holding-anchor lost,
> And half our sailors swallow'd in the flood?
> Yet lives our pilot still. . . .
> This speak I, lords, to let you understand,
> If case some one of you would fly from us,
> That there's no hoped-for mercy with the brothers
> More than with ruthless waves, with sands and rocks.
> Why, courage then! what cannot be avoided
> 'Twere childish weakness to lament or fear.

In scene v she and her son are captured and Prince Edward, a brave young prince, is brutally murdered by the Yorkist brethren. One feels that there is too much child-murder in this play, though the impression is not lacking that the bloody triumph of the house of York is destined to end in blood.

2. *Richard III.*

In Colley Cibber's version of *Richard III*, long on the stage and perhaps even yet destined to be enacted often, the sixth scene of the fifth act of *3 Henry VI* becomes the first scene of *Richard III*. In that play it is tremendously impressive. Richard prowls about the saintly Henry VI, debates with him cynically, and stabs him to the heart. Henry, who had the gift of prophecy, foretells what Richard will do to his family; Richard reannounces his Machiavellianism, and in the last scene Edward IV turns to self-indulgence. The scene affords an excellent introduction to the later, greater play.

Shakespeare had thus introduced Richard Duke of Gloucester into *3 Henry VI* and had, so to speak, got the feel of the character before he

wrote *Richard III*. It has been plausibly said that Marlowe furnished a
model for this play in the creation of dramas controlled by a single dominant character; but it may be that Shakespeare's experience in writing the
earlier plays caused him to do the particular things he did in writing
Richard III. Richard's dominance is a different sort of dominance from
that of Marlowe's heroes. It is more organic, more immediately related
to family and government. Richard is not so much a Machiavel and enemy
of mankind as the enemy of a particular group, mainly his own family,
and an enemy of divine order within a kingdom. Richard is immersed in
this group, and the play takes its realistic quality from the things he does
to this group. To Shakespeare Richard was an authentic historical character,
and in him Shakespeare could see what God had done to a kingdom in
punishment for having laid hands upon His anointed. *Richard III* is thus
a more realistic drama, more like *King Lear* and *Macbeth*, than are the
plays of Marlowe, even *Edward II*. It is significant that the sinister character and disposition of Richard appear not throughout the whole of 2 and
3 Henry VI, but suddenly in a soliloquy at the end of the second scene
of the third act of *3 Henry VI*. It is not as if Shakespeare were following
the pattern of Marlowe, but as if, after having read More's *Life of Richard
III*, he had just realized the dramatic possibilities of Richard's special
villainies. *Richard III* clearly looks forward and not backward. Richard
and his villainies seem to be a new theme in the story and may well be
in some sense revisional.

As one begins the reading of *Richard III* with that most famous opening soliloquy, one is confronted by two ideas of some importance in the
interpretation of the play. The first of these is a mere convention, but one
continually employed in Elizabethan drama, namely, that of open and
informative confession in soliloquy. No unrepentant person ever described
himself as a villain. On the contrary, prisons are full of good men who
have been wronged, better men, by their own account, than those who still
enjoy their liberty. Chaucer has his Pardoner accuse himself of base
character and conduct, and we may believe that for him to do so was
merely Chaucer's way of informing his readers about these matters. So
in the plays, in the case of Richard, other villains, and some good men,
Shakespeare used the soliloquy merely as a means of informing his
audience and sometimes revealing a character. Richard had shown himself
an opportunist and had uttered the sentiments and intentions of a

Machiavel in *3 Henry VI*. In *Richard III* he implements them with a definite program of wickedness. He will dispose of his brother George, who stands between him and the crown, and proceed from that, as opportunity offers, to break down all other barriers.

The second idea of which Shakespeare makes use is the Platonic doctrine of a fair soul in a fair body, or, in this case, a crooked and evil soul in a deformed and crooked body (I, i, 12-30):

> He [Edward] capers nimbly in a lady's chamber
> To the lascivious pleasing of a lute.
> But I, that am not shap'd for sportive tricks,
> Nor made to court an amorous looking-glass;
> I, that am rudely stamp'd, and want love's majesty
> To strut before a wanton ambling nymph;
> I, that am curtail'd of this fair proportion,
> Cheated of feature by dissembling nature,
> Deform'd, unfinish'd, sent before my time
> Into this breathing world, scarce half made up,
> And that so lamely and unfashionable
> That dogs bark at me as I halt by them;
> Why, I, in this weak piping time of peace,
> Have no delight to pass away the time,
> Unless to spy my shadow in the sun
> And descant on mine own deformity:
> And therefore, since I cannot prove a lover,
> To entertain these fair well-spoken days,
> I am determined to prove a villain
> And hate the idle pleasures of these days.
> Plots have I laid, inductions dangerous, . . .

Richard was not so black as he is painted in the Lancastrian chronicles; perhaps few men have ever been so black. He was a competent soldier, something of a statesman, and not much more criminal than his brothers or his enemies. He was loyal to King Edward IV and probably under Edward's orders brought about the murder of Henry VI. He did not contrive the murder of Clarence but probably did not exert himself to save him. Richard did not murder his wife, but he did obtain the crown by political trickery and seems also to have been responsible for the blackest crime of all, the murder of the little princes. In part from the suspicion of that act came his downfall. Again we have to do only incidentally with the truth of history, but must, like Shakespeare himself, accept romance for historical truth.

The play of *Richard III* overflows with startling action. Perhaps no scene is more sensational than the wooing of the Lady Anne, which occupies the second scene of the second act. It is a masterpiece of irony, the idea for which, as Professor R. A. Law suggests, is borrowed from Holinshed's account of Richard's suing to Queen Elizabeth for the hand of his niece, the Princess Elizabeth. Bacon says of boldness, "nevertheless it doth fascinate and bind hand and foot those that are either shallow in judgment or weak in courage, which are the greatest part." Richard lays his breast open and hands the Lady Anne his sword. He had no right to appoint her his executioner, but she forgets that. Having bred confusion in her mind, he goes further and offers at her bidding to slay himself, but she does not speak the word. She only says,

> I would I knew thy heart.

Well may Richard recall those favorite words of the age:

> Was ever woman in this humour woo'd?
> Was ever woman in this humour won?

Clarence's dream (I, iv, 1-74) is one of the most famous passages in Shakespeare. We have to do here with simple, plain Clarence, and it looks as if Shakespeare had seen more deeply into that character than he did when he wrote *3 Henry VI*. Clarence is deeply smitten in conscience, and there is a Poe-like horror in his vision (ll. 24-33, 47-62):

> Methought I saw a thousand fearful wrecks;
> Ten thousand men that fishes gnaw'd upon;
> Wedges of gold, great anchors, heaps of pearl,
> Inestimable stones, unvalued jewels,
> All scatter'd in the bottom of the sea:
> Some lay in dead men's skulls; and, in those holes
> Where eyes did once inhabit, there were crept,
> As 'twere in scorn of eyes, reflecting gems,
> Which woo'd the slimy bottom of the deep,
> And mock'd the dead bones that lay scatter'd by. . . .
> The first that there did greet my stranger soul,
> Was my great father-in-law, renowned Warwick;
> Who cried aloud, 'What scourge for perjury
> Can this dark monarchy afford false Clarence?'
> And so he vanish'd: then came wandering by
> A shadow like an angel, with bright hair
> Dabbled in blood; and he squeak'd out aloud,

'Clarence is come; false, fleeting, perjured Clarence,
That stabb'd me in the field by Tewkesbury;
Seize on him, Furies, take him to your torments!'
With that, methoughts, a legion of foul fiends
Environ'd me about, and howled in mine ears
Such hideous cries, that with the very noise
I trembling waked, and for a season after
Could not believe but that I was in hell.

The murderers of Clarence show in a gruesome way and at a high level Shakespeare's talent for handling common men. The Second Murderer's remarks on conscience are in the true vein (ll. 137-48):

I'll not meddle with it: it is a dangerous thing: it makes a man a coward: a man cannot steal, but it accuseth him; he cannot swear, but it checks him; he cannot lie with his neighbour's wife, but it detects him: 'tis a blushing shamefast spirit that mutinies in a man's bosom; it fills one full of obstacles: it made me once restore a purse of gold that I found; it beggars any man that keeps it: it is turned out of all towns and cities for a dangerous thing; and every man that means to live well endeavours to trust to himself and to live without it.

The second act is dramatically perfect in its depiction of Richard's steady advance upon his object. King Edward IV, who has reveled out his life, is anxious that, when he is gone, there should be no more wickedness. The irony of the situation, Edward's deathbed piety, is climaxed by Richard's informing him that Clarence has been put to death, a matter to which Richard himself has given careful attention. The only cool head in the lot, he takes advantage of the fright in his enemies' faces to cast suspicion upon them.

One after another he disposes of those who have been serviceable to him as soon as they cease to obey his will. Hastings is willing to have Richard wreak vengeance on the Queen's kindred, whom he hates, but is not willing for Richard to seize the crown away from the lawful heir, Prince Edward, and Hastings pays with his head for his scruples. His execution is notorious for its cynicism (III, iv, 69-79).

Buckingham is willing to have Richard crowned and assists in the achievement; but he is not willing to have the little princes murdered, and his hesitancy is his end. The scene of his rejection (IV, ii, 86-121), though it occurs only in the poorer text of the quarto, certainly came from Shakespeare's hand:

My lord, I claim your gift, my due by promise,
For which your honour and your faith is pawn'd;
The earldom of Hereford and the moveables
The which you promised I should possess. . . .
Buck. My lord!
K. Rich. Ay, what's o'clock?
Buck. I am thus bold to put your grace in mind
Of what you promised me.
K. Rich.   Well, but what's o'clock?
Buck. Upon the stroke of ten.
K. Rich.   Well, let it strike.
Buck. Why let it strike?
K. Rich. Because that, like a Jack, thou keep'st the stroke
Betwixt thy begging and my meditation.
I am not in the giving vein today.

The fourth act is, as fourth acts should be, filled with the consequences
of the climactic action of the third act—here Richard's usurpation of the
crown. The princes are murdered, and the reader feels the loss personally,
since he has seen them and heard them speak—the young King grave,
sensible, and aspiring; the little Duke of York a playful, irresponsible,
delightful child. Shakespeare has spared us the necessity of hearing their
screams and has in Senecan fashion reported their slaughter. Tyrrell
speaks (IV, iii, 1-22):

The tyrannous and bloody deed is done,
The most arch act of piteous massacre
That ever yet this land was guilty of.
Dighton and Forrest, whom I did suborn
To do this ruthless piece of butchery,
Although they were flesh'd villains, bloody dogs,
Melting with tenderness and kind compassion
Wept like two children in their deaths' sad stories.
'Lo, thus,' quoth Dighton, 'lay those tender babes;'
'Thus, thus,' quoth Forrest, 'girdling one another
Within their innocent alabaster arms:
Their lips were four red roses on a stalk,
Which in their summer beauty kiss'd each other.
A book of prayers on their pillow lay;
Which once,' quoth Forrest, 'almost changed my mind;
But O! the devil'—there the villain stopp'd;

> Whilst Dighton thus told on: 'We smothered
> The most replenished sweet work of nature,
> That from the prime creation e'er she framed.'
> Thus both are gone with conscience and remorse;
> They could not speak; and so I left them both,
> To bring this tidings to the bloody king.

"But didst thou see them dead?" asks Richard.

Senecan also is the great scene of grief (iv). All three of Our Ladies of Sorrow are there, and Queen Margaret makes the brain rock under conspiracies and tempests. One would like to think that in the interview between Richard and Queen Elizabeth, which follows the scene of lamentation, she had shown some gleam of subtlety or of honest resistance, but she does not. One would ask what Shakespeare thought of women if the Queen's acquiescence in Richard's shocking and unnatural proposal were not soundly based in the chronicle. As it is, one can only join Richard in his comment (1. 431):

> Relenting fool, and shallow, changing woman!

It is also to be noted that in this perfectly built tragedy the fourth act furnishes a suggestion that justice is not dead, that Richard's nemesis is on the way. Dorset escapes to Richmond (IV, i, 92), and at the end of the fourth scene Richard's hand for the first time falters. At the end of the third scene he had said (ll. 51-4):

> Come, I have heard that fearful commenting
> Is leaden servitor to dull delay;
> Delay leads impotent and snail-paced beggary:
> Then fiery expedition be my wing,

but in the fourth scene (ll. 433 ff.) when Ratcliffe and Catesby bring him news of the approach of Richmond, he gives confused orders to his officers and allows himself to be outwitted by Stanley. This is but the beginning of the panic which seizes him on the night before Bosworth field when the ghosts of all his victims visit his tent. Ghosts in Elizabethan plays were objective and played by actors in full view of the audience. Yet of course Richard was dreaming, and we are forced to believe that these supernatural visitors were accepted by the audience as the immaterial terrors of his conscience. Richard is as brave about ghosts as Macbeth himself, and his courage in battle is like that of Macbeth.

Richard III is a tragedy of the quest for power, of an insatiable appetite for dominance. In that respect it is very Marlovian. But it is broadened into a tragedy of state like the plays based on Plutarch. It is a tragedy of the recoil of humanity against tyranny, cruelty, and crime. Shakespeare, like us ourselves, certainly regarded this assertion of the eternal principles of justice in human nature as inevitable. *Richard III* fits into the concept of the romantic tragedy of Marlowe, and there is no clear pattern for such tragedies in the ancient world. The nearest proto-types are the Hercules plays of Seneca. Such plays do not fit into the scheme of tragedy laid down by Aristotle in the *Poetics*. Critics have said that we have to do with a villain-hero, and this is usually true; but perhaps a wider basis for thought is the idea that we have to do with the forward movement of a hero. There is no reason to think that both Marlowe's *Tamburlaine* and Shakespeare's *Henry V* do not belong to the same genre.

Looked at individually, these Yorkist plays, specifically *Richard III*, raise a question. We ask why any man should seek such power at such ι cost and by such means. Yet we know that men do continually in every age seek such power. We know that Machiavelli elevated this ideal to the utmost political importance, its methods fully worked out, in *The Prince*. We know, as apparently Machiavelli did not, that tyrants, political, economic, and domestic, degenerate. Shakespeare seems to have known that they did, although he nowhere definitely states the principle. Can we sympathize with tyrants? Can we sympathize with Richard of Gloucester? Tyrants drape their tyranny with pretenses of patriotism, the promotion of the general good, and what not; but it is doubtful if we can expand our sympathies to include them all. The matter seems to be relative. Machiavelli meant well, Shakespeare stakes his political faith on Prince Hal; but, where motives are selfish and evil, we have great difficulty in finding a motive, as in the case of Richard, which will save the humanity of such villains. Shakespeare almost succeeds in saving Macbeth, who retains to the end some measure of our sympathies, but the case is probably different with Richard. We may have to class him with Barabas in *The Jew of Malta* and Aaron in *Titus Andronicus*. Richard says in so many words: "I am determined to prove a villain." His way is the way of treachery and blood. To be sure, he has visitations of conscience and experiences horror in his dreams on the night before Bosworth field, and he seems even to show human confusion after his greatest act of abject villainy. We are willing to grant that a crown in Shakespeare's age seemed to be an overmastering goal of achievement.

Yet Richard's bravery made the world cry out:

> Give me another horse: bind up my wounds.

And yet Richard's wickedness is such that we sympathize with Richmond when he says, "The bloody dog is dead." Can we sympathize with such a hero even when we rejoice in his downfall? That would be a paradox and there is something paradoxical in such a dramatic spectacle. We seem forced to the verge of human nature. The truth is that Richard is fascinating even in his villainy. He has wit, cleverness, adroitness, a mordant humor all his own, and courage of the highest order. There is a Satan-like sublimity in his every move. He is not simply another bad man. It is unprofitable to involve oneself too deeply in the quicksands which surround the discrimination of literary forms, and yet we must have in *Richard III* and in some other romantic tragedies of the Renaissance a kind of tragedy not provided for by Aristotle and his commentators.

CHAPTER IV

Shakespeare's Theatrical Connections

KING JOHN AND THE TAMING OF THE SHREW

A S WE APPROACH the year 1594 and later years we need infor
mation about early theatres and dramatic companies. It is not
exciting information, but will prove itself useful in the study of
Shakespeare.

During the decade from 1580 to 1590 the stage and the dramatic
companies took on forms which were roughly characteristic throughout
the period of Elizabethan drama. One begins to hear of more plays and
players and of greater expenses of the Revels Office about the middle of
Queen Elizabeth's reign. These were her gayest years: Leicester was
her lover, and suitors for her hand were numerous. The situation at
court gave to actors an opportunity which they seem to have needed,
since their legal and social status was insecure and low. The application
to players, however, of the statute against rogues and vagabonds does not
mean that actors and entertainers had no place in Elizabethan society,
but only that the members of the craft of acting were expected to remain
in their ancient status of servants to the sovereign or to noble persons
able to maintain in their households musicians, minstrels, acrobats, actors,
and other entertainers. There was nothing unusual in the fact that the
Earl of Leicester in 1574 obtained for his servants a royal patent to perform plays within the City and liberties of London and in other cities,
boroughs, and towns. It was merely an extension in scope and a formal
recognition of a situation which had existed for generations. It is a more
significant fact that, because of a decree of the Common Council of London
(1574) forbidding the performance of plays within the City, James
Burbage, the leader of Leicester's company, built in 1576 the "Theatre"

in Shoreditch beyond the jurisdiction of the City. Here many of the plays of Shakespeare were performed. Shortly afterwards another playhouse, the Curtain, was built near by the Theatre, and a third at Newington Butts about 1580. Until the prohibitions of the City were enacted, dramatic companies seem to have performed their plays in the courtyards of various London inns. The corporation had been actuated by a desire to diminish the danger of plague infection, the neglect of divine service, the waste of time and money, and the conditions of vice and corruption which prevailed round about dramatic assemblies. The actors sought freedom from restriction by moving into the suburbs, but they still found it profitable to act in the City when they could; and courtyards at the Bull, the Bel Savage, the Cross Keys, and other inns seem to have continued in use. James Burbage modeled the Theatre after the inn courtyard: a platform for the actors at one end; common people on the ground, nobility and gentry at windows and in balconies above. This is, roughly speaking, the form of all Elizabethan public theatres.

An event of importance was the entrance of Philip Henslowe into the field of the theatre as the proprietor of playhouses. He built the Rose on the Bankside, on the south side of the river Thames. It was probably ready for occupancy in 1587. Other theatres migrated to the Bankside. Francis Langley built the Swan farther west (1594) than the Rose, and in 1598 the Burbages, Richard and Cuthbert, sons of James, having had trouble about the lease of the land on which the Theatre stood, tore down, somewhat illegally, the Theatre in Holliwell, Cripplegate, and used its timbers in the construction of the famous Globe on the Bankside. In 1600 Henslowe and his son-in-law, the actor Edward Alleyn, built the Fortune, not on the Bankside, but in Golders Lane, Cripplegate. The contract and specifications of the Fortune have been preserved, and from them much has been learned about the probable structure of the Globe and other public theatres. A second Globe on the old site succeeded the first after its destruction by fire in 1613. There were other public as well as private theatres. The reason for the distinction between the two kinds of playhouses is that they seem to have differed in their interior arrangements. The public playhouses had a stage projecting out into the pit, with the audience surrounding the players on three sides, and were open to the skies; the private theatres were roofed in and had a platform stage at one end of a hall. Certain differences, not well understood, in staging and in kinds of plays seem to have resulted from the physical features of the playhouses. The second Blackfriars theatre, occupied by Shakespeare's company in 1608, was a private playhouse; and the Globe, their regular playing place, was a public playhouse.

The Elizabethan theatrical company seems to have been made up of six leading actors, each of whom followed a conventional line. If there were more than six parts in the play, the actors had to double their rôles. T. W. Baldwin, speaking of the period before 1594, describes the composition of the original theatrical company as consisting of "two comedians, two more or less young men, and one usually humorous old dignitary." At a later time the company was expanded into seven major male parts, and still later into nine. From the earliest times there would have been one or more apprentices to play the parts of women. As the strolling players approach the court at Elsinore (*Hamlet*, II, ii, 332-40), Hamlet anticipates that there will be among them an actor to play the following parts: the king, the adventurous knight, the lover, the humorous man, and the clown, with a sixth, obviously a boy, to play the part of the lady. Bottom in *A Midsummer-Night's Dream* (I, ii) expects to play either a lover or a tyrant; he prefers the tyrant; Flute would like the part of the wandering knight, but has to content himself with the woman's part of Thisbe; Snout will play the father of Thisbe. There is here a sort of rough agreement on the number of five regular parts plus a youth to play the lady. Indeed, Baldwin has shown that older plays, many of them, were written for companies of this size and composition, and that dramatists planned their plays accordingly. As the stage prospered and companies remained on location for longer periods, the actors were increased in numbers, and plays were written which provided a larger and larger number of parts. The old major rôles persisted and are identifiable throughout the history of Elizabethan and Jacobean drama. Many of the additional actors were no longer principal members of the company, but hired men. The parts of women had been played from the beginning by the apprentices of the principal actors, and the practice continued, although as women's parts grew more varied and complicated, many successful actors of feminine rôles seem to have continued to play them long after their apprenticeship days were over.

Shakespeare's early plays still show quite plainly the six original parts, although in all of them the number of women is more than one, and it is clear that where the plot demanded it the numbers of actors playing certain types of characters have been multiplied. For example, the kingly and soldierly parts in the history plays are numerous. There are two clowns each in *The Two Gentlemen of Verona* and *The Comedy of Errors*, and several more in *A Midsummer-Night's Dream*, a play in which the lovers are also, as in *The Two Gentlemen*, increased to two. A primitive division of women into shrewish and amiable ladies appears in both *The Comedy of Errors* and *A Midsummer-Night's Dream*, and the device is used structurally in the plot of *The Taming of the Shrew*. Elizabethan actors thus had lines for which they were trained and selected.

There were many theatrical companies, and their histories and inter-relations are by no means fully known. It will suffice to say that the important children's companies were the Children of Paul's, the Children of the Chapel and the Queen's Revels, and the Children of the Royal Chapel at Windsor. Among the important adult companies were the Earl of Leicester's Men (1559-1588?). Tradition connects Shakespeare with this company, and it is certain that his later associates, the Burbages, had an original connection with it. The Earl of Sussex's company lasted from about 1569 until 1594. The Earl of Oxford's company was a still older one, which lasted until about 1590. Queen Elizabeth's men, a very popular company during the decade of the eighties, lasted until about 1592 and was later revived as one of the many provincial companies. It had many of the best plays of the period in its repertory. The famous clown, Dick Tarlton, was a member of it. Lord Strange's men are mentioned first about 1573-4 and existed probably until 1594. It is at least probable that Shakespeare belonged to this company, since it had so many of his future associates in it—Burbage, Pope, Phillips, Heminges, and others. Some authorities doubtfully assign Shakespeare to the Earl of Pembroke's company, a company certainly existent in 1592-1593. Dr. J. Q. Adams, in *A Life of William Shakespeare*, argues that when Shakespeare came to London he became a member of the Earl of Pembroke's company, mainly on the ground that Pembroke's men are known to have acted a *Hamlet*, *The Taming of a Shrew*, a *Titus Andronicus*, *The Contention betwixt the Two Noble Houses of York and Lancaster*, and *The True Tragedy of Richard Duke of York*, all plays or versions of plays appearing in Shakespeare's dramatic work. But *The Contention* and *The True Tragedy* and probably *The Taming of a Shrew* are degenerate stage versions of Shakespeare's *2* and *3 Henry VI* and of a lost original of *The Taming of the Shrew*. The *Hamlet* may have been the old play, probably by Kyd, which Shakespeare later rewrote; and the *Titus Andronicus* may not have been Shakespeare's play, since there were certainly plays on the subject by other dramatists. Pembroke's company went bankrupt in the year 1593, and another group with the same patronage, but apparently not the same in membership, appeared in 1597. A number of plays apparently from the Pembroke repertory fell, on the collapse of the company, into the hands of publishers. Several of them are versions of plays by Shakespeare, but a difficulty of assigning Shakespeare to that company arises from the fact that these plays, except *Titus Andronicus*, to which there seems to have been no clear title, are corrupt or so-called pirated versions. Pembroke's men were apparently not playing Shakespeare's original works, but only reported versions of certain of them.

When the theaters opened again in 1594, after having been long closed on account of the plague, there was a re-alignment of actors and companies, very difficult to trace. Two strong companies of actors of historical importance emerged and were of long continuance: the Lord Admiral's men and the Lord Chamberlain's men. We know far more about the activities of the former than of the latter, for Philip Henslowe set down in his famous *Diary*, a sort of account-book preserved with the Henslowe papers at Dulwich College, the names of the plays acted in his theaters, the sums taken in at performances, and also memoranda of payments to actors and dramatists. We know that Dekker, Drayton, Chettle, Porter, Hathway, Munday, Samuel Rowley, Day, and even Chapman, Jonson, Middleton, and Webster wrote plays for Henslowe; also that the leader of the Lord Admiral's men was the great tragedian Edward Alleyn. We also know the names of his associates in the company. We know from many performances at court, from title-pages of published plays, and from casual allusions a good deal about the Lord Chamberlain's men, the group to which Shakespeare belonged, but nothing like so much as we know of the Lord Admiral's. The Lord Chamberlain's company was not a proprietary but a joint stock company, whose shares were divided among a group of the principal actors, of whom Shakespeare was one. The Burbages held the largest number of shares. For this company wrote the greatest dramatists of the time—Shakespeare, Beaumont and Fletcher, Tourneur, Massinger, and Shirley. The company also acted plays by Jonson and Chapman. Largely from it came the group of anonymous plays collected as Shakespeare Apocrypha. The repertory of the company was dominated by

Shakespeare until he ceased to write or was succeeded in popularity by Beaumont and Fletcher. A great deal is known also about Shakespeare's "fellows," two of whom, John Heminges and Henry Condell, sponsored the great First Folio, a collection of Shakespeare's comedies, histories, and tragedies, in 1623.

During the years of the plague of 1592-1593 when the London theatrical companies went into the provinces, there is a plausible conjecture to the effect that Shakespeare did not go with them. At least that seems a time when the demand for new plays would not have been great and Shakespeare might have devoted himself to the composition of poetry. *Venus and Adonis* was published in 1593 and *The Rape of Lucrece* in 1594. Shakespeare was even then no mere beginner in the field, for Henry Chettle in 1592 apparently alluded to Shakespeare's skill in poetry when he speaks of Shakespeare's "facetious grace in writing." With this possible break in Shakespeare's activity as a playwright in mind, one may divide Shakespeare's early plays into those he probably wrote before the closing of the theaters and those he wrote during the period of the plague or soon after it was over. As to the first group, conjecture is difficult. On purely stylistic grounds one would be disposed to say that the earliest Shakespearean plays which have been preserved are *The Comedy of Errors* and *Titus Andronicus*. With them might be associated the stiff and rhetorical 2 *Henry VI* and probably 3 *Henry VI*. With these of course would be associated 1 *Henry VI*, although it is in part at least more mature in style than either of them. On purely internal evidence one would be disposed to regard *The Two Gentlemen* as certainly a play written before the plague. *Love's Labour's Lost* is much of a puzzle as regards date, since the version we have has been revised. Its likeness in style and temper to the poems tempts one to date it about the same time as the poems. *Richard III* must belong to the same impulse which produced the Henry VI plays, for its connection with 3 *Henry VI* is very close indeed. *Richard III* probably antedates 1594 and may antedate the plague. *A Midsummer-Night's Dream* in an original form may go back to a time before the theaters were closed. *Romeo and Juliet*, as we have seen, belongs to what Chambers calls "the lyrical group," and one would conjecture that it was certainly in existence by 1594.

This leaves two early plays whose dates are much in doubt, *King John* and *The Taming of the Shrew*. *King John* is a carefully written play,

formal in manner, but so is 2 *Henry VI*. *King John* is somewhat archaic
in style and surprisingly mature in thought and seems, on the whole, to
be an early play. Many critics, however, place it in date after *Richard II*,
a judgment which seems dubious. There has been of late a disposition to
regard *The Taming of the Shrew* as a very early play, but the reasons
are defective. If *The Taming of a Shrew* is, as Alexander contends, a
reported version of *The Taming of the Shrew*, then the latter play must
be very early, since *The Taming of a Shrew* was published in 1594. But
if, as seems more probable, the latter play is a reported version, not of
The Taming of the Shrew, but of the lost source of that play, the date
of *The Taming of the Shrew* becomes inconclusive. It will be convenient
to consider *King John* and *The Taming of the Shrew* as transitional
between the earliest group of Shakespeare's plays and those which clearly
belong to the period after the opening of the theaters in 1594.

1. *King John*.

   King John is thus a play apart. Its date and style are puzzling. It rests
immediately, not on the chronicles, but on an earlier play in two parts,
The Troublesome Raigne of John King of England, formerly acted by
the Queen's company and published in 1591. Shakespeare has condensed
the two parts into one, rewritten the old play throughout line by line,
changed the emphasis, and developed the characters. The anti-papistical
quality of *The Troublesome Raigne* and its defamation of the French
are gone, and Shakespeare has made *King John* into a play of transcendent
patriotism.

   King John has a uniformity and dignity of style beyond that of 2 and
3 *Henry VI*, but an undoubted stiffness and formality that recalls those
plays and compels one to regard it as an early effort. It is also a better
play than either of those, as witnessed by its actability and by its quite
respectable stage history. It has at least three good male parts—King John,
Pandulph, and Faulconbridge—and one female part of great tragic appeal,
that of Constance. There is also the lovely figure of Arthur, a sensitive
and intelligent child, and with him the repentant Hubert. The play has
much human interest and acts well. Garrick acted in it, as did John
Philip Kemble, Edmund Kean, and his son, Charles Kean. Henry Irving
was great as Pandulph, and Ellen Terry as Constance. No one who had
ever seen her in the rôle could forget the proudly tragic impression left

in the mind by her recitation of the lines of Constance (III, i, 67-74). Salisbury says to her, "I may not go without you to the kings" and her reply is,

> Thou mayst, thou shalt; I will not go with thee:
> I will instruct my sorrows to be proud;
> For grief is proud and makes his owner stoop.
> To me and to the state of my great grief
> Let kings assemble; for my grief's so great
> That no supporter but the huge firm earth
> Can hold it up; here I and sorrow sit;
> Here is my throne, bid kings come bow to it.

These important characters also have important things, both social and political, to say. The thought of *King John* has a surprising maturity about it, far ahead of the *Henry VI* plays and indeed of *Richard III*. This maturity may be derived from the fact that Shakespeare was rewriting a well thought out and, on the whole, excellent source in *The Trouble some Raigne*; but, however that may be, Shakespeare comes to grips with many questions important to the politics of sixteenth-century England —inheritance by primogeniture, the rights and duties of kings, and the relation between all kings and God's vicegerent on earth, the Pope of Rome. What Shakespeare's opinions were is not apparent, for he stands far outside the area of conflict but one would say that he knew the value of his native land, the quality of patriotism, and the behavior of men actuated by political motives, whether of selfish ambition or of social justice. *King John* is a great historical play, and nowhere does Shakespeare reveal more fully his vision of history as a stage whereon actual men of various sorts play many, many diverse parts. In no matter does the acting of the play bring a greater surprise than in the revelation of King John himself. To almost all readers he is a rather despicable character, uninteresting, inconsequential; but to those who see *King John* on the stage, the King becomes the central figure of the play—defeated, vacillating, and prone to evil, but unquestionably a man and a hero.

There is little that is lyrical in *King John*, but much that is finely rhetorical. The play excels in human interest. The first scene begins the revelation of Philip Faulconbridge. Philip is a bastard and as such was obliged to rebel against the social order, and he does so in many ways; but being a royal bastard, he is not villainous like Don John and Edmund. By his birth he must support the King and the country, but his alienation from society expresses itself in many ways. He despises courtiers and stands alone at court; he robs the church without compunction; he sees with his independence and common sense the essence of every issue, political or moral. As a bastard, he ought to be added to the studies of such persons in the Elizabethan drama. Unquestionably he belongs to wild and untamed nature, but to the beneficent aspects of such exuberant forces. The first scene shows his lack of shame and normal propriety. He is saying in his own way, and quite justifiably, "Now, gods, stand up for bastards!"

No play illustrates better than *King John* that drama is debate. The first act manages to introduce and establish Faulconbridge, to make clear the peculiar situation of domestic jealousy in the royal family, and to introduce Queen Elinor with her excessive favoritism for King John and her primitive jealousy of her daughter-in-law Constance, a jealousy which extends even to her own grandson Prince Arthur. Then in the second act we have debated before us the issue of compromise for the sake of commodity and betrayal of justice for the sake of gain. The third act, a great one, reveals the nature of the false settlement by showing its effect upon Constance. She has been greatly wronged, but she turns out to be the first of Shakespeare's sentimentalists. She suffers, no doubt, through the wrong done to her son, which is the only wrong she undergoes; but she suffers more from the wrong done to her through her son, for she loves herself in her son. His beauty, not himself, is the object of her affection. She grieves but enjoys her grief.

> You hold too heinous a respect of grief

says Pandulph, and she makes the unforgettable reply:

> He talks to me that never had a son.

And he replies,

> You are as fond of grief as of your child.

To be flattered by kings is no small inducement to villainy, and the naturally good Hubert yields to the blandishments of the ignoble John, and thus the third act is full of conspiracy, the murder of children, and the pillaging of churches. King John is here at his lowest ebb. It is a tribute to Shakespeare that he was thus willing to let history speak, for in Protestant England John had long been regarded as the champion

of his country against papal tyranny. The third act gives one also a
picture of the cool, resolute, devoted churchman, Cardinal Pandulph, the
Pope's legate, a part which was magnified into awe-inspiring power when
acted by Sir Henry Irving (III, i, 172-9, 191-4, 263-97; IV, ii, 131-40):

> Then, by the lawful power that I have,
> Thou shalt stand cursed and excommunicate:
> And blessed shall he be that doth revolt
> From his allegiance to an heretic;
> And meritorious shall that hand be call'd,
> Canonized and worshipp'd as a saint,
> That takes away by any secret course
> Thy hateful life. . . .
> It is religion that doth make vows kept;
> But thou hast sworn against religion, . . .
> Therefore thy later vows against thy first
> Is in thyself rebellion to thyself; . . .
> Upon which better part our prayers come in,
> If thou vouchsafe them. But if not, then know
> The peril of our curses light on thee
> So heavy as thou shalt not shake them off,
> But in despair die under their black weight. . . .

The fourth act is devoted mainly to Arthur, the first scene to the
moving struggle of Arthur in order that Hubert may not put out his
eyes, and the third to the child's death as he attempts to escape over the
castle wall. The first is a piece of emotional writing greater than anything
Shakespeare had yet done, unless this work follows rather than precedes
certain passages in *Romeo and Juliet*, such as Juliet's swallowing of the
sleeping potion and the events of her awakening in the tomb; and yet
there is a difference. The passages in *King John* have the stark immediacy
of Marlowe when he depicts the death of Edward II, and those of
Romeo and Juliet are relieved in their poignancy by poetry and romantic
setting.

Shakespeare had probably already depicted the little princes in *Richard
III* and had revealed his power to see into the lives and motives of
children. The speech and the manner of his children had always the
stiffness and grown-up quality attributed to them by an age which still
believed that each child was born with a fully matured soul. The painters
of the age did not even realize that the physical form of childhood differs
from that of adulthood—witness the children painted by Giotto and

even by Van Dyck—but they and Shakespeare manage somehow to be convincing. Arthur ranks with Mamillius among Shakespeare's children. There is a childishness in Arthur's imagery and his point of view, although, because his words and ideas are inappropriately mature for childhood, he seems unnatural. Take, for example, his greatest speech (IV, i, 41-58):

> Have you the heart? When your head did but ache,
> I knit my handkercher about your brows,
> The best I had, a princess wrought it me,
> And I did never ask it you again;
> And with my hand at midnight held your head,
> And like the watchful minutes to the hour,
> Still and anon cheer'd up the heavy time,
> Saying, 'What lack you?' and 'Where lies your grief?'
> Many a poor man's son would have lien still
> And ne'er have spoke a loving word to you;
> But you at your sick service had a prince.
> Nay, you may think my love was crafty love
> And call it cunning: do, an if you will:
> If heaven be pleased that you must use me ill,
> Why then you must. Will you put out mine eyes?
> These eyes that never did nor never shall
> So much as frown on you.

The plea is perfect. It is like the child to remember the "handkercher" and that he never got it back, but it is not so natural for him to introduce the abstract thought that it was more precious because a princess wrought it for him. It is like a child to despair quickly even when the case is won, and in the rather commonplace words, "Will you put out mine eyes," there is the hysterical shriek of childhood in pain.

One hesitates to build too much on the nemesis wrought upon John by Arthur's death, and yet it is there. Shakespeare preaches so little that one cannot hear him say, "This is what comes to you for murdering children." And yet the defection of the nobles is clearly due to John's crime, and the Bastard seems to know this when he says (IV, iii, 140-2):

> I am amazed, methinks, and lose my way
> Among the thorns and dangers of this world.
> How easy dost thou take all England up!

King John differs from *The Troublesome Raigne of John King of England* in the fact that it is less anti-papistical, and some critics have wished to argue from this fact that Shakespeare was more refined and more tolerant than was the older author. These critics may be right, but there is at least some slight evidence that Shakespeare may have written scenes of the despoiling of the monasteries in his original version and that these scenes were canceled at the time of some revival of *King John* after the passage of the *Act to Restrain Abuses of Players* on May 7, 1606, or perhaps in consequence of some change in official sentiment toward the Catholic Church in the reign of James I. As the play now stands, it is incomplete in the fifth act. We get no account of the motives of the monk of Swinstead who tasted to King John, "a resolved villain, whose bowels suddenly burst out." It is not like Shakespeare to leave his story imperfect, and, if one lays *King John* and *The Troublesome Raigne* side by side, one finds, except in this part of the story, an almost scene-for-scene agreement. Moreover, it will be observed that almost all the scenes of *King John* are rounded out with the final cueing couplet, except the third, the fifth, and the sixth scenes of the fifth act. It is natural to ask if these scenes have not suffered cuts. It is also true that one scene of the despoiling of monasteries which occurred in *The Troublesome Raigne* is not represented in *King John* at all. So it may be that Shakespeare's original play followed its sources even in the oppression of the church. That he would have presented such matters more modestly and more artistically than the old play did may well be granted, but there are at least some slight indications that in his rewriting Shakespeare did not omit all mention of necessary parts of the action. Another possibility is that after the act of 1606 the theater would have refrained from showing in detail the poisoning of an English king.

The patriotic sentiment of the later part of the play is hard for us to appreciate. King John as a patriot seems a rather sorry spectacle, and yet there is no doubt that it is strongly played up. The French lords acknowledge the King's greatness. The English lords are reconciled to him and rejoice in his victory over the French invaders, but the modern reader responds only to the heroism of Faulconbridge. His words, the final words of the play, still live in the minds of his countrymen:

> This England never did, nor never shall,
> Lie at the proud foot of a conqueror,
> But when it first did help to wound itself.
> Now these her princes are come home again,

Come the three corners of the world in arms,
And we shall shock them. Nought shall make us rue,
If England to itself do rest but true.

2. *The Taming of the Shrew.*

As we shift to *The Taming of the Shrew*, which we have chosen to
treat in the same chapter with *King John*, we remark that the form followed in the *Shrew* is that of Latin comedy. The plays of Plautus and
Terence do not, however, constitute the main stem of Renaissance comedy,
although there is no doubt that they were a shaping influence. Plautus
and Terence were acted in English schools from the beginning of the
sixteenth century, and the characters and situations of Latin comedy were
frequently employed in English comedy, but in specific cases it is often
difficult to tell whether one has to do with Plautus and Terence themselves or with the many Italian, French, or Low German adaptations
of them.

Among the dramatic achievements of the mid-sixteenth century drama
are, for example, two latinate comedies of unusual interest, *Ralph Roister
Doister* and *Gammer Gurton's Needle*. Both show the influence of Latin
comedy, and both arose from the custom of sixteenth-century school-
masters of having Plautus and Terence, or imitations of them, acted on
stages in their schools with schoolboys as actors. *Ralph Roister Doister* is
one of the first plays of the period in which there is a clearly constructed
plot, a rapid, natural dialogue, and a set of characters so conceived as to
furnish dramatic conflict. To be sure, the characters are largely types borrowed from Latin comedy, but are sufficiently adapted to their English
situation to bring the comedy through satisfactorily and make of it an
English play. *Gammer Gurton's Needle* is a realistic comedy in English,
almost but not quite free from Plautine influences, and the only one of
its kind. It has about it a roaring, farcical quality suggestive of a sixteenth-
century English village in all its naturalness. Thus *Ralph Roister Doister*
and *Gammer Gurton's Needle* together present the two elements which
enter into *The Taming of the Shrew*—literary comedy of the Renaissance
based on Plautus and Terence but with native English significance.

One associates with these two early comedies various others. George
Gascoigne made a translation of Ariosto's Italian comedy *Gli Suppositi* as
The Supposes, which was acted by the students of Gray's Inn in 1566. It

is a skillful comedy of disguises, of great importance in the history of English drama. It became the source of the minor plot of *The Taming of the Shrew*. It occupies the same imitative relation to Plautus and Terence as does *Ralph Roister Doister*, but it shows much better dramatic art than that play.

Intrigues of love and friendship such as appear in *The Two Gentlemen of Verona* are not absent from *The Taming of the Shrew*, which has, like *Love's Labour's Lost* and *The Two Gentlemen*, a group of gay young gentlemen full of puns, witticisms, *double-entendres*; but *The Taming of the Shrew* belongs in its major plot to a more popular type of comedy of which there are traces in Shakespeare's early work, comedy for the popular rather than for the courtly portion of his audience. The major plot is a refined treatment of the old farcical theme of the taming of the curst wife, but it is a mistake to conceive of the play in purely farcical terms. Petruchio is no wife-beater like the hero of the popular ballad on which the plot rests. He is a gentle, clever man of the world, a profound humorist and the best of actors.

We have seen in recent years various truly farcical presentations of *The Taming of the Shrew*, and there is no doubt that the play lends itself to treatment as a farce. Indeed, in Petruchio's dress, behavior, and equipage at his wedding and in his behavior in the country, there is actual slapstick comedy; but the minor plot is the Italian comedy of *The Supposes*, sufficiently respectable, and back of Petruchio's ridiculous behavior is a serious romantic purpose. This purpose is stated emphatically in the last scene of the play. The major plot is also not without significance in character development. Katharina has never seen herself as others see her. In order to make her aware of the true nature of her behavior Petruchio burlesques Katharina's unreasonable conduct, and thus shows her a picture of herself. When the couple are on their way to Padua, Kate still without food, he makes her agree that the sun is the moon (IV, v, 2-22); and something entirely new happens in Kate's mind. She sees the joke.

> Forward, I pray, since we have come so far,
> And be it moon, or sun, or what you please:
> An if you please to call it a rush-candle,
> Henceforth I vow it shall be so for me.
> *Pet.* I say it is the moon.
> *Kath.*   I know it is the moon.

In fact she makes a joke herself, and a very good one, when she says,

> Then, God be bless'd, it is the blessed sun;
> But sun it is not, when you say it is not;
> And the moon changes even with your mind.

She has always behaved like a fool, although she is not a fool, and her new sense of humor is an indication of a profound change within her. The major plot of *The Taming of the Shrew* is not therefore a farce. As to the minor plot, it is pretty consistently Italianate comedy. Differences between the two plots have given rise to a widespread theory of collaboration, but there is no compulsive reason to think that the minor plot is by another hand than Shakespeare's. The plots are almost too closely knit together for collaboration.

The intense conservatism of the most weighty kind of Shakespeare scholarship is no doubt an excellent thing, and yet one cannot help feeling some disappointment that so little progress is made in the acceptance of the results of much careful study. The scarcity of the materials of proof, if proof must rely on record and testimony alone, has brought it about that resort is had to probability. Probability is not to be despised, for, as Bishop Butler remarks, "Probability is nine-tenths of life." One wonders if, in at least certain cases, such as *The Taming of the Shrew* and some others, probability has not become so strong that some issues over disputed matters in Shakespeare scholarship may have reached a stage where sufficiently well answered to satisfy the minds of reasonable men. solutions may be said to be so obvious as to be generally accepted; indeed, whether some questions still in dubiety may not already have been

It is suggested that the long debate over the relation between *The Taming of the Shrew* and *The Taming of a Shrew* may have come to such a satisfactory end. *The Taming of the Shrew* first appeared in print in the First Folio in 1623. However, a play, *The Taming of a Shrew*, closely related to *The Shrew*, was published in 1594, 1596, 1607, 1631. There has been a long dispute over the relation between these two plays. If one disregards the unnecessary theory that the original shrew play was an early work of Shakespeare's, one sees that ten Brink had the right idea about the matter, since he suggested that the plays were not immediately derived one from the other, but went back to a common original. But ten Brink's theory has not been accepted. F. G. Fleay saw three hands in *The Taming of the Shrew*: an unknown author of *The*

Taming of a Shrew, Shakespeare himself, and a collaborator with Shakespeare. Fleay has been followed by R. W. Bond in his edition of the play and by most editors. Against this view is the careful study by E. P. Kuhl, who argues that the entire play is from Shakespeare's hand. That *A Shrew* is the source of *The Shrew* has been long and widely held. Chambers adheres to this view. To Shakespeare he makes the customary assignments of the part of Christopher Sly and the Petruchio and Katharina scenes. A collaborator, he thinks, is responsible for Bianca and her wooers. He finds collectively significant stylistic differences in the two parts, and complains of pedestrian verse, faulty stresses, and overabundant classical tags in the work of the collaborator. Chambers minimizes the inconsistencies usually said to characterize the text of *The Shrew*, a circumstance which makes his explanation the more unsatisfactory.

We may, like ten Brink, fairly start with an hypothesis of a lost original shrew play as the source of both the shrew plays preserved. This lost play may be dated in or before 1589 because of an allusion in that year to such a play both in Greene's *Menaphon* and in Nashe's prefatory epistle to that work. The contents of the original shrew play, we may suppose, were roughly the same as those of *A Shrew*, but it was presumably free from the confusion in the placement of scenes which Raymond A. Houk has discovered and pointed out. The old play may well have had a continuous time-scheme after the Plautine model, and, if it did, the inconsistencies in *A Shrew* pointed out by Mr. Houk may perhaps better be regarded as confusions of the original shrew play than as confusions of *The Shrew*; for *The Shrew* may, as regards the time scheme, have followed the original shrew play correctly, and *A Shrew* may have failed to do so.

We may suppose that the original was a play of formal construction and that it had a full induction telling the story of "The Sleeper Awaked." It must have contained principally the story of the taming of the shrew, to which had been added, by way of amplification, the story of the father who had three daughters, one a shrew, all provided with lovers. There is no reason to think that in composing this play the author of it resorted to Gascoigne's *The Supposes*, or to its original Ariosto's *Gli Suppositi*. The formal arrangement of having a fixed number of ladies and of lovers was characteristic of the drama of the time and appears, for example, in Shakespeare's early comedies. It was when Shakespeare rewrote the old shrew play that resort was had to *The Supposes*, and the dramatic purposes of that resort are still evident.

The original shrew play probably belonged to Lord Strange's Company and passed from them to the Lord Chamberlain's company, although, when it was revived at Henslowe's theater on June 11, 1594, the Lord Admiral's and the Lord Chamberlain's men were both acting for Henslowe, so that it is impossible to say definitely to which company it belonged. Since a version of the play finally shows up as the property of the King's Company (successors to the Lord Chamberlain's company) in 1623, it is likely that the Lord Chamberlain's company were the owners in 1594. Although it is impossible to say that the revival at Henslowe's theater in 1594 was Shakespeare's play, the name, "the Tamynge of a Shrowe," seems to suggest that it was not.

In 1592 a company of players under the patronage of the Earl of Pembroke appear in the records. Chambers thinks that it was a troupe made up of actors from various companies then disorganized because of the existence of plague in London and the consequent closing of the theaters. However that may be, Pembroke's company went bankrupt in 1593, and a group of plays claiming on their title pages that they had been acted by Pembroke's men came on the market and were published about 1594. Among them was *The Taming of a Shrew*. This, however, was probably not the original shrew play, for Alexander has shown conclusively that *A Shrew* is a reported play or "bad" quarto. Several others of the plays from the repertory of the defunct Pembroke's company are also "bad" quartos, and if they are representative of their list, that company must have acted mainly reported versions of plays and not originals.

If *A Shrew* is a "bad" quarto, not of Shakespeare's play but of the original shrew play (now lost) called for in ten Brink's hypothesis, practically all difficulties are overcome. For example, it is easy to see why *A Shrew* is formally more perfect in structure than is *The Shrew*, although much more confused in time-scheme. It would follow also that, as a reported version of the original shrew play, it would retain, perhaps imperfectly, but with rough faithfulness, the names of the characters and the place names of the old play. Athens was a popular location for old comedies, because perhaps of association with Greek romance and Latin comedy. *A Shrew*, in short, is a bad quarto made up for an unfortunate company from an original shrew play whose plot it probably reproduces with a fair degree of correctness, especially the complete formal Induction, the balanced love-plot, and the names of characters and places. It is doubtful if Shakespeare ever saw it, but he did rewrite its original.

We know that Shakespeare rewrote certain old plays the proprietorship of which was in his company—probably *Henry V, Hamlet*, and *King Lear*; possibly *King John, The Merry Wives of Windsor, Much Ado about Nothing*, and others. At some time, possibly in 1594 or earlier, Shakespeare rewrote the original shrew play. Perhaps because it was an old story by this time, he called his version *The Taming of the Shrew*. In rewriting it he blended it for its own good with Gascoigne's *The Supposes*, and in so doing he changed, sharpened, and rendered dramatic the whole minor plot. The major plot, as a plot, he left pretty much as it was, as also the Induction. If he carried the Induction through to logical completeness, the latter part was probably canceled on the occasion of some revival. Shakespeare in his rewriting shifted the scene to Italy, which by that time he had used as the setting for *The Two Gentlemen of Verona* and for *Romeo and Juliet*. Some names he got from Ariosto, the name of Kate he kept (perhaps for the sake of puns) from the old play, but most of the names he invented. On this hypothesis it is likely that Shakespeare rewrote the whole play with great thoroughness, since otherwise there would have been closer parallels with *A Shrew*, a reported version of the original shrew play. The Katharina-Petruchio plot and the Induction he did under the full swing of his comic genius. The other parts he imitated somewhat lamely from *The Supposes*, and later touched up the part borrowed from Gascoigne to make it connect better with the major plot. These modifications are the revisions for which Mrs. Ashton found evidence.

Ten Brink's is a very plausible hypothesis, since it settles so many questions and has the advantage of showing that all the critics are right and all of them are wrong. That is, *A Shrew* might readily be mistaken for the source of *The Shrew*, because *A Shrew* is a version of its source. It might readily be regarded as a "bad" quarto of *The Shrew*, because it is a "bad" quarto of the source of *The Shrew*.

It is a pity that Shakespeare tired of the Induction, which is the solitary point in which the old shrew play is superior to *The Taming of the Shrew*; or, what is more likely, it is a pity that in the exigencies of some revival before the publication of the play in the First Folio of 1623 his version of the complete story of Christopher Sly was omitted and so lost. Sly does not speak after the end of the second scene of the first act and is simply lost. In his comment on the play there is an unforgettable piece of dramatic criticism, one that often echoes in our hearts at symphonies, operas, and plays:

> 'Tis a very excellent piece of work, madam lady; would 'twere done!

The tinker Sly is an interesting fellow and the embodiment of naturalness. Found drunk on the doorstep of an inn by a nobleman, he is carried to a fine chamber, dressed in rich clothes, and ultimately persuaded that he is himself a noble lord just recovered from a fit of insanity which has lasted fifteen years. He is not prone to believe this, but is incredulous and has a lively sense of himself. "The Slys are no rogues," he says. "Look in the chronicles; we came in with Richard Conqueror." But all men are anxious to believe the best about themselves, and Sly is no exception. The physical facts and the gorgeous environment are too much for his realism; with Christopher Sly seeing is believing. He becomes convinced and at once begins to speak blank verse (ii, 70-7):

> Am I a lord? and have I such a lady?
> Or do I dream? or have I dream'd till now?
> I do not sleep: I see, I hear, I speak;
> I smell sweet savours and I feel soft things:
> Upon my life, I am a lord indeed
> And not a tinker nor Christophero Sly.

The minor plot is not the poor thing some critics would have us believe. Shakespeare has borrowed it from the fourth and fifth acts of Ariosto's comedy and has bettered it in the borrowing. It is a lively and complicated example of the Italian comedy of intrigue which had grown up in Italy on the basis of Plautus and Terence. Fault has been found justifiably with the style of the minor plot of *The Taming of the Shrew*. Perhaps it was hastily adapted from Ariosto and touched up finally in only a few places. But the changes that Shakespeare made in it are matters of genius. In the old play the father of Kate has three daughters. In Shakespeare he has but two. One has lovers, the other not, and the father, the rather prying, greedy Baptista, has in Shakespeare's version the intention of finding a husband for Kate before he lets Bianca go. He does not want Kate left on his hands, and Shakespeare knows the humiliation such an arrangement inflicts on Katharina. Lucentio is a Shakespearean figure, a young lover who loves at first sight and dashingly enters the contest for Bianca's hand, bringing with him a mob of stock characters from Italian comedy. The first and foremost of these is his servant-companion, Tranio, ready to play his master's part, look after his affairs, and act independently in his behalf. There is also the elderly suitor or pantaloon, Gremio, and a younger lover, Hortensio, who would normally defeat Gremio but is destined to be tricked by Tranio and defeated by Lucentio. The pedant, an Italian type, belongs with the group as does Baptista himself. The new situation enables Shakespeare to introduce an elopement and to render his whole play more exciting. All through, the detail of the Italian source is vivified and rendered intelligible in its relation to English life. The minor plot is anything but stupid.

It is, moreover, brilliantly integrated with the major plot concerning the taming of the shrew. Petruchio, whose name is borrowed from Ariosto, is an original creation, and one sees no reason why he should be regarded or presented as a too boisterous and primitive character. It is certain that Shakespeare did not so conceive of him. In the old shrew play Ferando is a rather mercenary wooer who pays court to Kate because her father has offered him six thousand crowns in case he can succeed in conquering her. Petruchio, to be sure, professes mercenary motives (I, ii, 65-76), but we are hardly expected to take him seriously. He has just been left heir to his father's property. He has travelled widely and found danger by land and sea, a wise adventurer and a man of the world. A mercenary motive will do as well as another for such a man in pursuit of a wife, but he is plainly interested in the enterprise because it offers difficulty, is adventurous. Almost all that he does to win Katharina may be summed up under the statement that he is really her friend. Although the stupid wife-taming, through hunger and cruelty, of the source is preserved as the machinery of the plot, it has lost its essential quality. Petruchio offers Kate a grand travesty of her own temper and way of life, preserving the business about taming her by hunger as one tames a falcon, and she eventually comes to appreciate his art and him. Thus in contradiction to the text Shakespeare does successfully put new wine in old bottles. It is interesting to see how even the scriptural teachings of the old play are retained in

Katharina's final definitive speech; and yet they too suggest, not the dreary bullying of other plays and stories on the theme, but the actual basis, the real scriptural basis, of all successful marriages, namely, that husbands and wives are meant to be partners in the enterprise of living. It means that normally men labor and women share the fruits of that labor and lighten its burden.

CHAPTER V

Poems and Sonnets

THE drama was a popularized and commercialized form of literature in the Age of Queen Elizabeth, so that Shakespeare's bid for
fame was as a poet rather than as a dramatist; but the plays, both
in quantity and greatness, have overwhelmed the poems. The world has
decided that he was greatest as a playwright, and yet it has not denied
greatness to him as a poet. He wrote his poetical works during the earlier
part of his career. We have the dates and dedications of Shakespeare's
Venus and Adonis and his *The Rape of Lucrece*. They belong to the period
of the early plays, that is, 1592 to 1594, and the literary relations between
the poems and the early plays are very close. Not only are there many
parallels in style and sentiment between them, but there is an almost
identical poetic attitude in the two groups. This will appear in a brief consideration of epic poetry in the age of Queen Elizabeth.

During the later years of the Queen's reign the succession to the crown
was not fully determined, and there was much political uneasiness in the
nation. Indeed, there was a wave of national anxiety. Such subjects as the
fates and fortunes of kings, royal succession and the principle of primogeniture, and the terrors of civil war occupied the minds of all men. Poets
and playwrights, notably Shakespeare himself, responded to this feeling
and produced a great body of historical and patriotic literature. It is natural
that there should have been revived the conception of history, with biogra-
phy, as a mirror wherein living men and peoples might view themselves
as in a glass and thus avoid the doom which in all ages had befallen great
men and great nations when they sinned against reason, the welfare of
commonwealths, and the will of God. In the ancient world the downfall
of heroes had been largely a matter of fate or fortune, but in the modern

world it had come to be linked with conduct. The mirror concept took thus a deep hold on men's minds in Shakespeare's day.

He devoted his powers as a historical dramatist to these great matters of state, and his poems are not remote from his plays. The *Mirror for Magistrates* was full of significant stories and was widely imitated. Thomas Churchyard's *Shores Wife*, called *Jane Shore* when it was separately published in quarto, is a moving story which introduces elements of passion not found in many of the historical accounts of the downfalls of princes and men of high estate. *The Civil Wars between the Two Houses of Lancaster and York* (1595, 1609) by Samuel Daniel stands out as the typical and most meritorious Elizabethan historical epic. It is worthy of comparison with the historical plays of Shakespeare. The poets of the time retold many of the stories of mainly English history, both in series and as single tales. It is said with approximate truth that Churchyard's *Jane Shore* influenced Daniel's *The Complaint of Rosamond* (1592) and that that in turn influenced Shakespeare's *The Rape of Lucrece* (1594). At any rate, there was a flood of these historical epics, and they seem to be the core of the literary movement in which Shakespeare's poems find their places.

There were, however, two kinds of Elizabethan epic, the one historical, as above, the other Ovidian, mythological, amatory, sometimes Platonic. The two kinds are not always distinguishable except in subject matter, and they seem to be parts of one literary movement. To the less numerous non-historical class belong Lodge's *Scillaes Metamorphosis* (1589), Marlowe's *Hero and Leander* (1592?), Shakespeare's *Venus and Adonis* (1593), Drayton's *Endimion and Phoebe* (1595), Barnfield's *Cassandra* (1595), and others. *Scillaes Metamorphosis*, or, as it is usually called, *Glaucus and Scilla*, is based on Ovid's *Metamorphoses* (xiii, 900-960) and is composed in the same six-line stanza as is *Venus and Adonis*. *Glaucus and Scilla* was no doubt Shakespeare's chief model, yet the greatest and most influential romance of this sort was Marlowe's *Hero and Leander*, a strikingly beautiful poem which apparently Marlowe did not live to complete. Marlowe was killed by Ingram Frisar in a tavern at Deptford in 1593, and *Hero and Leander* was not published until 1598, in which year it appeared as a fragment and also in a form completed by George Chapman. Marlowe's poem must, however, have been known in manuscript. The story of Hero and Leander, a favorite theme, appears in Ovid's *Heroides* (xviii, xix) and is also the subject of a Greek poem of the fifth century A.D. by Musaeus, which had been translated into Latin, French, and Italian and had been frequently published.

Venus and Adonis was on an even better known subject, also in Ovid (*Metamorphoses*, x, 519-59), also re-told in many versions in the chief modern languages. The story, which is said to be of Phoenician or Assyrian origin, was part of the mythology of the Greeks, and there was no more popular elegiac subject than the death of Adonis. Although modern mythologists make of Adonis a spirit of vegetation whose death and return to life represent the decay of nature in winter and the rebirth in spring, the tale as thought of in poetry and fiction and as told by Shakespeare was merely a love story. Venus seeks the love of the youth Adonis, given to hunting the boar; he is a model of beauty. She detains him from the chase, woos him, but cannot win his love. She begs him to meet her the next morning, but he insists on hunting the boar. On the morrow she hears his hounds at bay. Filled with alarm, she goes to seek him, only to find that he has been killed by the boar. Zeus, on her entreaties, decrees that Adonis shall spend the half of each year in Elysium and the other half in Hades. It is thought that Shakespeare resorted to another Ovidian tale, *Hermaphroditus and Salmacis*, for the idea of the coldness of Adonis when wooed by Venus, but this feature had already been associated with the story; it appears, for example, in the early lines of Marlowe's *Hero and Leander*, where we are told of Hero's dress:

> The outside of her garments were of lawn,
> The lining purple silk, with gilt stars drawn;
> Her wide sleeves green, and bordered with a grove,
> Where Venus in her naked glory strove
> To please the careless and disdainful eyes
> Of proud Adonis that before her lies.

Shakespeare's primary sources for *Venus and Adonis* really make very little difference, since amplification is the special characteristic of his poem. He enlarges Ovid's story, seventy lines long, to 1200 lines and adds many features of his own, such as the horse and the jennet, and the hunting scenes of the fox and the hare; so that the poem is given a variety like life itself. Coleridge declared on the basis of *Venus and Adonis* that Shakespeare possessed "the chief, if not every requisite of a poet—deep feeling and exquisite sense of beauty, both as exhibited to the eye in the combinations of form and to the ear in sweet and appropriate melody; that these feelings were under the command of his own will; that in his very first productions he projected his mind out of his own particular being, and felt, and made others feel, on subjects no way connected with himself, except by force of contemplation and that sublime faculty by which a great mind becomes that on which it meditates." "To this," he says later, "must be added that affectionate love of nature and natural objects, without which no man could have observed so steadily, or painted so truly and passionately, the very minutest beauties of the external world." He then quotes the following stanzas from *Venus and Adonis* (ll. 679-708):

> And when thou hast on foot the purblind hare,
> Mark the poor wretch, to overshoot his troubles
> How he outruns the wind and with what care
> He cranks and crosses with a thousand doubles:
>   The many musets through the which he goes
>   Are like a labyrinth to amaze his foes.
>
> Sometime he runs among a flock of sheep,
> To make the cunning hounds mistake their smell,
> And sometime where earth-delving conies keep,
> To stop the loud pursuers in their yell,
>   And sometime sorteth with a herd of deer:
>   Danger deviseth shifts; wit waits on fear:
>
> For there his smell with others being mingled,
> The hot scent-snuffing hounds are driven to doubt,
> Ceasing their clamorous cry till they have singled
> With much ado the cold fault cleanly out;
>   Then do they spend their mouths: Echo replies,
>   As if another chase were in the skies.
>
> By this, poor Wat, far off upon a hill,
> Stands on his hinder legs with listening ear,
> To hearken if his foes pursue him still:
> Anon their loud alarums he doth hear;
>   And now his grief may be compared well
>   To one sore sick that hears the passing-bell.
>
> Then shalt thou see the dew-bedabbled wretch
> Turn, and return, indenting with the way;
> Each envious brier his weary legs doth scratch,
> Each shadow makes him stop, each murmur stay:
>   For misery is trodden on by many,
>   And being low never relieved by any.

Coleridge says again, "In this beautiful poem there is an endless activity of thought in all the possible associations of thought with thought, thought with feeling, or with words, of feelings with feelings, and of words with words." With this ingenious statement Coleridge quotes the first stanza of the poem:

> Even as the sun with purple-colour'd face
> Had ta'en his last leave of the weeping morn,
> Rose-cheek'd Adonis hied him to the chase;
> Hunting he loved, but love he laugh'd to scorn;
>   Sick-thoughted Venus makes amain unto him,
>   And like a bold-faced suitor 'gins to woo him.

These words of Coleridge with their accompanying quotations I used many years ago as an introduction to *Venus and Adonis*. I use them again, since I have found nothing more suggestive of the nature and greatness of Shakespeare's poem.

Venus and Adonis was issued in 1593 from the press of Richard Field, a native of Stratford and at that time a successful London printer. The poem is dedicated to the third Earl of Southampton, who was then in his twentieth year and was recognized at court as a brilliant and promising youth:

Right Honourable,

I know not how I shall offend in dedicating my unpolished lines to your lordship, nor how the world will censure me for choosing so strong a prop to support so weak a burden: only if your honour seem but pleased, I account myself highly praised, and vow to take advantage of all idle hours, till I have honoured you with some graver labour. But if the first heir of my invention prove deformed, I shall be sorry it had so noble a god-father, and never after ear so barren a land, for fear it yield me still so bad a harvest. I leave it to your honourable survey, and your honour to your heart's content; which I wish may always answer your own wish and the world's hopeful expectation.

Your honour's in all duty,

WILLIAM SHAKESPEARE.

This dedication, although marked by the rich complimentary style of such documents, is not fulsome or lacking in self-respect. Shakespeare deprecates his effort, but not unduly, and promises, if this is well received, "some graver labour." The epistle is written with some diffidence, as if Shakespeare were not well acquainted with Southampton or as if the dedication had been made without Southampton's definite permission. In this respect it offers a contrast to the dedication to the same nobleman of *The Rape of Lucrece*, which followed in about a year. There has been apparently great growth in intimacy between the poet and his patron during that time. The dedication to *Lucrece* is gayer, more confident, and more affectionate, as if Shakespeare had grown sure of his ground:

> The love I dedicate to your lordship is without end; whereof this pamphlet, without beginning, is but a superfluous moiety. The warrant I have of your honourable disposition, not the worth of my untutored lines, makes it assured of acceptance. What I have done is yours; what I have to do is yours; being part in all I have, devoted yours. Were my worth greater, my duty would show greater; meantime, as it is, it is bound to your lordship, to whom I wish long life, still lengthened with all happiness.
>
> Your lordship's in all duty,
>
> WILLIAM SHAKESPEARE.

Mr. J. A. Fort, assuming that Southampton was the "fair friend" addressed by Shakespeare in the *Sonnets*, bases the chronology of the *Sonnets* on the dedication of *Lucrece* and Sonnet No. xxvi. That sonnet says, "To thee I send this written embassage," and Mr. Fort conjectures, not implausibly, that the written work referred to was actually *The Rape of Lucrece*. This would have the effect of dating the sonnet in 1594.

Venus and Adonis was very popular, running through five editions subsequent to the first by the year 1602. It was, however, criticized from the first on account of its amatory quality. Gabriel Harvey, for example, noted in the margin of his copy of Speght's Chaucer at some time probably between 1598 and 1601:

> The younger sort takes much delight in Shakespeare's Venus and Adonis; but his Lucrece and his tragedy of Hamlet, Prince of Denmark, have it in them to please the wiser sort.

It may have been in response to censure that Shakespeare wrote his *Lucrece*, or it may have been merely in fulfillment of his promise to honor Southampton with "some graver labour." The poem is professedly written in celebration of the virtue of chastity. *The Rape of Lucrece* is a finished and elegant poem written in rhyme royal, a seven-line five-foot stanza rhyming *ababbcc*. The verse form and the style of the poem are marked by dignity as well as sweetness. *Lucrece* is superior in care and elaboration to *Venus and Adonis*, but it lacks the naturalness and brilliancy of the earlier poem. *Lucrece* celebrates the fame of the Roman lady Lucretia, daughter of Lucretius and wife of Tarquinius Collatinus, whose beauty inflamed the passions of Sextus, son of King Tarquin of Rome. She is attacked with threats and overcome with violence. Lucretia informs her father and her husband of what has happened, begs them to avenge her wrongs, and takes her own life. This famous event brought to a head the rebellion against the tyranny of the King and led to the expulsion of the Tarquins and the establishment of the Roman Republic. The total significance of the story of Lucrece would not have been lost on an Elizabethan public. Rather numerous sources for Shakespeare's poem have been cited, and it is probable that, since he apparently worked with the greatest care and thoroughness, he consulted every version he could lay his hands on. In any case, he is thought to have followed Livy's *History of Rome* (I, 56-60), Ovid's *Fasti* (II, 711-852), Chaucer's *The Legend of Good Women* (ll. 1680-1885), and Painter's *The Palace of Pleasure* (second novel), with various parallels in other works.

Of the greater Shakespearean critics Coleridge alone seems to have taken *Lucrece* with sufficient seriousness. He was justified in so doing, for the poem gains in effectiveness and beauty when it is perceived that Shakespeare wrote it throughout in a spirit of reverence. The following passage from *Biographia Literaria* reveals Coleridge's clear understanding of both of Shakespeare's poems and of their relation to each other, as well, of course, as his fine appreciation of poetic detail:

> The Venus and Adonis did not perhaps allow the display of the deeper passions. But the story of Lucretia seems to favor, and even demand their intensest workings. And yet we find in *Shakespeare's* management of the tale neither pathos, nor any other *dramatic* quality. There is the same minute and faithful imagery as in the former poem, in the same vivid colors, inspirited by the same impetuous vigour of thought, and diverging and contracting with the same activity of the assimilative and of the modifying faculties; and with yet a larger display, a yet wider range of knowledge and reflection; and lastly, with the same perfect dominion, often domination, over the whole world of language.

The following sentence is repeated from the Variorum edition of the *Poems*. It is from F. P. G. Guizot:

> Thus Lucrece, weighed down by a sense of her shame, after a night of despair, summons a young slave at dawn of day, to dispatch him to the camp with a letter to call her husband home; the slave, being of a timid and simple character, blushes on appearing in the presence of his mistress; but Lucrece, filled with consciousness of her dishonor, imagines that he blushes at her shame; and, under the influence of the idea that her secret is discovered, she stands trembling and confused before her slave.

Dowden has this to say about *The Rape of Lucrece*:

> In "Lucrece" the action is delayed and delayed that every minute particular may be described, every minor incident recorded. In the newness of her suffering and shame Lucrece finds time for an elaborate tirade appropriate to the theme "Night," another to that of "Time," another to that of "Opportunity." Each topic is exhausted. Then studiously a new incident is introduced, and its significance for the emotions is drained to the last drop in a new tirade. We nowhere else discover Shakspere so evidently engaged upon his work. Afterwards he puts a stress upon his verses to compel them to contain the hidden wealth of his thought and imagination. Here he displays at large such wealth as he possesses; he will have none of it half seen. The descriptions and declamations are undramatic, but they shew us the materials laid out in detail from which dramatic poetry originates.

Dowden's opinion is widely held and, being interpreted, means that *The Rape of Lucrece* is a failure; and yet we have the spectacle of Shakespeare exercising with maximum care his greatest powers, a thing which can hardly be associated with failure. It must rather be that we have to do with a great change in literary ideals and that we cannot without effort appreciate at its full value the beauty and power of Shakespeare's poem. Literary appreciation is in some respects a relative matter. The fault is perhaps with us, but not entirely so. There is much in Shakespeare which does not readily appeal to modern taste. We do not enjoy the leisurely and meticulous treatment of detail in *The Rape of Lucrece*. We are perhaps too insistent on the dramatic, the immediate, and the pungent; and, although we recognize these qualities in Shakespeare's poem, we are inhospitable to the quiet, detailed, unhurried, and long-winded manner in which Shakespeare has worked. If we had more patience, we should enjoy the poem more than we do. If we were more contemplative than we are, we might be provoked to pleasant thought. *Lucrece* is a formal exaltation of chastity, which, in the light of the morals of his plays, Shakespeare was entitled to make.

In spite of the lukewarm attitude of the critics, one may nevertheless confess great admiration for the poetical excellence of *The Rape of Lucrece* and without hesitation place many parts of it with the more sententious passages of the *Faerie Queene*. The following stanzas will give as well as perhaps any others the style and temper of Shakespeare's poem (ll. 134-68):

> Those that much covet are with gain so fond,
> For what they have not, that which they possess
> They scatter and unloose it from their bond,
> And so, by hoping more, they have but less;
> Or, gaining more, the profit of excess
>   Is but to surfeit, and such griefs sustain,
>   That they prove bankrupt in this poor-rich gain. . . .
>
> Now stole upon the time the dead of night,
> When heavy sleep had closed up mortal eyes:
> No comfortable star did lend his light,
> No noise but owls' and wolves' death-boding cries;
> Now serves the season that they may surprise
>   The silly lambs: pure thoughts are dead and still,
>   While lust and murder wake to stain and kill.

Besides *Venus and Adonis* and *The Rape of Lucrece*, the canon of Shakespeare is usually made to include a few shorter poems. A collection of poems by various authors called *The Passionate Pilgrim* was published as by W. Shakespeare in 1599. It contains twenty poems including versions of *Sonnets* cxxxviii and cxliv and three poems from *Love's Labour's Lost*. The Globe edition includes as possibly by Shakespeare "It was a lording's daughter," "My flocks feed not," "When as thine eye hath chose the dame," and "As it fell upon the day." This inclusion is probably to be regarded merely as the expression of an opinion, since no one is as yet certain that Shakespeare wrote any of these lyrics. He certainly did not write "Live with me and be my love" and the first stanza of "The Nymph's Reply," which are assigned on fairly satisfactory grounds to Marlowe and Raleigh respectively. As to "The Phoenix and the Turtle," a poem marked with Shakespeare's name in Robert Chester's volume called *Love's Martyr* (1601), it is pretty generally accepted. It is a puzzling poem which may have some hidden topical significance. As it stands, it adds little to Shakespeare's fame.

When we come to the great subject of the *Sonnets*, there is much to say. Only a little of it will be said here, but the writings about the *Sonnets* are very great in volume. This is not unnatural, since in some of the *Sonnets* English lyrical poetry probably reaches its supreme height. It may throw some light on the work of Shakespeare for us to consider briefly the work of two other English sonneteers, Sidney and Spenser; of these Shakespeare owes most to Sidney.

In spite of its obvious resemblance as a whole and in detail to Petrarch, Ronsard, Du Bellay, Marot, Desportes, probably Tasso, and others, Sidney's *Astrophel and Stella* is a cycle of beautiful sonnets which not only expresses the Petrarchan or neo-Platonic ideal of beauty and love with the conventional figures and devices of the *genre*, but, like Shakespeare's *Sonnets*, is a cycle with unmistakable individual features. *Astrophel and Stella*, probably written between 1575 and 1583, was published surreptitiously by Thomas Newman in 1591. In 1598 an improved edition under the auspices of the Countess of Pembroke made its appearance. *Astrophel and Stella* started the vogue of the sonnet in England. The cycle in its course traces the history of an emotion, beginning conventionally with admiration for Stella's spiritual and personal charms. In the early part the work is conventional and imitative. After the thirtieth sonnet, however, Astrophel comes to a realization of what he has missed in his failure to gain Stella for himself, love makes new inroads on his heart, and there is a hint that Stella also loves. Astrophel passes into resolution and expectant passion. The next stage is hope, followed by exultation and ecstasy over Stella's kiss (Nos. 74-84). In this situation virtue and reason assert themselves; discouragement takes the place of hope; and finally come resignation and philosophic consolation. True love, it seems, is its own excuse for being. There can be little doubt that the great sonnet, "Leave me, O Love, which reachest but to dust," and probably the sonnet denouncing desire, "Thou blind man's mark, thou fool's self-chosen snare," although not published as part of the sequence, were nevertheless intended to offer final commentary on an experience mainly imaginary but partly real.

Spenser's approach to the sonnet is different from that of Sidney. Spenser was concerned with poetic art, with the creation of beauty in the abstract, rather than with the expression of human emotions or the depiction of significant situations. Since he strove continually for the impersonal style and regarded his materials as the means of his art, he has been the leader and teacher of professional poets, like Milton and Keats. This objective quality is nowhere better illustrated than in the poetic record of his own experience in love, the *Amoretti*, with which is always associated the *Epithalamium*. Even the rhyme scheme of the sonnet invented by Spenser (*ababbcbccdcdee*) is evener, more continuous, less dramatic than either the Petrarchan or the Shakespearean forms.

Not long after Spenser's return to Ireland in 1591 he fell in love with Elizabeth Boyle and, after a courtship of twelve months or more, he was married to her on June 11, 1594. The *Amoretti* is an idealized account of the courtship, and the *Epithalamium* (1595), one of the most beautiful poems in English literature, celebrates the marriage. *Amoretti* characteristically presents a doctrine of gradations in beauty analogous to the gradations of Platonic love presented by Sidney in *Astrophel and Stella*. The third sonnet in the cycle, for example, announces the power of beauty to purify the human soul; the forty-fifth presents the image of beauty as the enduring creative image in the soul of the lover; the seventy-ninth and eightieth show beauty in its second stage as "gentle wit" and "virtuous mind"; near the end of the cycle in the eighty-seventh sonnet we reach the third stage and learn that true beauty is realizable only through contemplation, an idea somewhat similar to Wordsworth's discovery of the power of beauty recollected in tranquility. This highest stage is Idea, the approach through beauty to union with the divine. In this we are at the heart of Spenser's Platonism. Shakespeare's Platonism is like that of both Sidney and Spenser.

The soul shapes for itself a body commensurate with its participation in beauty, so that a beautiful person has by inference always a beautiful soul. Sometimes, however, inferior matter is not obedient to the shaping influence of the soul, so that the virtue of a beautiful soul may not find complete physical expression. But the principle holds, for beauty flows into the soul through the eyes and actuates love in the heart; love in turn imparts warmth and form to cold and chaotic matter. With Spenser it is a question of emphasis. He dwells on beauty rather than on love, that is, on the cause rather than the effect. Thus in *Amoretti* we find expressed the gradations of beauty, whereas in Castiglione and in Sidney we find the familiar stair of love—love of the senses, love of the intellect, and love of the understanding or intuitive faculty of the soul. Stated in another way, these Platonic stages of the soul's advance explain Spenser's theory of heavenly love set forth in the *Foure Hymnes*.

The greatest of all sonnets are those of Shakespeare. Externally considered, they present many mysteries, but in themselves they are comprehensible, magnificent, and universal. The *Sonnets* seem not to have been finally and formally organized by their author and are yet unquestionably cyclic in their nature. The series is made up of groups of varying length, the groups being tied together by continuity of theme but not usually joined group to group. Themes, however, frequently recur. Between these groups, and not infrequently embedded within them, are sonnets of a personal nature whose interpretation is obscure, as well as others of an apparently formal or conventional character. One of the most plausible of modern opinions is to the effect that the *Sonnets* were written as a series of poetical epistles of two to five sonnets and gathered up, at least the first one hundred and twenty-six of them, roughly in the order in which they were composed. Within the groups the sonnets are usually tied together by continuity of subject or systematical connection. These short series themselves are usually set apart from each other by changes in subject at the end of each group. That they are not, as printed by Thorpe in 1609, in absolutely correct order has long been suspected. A plausible rearrangement of the order of the *Sonnets* has recently been made by the late Professor Tucker Brooke, and his corrections certainly make the story of the *Sonnets* far easier to understand. Attention is called to his suggested changes in the following outline.

The collection begins with a series of seventeen sonnets to a youth of beauty and nobility, to whom, indeed, the first one hundred and twenty-six are addressed. This youth is urged to marry so that his virtue may be perpetuated in his offspring. The next group of eight sonnets (xviii-xxvi) have to do with the poet's relation to the person addressed, and the last (xxvi) seems designed to accompany a gift, a "written ambassage." Nos. xxvii-xxxii mark a period when the poet, apparently traveling, is absent from his friend. In this group appear "When in disgrace with fortune and men's eyes" (xxix) and "When to the sessions of sweet silent thought" (xxx). Nos. xxxiii-xxxv and xl-xlii constitute a group having to do with the Dark Lady, the poet's mistress who has been taken away from him by his friend. The designation comes from sonnet cxliv, which begins,

> Two loves I have of comfort and despair,
> Which like two spirits do suggest me still:
> The better angel is a man right fair,
> The worser spirit a woman colour'd ill.

This sonnet belongs to a second sequence of Shakespeare's *Sonnets* (cxxvii-clii) which treats at length the episode of the Dark Lady. There is no valid reason for thinking that the episode there dwelt upon is not the same as that presented in the first sequence. One must, of course, recognize that the whole event brings into play the conventional Renaissance theme of the warfare between love and friendship. This group begins with "Full many a glorious morning have I seen" (xxxiii). Nos. xxxiv-xxxix and xliii-xlvii come from a period of absence, apparently from London, of the friend, and xlviii-lv from a second absence of the poet. The last sonnet of the latter group begins, "Not marble, nor the gilded monuments." Nos. lvi-lviii and lxi have been put together by Professor Brooke as a group on loneliness and Nos. lxii-lxv and lix-lx as a masterly series on beauty and time. Here appear "When I have seen by Time's fell hand defaced" (lxiv), "Since brass, nor stone, nor earth, nor boundless sea" (lxv), and "Like as the waves make towards the pebbled shore" (lx). The vein seems to be continued in Professor Brooke's next group (lxvi-lxx, xciv-xcvi), which deals specifically with the corruptions of the world. There follows a series on death (lxxxi, lxxi-lxxiv), in which are to be found "No longer mourn for me when I am dead" (lxxi) and the immortal sonnet on immortality, "That time of year thou mayst in me behold" (lxxiii). Nos. lxxviii-lxxx, lxxxii-lxxxvi are devoted to a "Rival Poet," evidently a person of learning and importance. The author reproaches his patron for the favor he has bestowed upon another poet, whose name we do not know. Nos. lxxvii-xciii continue the theme of estrangement, now a personal matter, the loss of loving confidence rather than of mere patronage. The first sonnet of this group is "Farewell! thou art too dear for my possessing." Sonnets xcvii-ciii come from a third absence of the poet. The group begins "How like a winter hath my absence been" and contains "O truant Muse, what shall be thy amends" (ci). Sonnets civ-cviii, cxv-

cxvi, which are loosely connected with one another, are mainly congra
latory. Among them are some of the finest of Shakespeare's sonnets, su
as "To me, fair friend, you never can be old" (civ), "Let not my love b
called idolatry" (cv), "When in the chronicle of wasted time" (cvi), and
"Let me not to the marriage of true minds" (cxvi). They are accompanied
by two sonnets (cxiii, cxiv) on the poet's fourth absence. The remaining
sonnets of the sequence (cix-cxii, cxvii-cxxv) seem devoted to a restoration
of loving relations between the poet and his friend. They excuse the poet
for seeming transgressions, reassert the poet's devotion, and defy slander
and misrepresentation. Sonnets of worldwide fame appear here: "O,
never say that I was false of heart" (cix), "Alas, 'tis true, I have gone
here and there,/And made myself a motley to the view" (cx), and " 'Tis
better to be vile than vile esteem'd" (cxxi).

Sonnets cxxvii-clii, the second sequence, introduce no new element into
the story and were apparently written during the same period as that
occupied by the first sequence. They must appear in their present position
because they were so placed in the printer's manuscript, for they are manifestly out of their order of composition. Professor Brooke regroups them
as follows: Nos. cxxvii-cxxviii, cxxx, as a group of "semi-jocose" compliment; Nos. cxxxi, cl, cxxxii, cxlviii, cxxxvii, cxxxix-cxlii, cxlix, as a group on
the poet's wooing; Nos. cxliii, cxxxv, cxxxvi, as the "Will" sonnets; Nos.
cli, cxxxviii, as sensual sonnets; Nos. cxliv, cxxxiii, cxxiv, as sonnets having
to do with the theft of the poet's mistress by his friend; Nos. clii, cxlvii,
cxxix, cxlvi, as sonnets of final vehement rejection by the poet of the Dark
Lady and all she stands for.

Whatever the order and whatever the relation of the Dark Lady sonnets to the first sequence, there can be no question of their power and of
their significance in the interpretation of Shakespeare. The confusion in
which they appear has kept these great poems from receiving the recognition they deserve. Of course, "My mistress' eyes are nothing like the sun"
(cxxx) is widely known, as are the two incomparable sonnets of renunci-
ation, "The expense of spirit in a waste of shame" (cxxix) and "Poor
soul, the centre of my sinful earth" (cxlvi); but the last two have been
thought of as individual poems and not as ultimate comment on a shatter-
ing personal experience. Brooke points out that the Dark Lady sonnets,
read in this way, reveal much, not only of Shakespeare's mind and art,
but also of the essential virtue of his character.

Whatever may be the truth with reference to the personal significance of cycles of sonnets written in compliance with a literary fashion and in accordance with an established literary convention, certainly the cycles of Sidney, Spenser, and Shakespeare hold out immediate promise of revealing the authors' real selves. There are also facts known or highly probable in each of these cases which seem to be reflected in the poems. Petrarch's sonnets were known to reflect the kaleidoscopic emotional situations in which, as a lover, he found himself, and some autobiographical significance was presumed as a part of the sonnet convention. Probably therefore *Astrophel and Stella* is not a mere exercise in Petrarchism, or a mere illustration of the theory of Platonic love, but does vaguely and with some mystification reflect a love affair between Sidney and Lady Rich. Something similar is probably true of the *Sonnets* of Shakespeare, which seem to be, not merely conventional exercises in Petrarchism, but rather the moving record of personal experience.

In 1598 Francis Meres speaks admiringly of Shakespeare's "sugred Sonnets among his priuate friends." The *Sonnets* must by that time have been circulating in manuscript. They were not, however, printed until 1609, when they were set forth in quarto by the printer Thomas Thorpe. The volume has as a full page this puzzling dedication:

> TO. THE. ONLIE. BEGETTER. OF. THESE. INSVING. SON-
> NETS. MR. W. H. ALL. HAPPINESS. AND. THAT. ETERNITIE.
> PROMISED. BY. OVR. EVER-LIVING. POET. WISHETH. THE.
> WELL-WISHING. ADVENTURER. IN. SETTING. FORTH. T. T.

Obviously "T. T." stands for Thomas Thorpe, the "adventurer" in print-ing, but who "Mr. W. H." is has been a matter of much speculation. One group of critics has held the now almost discarded theory that the initials W. H. stand for William Herbert, Earl of Pembroke, who, if one may judge from the dedicatory epistle to the First Folio, was Shakespeare's patron. A more recent supposition has made them stand for one William Hall, a person known to have supplied manuscripts to publishers. It has also been long believed that "W. H." are the inverted initials of Henry Wriothesley, Earl of Southampton. In any case, it is absurd to interpret the words, "the onlie begetter of these insving sonnets" as referring to anyone other than the man to whom the *Sonnets* were addressed. Thorpe plainly states that that man supplied the manuscripts. Southampton's **case** is the best, and is so good in fact that all other persons may be disregarded. If Southampton supplied the manuscript, we do not know what motives he may have had for disguise and what instructions he may have given to Thorpe.

Mr. J. A. Fort has suggested that, since there is a resemblance in the wording of the gift sonnet (xxvi) to the epistle dedicatory to Southampton prefixed to *The Rape of Lucrece*, the "written ambassage" referred to in the sonnet was *Lucrece*. Since sonnet civ marks a third year of the poet's attachment to his friend, Mr. Fort would count three years forward from the date of *Venus and Adonis* (1593) and fix the date of sonnet civ as 1596. This determination is supported by other evidence. The identification of Southampton as "the onlie begetter of these insving sonnets" and as the youth of nobility and beauty to whom they are addressed is in every way worthy of credence.

With the Pembroke hypothesis came the identification of the Dark Lady with Mary Fitton; with Southampton came Mrs. Davenant, innkeeper's wife at Oxford. For neither identification is there so far a shred of really convincing evidence.

All Shakespeare critics have had their say about the *Sonnets*, devoting themselves mainly, but not exclusively, to the Friend, the Dark Lady, the Rival Poet, the proper order of the individual poems, and the autobiographical aspects of the series. No works of Shakespeare, except certain of the very greatest dramas, have had so extensive a vogue over the whole world.

All critics agree that the *Sonnets* are cast in a mold of convention. Among the great mass of Italian, French, and English sonnets parallels have been found for almost every situation, every image, and every conceit; and yet it is uniformly agreed that Shakespeare has personalized his work and infused into it thoughts, feelings, and aspirations of the soul which must be his own. He has never ceased to be himself. The language, harmony, and style are peculiar to him. "The language of Shakespeare's sonnets," says Tucker Brooke, "is perhaps the simplest by which any English poet has achieved comparable effects, and in the couplets it is, if possible, simpler than in the quatrains." It is acknowledged also that the *Sonnets* have an almost unequaled range of subjects and breadth of treatment. They present human situations and relations of the most universal occurrence. This, indeed, is not to be wondered at since just such universality finds expression in *Romeo and Juliet*, *Hamlet*, *King Lear*, *Antony and Cleo-patra*, and *The Tempest*, and is the greatness of these plays. As Professor Mark Van Doren says, Shakespeare in the *Sonnets* "is writing about the world, the largeness of which he has perhaps only recently discovered, and his power to release which in a line he may be only now discovering. The sonnets are not, finally, love poems. They are poems. Their subject is the greatest possible subject, existence: beautiful or ugly, near or remote, celestial or domestic, and sometimes so awesome that its force can be no more than hinted at."

Professor T. M. Parrott describes the *Sonnets* realistically, as follows:

> This [i.e. his praise of the *Sonnets*] is not to say that all the sonnets are of great and equal value; on the contrary many of them are slight things, occasional verses, too often marred by the Elizabethan fond-ness for strained conceits. But when the poet is strongly moved he rises to very lofty heights of thought and to such perfection of expres-sion as is matched, if matched at all, only in his own plays. What moves him most and stirs him to such expression is the Renaissance theme of Beauty, beauty revealed in the person of his friend, beauty that irresistibly evokes love, beauty warred upon by Time, love tri-umphing over the wreckage of Time, and conferring immortality on the beautiful beloved in enduring verse.

Finally, as regards the style of the *Sonnets*, consider the following judi-cious statement by Gustave Landauer, as reproduced in the Variorum edition:

> [Many sonnets by Shakespeare's contemporaries] are structurally perfect, but they are of little importance, because they have seldom come out of a personality, because there was no need in them to restrain exuberance. Thus in content they are mainly allegorical, mythological, bombastic, or in some way rhetorical or artificial. In Shakespeare's most perfect sonnets, of which there are many, the diction is in direct contrast to the turgidity and the pathetically baroque extravagance in comparisons which was fashionable in his day, and which he himself understood and employed in grandiose manner even to grotesqueness in some of his plays and in the narrative-lyric poems. In the sonnets, however, as befits this form, we have an approxima-tion of the language, in diction and syntax, to prose, which through the compactness of the structure, the highly rhythmical symmetry, the parallelism of the rimes, is elevated into a poetry, in which the

structure of language never becomes rhetoric or tirade but always plastic art and music.

Landauer adds also the following suggestion of the place the *Sonnets* hold in Shakespeare's stylistic development. It may be that practice in the sonnet form is to be connected with the new highly condensed style which made its appearance in Shakespeare's plays about the time he finished writing the *Sonnets*, about the year 1600. Landauer says:

> And Shakespeare, who came out of that frothy bombast, which was determined by his nature, by youthful habit, and by fashion, and in which pathos, richness of imagery, choice of rare phrases, affectation and studied mannerism, antithesis and wit, mingled oddly and seldom truly balanced one another, could want no better taskmaster than the sonnet.

CHAPTER VI

Success in the Theatre

ROMANTIC COMEDIES:

THE MERCHANT OF VENICE
MUCH ADO ABOUT NOTHING
AS YOU LIKE IT

THE GREAT TETRALOGY:

RICHARD II
THE HENRY IV PLAYS
HENRY V

D URING the period when Shakespeare was writing his greatest history plays he was also engaged in writing the best and brightest of his comedies. He was winning his way, and it must be that for a time toward the end of the sixteenth century he was the leading London dramatist, not yet rivaled and surpassed in popular favor by Ben Jonson, Marston, Middleton, Dekker, and Webster. We think of him as traveling the high road of general human appeal and so operating within the range of the probable in his characters and his plots. We think of his rivals as having in general shifted to the right or the left—toward realism or romance, toward eccentricity or specialized traits. We do not think of them as necessarily inferior to Shakespeare or degenerate and immoral. Their works were merely what all literary works become after the climax of a literary *genre*. These dramatists tended to leave the open highway for by-paths and sensational adventures in traveling. This divagation was prompted no doubt by the circumstance that the later dramatists were writing to please the courtly circle, a part only of Elizabethan society, whereas Shakespeare was still addressing the whole people.

1. *The Merchant of Venice.*

It may be that Shakespeare took his stand as a writer of typical romantic comedy in *The Merchant of Venice*. Earlier elements are there merged, and in the plot several different themes are again woven together into one story. These several parts dictate the acts of various characters who, nevertheless, seem to be embarked upon one enterprise. The story of the bond and the story of the rings (these two joined already in *Il Pecorone*), the story of the choice of caskets, and the story of the elopement of Jessica make up the plot. *The Merchant of Venice* is a play of the Renaissance, devoted to the exploitation of two popular Renaissance topics, the nature of true love and the relative power of love and friendship. Mere sensual love is illustrated by Morocco, love controlled by intellect by Arragon, and love resting humbly on its own intuition by Bassanio. The story of the pound of flesh, originally secondary, serves to endanger the friend under trial. Shakespeare, guided by the universality of his genius, has, however, made Shylock into a significant human being, and, to many, a sympathetic figure. This fact has made some critics distort the play and interpret it on and off the stage as a tragedy of Shylock, than which nothing could be further from Shakespeare's intention. The play is meant to be rounded out into a complete comedy by the ring episode, sometimes omitted on the stage, which shows that friendship may have greater strength than love; that true love must be forgiving. In the Lorenzo-Jessica plot Shakespeare has re-avowed his liking for true and natural love. By sending Lorenzo and Jessica to be housekeepers at Belmont he has provided his customary place of assembly in comedies, by means of which he may complete the action of the play.

Shakespeare's part seems to have been, not the making of new combinations of plots, but the enrichment of plots. If we judge by his characteristic interests, we may be reasonably sure that he developed the bond story by adding its Hebraic qualities. He meant to make Shylock a Jew as he understood Jews and to make of him in some respects a noble, or at least a typical, specimen of his race. Thus Shylock is an advocate of Justice instead of Mercy and otherwise an adherent of the Old Law. Shylock is not only a practiser of usury, but, like most men of the commercial world, a believer in it. This has brought about the antipathy between Shylock and Antonio, since Shylock is a proponent of what Antonio regards as a sinful social practice. Shylock plays a villain's part, and Shakespeare plainly thinks him wrong; but it is a mistake to say, as some modern critics do, that Shylock is a villain only, a part fit to be enacted in a red beard, like Judas. Shylock is plainly conceived of as a man with a man's feelings and deservings, a man, moreover, who has a cause which he is not ashamed to advocate.

Shakespeare, like other Elizabethans, was used to disputation and was a genius at seeing both sides of every issue, and it is the excellence of Shylock's defense which has perplexed the critics and set the play awry.

The proper interpretation of Shylock's character has been much discussed. He is conceived of fundamentally as a cool and scheming villain, speaking with a certain weightiness of self-defense and a certain suggestion of Hebraic dignity, who has an intelligent understanding of the ancient and consistent nature of his own social, religious, and personal position. He goes through his rôle of villainy and is properly and severely punished at the end. It may be pointed out that these narrative parts are mainly in blank verse. They offer no trouble in interpretation. The trouble arises from certain scenes and passages in prose, all of which serve to humanize Shylock and make us sympathizers when we may be sure the Elizabethans would have merely laughed at him. Are these passages revisions, possibly at the time of composition? Are they concessions to the actor who played Shylock, in the fattening of his part? Toward these passages, which are doubtfully consistent with the rest, we must direct our attention if we wish to come to a better understanding of the problem.

The first forty lines of the third scene of the first act are in prose. They are very lively. Shylock discusses granting the loan of three thousand ducats to Antonio, reveals a knowledge of the state of Antonio's business, speaks picturesquely to the effect that ships are but boards, sailors but men. He declines to dine with Christians. He will not smell pork or "eat of the habitation which your prophet the Nazarite conjured the devil into." He is a wittier, less dignified Shylock than he becomes when Antonio enters. The famous speech of malice beginning "How like a fawning publican he looks!" is in blank verse and is part of the serious Shylock plot. The humorous account of Shylock's ravings given by Salanio (II, viii) is the beginning of the comic Shylock, and the first scene of the third act, which contains the tauntings of Salanio and Salarino, may have been intended to carry this comic business on; but the case is not clear. It is hard to believe that even an Elizabethan audience could have found anything funny in Shylock's speech about Jews and Christians, and it looks as if Shakespeare's sympathies had gone over at least temporarily to the side of the tormented. Indeed, it is hard to imagine any more completely human appeal than Shylock's (III, i, 61-76):

I am a Jew. Hath not a Jew eyes? hath not a Jew hands, organs, dimensions, senses, affections, passions? fed with the same food, hurt with the same weapons, subject to the same diseases, healed by the same means, warmed and cooled by the same winter and summer, as a Christian is? If you prick us, do we not bleed? if you tickle us, do we not laugh? if you poison us, do we not die? and if you wrong us, shall we not revenge? If we are like you in the rest, we will resemble you in that. If a Jew wrong a Christian, what is his humility? Revenge. If a Christian wrong a Jew, what should his sufferance be by Christian example? Why, revenge. The villainy you teach me, I will execute, and it shall go hard but I will better the instruction.

It is a trifle hard to believe that every man in the audience laughed when Tubal said (III, i, 123-4), "One of them showed me a ring that he had of your daughter for a monkey" and Shylock replied,

> Out upon her! Thou torturest me, Tubal: it was my turquoise; I had it of Leah when I was a bachelor: I would not have given it for a wilderness of monkeys.

It looks very much as if Shakespeare were at his favorite game of sympathizing with the underdog and revealing the humanity in persons not popularly considered entitled to it. Gratiano taunts Shylock in his own words in the trial scene (IV, i), and there is no doubt that the audience crows over the thwarted villain. In many performances of the play, however, Gratiano is played by a weak-voiced, inconspicuous actor who is not often allowed to make himself felt, in deference to some great star who is playing Shylock.

The truth of it is that Shakespeare wrote one play, and we insist on reading another. He wrote a comedy of true love and true friendship, and we insist on making it into a tragedy of a wronged individual and a wronged race. Shakespeare is not to blame for this, although it is a penalty of his genius that he should have revealed issues and ideas perhaps far beyond his intention. It is, however, possible, as Granville-Barker shows, to interpret and to act *The Merchant of Venice* with such fair appraisal of all its parts that all contradictions disappear.

2. *Much Ado about Nothing.*

In *Much Ado About Nothing* Shakespeare returned to social comedy and reached with Beatrice and Benedick in their wit-combats, their inconsistencies, and their general aptness and charm what is perhaps his highest point in that form. He also continued his practice of placing in the plot a serious element which for a time threatens the happiness of a group of good people, especially, in this case, the happiness of the innocent Hero. Social comedy and domestic tragedy are especially liable to be distorted for us by the changes which have taken place in the conventions of society. In *Much Ado* Claudio suffers from such distortion. Something can be said, however, to render his actions intelligible if not acceptable. Sensational plots, such as the rejection of a bride at the altar, were common enough. Italian fiction supplied many of them. A cruelty of the kind perpetrated by Claudio would not, in the light of the exaggerated conception of marital fidelity, have seemed a cruelty if practiced on an unchaste maid or on one thought to be unchaste. Seeing is believing, and Claudio thought he had seen. Shakespeare, moreover, does much to make Claudio attractive by representing him as young, brave, handsome, a lover who falls in love at first sight; by depicting him later as a youth deeply smitten with contrition when he realizes his mistake. The modern reader might ask why he offers himself in the fifth act so readily as the husband of another woman, sight unseen; but we can hardly estimate the businesslike aspect which marriage had in Elizabethan England. There would have been no feeling in the audience that Claudio, guilty though he is, should remain single and forever faithful to Hero's memory. A modern romantic hero would have to do that. But Claudio had sung his dirge and was ready to do his part in expiation. He was showing a truly just and generous spirit in bestowing himself as a husband on another member of Leonato's family. It has been suggested that the Hero-Claudio part may be less plausible because of excisions; that is, that details which would have made us more sympathetic toward Claudio have been omitted.

The major plot of *Much Ado*, the tale of a stratagem to break off the engagement of an innocent girl by making it appear that she was receiving a lover into her bedchamber, was widely distributed. It appears in Ariosto's *Orlando Furioso*, in Spenser's *Faerie Queene* (II, iv), and elsewhere. It is told in one of the novels of Bandello which was adapted into French by Belleforest in *Histoires Tragiques* (1582). There are allusions in Shakespeare's play to earlier meetings of Benedick and Beatrice, and it may be that Shakespeare was following an earlier play now lost. Whatever his source may have been, he apparently started out to write a rather serious poetical comedy on the old theme. But he introduced two characters with an issue of marriage between them, and the sideshow swallowed the circus. The scenes between Benedick and Beatrice are actually funny, and it is not unusual for modern audiences of the play to laugh heartily, not because it is a Shakespearean comedy and they are supposed to laugh, but because they are actually amused. J. Dover Wilson in his introduction to the play suggested very plausibly that Shakespeare, having made a great hit on the stage with the merry war of courtship between a resolved old bachelor and a woman who was a man-hater, modified the play, probably while it was on the stage, by fattening these parts and, in order to find room for the new matter, which is written in prose, abridged the major plot, which had been written mainly in verse. This would account for various inconsistencies in the major plot. The scenes between Benedick and Beatrice are not only surpassingly witty, but vivid, lifelike, and interesting. There is hardly a sharper climax to be found in Shakespeare than that which arises between them in the first scene of the fourth act (ll. 288-91). They have been tricked into a relationship which is artificial. They are not quite comfortable in it, and of course a love union on a basis of deceit, however well intended, will not do. But they agree in principle in that they both side with the wronged Hero. Beatrice says,

> I love you with so much of my heart that none is left to protest.

And Benedick replies,

> Come, bid me do any thing for you.

And Beatrice shoots at him the surprising words:

> Kill Claudio.

He does not kill Claudio, but he busies himself about Hero's defense and thus wins Beatrice's as yet reluctant heart. One feels that the future happiness of Benedick and Beatrice is pretty well assured in spite of their talent for sharp talk.

In low comedy it is doubtful if Shakespeare ever did anything better than Dogberry. His is a kind of clownage akin to the roughness of the older drama and yet carried by skill in characterization from the realm of farce into the realm of comedy. The very idea of having such a constable apprehend a criminal is profoundly humorous, unequaled outside *Don Quixote*. Shakespeare wrote the part of Dogberry for Will Kemp, for whom also he had written the parts of Bottom, Launcelot Gobbo, and other simple, rough, or rustic clowns. Sheer, pompous stupidity becomes a rapier in the hands of Dogberry. He gives the Watch their famous charge (III, iii, 20-95) and ends by bidding them watch about Signior Leonato's door, because "there is a great coil tonight"; they there overhear the plottings of Borachio and Conrade, and, much to the disgust of these two courtly gangsters, arrest them. Dogberry, like a character in Jane Austen, can create an impression of interminable boredom in very brief time, and it is his tediousness that prevents the discovery of Don John's plot in time to forestall the rejection of Hero at the altar. The famous examining trial (IV, ii) is a model of ineptitude. Sexton manages to make it adequate, but it is Dogberry who takes the credit. Now, Dogberry is obviously on the side of the angels, and his indignation at having been called an ass and his consternation that no record of the insult has been made provoke a truly memorable outburst (IV, ii, 75-90):

> *Con.* Away! you are an ass, you are an ass.
> *Dog.* Dost thou not suspect my place? dost thou not suspect my years? O that he were here to write me down an ass! But, masters, remember that I am an ass; though it be not written down, yet forget not that I am an ass. No, thou villain, thou art full of piety, as shall be proved upon thee by good witness. I am a wise fellow, and, which is more, an officer, and, which is more, a householder, and, which is more, as pretty a piece of flesh as any is in Messina, and one that knows the law, go to; and a rich fellow enough, go to; and a fellow that hath had losses, and one that hath two gowns and every thing handsome about him. Bring him away. O that I had been writ down an ass!

Perhaps nowhere is there such a revelation of the *amour propre* and such insight. He is "a fellow that hath had losses, and one that hath two gowns and every thing handsome about him"!

3. *As You Like It.*

Kemp left the Lord Chamberlain's company about 1598, and his place as chief clown was taken by Robert Armin, a comic actor of a different style, a court fool rather than a clown. We know of course that Armin also played the part of Dogberry, but his particular style was a more refined one. He himself was the author of comedies and of books on clowns and clownage. It seems probable that Armin's appearance in Shakespeare's company invited the creation of Shakespeare's later set of comic parts—Touchstone, Feste, the Fool in *King Lear*, and Lavache in *All's Well That Ends Well*.

Touchstone would be an ornament to any comedy. He has in him a certain fidelity and satirical honesty which wins sympathy. He is possessed of more than a dash of amusing roguery, conceit, and bravado, and of a vein of nonsense at once professional and spontaneous. One of the set pieces in *As You Like It*, as a pastoral comedy, is the issue between the city and the country, between the court and the forest. Touchstone attacks this issue on the flank, for he embodies certain traits of the courtier which were never meant to be brought into the debate. The one whose profession at court had been folly becomes a philosopher in the forest. For the creation of Touchstone and other parts for Armin, Shakespeare must be credited with further advances in Elizabethan drama.

As You Like It is a pastoral play filled with the freedom and naturalness of Sherwood forest. It is based on Lodge's *Rosalynde*, which in turn rests upon the excellent Robin Hood romance of *Gamelyn*. The fact that *As You Like It* is a dramatized novel makes the play possibly more static than most of Shakespeare's comedies. Many persons read it, for example, without realizing that the climax of the plot is in the scene (IV, i) in which Rosalind, disguised as a man, compels Orlando to woo her as if she were Rosalind, as indeed she is. The character Jaques is an innovation in the play. Jaques, according to current fashion a malcontent, has nothing to do in the comedy and yet is dramatically important. His importance arises from the fact that he is an impartial commentator, hardly as yet the dramatist's voice, but the first of a series of chorus-like characters of growing effectiveness in Shakespeare's plays and in those of other dramatists.

The melancholy Jaques is not popular in Arden with anybody but Shakespeare. Jaques is often thought of as the harbinger to his creator of much sadness and disillusionment in the years to come. Shakespeare has done well by him and has put into his mouth unforgettable speeches by the score. The chief of these is

> All the world's a stage,
> And all the men and women merely players:
> They have their exits and their entrances;
> And one man in his time plays many parts,
> His acts being seven ages. . . .

He is the first of a series of characters who serve as commentators and whose words cut across the current sentiment of the play with a differing point of view, usually with the thought of the seven ages of man. Jaques and with him other spectator-like characters who have little to do with the action are perhaps another of Shakespeare's inventions.

Hamlet, himself a principal character, utters words of general significance. His voice seems to be, not only that of the dramatist, but of wisdom and human experience. Timon also has his say about the evils of existence and the wicked ways of the world. Macbeth too is a thinker in the midst of his furious passion, and Prospero is commentator general. Enobarbas in *Antony and Cleopatra* and Menenius Agrippa in *Coriolanus* are in their functions also chorus-like, each of course in ways different from those of Jaques and yet each suggesting that we are hearing the dramatist's voice.

One need not take Jaques too seriously. He is out of place in *As You Like It*, and that is why he is there. Rosalind, with her interest in marrying Orlando and living happy ever afterwards, cannot abide Jaques. She makes him the target of her wit (IV, i), but he succeeds nevertheless in giving her a very interesting, though incomplete, definition of his melancholy. It is, he says, neither the melancholy of the scholar, the musician, the courtier, the soldier, the lawyer, the lady, nor the lover: "but it is a melancholy of mine own, compounded of many simples, extracted from many objects." Jaques is not without a victory in his refusal to leave the forest. He will not admit that there will be no more troubles and no more vanities in the world because a particular problem has been happily solved. He will join the newly exiled Duke:

> *Jaq.* To him will I: out of these convertites
> There is much matter to be heard and learn'd.

4. *Richard II.*

During the period in which *The Merchant of Venice* and *Much Ado About Nothing* were in the making Shakespeare continued his activity in the field of English history. He had told the violent story of the Wars of the Roses, in which there had been little comedy. And, when he began again, there was no comedy to be found in *Richard II*, the first of the plays which deal with the rise of the house of Lancaster. In the Henry IV plays, however, Shakespeare combined the two dramatic *genres* with great gusto and great skill, as we shall see.

Richard II is tragic; indeed Shakespeare made in that play a forward step in the development of Elizabethan tragedy. Marlowe had treated an almost precisely similar plot in his great play *Edward II*, and Marlowe had gone as far in objective treatment as Shakespeare or any dramatist could hope to go. In taking up the same problem Shakespeare was forced to find a new solution. He could not merely follow Marlowe's method. The result of his effort was the discovery or rediscovery of the tragedy of character. He had to go inside his hero for the real antagonist. Richard II was, if we may believe the testimony of the time, a beautiful person, a man of charm, capable of attaching others to him. These traits he shared with Marlowe's hero, and with him also the defects of being a bad king, one misled by flatterers and one almost incapable of appropriate action. Edward II is overthrown by actual enemies and goes down lamenting his crown and his power. Richard II is overcome not by external forces but by what he himself was. His character is his fate. The essential tragedy is brought about by the mere action of his mind upon itself, for he is a sentimentalist, self-defeated, though still a king in nature, feelings, and trappings. *Richard II* deserves to be regarded as the first consciously developed character tragedy in English drama. Richard himself is the forerunner of Brutus, Hamlet, Macbeth, Antony, and Coriolanus, all men, in a certain sense, who are architects of their fate, as are Agamemnon and other heroes of Greek tragedy.

There underlay the stories of both Edward II and Richard II the question of whether or not a king might in any circumstances be dethroned, since a king's title came from God and since it was for God and not for man to punish him if he were wicked. Marlowe ignores this question, or rather lets it settle itself by legitimate succession. Shakespeare makes the problem abundantly clear but does not attempt any solution except that furnished by fact and human conscience. He provides a representative of each side of the issue. In *Edward II* there is one protagonistic figure set over against a series of secondary figures; but the story of King Richard II, as told in the chronicles and in Daniel's *Civil Wars*, caused Shakespeare to do a very different and a very significant thing. It caused him to unite in the person of Bolingbroke the antagonistic forces opposed to Richard. To have embodied opposite and irreconcilable forces in two opposing characters contributed to the tragic quality of the play. To do this was a new thing in Elizabethan tragedy, and Shakespeare had discovered from his experience a masterly device which he subsequently used in Brutus and Cassius, Hamlet and Claudius, Iago and Othello, Macbeth and Macduff, Octavius and Antony. Such dramatic opposites appear also in the plays of other tragic writers.

One difficulty for the modern reader of *Richard II* is that the play depends on a famous historical situation perfectly familiar to Shakespeare's audience and not only not presented in the play but merely alluded to as a matter of more or less common knowledge. The fact that it serves as a concealed personal and political motive in the first scene makes that scene difficult to understand. Thomas, Duke of Gloucester, the King's uncle, had been imprisoned on the charge of treason at Calais castle and had been mysteriously murdered. It was an open secret that Richard II was responsible for his uncle's death. This episode really constitutes the first part of the tragedy of King Richard II and was so treated apparently in a number of plays, one of which, *Woodstock*, has been preserved in manuscript. If Shakespeare wrote a first part of *Richard II*, no trace of it has survived, but *Richard II* is none the less part two of a two-part play. As the play opens, the uncles of the King, John of Gaunt, Thomas of Woodstock, and to a moderate extent Edmund of York, together with the Duke of Northumberland and other nobles, had been ousted from power by a group of greedy and corrupt royal favorites, of whom Bushy, Bagot, and Green are the principal members. Aumerle, son of the Duke of York, is also one of the King's new party. The first scene is really a move on the chess board of politics. John of Gaunt is very old, and his eldest son, Henry, Duke of Hereford, called "Bolingbroke," is the leader of the opposition to the King's party. He is a remarkable man, who says little in the play, but is felt from the beginning as a powerful force. Bolingbroke has seen in Gloucester's murder a fulcrum for his lever to shake or upset the throne. Whether he planned from the beginning to dethrone the King is uncertain; probably not, although that idea may have been present in the King's mind when he exclaimed (I, i, 109),

> How high a pitch his resolution soars!

He sees that the point of attack on the King is Thomas Mowbray, Duke of Norfolk, who when Gloucester was murdered had been keeper of Calais castle and therefore responsible for the safety of his prisoner. At some time before the opening of the play Bolingbroke has preferred charges against Mowbray, and in the first scene the two men are, according to the customs of chivalry, brought face to face in the presence of the King. Richard, we may imagine, was so occupied with his pleasures and his plans that he did not realize the nature of Bolingbroke's attack, for as a man Richard is conspicuous for over-confidence and false security. He simply cannot believe that his interests are in jeopardy, and, besides, he loves the pomp of his office, else he would hardly have suffered Bolingbroke and Mowbray to meet. Richard's crooked thinking appears in almost the first words he says (I, i, 25-7),

> We thank you both: yet one but flatters us,
> As well appeareth by the cause you come;
> Namely, to appeal each other of high treason.

The truth of what he says does not follow, since they both may have been innocent or both guilty.

When Bolingbroke makes his four charges (I, i, 30-150), three of them turn out to be trumped up. The first is,

> Thou art a traitor and a miscreant.

There is nothing unusual in calling a political enemy a traitor and a miscreant. Mowbray makes the only possible answer,

> I do defy him, and I spit at him.

The second charge is,

> That Mowbray hath received eight thousand nobles
> In name of lendings for your highness' soldiers,
> The which he hath detain'd for lewd employments.

This also gives Mowbray no concern. These accounts have been audited. The charge amounts to nothing. The third charge is like the first,

> That all the treasons for these eighteen years
> Complotted and contrived in this land
> Fetch from false Mowbray their first head and spring.

The fourth charge, which is the occasion for all the rest, touches very nearly the King as well as Mowbray,

> That he did plot the Duke of Gloucester's death,
> Suggest his soon-believing adversaries,
> And consequently, like a traitor coward,
> Sluiced out his innocent soul through streams of blood·
> Which blood, like sacrificing Abel's, cries,
> Even from the tongueless caverns of the earth,
> To me for justice and rough chastisement.

Abel was slain by his brother Cain, and the allusion to him is a covert accusation against the King. Mowbray's reply to this charge is interesting. He might have shielded the King had he taken the blame of Gloucester's death upon himself, or denied the matter and offered to fight. Instead of following either of these false policies he speaks the truth,

> For Gloucester's death,
> I slew him not; but to my own disgrace
> Neglected my sworn duty in that case.

The deep passion of his sincerity appears pathetically in his unasked-for confession that he had once planned the death of John of Gaunt, but had repented, confessed his sin, and taken the sacrament. Richard gains time by ordering the opponents to appear in the lists at Coventry upon St. Lambert's day and submit their difference to trial by combat.

At Coventry, Richard, who spent his life, not living, but playing parts, participates up to the crucial moment in a great spectacle. He goes proudly through all the ceremonies, but when the combatants are poised for their duels, and actualities are about to appear, he throws his truncheon down and stops the fight. Why does he do this? If Mowbray had won, Bolingbroke would have been silenced. If Bolingbroke had won, the King would have been rid of a follower who, he feared, would betray him, and he would have been at least no worse off as regards Bolingbroke. Then, too, in the decision of the council, which Richard has dictated, he follows the one course of conduct that was sure to do injustice to both appellants; and, most cruelly and unnaturally, he inflicts the heavier penalty on Mowbray, who has had no ulterior motive and has been honest and faithful. That the King is playing with dangerous weapons and does not know it appears in an almost casual manifestation of his vanity while he is pronouncing the sentences of banishment. He looks at John of Gaunt and, seeing grief and consternation in his face, changes Bolingbroke's exile from ten years to six. One cannot believe that he has any deep sympathy for old Gaunt. One must believe that he is making for his own enjoyment a brilliant exercise of kingly power. Bolingbroke understands, and there is something ominous in his words (I, iii, 213-15),

> How long a time lies in one little word!
> Four lagging winters and four wanton springs
> End in a word: such is the breath of kings.

Richard's interview with the dying Gaunt serves to bring out the famous speech (II, i, 31-68) in praise of England. It contains the lines said to have been recited by many patriots of English blood in the trials and tribulations of war. which that country has gone through in recent years:

> This royal throne of kings, this scepter'd isle,
> This earth of majesty, this seat of Mars,
> This other Eden, demi-paradise,
> This fortress built by Nature for herself
> Against infection and the hand of war,
> This happy breed of men, this little world,
> This precious stone set in the silver sea,
> Which serves it in the office of a wall . . .

The speech is not, however, patriotic only; it is also deeply dramatic in its indictment of Richard as an unworthy king and in its warning from true and aged lips. Gaunt's later speech (ll. 93-114) in which he reproves Richard serves to show the audience how hopeless the case is. One test of the sentimentalist, the man who refuses to live in any world but that of his own vain imagination, is the sudden anger of such persons when they are shocked into seeing the actual truth. This may be observed in ordinary life. When Gaunt says to Richard,

> Landlord of England art thou now, not king:
> Thy state of law is bondslave to the law;
> And thou—

Richard breaks out into incontrollable anger against the dying man, his uncle, his guardian:

> A lunatic lean-witted fool,
> Presuming on an ague's privilege,
> Darest with thy frozen admonition
> Make pale our cheek, chasing the royal blood
> With fury from his native residence.
> Now, by my seat's right royal majesty,
> Wert thou not brother to great Edward's son,
> This tongue that runs so roundly in thy head
> Should run thy head from thy unreverent shoulders.

Note also that here and elsewhere Richard's vanity makes him conscious of his complexion, for sentimentality is highly self-conscious.

Richard II might have had much vanity without much harm; it is his blind folly that matters. He is bound for Ireland, and he insists on leaving his aged uncle York in charge of his kingdom. York is faithful enough, but he is incompetent and deeply wounded in the injuries done his family—Bolingbroke banished and hindered in his marriage, Gaunt dead in disgrace and his estate confiscated; but Richard makes York viceroy in spite of York's protests, and, as if to make sure of disloyalty at home, levies illegal taxes to support his campaign.

When Bolingbroke has landed and gathered followers and York has yielded to him, Richard returns from Ireland. The second scene of the third act is unforgettable in its picture of the King. As a sentimentalist, and like all egotists, bigots, and fanatics, he has only two extreme moods, with no intermediary emotional states. Although things are in a very bad way Richard refuses to believe that there is anything the matter. He treats Aumerle and the Bishop of Carlisle to the spectacle of how an ideal king might behave when he returns to his kingdom after an absence. To him it is a mystical and all-important event. Is he a patriot? Does he love his country? This is worth asking because of the interpretations recently offered by great actors and critics. Of course he loves England, but he loves it as an appendage to himself (ll. 3-11):

> *Aum.*   How brooks your grace the air,
> After your late tossing on the breaking seas?
> *K. Rich.* Needs must I like it well: I weep for joy
> To stand upon my kingdom once again.
> Dear earth, I do salute thee with my hand,
> Though rebels wound thee with their horses' hoofs:
> As a long-parted mother with her child
> Plays fondly with her tears and smiles in meeting,
> So, weeping, smiling, greet I thee, my earth,
> And do thee favours with my royal hands.

It is little that the earth cares for being saluted with any mortal hand. When the bishop says (ll. 27-30),

> Fear not, my lord: that Power that made you king
> Hath power to keep you king in spite of all.
> The means that heaven yields must be embraced,
> And not neglected;

Richard, who is enjoying his impractical vision to the utmost, does not even know what Carlisle is talking about. Aumerle explains:

> He means, my lord, that we are too remiss;
> Whilst Bolingbroke, through our security,
> Grows strong and great in substance and in power.

But Richard is deaf to common prudence. He compares his return to the rising of the sun (ll. 47-62):

> So when this thief, this traitor, Bolingbroke,
> Who all this while hath revell'd in the night
> Whilst we were wandering with the antipodes,
> Shall see us rising in our throne, the east,
> His treasons will sit blushing in his face, . . .
> Not all the water in the rough rude sea
> Can wash the balm off from an anointed king; . . .
> For every man that Bolingbroke hath press'd
> To lift shrewd steel against our golden crown,
> God for his Richard hath in heavenly pay
> A glorious angel: then, if angels fight,
> Weak men must fall, for Heaven still guards the right.

From this pinnacle of self-conceit Richard is doomed to fall quickly into his other mood, the mood of complete despair. Salisbury enters to say that the Welsh soldiers, frightened by portents and false news, are dispersed and fled, and Scroop to tell about Bolingbroke's rising power. Aumerle asks (l. 143),

> Where is the duke my father with his power?

And Richard, in spite of the fact that all is not lost, gives up the fight.

> No matter where; of comfort no man speak:
> Let's talk of graves, of worms and epitaphs; . . .
> For God's sake, let us sit upon the ground
> And tell sad stories of the death of kings: . . .
> How can you say to me, I am a king?
> *Car.* My lord, wise men ne'er sit and wail their woes,
> But presently prevent the ways to wail. . . .
> *K. Rich.* Thou chidest me well: proud Bolingbroke, I come.

But Scroop says,

> Your uncle York is join'd with Bolingbroke.

And Richard, having now a fascinating new part to play, that of a deposed ruler, resolves to surrender. As confirmation of his sentimentality, his enjoyment of his play-acting, note his words (ll. 204-5):

> Beshrew thee, cousin, which didst lead me forth
> Of that sweet way I was in to despair!

At Flint castle Richard has one manly impulse, but he rejects it (III, iii, 127-30),

> We do debase ourselves, cousin, do we not,
> To look so poorly and to speak so fair?
> Shall we call back Northumberland, and send
> Defiance to the traitor, and so die?

Such a resolution on his part might have upset Bolingbroke's plans. Bolingbroke could hardly have become king of England by war against the King, but Richard plays into his hand and offers to resign. Bolingbroke, having got a taste of power, insists that the resignation shall be ceremonious, and this gives rise to one of the most remarkable scenes in Shakespeare (IV, i). It begins with impeachments for treason and charges against Aumerle. Aumerle is not an admirable character, but one must admire his courage. He has been challenged to combat by two knights, and when Fitzwater also challenges him he cries (l. 83),

> Some honest Christian trust me with a gage.

One wonders if Shakespeare realized that the brave Duke of York who dies nobly in battle in *Henry V* is none other than this rather shifty Aumerle.

The deposition scene does not occur in the first two quarto editions of the play, and when it appears in the third quarto of 1608 it is in a somewhat imperfect form. It has been supposed that it had been censored in the earliest versions, but it is at least possible that the famous scene was composed on the occasion of the revival of the play at the time of Essex's rebellion in 1601. The scene is, however, perfectly in the vein of Richard. He has prepared himself to abdicate in ideal fashion and is rather obliging about it. He calls for the crown with the idea of making a hand-to-hand surrender of it. He has two styles, and in his plain style he asks Bolingbroke to enter into the ceremony with him by placing a

hand upon the crown. Bolingbroke is apparently embarrassed and
reluctant (ll. 181-2).

> Give me the crown. Here, cousin, seize the crown;
> Here, cousin.

Then in the magniloquent language of his set speeches he goes on.

> On this side my hand, and on that side yours.
> Now is this golden crown like a deep well
> That owes two buckets, filling one another,
> The emptier ever dancing in the air,
> The other down, unseen and full of water:
> That bucket down and full of tears am I,
> Drinking my griefs, whilst you mount up on high.

Bolingbroke, no play-actor, says in exasperation,

> I thought you had been willing to resign.

When Richard has signed the articles of abdication, he, conceiving of
himself as a man of deepest woes, calls for a mirror in which to see his
face. Bolingbroke, tired of the foolery, says impatiently (l. 268),

> Go some of you and fetch a looking-glass.

When the mirror comes and Richard looks at his countenance, he is very
much disappointed. His face shows no marks of care, and why should it?
He has been having a pleasant time, just as do millions of sufferers from
imaginary woes in daily life. Richard dashes the mirror against the ground
and says,

> Mark, silent king, the moral of this sport,
> How soon my sorrow hath destroy'd my face.

Whereupon Bolingbroke says almost the only good thing he utters in
the play,

> The shadow of your sorrow hath destroy'd
> The shadow of your face.

This pleases Richard, who has no doubt found Bolingbroke an unrespon-
sive vis-à-vis in their dialogue, and he says appreciatively, like a child,

> Say that again.

For some odd reason, in spite of constant and interwoven folly, one likes Richard better than one likes Bolingbroke.

Richard's real troubles have now begun, but, when we later see him in prison (V, v), he is the same Richard. From this scene it dawns on us that we have to deal in his case with a poet. He is represented in soliloquy (ll. 1 ff.) studying

> how I may compare
> This prison where I live unto the world.

He finds the comparison difficult and shows the great artist's persistent patience when he says,

> I cannot do it; yet I'll hammer it out.

The keeper of the prison at Pomfret enters ahead of the men hired to murder Richard. The keeper refuses to taste the food which he has brought, and Richard loses his temper and beats the keeper. Just then Exton with his servants rushes in. Richard cries (ll. 104-5),

> How now! what means death in this rude assault?
> Villain, thy own hand yields thy death's instrument.

The King snatches his assailant's axe and slays him. He kills another and cries,

> Go thou, and fill another room in hell.

Then Exton slays him. Thus in the last seconds of his life Richard II strikes an honest blow in his own defense, and we somehow feel that our belief has been justified, that somewhere in this vain and ineffectual king there was hidden the soul of a man.

The theme of the play is embodied in the character of Richard. His enjoyment of his own emotions and his refusal to see any world but a world of ideas, his idea of what is real and not reality itself, overthrow him. He is so eloquent, so sincere, so personally attractive, so spiritually courageous in his adherence to his insecure doctrine of divine vicarship, so surely possessed of a nobler nature, that his downfall is deeply tragic. Coleridge has found in York an admirably drawn character; and the picture of Bolingbroke, with his keen, impersonal intellectuality, has never received the recognition it deserves as a masterpiece of character portrayal. With his feet solidly planted on the ground he advances toward his object with remorseless steadiness and patience, quietly sarcastic, a good judge of men, subtly playing on the feelings of others to achieve his purpose, a treasonous purpose; and yet, withal, he is the man of his time, just and masterful, needed by his country in the crisis where she stood. Shakespeare does not pronounce judgment on the moral issue between Bolingbroke and his king, and yet he must have shared the belief of his countrymen that because of the sinful rejection of a divinely anointed king the soil of England had been bathed in blood during the long and bitter Wars of the Roses. Richard's fall seemed inevitable; England demanded it; and yet Shakespeare does not exculpate Bolingbroke from treason and regicide.

Shakespeare had evidently planned a series of plays, of which *Richard II* was the first. In *1* and *2 Henry IV* and in *Henry V* he harks back again and again to *Richard II*, but in *Richard II* there is only one rather amusing little scene (V, iii) which seems to look forward to the plays to come. Bolingbroke asks Percy and other lords bitterly (ll. 1-12),

> Can no man tell me of my unthrifty son?
> 'Tis full three months since I did see him last:
> If any plague hang over us, 'tis he.
> I would to God, my lords, he might be found:
> Inquire at London, 'mongst the taverns there,
> For there, they say, he daily doth frequent,
> With unrestrained loose companions,
> Even such, they say, as stand in narrow lanes,
> And beat our watch, and rob our passengers;
> Which he, young wanton and effeminate boy,
> Takes on the point of honour to support
> So dissolute a crew.

Jack Falstaff is one of those "unrestrained loose companions," and the prince's "support" of the dissolute crew is probably an allusion to a well known story, never presented by Shakespeare, of how Prince Hal had slapped the face of a justice because he refused to release from detention Bardolf, who had committed some misdemeanor.

Percy says that he has seen the Prince and asked him if he meant to attend the coronation festivities to be held at Oxford. Bolingbroke asks,

> And what said the gallant?
> *Percy.* His answer was, he would unto the stews,
> And from the common'st creature pluck a glove,

And wear it as a favour; and with that
He would unhorse the lustiest challenger.
Boling. As dissolute as desperate; yet through both
I see some sparks of better hope, which elder years
May happily bring forth.

The "sparks of better hope" he sees are probably a realization of a characteristic of Prince Hal which we sometimes fail to observe. Undoubtedly it was written down to Prince Hal's credit that he despised the society life of the court, lived a common life, and had about him a frank quality of plain manhood. Strangely enough, this appears most obviously at the end of *Henry V* when the victorious King woos the Princess Katharine in the plain terms of a downright soldier. It may be that Prince Hal's absenting himself from court and courtly society was credited to him as a bluff and hearty man of deeds.

5. *The Henry IV Plays.*

Richard II thus seems to look forward to the life story of England's great hero, the victor of Agincourt, King Henry V. There had grown up about the career of this king a traditional romance about a wild young manhood marked with escapades of rioting and even highway robbery. Such a fiction had been embodied in an apparently very early chronicle play of Henry V. An abridged and degenerate version of that play is preserved as *The Famous Victories of Henry V*, licensed for printing in 1594. We need not, however, believe that Shakespeare followed this bad version but rather that he worked from an original Henry V play now lost. On the basis of this story Shakespeare constructed a hero play in three parts, *1* and *2 Henry IV* and *Henry V*. The general tenor of Prince Hal's life, its chief episodes, his reformation, his conquest of France, and his marriage to the Princess Katharine are all provided for in this source, even as represented in *The Famous Victories*. But Shakespeare seems to have been moved also by a serious historical purpose, and he uses actual history in these major episodes to afford occasion for his hero to develop his true quality. He does not, for example, permit Prince Hal to engage in actual highway robbery and seems anxious to show, if one may judge by the early scenes of *Henry V*, that Prince Hal had had ambition to be a great king all the time and had trained himself for his duties, but had done so in secret and kept himself away from the court and the public eye. Shakespeare was thus anxious to correct the erroneous popular view. He reminds us of it often, but nowhere so obviously as at the end of the second scene of the first act of *1 Henry IV* when Prince Hal stays behind and addresses the audience in a soliloquy (ll. 218-40):

> I know you all, and will awhile uphold
> The unyoked humour of your idleness:
> Yet herein will I imitate the sun,
> Who doth permit the base contagious clouds
> To smother up his beauty from the world, . . .
> So, when this loose behaviour I throw off
> And pay the debt I never promised,
> By how much better than my word I am,
> By so much shall I falsify men's hopes;
> And like bright metal on a sullen ground,
> My reformation, glittering o'er my fault,
> Shall show more goodly and attract more eyes
> Than that which hath no foil to set it off.
> I'll so offend, to make offense a skill;
> Redeeming time when men think least I will.

Now, when considered as a speech of Prince Hal, that is the speech of a prig, and Shakespeare cannot have meant to degrade his hero. The truth of the matter is that it is a speech addressed by the author to the audience in order to inform them and set them right. He is disabusing the minds of those in the audience who may think that a great prince such as Prince Hal could ever have been truly a tavern roisterer. Shakespeare, as he so often does, is using the soliloquy merely to give his no doubt motley audience a true conception of the play. "This prince," he is saying to them, "is only amusing himself. You shall witness his reformation, and everybody will be all the more surprised because they have expected nothing."

Henry IV, Part I, presents, then, the first great stage of Prince Hal's reformation, and to bring it about Shakespeare chooses from Holinshed's *Chronicles* the story of the rebellion of the Percy family. Both the head of the house, the Earl of Northumberland, and his son, the valiant Hotspur, have assisted Henry IV to overthrow Richard II, and are jealous of the power and influence to which they think they are entitled. This part of the rebellion is so dramatic, so unified in the temper and character of Hotspur, that it becomes, not only a first stage in the hero play of

Henry V, but the rather pitiful tragedy of the noble but erring Hotspur. The central episode of 2 *Henry IV* is a poor thing compared to Hotspur's rebellion. It follows immediately on the first play and concerns itself with the mopping up of the remaining members of the Percy group. The rebels are wretchedly tricked by Prince John of Lancaster, and, because they are in rebellion against the King, no sympathy is shown them by Shakespeare or anybody else. No faith need be kept with any rebel, and we have illustrated in this play better than anywhere else in Shakespeare the Tudor dread of insurrection. Sir John Cheke's *The Hurt of Sedition*, widely read in the sixteenth century and included in Holinshed's *Chronicles*, expresses the point of view. Prince Hal in 2 *Henry IV* undergoes confirmation of good character. He has little to do with the rebellion, comes to a complete and final understanding with his father, assumes the crown, and rejects Falstaff. *Henry V* practically throughout is the story of a hero. There is no genuine dramatic motive in the play. In all three parts, however, Shakespeare, in spite of many comic matters, writes serious history seriously.

In the Henry IV plays, as in *Richard II*, Shakespeare made a great advance as creator and founder of Elizabethan drama. In *The Famous Victories of Henry V*, and of course in the original play, of which it is a bad version, there was a character intended to represent Sir John Oldcastle, who is there because of his supposed connection with the youthful wantonness of King Henry V; for the reputation of Oldcastle, the Lollard martyr, had been blackened by later generations, and he had come to be regarded as a religious hypocrite and a misleader of the young Prince Hal. The story is told by Sir Thomas Elyot in *The Gouernour* and elsewhere. Shakespeare knew the old play, and when he wrote his dramas on Henry IV and Henry V, he made wide use of it, along with serious historical matter from Holinshed's *Chronicles*, not only as a comic accompaniment, but also as a structural source for his depiction of the life of Henry V.

According to the studies of Mr. A. E. Morgan, Shakespeare seems first to have written a play in two parts on the reign of King Henry IV, plays largely in verse, in which Falstaff was known as Oldcastle. The popularity of the Oldcastle parts on the stage probably caused Shakespeare to expand them and enrich them in the free prose style with which we are familiar in the Falstaff scenes. Offense taken by the Earl of

Cobham, a descendant of Oldcastle, caused Shakespeare to change the name of his character from Oldcastle to Falstaff. Morgan is right in his general contention, although it is probable that Shakespeare first wrote a single play of Henry IV and later expanded it into two.

What then is the provenance of Falstaff? He was built up in four stages—the tradition of the Lollard hypocrite, the old Henry V play, the Oldcastle form of Shakespeare's play, and the final form. Falstaff has been regarded as a character of puzzling complexity, and with such an origin he has a right to be. He is as puzzling as life itself, and his dramatic history is as complicated as any life story. He nevertheless hangs together as an actual man. He is Shakespeare's and the Elizabethan drama's first great synthetic character. In his wake come Hamlet, Antony, Cleopatra, and Prospero. One can in a manner see how Falstaff was made, how apparently discordant elements were by repeated contact and long acquaintance fused into a single character. The fact that he was gradually arrived at and had earlier forms based on a false though credible tradition of a real man will keep us from making the mistake of thinking of him either as an actual person such as occurs in history, or as a new creation struck out at one forging from a clear-cut and definite pattern in Shakespeare's brain. Falstaff is, from the point of view of literary history, almost a happy accident, but an accident which gave Shakespeare opportunity to develop his powers of character synthesis. Falstaff is the most lifelike of dramatic characters, and his creator worked from the qualities and actions of living men.

There has been much controversy about the proper interpretation of the character of Falstaff. After Maurice Morgann's famous *An Essay on the Dramatic Character of Sir John Falstaff* (1777) Falstaff came to be regarded with great sympathy by many critics. Indeed, he became something of a hero to sentimental commentators. This anachronistic practice was emphatically rejected by Professor Stoll (1914), and a moderate view was expressed by A. C. Bradley in his chapter called "The Rejection of Falstaff" in his *Oxford Lectures on Poetry* (1909). Some light on the Elizabethan point of view may be had from C. R. Baskervill's paper "The Quarrel of Benedick and Beatrice" (1917). It has been debated whether Falstaff is to be regarded as a rogue or a gull, both of which parts he seems at times to exemplify. The suggestion here is that Shakespeare performed the miracle of synthesizing all sorts of things in one character. Falstaff is original precisely as he escapes pigeon-holing as rogue, or gull, or braggart captain, or what not. Shakespeare in various stages and under various influences entered into the mind and heart of his character and produced the most lifelike effect ever seen on the stage up to that time. There are probably no cut and dried recipes for constructing characters. Certainly there are none which are adequate in the criticism of life. One would merely say that, as Rabelais, Montaigne, and Cervantes, or Thackeray, Dickens, and Meredith succeed in presenting lifelike characters of a paradoxical kind, so also did Shakespeare, and his achievement marked a great advance in dramatic art. Shakespeare had before him the type, a conventionalized general judgment as to what men are like; and there had always been also well rounded historical portraits—Socrates, Alcibiades, Cicero, Petronius, and more recent figures. What Shakespeare did, with the complexity of qualities and events pertaining to this Oldcastle-Falstaff person before him, was to make a probable synthesis on the broadest possible basis and put his man in action. This is a very different thing from the modern idea of constructing characters by adding trait to trait as if one were preparing a dish for the table. There is no stream-lining in Falstaff. Shakespeare operates in the broad highway of probability. Does it matter whether or not Morgann's paradoxes are sound?

> A man at once young and old, enterprising and fat, a dupe and a wit, harmless and wicked, weak in principle and resolute by constitution, cowardly in appearance and brave in reality; a knave without malice, a liar without deceit; and a knight, a gentleman, and a soldier, without either dignity, decency, or honour.

The question is not whether these judgments are individually correct, but whether Falstaff is a credible creature. Why sternly say with some of our severe modern critics, who rather doubtfully regard Falstaff as funny, that he is a mere stage mechanism compounded of rogue and gull and that the whole question of his integrity as a character is anachronistic and not pertinent? Of course Falstaff is a character in drama, but, after all, drama is an art of communication; and the real question is what the drama says, what impression as to a given character it makes on the reader and spectator. As to inconsistencies, ordinary men as well as other dramatic characters offer abundant examples. Prince Hal is inconsistent, so is Dame Quickly, so are you and I and perhaps even some of the historical critics. It is even possible that Shakespeare was inconsistent.

Justice Shallow of 2 *Henry IV*, apparently almost as popular in his day as Falstaff, wins his way because he is so excellent a type, so life-like a caricature. He is Falstaff's moon and shines by reflection of Falstaff himself. Bardolf is primarily a drunkard, but something more than a drunkard. He is certainly an excellent foil to Falstaff, for example, in the third scene of the third act of *1 Henry IV* where Falstaff in an idle, melancholy mood falls to berating Bardolf for want of something else to do (ll. 1-28):

> Bardolf, am I not fallen away vilely since this last action? do I not bate? do I not dwindle? . . . An I have not forgotten what the inside of a church is made of, I am a peppercorn, a brewer's horse: . . . Company, villainous company, hath been the spoil of me. . . .
> *Bard.* Why, you are so fat, Sir John, that you must needs be out of all compass, out of all reasonable compass, Sir John.
> *Fal.* Do thou amend thy face, and I'll amend my life.

In *Henry V* it is Bardolf who pays the greatest tribute to good company ever paid. Falstaff is dead, and Bardolf says,

> Would I were with him, wheresome'er he is, either in heaven or in hell.

Falstaff had to have great qualities, such as perfection in repartee and adeptness in escape, in order that he serve in his rôle as misleader of princes. The question is, has Shakespeare overdone this and made us unwilling to have Falstaff offered up as a sacrifice to the character development of any youthful prince? He certainly has with many honest and intelligent readers. Was Prince Hal sorry to dismiss him? Wasn't the new king strong enough to conquer France in spite of the rascalities of Sir John? Shakespeare seems at one time to have thought he was, for he says quite plainly in the epilogue to *2 Henry IV*.

> If you be not too much cloyed with fat meat, our humble author will continue the story, with Sir John in it, and make you merry with fair Katharine of France: where, for any thing I know, Falstaff shall die of a sweat, unless already a' be killed with your hard opinions; for Oldcastle died a martyr, and this is not the man.

Sentimental critics have tried to tell us that Shakespeare was afraid to take Falstaff along to France for fear he would steal the show which Shakespeare wished to devote to the glorification of his hero king and of his country. It is doubtful if he was so. He knew enough of policy to know that the rejection of Falstaff, which he had already described, was a symbolic act appropriate to the new king. It is more probable that Shakespeare saw that Falstaff had served his turn and that there was no need for him in France. Falstaff has been more than a comic character; he has been a personality; Shakespeare has the genius to provide him with an appropriate end (*Henry V*, II, iii). This killing of Falstaff was a very brilliant thing to do and may be attributed, not to the exigencies of drama, but to Shakespeare's genius.

But did Prince Hal care, or rather did Shakespeare leave any indication that he cared? The new king is in a stern, official mood. He has thrown off his loose behavior, and every eye is on him. And yet the scene of the rejection (2 *Henry IV*, V, v) is not totally without a normal human element. As the coronation procession leaves Westminster Abbey, and Falstaff pushes himself forward to cry (l. 50),

> My king! my Jove! I speak to thee, my heart!

he is not moved by tactless impertinence. He has wagered a show of zeal against a more prudent approach, and he has lost his wager. The King's words are rather awful:

> I know thee not, old man: fall to thy prayers;
> How ill white hairs become a fool and jester!
> I have long dream'd of such a kind of man,
> So surfeit-swell'd, so old and so profane;
> But, being awaked, I do despise my dream.
> Make less thy body hence, and more thy grace;
> Leave gormandizing; know the grave doth gape
> For thee thrice wider than for other men.
> Reply not to me with a fool-born jest:
> Presume not that I am the thing I was;
> For God doth know, so shall the world perceive,
> That I have turn'd away my former self;
> So will I those that kept me company.
> When thou dost hear I am as I have been,
> Approach me, and thou shalt be as thou wast,
> The tutor and the feeder of my riots:
> Till then, I banish thee, on pain of death,
> As I have done the rest of my misleaders,
> Not to come near our person by ten mile.

For competence of life I will allow you,
That lack of means enforce you not to evil:
And, as we hear you do reform yourselves,
We will, according to your strengths and qualities,
Give you advancement.

"Reply not to me with a fool-born jest!" The unuttered jest! The King saw it in the eye of the greatest of all wits. Falstaff, thus under fire, could not safely be allowed to speak. The King promises material support to Falstaff and offers opportunity for advancement. Surely there's an inconsistency here. The idea of Falstaff as a virtuous and hard-working public servant winning his way up to preferment is inconsistent with the play as we have it. This speech and this scene must belong to an earlier form of the play and an earlier conception of the relations between Falstaff and Prince Hal. We know that Prince Hal has long ago solved his problems of conscience and that he has been merely amusing himself. Why then does he express such fear and such loathing? He is perhaps talking out of a more serious early situation, from the conception in a play which treated more seriously the danger of a prince's being misled by wicked contrivers. The speech does not fit. The new king was in no such danger as he says, and his sins were by no means so grave. In Shakespeare's revision of the play his idea of the relation of the prince and his companions has grown and changed. This scene has the patriotic sternness of an earlier conception of the career of the hero monarch.

1 Henry IV is no doubt Falstaff's play, but it is not without another kind of interest. Indeed, it is doubtful whether the dramatic interest of history ever rose to a higher point in Shakespeare than it does in the story of Hotspur.

Hotspur was a rebel and, as such, beyond the point where an Elizabethan might wish him success in his enterprise. He was therefore foredoomed to tragic failure. He has his grievances, and they are political; but, although they are not presented in the play, one has no reason to regard them as irreconcilable. These grievances are mainly embodied in Hotspur's uncle, the Earl of Worcester. In the case of Henry IV the Percys feel that since they have been kingmakers, they ought to count for more at court than they do. The King himself very naturally resents their attitude. Northumberland is represented as old and peaceable. Worcester is irate and rebellious in his attitude. Hotspur is not hostile to the King except as he is urged on by Worcester. Thus the law of saving the hero from blame puts Worcester in the rôle of villain. Hotspur is unstable, and his character makes him easy to persuade to a wrong course.

No doubt Shakespeare had in mind with reference to Hotspur such an ethical analysis as Aristotle's *Ethics* would have supplied. Hotspur is prone to go to extremes. His courage runs readily into foolhardiness, and his indignation into rage, excessive anger. According to doctrine, reason dwells with the golden mean. Hotspur continually acts unreasonably. He has charming traits of character; he is noble in principle, generous to a fault, witty in speech, and brave as a lion. This conception of the way in which the faults of Hotspur serve to undo him is manifested over and over again. Hotspur has also the quality of being impatient and splenetic, and, since he is also witty, he does himself and his cause harm by over-indulging his turn for satire. In this respect also he shows his lack of balance. Hotspur's weaknesses are human, and he is one of the most sympathetic of Shakespeare's unfortunate men. He requires indulgence, and the thing that sets him off on the wrong course is his encounter with King Henry IV, that stern man to whom the very idea of indulgence was unknown.

There is a question of prisoners. Hotspur has taken various prisoners in his fight against the Scotch at Holmedon. These he has not turned over to the King, and, probably at the instigation of Worcester, has refused to do so unless the King will ransom from the Welsh the Earl of March. Henry IV does not wish to do this. The Earl of March is his political enemy and is himself a claimant to the crown. Nevertheless the matter was capable of adjustment, and Hotspur's attitude is not rebellious. In his sprightly way he offers ground for negotiation (I, iii, 29-69):

> My liege, I did deny no prisoners.
> But I remember, when the fight was done,
> When I was dry with rage and extreme toil,
> Breathless and faint, leaning upon my sword,
> Came there a certain lord, neat, and trimly dress'd,
> Fresh as a bridegroom; and his chin new reap'd
> Show'd like a stubble-land at harvest home; . . .
>   and still he smiled and talk'd,
> And as the soldiers bore dead bodies by,
> He call'd them untaught knaves, unmannerly,

To bring a slovenly unhandsome corse
Betwixt the wind and his nobility.
With many holiday and lady terms
He question'd me; amongst the rest, demanded
My prisoners in your majesty's behalf.
I then, all smarting with my wounds being cold,
To be so pester'd with a popinjay,
Out of my grief and my impatience,
Answer'd neglectingly I know not what,
He should, or he should not; for he made me mad
To see him shine so brisk and smell so sweet
And talk so like a waiting-gentlewoman
Of guns and drums and wounds,—God save the mark!—
And telling me the sovereign'st thing on earth
Was parmaceti for an inward bruise; . . .
This bald unjointed chat of his, my lord,
I answer'd indirectly, as I said;
And I beseech you, let not his report
Come current for an accusation
Betwixt my love and your high majesty.

This charming apologia from a brave man would have won over almost
anybody, but not Bolingbroke, who says (ll. 77-8),

Why, yet he doth deny his prisoners,
But with proviso and exception.

And he adds to that an insult in his refusal to ransom home "revolted
Mortimer." Mortimer was Hotspur's brother-in-law, and Hotspur defends
him; but the king is obdurate, and Hotspur's rage begins. Worcester
enters and feeds the flames. Hotspur is crazy with anger, and all hope
of reconciliation with the King vanishes. Hotspur is to blame, and yet
Worcester and the King himself are chargeable.

When we see Hotspur again (II, ii) he is reading letters from persons
whose assistance he has sought in his rebellion against the King. The
letters ought to have discouraged him, yet the quality of his unreason
is such that the more he stands alone the more determined he becomes
to fight. Prudence is another name for reason, and Hotspur is totally
lacking in prudence. Lady Percy tries to dissuade him in vain in a scene
of extraordinary charm. But his worst error is his treatment of Glendower. Glendower is a warrior and a magician who thinks well of him-

self in both capacities, and Hotspur cannot restrain his spleen. He dis-
likes pompous fools as much as he does fops, and forgets that the success
of his enterprise is dependent on Glendower's aid. The three chief rebels
sit down at conference to divide up the soil of England among them.
This, as a spectacle, we may believe would be most objectionable to
Englishmen. Glendower is disposed to be pleasant with Hotspur, who,
however, checks him at every turn (III, i, 53-55):

> *Glend.* I can call spirits from the vasty deep.
> *Hot.* Why, so can I, or so can any man;
> But will they come when you do call for them?

Glendower does not appear with his troops, and, as the battle of
Shrewsbury approaches, Hotspur receives news of further defections
(IV, i). Hotspur greets each one as if it were a gain. He had said before
(I, iii, 201-2),

> By heaven, methinks it were an easy leap,
> To pluck bright honour from the pale-faced moon,

and, confronted now by the absence of Northumberland, he says,

> I rather of his absence make this use:
> It lends a lustre and more great opinion,
> A larger dare to our great enterprise,
> Than if the earl were here.

And so he goes forward to defeat in battle and to death at the hands
of Prince Hal, a noble sacrifice to the exaltation of that worthy. But
Shakespeare nevertheless does take Hotspur seriously as a tragic hero,
as witnessed by a moment of final suspense which he arranges. After
the fashion of heroes, Prince Hal offers to fight the issue out with
Hotspur in single combat (V, i). In such a meeting a happy solution
might have been found, and there are also gleams of hope of reconciliation
in the third scene of the fourth act. It is evident that to Shakespeare the
fall of the gallant Hotspur was a matter of note.

In proportion as the serious historical interest goes down, as it does
in *2 Henry IV*, the comic scenes increase. The humor in that play is more
varied and profound, though perhaps more conventional, than is that of
1 Henry IV. Falstaff is given a page to set him off, so diminutive that
Falstaff says (I, ii, 11-12),

> I do here walk before thee like a sow that hath overwhelmed all her litter but one.

Indeed, the baiting of Falstaff has become a regular feature of the comedy (ll. 6-11):

> Men of all sorts take a pride to gird at me: the brain of this foolish-compounded clay, man, is not able to invent any thing that tends to laughter, more than I invent or is invented on me: I am not only witty in myself, but the cause that wit is in other men.

The relation with the judge of the law, here called Lord Chief-Justice, which had come down from the original Henry V play, is exploited in *2 Henry IV*. It was recounted in the story as a scandal how the young prince, seeking a release from the clutches of the court for an offending follower of his, probably Bardolf, had struck a justice on the bench and, prince though he was, had been punished by the judge. The episode as such does not appear in these plays, but is referred to a number of times. In the second scene of the first act is a memorable interview between Falstaff and the Chief-Justice (ll. 62 ff.). Falstaff at first pretends to be deaf, with very comic effect; but later the defect disappears (ll. 185-221) and Falstaff escapes by a most intelligent use of his privilege as a soldier:

> *Ch. Just.* You follow the young prince up and down, like his ill angel.
> *Fal.* Not so, my lord; your ill angel is light; but I hope he that looks upon me will take me without weighing: and yet, in some respects, I grant, I cannot go: I cannot tell. Virtue is of so little regard in these costermonger times that true valour is turned bear-herd: pregnancy is made a tapster, and hath his quick wit wasted in giving reckonings: all the other gifts appertinent to man, as the malice of this age shapes them, are not worth a gooseberry. You that are old consider not the capacities of us that are young; you do measure the heat of our livers with the bitterness of your galls: and we that are in the vaward of our youth, I must confess, are wags too.
> *Ch. Just.* Do you set down your name in the scroll of youth, that are written down old with all the characters of age? Have you not a moist eye? a dry hand? a yellow cheek? a white beard? a decreasing leg? an increasing belly? is not your voice broken? your wind short? your chin double? your wit single? and every part about you blasted with antiquity? and will you yet call yourself young? Fie, fie, fie, Sir John!
> *Fal.* My lord, I was born about three of the clock in the afternoon, with a white head and something a round belly. For my voice, I have

lost it with halloing and singing of anthems. To approve my youth further, I will not: the truth is, I am only old in judgement and understanding; and he that will caper with me for a thousand marks, let him lend me the money, and have at him!

Some of the scenes of the comedy are continuations of the themes and situations of *1 Henry IV*, such, for example, as the Hostess's attempt to have Falstaff arrested for debt (II, i) and the second and fourth scenes of the same act, all of which are noteworthy examples of Shakespearean comedy. The second shows the Prince's return to Eastcheap and contains Falstaff's famous letter (ll. 130-46):

> *Poins.* [*Reads*] 'Sir John Falstaff, knight, to the son of the king, nearest his father, Harry Prince of Wales, greeting.' Why this is a certificate. . . . 'I will imitate the honourable Romans in brevity:' he sure means brevity in breath, short-winded. 'I commend me to thee, I commend thee, and I leave thee. Be not too familiar with Poins; for he misuses thy favours so much, that he swears thou art to marry his sister Nell. Repent at idle times as thou mayest; and so, fare-well.
>   'Thine, by yea and no, which is as much as to say, as thou usest him, *Jack Falstaff* with my familiars, *John* with my brothers and sisters, and *Sir John* with all Europe.'

The fourth scene of this great comic act is perhaps the most Rabelaisian scene in the plays. It shows Falstaff in his glory as master of his domain in Eastcheap. The Boar's-Head Tavern is not Poosie-Nansie's, but here is staged the low point in Prince Hal's youthful wildness. So vicious is it that some critics have entertained the absurd idea that this scene and other low comedy scenes in the play are intended to present the degeneration of Falstaff, although Falstaff from the beginning thrives on degeneracy. In this scene the Ancient Pistol makes his appearance, and we become acquainted with Doll Tearsheet. One bit is unforgettable in its depiction of command (ll. 189-217). Pistol remarks with his characteristic inconsequentiality,

> Die men like dogs! give crowns like pins! Have we not Hiren here?

Hostess, alarmed and desirous as usual to keep the peace, replies,

> O' my word, captain, there's none such here. What the good-year! do you think I would deny her? For God's sake, be quiet.
> *Pist.* Then feed, and be fat, my fair Calipolis.
> Come, give's some sack.

'Si fortune me tormente, sperato me contento.'
Fear we broadsides? no, let the fiend give fire:
Give me some sack: and, sweetheart lie thou there.
                    [*Laying down his sword.*
Come we to full points here; and are etceteras nothing?
Fal. Pistol, I would be quiet.
Pist. Sweet knight, I kiss thy neif: what! we have seen the seven stars.
Dol. For God's sake, thrust him downstairs: I cannot endure such a
fustian rascal.
Pist. Thrust him downstairs! know we not Galloway nags?
Fal. Quoit him down, Bardolf, like a shove-groat shilling: nay, an a'
do nothing but speak nothing, a' shall be nothing here.
Bard. Come, get you down stairs.
Pist. What shall we have incision? shall we imbrue?
                    [*Snatching up his sword.*
Then death rock me asleep, abridge my doleful days!
Why, then, let grievous, ghastly, gaping wounds
Untwine the Sisters Three! Come, Atropos, I say!
Host. Here's goodly stuff toward!
Fal. Give me my rapier, boy.
Dol. I pray thee, Jack, I pray thee, do not draw.
Fal. Get you downstairs.

Having, so to speak, exhausted the possibilities of the older group,
Shakespeare resorts to Justice Shallow and his *ménage* or *entourage.* The
Justice Shallow scenes are rich in rather general satire. Justice Shallow is
vain and fussy, is, as somebody said, "a selfish and greedy gull." In him
the country justice of the peace, a contemporary "character" like those
in Overbury, is presented for exploitation by the shrewd old rascal from
the city. With it is combined the also current satire of the abuse of the
king's press. Falstaff, with Bardolf's help, accepts only those draftees
who are unable to buy themselves out. Falstaff pockets the money. He
continually enlightens the audience about Shallow, who has many of the
qualities of the "old grad" (III, ii, 325-55).

The scene of the famous ragged regiment (*1 Henry IV*, VI, ii) fits
in with the corruption of the draft, and one would say that Falstaff has
a genius for luck, were it not for his amazing ability to make use of
the material at hand. For example, he has wasted so much time in Glouces-
tershire that he arrives late for the battle, or rather the settlement.
Prince John of Lancaster is ready to fall upon him, but Falstaff has

captured Coleville of the Dale (IV, iii); that famous rebel gave himself away gratis, and the disciplinarian hand is stayed. Not that Prince John is gracious; Falstaff stays behind to account for the Prince's surliness on the ground that he abstains from sack (ll. 92-135). *2 Henry IV* is a triumph of Shakespeare's humor.

The historical plot of the play, however, is of no value, a mere tractate on rebels, so that one turns for the serious excellence of the play to the old romantic episode of Hal's removal of the crown from the bedside of his dying father (IV, v). This Shakespeare's genius has made into a scene of deep human significance. The father-son relationship, not without its repeated conflicts in the world, is perfectly presented. Henry IV shows his characteristic sternness in his reproaches against his son, and the new greatness of that youth nowhere shines out more magnificently than in the manner in which he receives his father's reproaches. The King, and with him England, has won. The wild young Prince has somehow developed qualities which will make him the greatest of English kings.

6. *Henry V.*

To understand what it is that Shakespeare has done with his favorite character it is necessary to resort to a common doctrine of the Renaissance, the qualities of the true prince. Normal, moral, efficient manhood seems often to be the commonplace thing. Shakespeare had the task of making his audience realize the significance of normal virtues. Milton had this same demonstration to make in the case of Adam; and Thackeray came near succeeding with it in Henry Esmond. Shakespeare displays his king in the framework of Justice, Temperance, Fortitude, and Wisdom. The idea of the perfect prince or governor was an old one in Shakespeare's day and is still an idea of great importance. *Henry V* illustrates these virtues in the action of the play, not formally in terms of the four Platonic virtues, but essentially in the conduct of the King. No doubt Shakespeare has heightened his effort to exalt the commonplace by his splendid gift of eloquence and his deep appeal to patriotic feeling. These enabled him to cast a light of glory over his hero and his deeds, and Shakespeare uses every occasion to endow his hero with his own knowledge about life. He had learned the fundamental importance and the wide appeal of human nature, or humanity. He therefore loses from beginning to end no opportunity to show how human his hero is.

Shakespeare begins the play of *Henry V* with his usual ideational clarity. The dialogue between the Archbishop of Canterbury and the Bishop of Ely (I, i) brings out the kingly accomplishments of the new monarch. Henry V, we are given to understand, has the qualities of a real king as the Renaissance understood the matter. He is a scholar—knows divinity, commonwealth affairs, war, and policy. When he speaks we discover that he is an orator. The second scene of the first act reveals the new king's careful sense of justice. He investigates his claim to the French crown and gets advice from the best authorities, and in this area of justice, the particular field of kings, one sees him strong, not only in distributive justice, but in corrective justice. He punishes the traitors, Scroop, Cambridge, and Grey, displaying, as he does so, natural, righteous indignation. His judgment is in the form of an invective (II, ii, 79 ff.).

The brilliant assault on Harfleur (III, i) shows King Henry's courage and his mastery of the psychology of combat (ll. 5-17):

> But when the blast of war blows in our ears,
> Then imitate the action of the tiger;
> Stiffen the sinews, summon up the blood,
> Disguise fair nature with hard-favour'd rage;
> Then lend the eye a terrible aspect;
> Let it pry through the portage of the head
> Like the brass cannon; let the brow o'erwhelm it
> As fearfully as doth a galled rock
> O'erhang and jutty his confounded base,
> Swill'd with the wild and wasteful ocean.
> Now set the teeth and stretch the nostril wide,
> Hold hard the breath and bend up every spirit
> To his full height.

Henry's courage is, however, properly tempered with prudence, so that it is true fortitude. He would rather not fight at Agincourt, because he is ill-prepared to do so; but, if he has to fight, he will fight bravely and in the wisest way (III, vi, 173-4):

> We would not seek a battle, as we are;
> Nor, as we are, we say we will not shun it.

Henry V is definitely religious, and no man could show a greater zeal to get God on his side. His private prayer on the night before the battle of Agincourt (IV, i, 306-22) is a model of humility and confession:

O God of battles! steel my soldiers' hearts;
Possess them not with fear; take from them now
The sense of reckoning, if the opposed numbers
Pluck their hearts from them. Not to-day, O Lord,
O, not to-day, think not upon the fault
My father made in compassing the crown!

He has no foolishness in his heart as regards the superiority of kings.
He knows, just as Shakespeare knew, that kings are men. In the wise and
reasonable words he says to the soldiers while he is walking among them
in disguise (IV, i, 103-246) and in the soliloquy that follows, he puts
stress, as Shakespeare does elsewhere, on the overwhelming responsibilities
of kings. Surely these opinions on kingship which Shakespeare attributes
to his great hero at a crisis in his life are very close to Shakespeare's own
opinions. The allegiance of his soldiers means merely that the battle in
which they are about to engage is a common enterprise, not the King's
battle only or mainly. There are moving scenes within the English camp,
and in the battle the King shows himself wise, merciful, appreciative of
the service of others, and yet stern where sternness is required. The play
ends in the glory of national victory, presented, not as conquest, but as
justice and the will of God, as if it were regarded as the restoration of a
rightful king to his kingdom.

In the last scene of the play we have presented an aspect of Henry V's
character for which this play and its predecessors have hardly prepared
us. It no doubt fulfilled an ideal of Shakespeare's age to show this king
without a trace of sentimentality. He will lay firm hands on that which
belongs to him. He loves France so well that he will not part with a
village of it. That disposition to claim his rights belonged to him and
no doubt made him more attractive to the audience. But his manners are
another matter. Although his wooing of the Princess Katherine is a very
funny scene, very charming on the stage, one is hardly prepared to see
him suddenly become actually bluff and boisterous, qualities admired in
King Henry VIII and of course attractive to the Elizabethan audience.

Henry V has in it little dramatic conflict, but is a positive hero play
almost epic in its nature. One would not minimize the greatness of
Shakespeare's representation or the splendid character of his hero. King
Henry V has his personal struggles, which display his courage, his wisdom,
his essential democracy, his piety, and his charm. The play, moreover, has

great variety. The humor of the play is second only to that of the Henry IV plays. Ancient Pistol takes the lead and goes through triumphantly (V, i, 90-4):

> Well, bawd I'll turn,
> And something lean to cutpurse of quick hand.
> To England will I steal, and there I'll steal:
> And patches will I get unto these cudgell'd scars,
> And swear I got them in the Gallia wars.

The rest of the Falstaff group disappear, and one quotes with pleasure Dr. Johnson's note:

> The comic scenes of The Histories of Henry the Fourth and Fifth are now at an end, and all the comic personages are now dismissed. Falstaff and Mrs. Quickly are dead; Nym and Bardolf are hanged; Gadshill was lost immediately after the robbery; Poins and Peto have vanished since, one knows not how; and Pistol is beaten into obscurity. I believe every reader regrets their departure.

But Fluellen must have gone back to Wales and talked mightily to the effect that the mines and their concavities should be according to the true disciplines of the wars. He must have talked also about Alexander the Pig and about the ceremonies of the wars, and the cares of it, and the forms of it, and the sobriety of it. He no doubt said again and again that there was no tiddle taddle or pibble pabble in the camp of Pompey the Great.

Fluellen's humor and that of the wooing of the princess accord well with the temper of the last member of the great Lancastrian tetralogy, which begins with *Richard II* and ends with *Henry V*. The last of the group is a play of noble sentiment, exalted rhetorical poetry, and deep human appeal.

CHAPTER VII

The End of the Century

THE MERRY WIVES OF WINDSOR
TWELFTH NIGHT
JULIUS CAESAR

1. *The Merry Wives of Windsor.*

AS WE have thus far traced Shakespeare's development in drama we have seen him as an original genius transforming nearly everything he touched and creating by his inventiveness the greatest features of a great age of the drama. The story is not all told, and we shall see that Shakespeare at the end of the sixteenth century had still further progress to make. Meanwhile we have for consideration three workmanlike plays of great popular appeal. The first of these is *The Merry Wives of Windsor,* which might have been treated along with the Falstaff plays, but which, because it is not in entire harmony with those plays, has been reserved until now. It is an excellent play on the stage, and has a long history of theatrical success all over the world. It is not, however, a great literary performance. The style is not usually distinguished. The action is not altogether consistent. There are relatively few memorable passages in the play. One recalls the Welsh parson's remark that "Seven hundred pounds and possibilities is goot gifts." "We burn daylight" is a phrase that everybody knows, and most people know "Happy man be his dole!" Other expressions, like "Your hearts are mighty and your skins are whole," and "I have a kind of alacrity in sinking," are not forgotten.

There are two versions of the play; neither one is very satisfactory, and yet they seem both to be necessary in order to make up as true a modern text as is possible. There is a version in quarto published in 1602, and there is also the longer, better text appearing in the First Folio of 1623. The relation of these versions has long been debated, and, on this occasion, one cannot argue about origins and versions, but can only state what seems to be plausible and probable.

At some date, probably in the spring of 1597, Shakespeare wrote *The Merry Wives of Windsor*. A tradition reported by Charles Gildon (1710), following Dennis (1702) and Rowe (1709), declares that Shakespeare wrote the play to please Queen Elizabeth, "who had obliged Shakespeare to write a Play of Sir John Falstaff in Love." Gildon adds, "which I am very well assured he performed in a fortnight." A reason for believing in the truth of this story is that the play shows evidence of haste in composition. Shakespeare evidently seized upon an old play which combined a number of Italian stories and rewrote it to serve the Queen's turn. It has been suggested that the old play which Shakespeare revived was the "Jealous Comedy," now lost, which belonged to Shakespeare's company. This may be true, but there is no way of determining the matter.

No one version of the widely disseminated story parallels the plot of *The Merry Wives*, but they all present the incident of a lover's courting two or more women at the same time. The women confer, and, when the gallant arranges love intrigues with two of them on the same night, he is involved, as Falstaff is, in consequences more or less disastrous, or at least humiliating, to himself. There is also usually the feature of the jealous husband. It looks as if Falstaff had been, as it were, thrust into an old play, some parts of which may actually have been left standing as in the original. The picture of Falstaff is a disappointment to those who appreciate the masterful quality of that character in the Henry IV plays. Falstaff is fooled by some very ordinary people and made too much of a butt; he usually talks like himself, but not always. Sometimes he seems to utter words written apparently for the silly philanderer who played his rôle in the intrigue of the old comedy, and the impression made on the reader is most offensive. It may be, of course, that Shakespeare had not learned to interpret the character of his own comic hero, but it seems more likely that Shakespeare was in a great hurry. *The Merry Wives of Windsor* is unique in the convincing picture it draws of the lives of ordinary Elizabethan citizens.

It seems likely that the First Folio version, with a certain rather large amount of error, preserves the play as Shakespeare wrote it, the corruptions being in part due to a bad manuscript, which may have had in it, when it was set up by the Folio printers, pages from the source play. Of course, the manuscript being in bad shape, Heminges and Condell, the compilers of the First Folio, may have had it transcribed for the printer. Such a transcription would account for the gathering together at the opening of each scene of the names of the characters who were to participate in the scene instead of the usual practice of recording the entries of the late comers when they appear. This form in the copying of plays was used for Latin comedy and for Jonson's plays. A transcriber following such a method may also have omitted stage directions, many of them because they were illegible or considered unnecessary in a printed play. It is hardly necessary to believe with Dover Wilson that the copy for the play was assembled by piecing together actors' parts. The quarto of 1602 has not these defects, but has numerous faults of its own. It does not seem to be based immediately on the Folio version, but possibly on an earlier draft of the play by Shakespeare. It has features and words which are perhaps derived from the source play, and it may have been merely an acting version of the play as Shakespeare first wrote it.

Shakespeare's work in revamping the old play was much more carefully done in the earlier parts than in the later. It needed to be so in order to implant in the play Falstaff and his followers—Bardolf, Pistol, Nym, and Mistress Quickly. The followers are all brought over neatly and naturally enough except Mistress Quickly, who has been much elevated socially. She is here a quite respectable person. The truth of it is that she is playing another rôle, a sort of Italian *balia* type, a person who makes herself useful in arranging matters of courtship and marriage. The latter part of the old comedy would not need much alteration and might in part have been allowed to stand. It may have been known to the actors and would have saved time in rehearsal. The chances are that Shakespeare's hand was withheld from the latter part of the play, or hastily employed in order to save time, although there are Shakespearean touches throughout. Certainly the minor escapades at first planned for Bardolf, Pistol, and Nym are simply let slide. The old play must have been prepared for enactment at Windsor, and Shakespeare worked very badly and very hastily on those parts of the fifth act which serve to give a Windsor setting. One wonders whether or not the episode of Herne the Hunter appeared in the original comedy. Perhaps it did.

The Folio version is bad toward the end; so is the quarto version, and so are many Elizabethan plays. Memories broke down toward the end of a play, and prompt-books had to record the plays as they were intended to be spoken. The quarto of 1602 is apparently an ordinary stage version made up about 1597 from something very like the Folio version, in order to be carried in the repertory of a traveling company; at any rate Shakespeare had changed the name of "Oldcastle" to Falstaff before the quarto copy was made up. This road company was unfamiliar with certain scenes of the original, and they may have supplemented their play with parts of the old comedy, with which they may have been familiar. These problems are very puzzling, but one may justify oneself for writing thus much about them on the ground that readers of Shakespeare anxious to form right views of the great master need warning when they approach *The Merry Wives of Windsor*, a play touched with Shakespeare's finest comic genius and yet a hasty piece of work and not completely his. This comparatively simple explanation of Shakespeare's handling of the Falstaff plot saves the necessity of believing in various traditional theories: as, for example, that Shakespeare in *The Merry Wives* consciously depicted a further degeneration of his comic hero, or that he meant to write a caricature of his own treatment of Falstaff in the Henry IV plays. The suggested theory, in other words, attempts in the light of probable circumstances to ascertain what is the actual content of *The Merry Wives* and to suggest what probably happened in its composition.

One must, however, remember that we have to do in *The Merry Wives of Windsor* with a comedy of real dramatic merit. It is one of the liveliest comedies in dramatic literature. It has greatness in dramatic situations; and situations, rather than wit, are the basis of English comedy. There is a wealth of incidents, all presented in a breathless bustle. Falstaff's plot against the virtue of Mistress Ford, for example, is betrayed to Ford by the unexpected treason of Nym and Pistol. They might have done such a thing, although it seems out of character. Of course, they are merely taking over rôles from the old comedy. Ford disguises himself as Brook and makes up to Falstaff, whose ironic abuse of Ford to his face is a joy to hear. Falstaff's two escapes, or near-escapes, are simply marvels of ingenuity—one in the buck-basket with the soiled linen (ending in the Thames) and the other as the witch of Brainford (when he is beaten justly though in altered guise). Of course, Falstaff is the same Falstaff.

His casual comments prove it, and we only wish that he had made more of them. Does he not say in his unmistakable voice (V, i, 23-5):

> He beat me grievously, in the shape of a woman; for in the shape of man, Master Brook, I fear not Goliath with a weaver's beam; because I know also life is a shuttle.

Falstaff is less certainly himself in the fifth act when he says (V, v, 51-2),

> They are fairies; he that speaks to them shall die:
> I'll wink and couch: no man their works must eye.

He is evidently speaking (in verse, mind you) words written for his silly predecessor. But one does recognize his own incorrigible insolence when he says (in prose): "Heavens defend me from that Welsh fairy, lest he transform me to a piece of cheese!"

It is not the major plot only that makes *The Merry Wives* successful on the stage. The minor plot is very delightful and is fitted into the major plot perfectly, serving there as a perfect foil. The Pages have a charming daughter, Anne. Page wants to marry her off, for the sake of the dowry, to a vapid simpleton, Abraham Slender, cousin to Justice Shallow. Slender is merely the Silence of *2 Henry IV* renamed. Of course, Slender is a mere type in comedy, a fool with lands and beeves, like Sir Andrew Aguecheek in *Twelfth Night*, who is offering himself, or in this case being offered, as a husband for an eligible lady. Anne is amused at Slender, and Mistress Page treats him like a stray dog. Mistress Page disagrees with her husband. She wishes to marry Anne off to a peppery French doctor named Caius, whom Anne has no intention of accepting. Anne prefers a gentleman named Fenton, very sympathetically presented, although he too is a common enough type in the comedy of the time. He has wasted his own fortune in gay living. Elizabethans loved the spectacle of the young gentleman sowing his wild oats and were always happy to see him recoup his fortune by marrying a rich wife. Bassanio himself is such a type. But Anne Page accepts Fenton as her choice and elopes with him, so to speak, from under the noses of her parents and their lieutenants. Shakespeare was conscious of parental authority, but he always sides with true love. The abortive duel between the fiery Welsh parson, Evans, and the mercurial Frenchman, Dr. Caius, is a masterpiece entirely comparable to the encounter between Viola, disguised as Caesario, and Sir Andrew Aguecheek, a coward both in nature and by instinct, in *Twelfth Night*.

2. *Twelfth Night.*

Twelfth Night, first mentioned in Manningham's *Diary* on February 2, 1601-2, is often regarded as Shakespeare's most perfect comedy. It is certainly a drama of very careful workmanship. It has behind it a complexity of slightly differing sources which have been carefully fused together. Like *The Merchant of Venice* it has something allegorical to say about the nature of true love, and like *As You Like It* it has a great clown. An added feature is an episode in contemporary satire in which Shakespeare ridicules and punishes an upstart servant, Malvolio. The spectacle of the over-ambitious servant aspiring beyond his station was no doubt abominable in the eyes of the Elizabethan upper-classes; and here again, as in *The Merchant of Venice,* a change in social sentiment has caused even great actors to distort the comedy by making Malvolio unpleasantly threatening, if not actually tragic.

Twelfth Night is indeed excellent in workmanship—in plot and minor plot, liveliness and variety of incident, and sharply drawn characters. Structurally it is a joy. No wonder it has been singled out as Shakespeare's most perfect comedy. Those who have so regarded it have usually had in mind, not only that Shakespeare has outdone himself, but that in *Twelfth Night* he has approached most nearly the hard and glittering objectivity of Latin comedy, and of Jonson, Molière, and Congreve. The so-called pure comedy of these worthies, much admired, refuses to have pity for folly, or even for misfortune of a sort. It takes no sides in the issue between the rogue and his dupe. It likes the spectacle of the biter bit, but it also adds "the rod for the fool's back." The idea that *Twelfth Night* is Shakespeare's nearest approach to the comedy of wit and the comedy of spectacle is attractive enough; and yet, for all that, *Twelfth Night* is a romantic comedy. The impression of its detachment arises in part from the fact that it is the most realistic of Shakespeare's Italianate comedies. This comedy of romance and ideal love is played against a background of what many believe was a familiar upper-class English household, that of the Lady Olivia, with some contributions from the Duke's *ménage.* There are also two sea captains, both of an honest, kindly type perhaps not unfamiliar on the streets of London.

These minor characters are all strongly worked out. Sir Toby Belch is highest in point of rank, since he is a cousin of Olivia. He makes her mansion his own and disturbs it with his rioting. He is often called a less effective Falstaff and he is played so on the stage; but the conception of him is different. He is better established in the community, more of a Will Wimble, more gratuitously mischievous than Sir John, and probably younger. Shakespeare thinks well enough of Sir Toby to marry him off to the lively and attractive little Maria. It is notable that, having had his head broken by Sebastian, he repudiates drunkenness and abusively rejects Sir Andrew Aguecheek (V, i, 206-14). Sir Toby is much less of a veteran in vice than Sir John and certainly is much less complex. Reformation for Sir Toby would be an entire possibility. He guzzles outrageously, loves to play pranks, and in an unvicious sort of way fleeces the foolish knight, Sir Andrew, who adores him. Sir Toby is unscrupulous, but his treatment of his dupe is not so much for greed and villainy as for the fun he gets out of it. That fatuous cavalier Sir Andrew Aguecheek is the ordinary gull of comedy, but Shakespeare, as usual, has individualized him. Sir Andrew is very self-conscious, with just brains enough to have an inferiority complex, which, we may believe, does not require exceptional brains. He desires to excel in all knightly accomplishments, but is not only riotously inept, but has a genius for getting things wrong. He says of Malvolio (II, iii, 135-8):

> 'Twere as good a deed as to drink when a man's a-hungry, to challenge him the field, and then to break promise with him and make a fool of him.

He wants to dance and evidently cuts the most ridiculous capers. He even envies the Fool his voice (II, iii, 19-22):

> By my troth, the fool has an excellent breast. I had rather than forty shillings I had such a leg, and so sweet a breath to sing, as the fool has.

With great difference in "humour" and unbecoming lack of courage, he is much like Stephen in *Every Man in his Humour*; and his part along with Sir Toby and the others in the group justifies one in saying that the underplot of *Twelfth Night* is indeed an excursion on Shakespeare's part into the field of the pure comedy of Jonson. Sir Andrew in his main function is, like Slender, a prime example of the foolish wooer, very well individualized. Fabian is a colorless but useful character.

The steward, Malvolio, was Shakespeare's nemesis in pure comedy. His very name seems to indicate that Shakespeare regarded him as an ill-natured person, and he is. Malvolio is a precisian—Shakespeare refuses to call him a Puritan—a precisian not from scrupulous morals but from jealousy of the pastimes of others. Sir Toby hits him and his kind off to the world's satisfaction when he says, "Dost thou think, because thou art virtuous, there shall be no more cakes and ale." In his capacity as a steward Malvolio is not without dignity (of a self-conceited kind), responsibility, and usefulness, so that the Lady Olivia says she would not have him miscarry for half her dowry, but it is she who tells him he is "sick of self-love." He is a prig and belongs to the well-hated class of upper-servants who persecute their inferiors and seek to extend their authority into fields where it has no necessity or propriety. He is called an "affection'd [or affected] ass," and his exaggerated superior bearing offers opportunity for caricature. There is no reason for picking Malvolio from this group of pure comedy characters to become the hero of a minor tragedy.

There is also the pert, witty, tiny Maria, "the youngest wren of nine," she who is nicknamed "Penthesilea" after the Queen of the Amazons. She is described in the bill as "Olivia's woman," but it is not correct to think of her as an ordinary servant. As companion to her mistress, she would have belonged to a respectable family, and in Shakespeare such women have matrimonial prospects. She is educated, is well steeped in the ways of the world, and is evidently a favorite of her creator. Those rather snobbish critics who declare that Sir Toby is "entangled" because of his own naughtiness and is punished by making a *mésalliance* with a "servant" are certainly reading their own social scruples into the play. Maria is no doubt socially and certainly culturally quite the equal of Sir Toby Belch. He needs a manager and does well by himself in securing the clever Maria.

Finally, in this realistic world, there is Feste the Clown, the perfect clown, equipped, like Armin, for whom the part was written, with a theory of clownage. Like Touchstone in *As You Like It* (V, iv, 111-12),

> He uses his folly like a stalking-horse and under the presentation of that he shoots his wit.

But Feste goes further, for Viola thus describes him (III, i, 67-72):

> This fellow is wise enough to play the fool;
> And to do that well craves a kind of wit:
> He must observe their mood on whom he jests,

> The quality of persons, and the time,
> And, like the haggard, check at every feather
> That comes before his eye.

Feste likewise has his authorities on whom he calls. There is Pigrogro-
mitus, of whose works we have no trace except that he seems to be an
authority on "the Vapians passing the equinoctial of Quebus," and Qui-
nalpus, from whom Feste has preserved the gem, "Better a witty fool
than a foolish wit." Feste is a master of language, and to him must be
assigned that masterpiece of pig-Latin: "I did impeticos thy gratility."
He sings, he jests, he executes practical jokes, and in his comments on
action and character succeeds in his own way the melancholy Jaques. By
his songs he does no small amount in bridging the gap between the
ordinary world of the underplot and the elevated romantic world in which
the major characters move. Please observe that it is Feste who sings, "O
mistress mine, where are you roaming?" and "Come away, come away,
death." He closes the play with the quaint and gay note of

> When that I was and a little tiny boy,
> With hey, ho, the wind and the rain,
> A foolish thing was but a toy,
> For the rain it raineth every day.

Before we consider the romance of that world, we might call attention
to the fact that the low comedy of Shakespeare was usually not slap-stick
stuff, and that no comedy suffers more on our modern stage than does
Twelfth Night by having applied to it the technique and make-up of the
comic strip. Scenes of revelry in the play, such as the third scene of the
second act and the second scene of the fourth, are usually played so
grotesquely and with such affected utterance that they are unintelligible.
In point of fact, the dialogue of *Twelfth Night*, even in such scenes as
these, has, perhaps, more allusions, witticisms, innuendoes, and general give
and take than the dialogue of any other play. This witty dialogue must
have been written by Shakespeare to be understood and appreciated, and,
although much of it has no doubt lost its point and application, it is certain
that our way of acting scenes of low comedy was not the Elizabethan way.

The worship of love has its own ritual, its own liturgy, and in the love
plot of *Twelfth Night* there is much beautiful poetry. The blank verse
itself is on a high level expressive of exalted sentiment, and it is this senti-

ment, its genuineness and sincerity, which makes *Twelfth Night* as a whole a romantic comedy like *As You Like It* and *Much Ado*. The first scene is like the overture of an opera, which suggests that we are, so to speak, in fairyland and that, in that land, values, motives, and behavior will be different. The fact that we later learn that Orsino's passion is not to be taken too seriously should not interfere with our immediate acceptance of him as a lover. He is a refined, youthful, sentimental character, endeavoring, to be sure, to languish away as best he can because of unsatisfied love. He is nevertheless *euphues*—handsome, well-born, noble in principles. His education has taught him the lore of love such as that possessed by sonneteers (I, i, 1-15):

> If music be the food of love, play on;
> Give me excess of it, that, surfeiting,
> The appetite may sicken, and so die.
> That strain again! it had a dying fall:
> O, it came o'er my ear like the sweet sound,
> That breathes upon a bank of violets,
> Stealing and giving odour! Enough; no more:
> 'Tis not so sweet now as it was before.
> O spirit of love! how quick and fresh art thou,
> That, notwithstanding thy capacity
> Receiveth as the sea, naught enters there,
> Of what validity and pitch soe'er,
> But falls into abatement and low price,
> Even in a minute: so full of shapes is fancy
> That it alone is high fantastical.

His attitude toward his mistakenly chosen beloved is noble (ll. 33-41):

> O, she that hath a heart of that fine frame
> To pay this debt of love but to a brother,
> How will she love, when the rich golden shaft
> Hath kill'd the flock of all affections else
> That live in her; when liver, brain and heart,
> These sovereign thrones, are all supplied, and fill'd
> Her sweet perfections with one self king!
> Away before me to sweet beds of flowers:
> Love-thoughts lie rich when canopied with bowers.

The conception of the play as a romantic comedy is borne out by the title—*Twelfth Night, or What You Will*. Twelfth Night was traditionally a time of jokes and merry-making. It is the feast of Epiphany, celebrating, on January 6, the visit of the Magi to the infant Jesus at Bethlehem. The title of the play suggests the unpredictable gaiety of the feast, and the reference is to the major plot; for we have as subject for *Twelfth Night* the rather improbable love-adventures of the identical twins, brother and sister, Sebastian and Viola. Various comic situations arise from the mistaking of one for the other, and all perplexities are ended when they finally meet and recognize each other. We may therefore anticipate that such a story turned into a comedy will move toward an assembly of characters in the last scene, and such is the construction of *Twelfth Night*. It is a comedy of errors, and the making of a play about an indistinguishable brother and sister is merely a sensational variant of the story of the identical brethren borrowed in *The Comedy of Errors* from the famous *Menaechmi* of Plautus. Even the variant used in *Twelfth Night* was widely distributed. Twice employed in Italian comedy, once as the anonymous *Gl' Ingannati* (1531), it was early translated into French, and into Latin as the comedy *Laelia*, acted at Queen's College, Cambridge, in 1595. The story appears in Bandello and in Belleforest. Shakespeare knew several versions of the story when he wrote his play, and among them certainly "Apollonius and Silla" by Barnaby Riche in his *A Farewell to the Military Profession* (1581). There are unmistakable parallels between Riche and Shakespeare. There seems also, as usual, to have been an old play, now lost, on the subject, which Shakespeare probably followed. That old play may be the original of the late German comedy *Tugend und Liebestreit*. Sources have been found for all episodes in *Twelfth Night* except the plot against Malvolio.

The plot management of *Twelfth Night* is really exquisite, so contrived as to bring into juxtaposition contrasts in character and point of view, usually ironical, but sometimes as natural as life. Orsino woos the rich Countess Olivia, and this wooing serves excellently to provide by delay for a happier solution than their union could ever have been. His wooing, except at the very end of the play, is by deputy, for his self-generated love is not of the kind that desires to confront the lady or could perhaps endure such an encounter. Orsino is in love with being in love.

Viola is a young lady who has a great deal of trouble. She contrasts well with both Orsino and Olivia. She has been shipwrecked off the coast of Illyria and has lost her brother, so she thinks, at sea. She goes for protection to the court of Orsino, and for further protection she puts on man's apparel. Very different is she from her prototype in the old story, who is a professed man-hunter. Viola merely goes so far as to admit that she has heard her father speak of Orsino; she falls in love with her master. She has yet the courage and honesty to carry out the bitter task of acting as Orsino's love messenger. There is nothing wooden about her; she is quite feminine, and there is no cleverer touch in the play than her insistence on seeing the face of her rival (I, v, 248-61):

> *Oli.* Have you no more to say?
> *Vio.* Good madam, let me see your face.
> *Oli.* Have you any commission from your lord to negotiate with my face? You are now out of your text: but we will draw the curtain and show you the picture. Look you, sir, such a one I was this present: is't not well done? [*Unveiling.*
> *Vio.* Excellently done, if God did all.
> *Oli.* 'Tis in grain, sir; 'twill endure wind and weather.
> *Vio.* 'Tis beauty truly blent, whose red and white
> Nature's own sweet and cunning hand laid on:
> Lady, you are the cruell'st she alive,
> If you will lead these graces to the grave
> And leave the world no copy.

It occurs to one that what Olivia really needs to awaken her out of her sentimentality is a wooer of the Caesario-Sebastian type and not of the type of Orsino. Viola has to go through the harrowing experience of appearing on the field of honor, and at the end her dear master considers taking her life because he thinks her a traitor. She has many troubles, and it is no wonder that she is a sad and wistful person. No hardship could be worse than being the companion and confidante of Orsino in his agonizing love for Olivia. Shakespeare has put Viola into a scene, even into a speech, very expressive of her situation. In one of the most beautiful episodes of the play (II, iv), after the clown has sung "Come away, come away, death," the Duke instructs Viola on the nature of love, a subject about which he really knows very little but thinks he knows everything (ll. 107-21):

> *Duke.* What dost thou know?
> *Vio.* Too well what love women to men may owe:
> In faith, they are as true of heart as we.
> My father had a daughter loved a man,
> As it might be, perhaps, were I a woman,
> I should your lordship.

Duke.   And what's her history?
Vio. A blank, my lord. She never told her love,
But let concealment, like a worm i' the bud,
Feed on her damask cheek: she pined in thought,
And with a green and yellow melancholy
She sat like patience on a monument,
Smiling at grief.

The Countess Olivia is the third of the major figures. We have heard of her as the object of Orsino's fruitless passion. When she appears it is in the midst of her lively and varied household in conversation with the Fool, who makes it appear that Olivia is also something of a sentimentalist, if not a fool. She mourns unreasonably the death of her brother, enjoys her grief, and, marriageable as she is, refuses to entertain the advances of any lover—something of an offense in Renaissance eyes. Cupid, however, takes a hand, and at the moment when she turns her back disdainfully on one who is suffering for love, she herself becomes a sufferer. She falls in love at first sight with Caesario.

Structurally the introduction of Sebastian is a matter appropriate to the first act, but for want of space we do not see him until the first scene of the second. After he appears, we have four individuals, the necessary number for two weddings, and our task from this time forward is merely to get them properly paired. Sebastian arrives on the coast in company with a sea captain, Antonio, devoted to Sebastian. Antonio follows Sebastian to the ducal court where there is a price on Antonio's head as an enemy to the state. The plot does not amount to a great deal; its complications are like those of *The Comedy of Errors*. On her very first visit Viola is not only loved by Olivia but receives an overture of love in the form of a ring. The ring is sent after Caesario by Malvolio; the scene between them is one that can be very funny on the stage. On her next visit the Countess makes love to Caesario openly—titivating feature of the identical brother-sister plot, since it shows one lady making love to another. Viola protects the lady's reputation, but the favor in which she is held is observed by Sir Toby. In order to keep Sir Andrew in line, he arranges to have Sir Andrew's famous challenge prepared, and the duel between mutually reluctant Viola and Sir Andrew follows. This serves to tie the two groups together with the utmost security and skill; for when Antonio, Sebastian's friend, sees a person whom he believes to be Sebastian, involved in a duel, he rushes to the rescue. This causes his arrest as an alien enemy and informs Viola that her brother still lives and is near at hand. It also begins the untying of the knot, and that suddenly. Sir Toby sees that Caesario is an acknowledged coward; even Sir Andrew sees it, and they resolve to pursue their vengeance. They see Sebastian, mistake him for Caesario, set upon him, and get their heads broken for their pains. The lady Olivia interferes, as she thinks, in behalf of her darling Caesario. When she offers him her hand and heart, Sebastian is bewildered but prompt in his acceptance. Those who wonder why he so readily absorbs the goods the gods provide will never understand the age of Queen Elizabeth. Sebastian and Olivia are promptly married.

The complications, however, are not entirely over. Viola is the heroine of *Twelfth Night*, and she has more to endure. She has in the nick of time accompanied her master, who has finally decided to pay his court in person. A change has taken place in him, and many believe sentimentally that it is due to the unconscious influence of Viola. He wants a wife, not merely wants to be in love—a very different state of mind. Olivia at once claims Caesario as her husband and has witnesses to prove that he (she) has married her. Orsino turns in a rage on Viola to take her troubled life, and she is quite willing to be a sacrifice; but Sebastian enters, brother and sister recognize each other, and explanations ensue. Orsino is delighted to find that the lovely boy to whom he has been so much attached and with whom he has had such soulful conversations about love and lovers, is really a woman. He accepts her joyously and immediately as his wife. We approve of this, but we do not like the suddenness of it. We quarrel with the Elizabethans for their sudden changes of mood and passion. There are two explanations, both of which are satisfactory. The faulty psychology of the Elizabethans provided for just such sudden changes by the belief that the heart, being full of the spirits of one passion, might be emptied at once like a cup emptied of one liquid and at once refilled with another. Then, too, Orsino has not been in love at all until that moment; he has merely thought he was. True love may have begun in his heart at that moment, and his affection for Caesario may have lent power and speech to his love for Viola.

The plot against Malvolio also comes to an end in the great assembly scene. It too is explained and Malvolio is liberated. He sees how he has been gulled, and his vanity is wounded. He leaves the stage saying, "I'll be revenged on the whole pack of you." The rôle of Malvolio is a deeply marked character part, interesting in the opportunity it gives those who act it. In this play there is no other part more attractive to mature actors. It has therefore been customary in revivals of *Twelfth Night* to cast in the part some great tragic actor. Such actors have almost uniformly made Malvolio's last exit an alarming thing unpleasantly suggestive of the cutting of throats. It was no trivial matter to have Sir Henry Irving leave the stage vowing vengeance. It must be wrong to end this comedy on such a sour note. It cannot have been Shakespeare's intention to arouse tragic sympathy by the punishment of Malvolio. Malvolio was an upstart servant aspiring to his mistress's hand and imagining himself fitted for the exalted station of gentility. That was enough to condemn him before an Elizabethan audience, for, try as we will, we cannot make the Elizabethans democratic. They loathed the word, and did not have in mind even the concept. Add also that Malvolio was a humourless, "affection'd ass," offensive to his fellows, a busybody, who got what was coming to him. Olivia says (V, i, 359-63),

> Prithee, be content:
> This practice hath most shrewdly pass'd upon thee;
> But when we know the grounds and authors of it,
> Thou shalt be both the plaintiff and the judge
> Of thine own cause.

And when he leaves, Orsino says (l. 389),

> Pursue him, and entreat him to a peace.

Shakespeare certainly meant that Malvolio was to be appeased, and let us hope he had learned his lesson.

3. *Julius Caesar.*

Besides *Titus Andronicus* and *Romeo and Juliet*, the only tragedy Shakespeare wrote before the end of the sixteenth century is *Julius Caesar*, a play widely removed from both the earlier works. He had by the year 1598, to which *Julius Caesar* is usually assigned, had further experience in the dramatization of history, and the poise and patience of the history plays appear in *Julius Caesar*. It is not a clear-cut tragedy like his earlier or later ones, but blends and combines its themes. He wrote it to some extent in the tradition of the neo-Senecan drama of France and Italy, which had treated Plutarch's great Romans. The Plutarchan conception which underlay these plays is still present in Shakespeare. Plutarch had learned from literature and tradition the Greek doctrine of Nemesis, namely, that Fate strikes down at their crest the favorites of fortune. Shakespeare has thus unified his tragedy in the figure of Brutus, for it is easy to see that Brutus in the one part is laying the basis of his downfall in the other. It is interesting to speculate upon whether or not Shakespeare when he wrote *Julius Caesar* had already begun to realize the great background of human destiny he was later so clearly to define in *Hamlet*.

In order to be able to think about human life as a unity, to comprehend it, and to generalize it, one has to have some sort of ideal form. Consider the differing results if one thinks about life as a school, a battle, a pilgrimage, or a journey. We must have some form by which we may organize our thought. To the Greeks life was typically either a tragedy, or, if comic, a burlesque entertainment or practical joke. Serious, significant life was organized by means of a rubric of tragedy: man in high station (obscure persons did not count) was born, grew to higher and higher station until he reached a summit, then declined to his end, which was wretchedness, failure, and destruction. Divinity ruled it so. The religion of the Greeks helped them to arrive at this concept, because their gods were jealous and fate was determined that no man should achieve permanent happiness and complete success on earth. Now this concept was a great and lasting invention. It still holds and always will. Nature itself seems usually to follow this pattern. There is a constant ebb and flow, action and reaction in physical nature. All life takes on the pattern of youth, maturity, and old age. Power grows up to a certain usually ascertainable point, then hesitates, then declines to extinction. Most enterprises of individuals and of races begin, grow to maturity, and then decline.

So widespread and so convincing was this concept of the Greeks that it lasted for hundreds of years, was taken over by the Romans, impressed itself on Christianity, and appeared in almost universal acceptance in the Renaissance, when the classics were revived. For our purpose it will be sufficient if we say that the late Greek writer Plutarch carried over the Greek idea of what a human life was like and presented an organization of the lives of famous Greeks and Romans in parallel series. Each Greek, such as Alexander the Great, usually had his parallel among the Romans, such as Julius Caesar. Now, life is not always like a Greek tragedy, but it often tends to take that form. It was necessary for Plutarch to reshape both Greek history and Roman history, Roman history particularly. He had to chop it out of the brush. Plutarch was a very popular author in the Renaissance, and it happens that Shakespeare knew and used repeatedly North's translation of Amyot's French translation of the *Bioi Paralleloi.* It was, as one will see, an excellent source, a source in which the spadework of writing tragedy had already been done.

But when we have spoken of the Roman plays of Shakespeare we are by no means through with the influence of the Greek or Plutarchan idea on Shakespeare. It happens that when Renaissance historians went to work to write history in the classical manner, they too recast and reconceived their princes and potentates of the more recent world in quite classical terms. To do so they had to reshape their history into Plutarchan or Greek forms. For example, Polydore Vergil, an Italian at the court of King Henry VII, reshaped the English chronicles, gave the Yorkists the blacker parts to play. Life can be trimmed here and expanded there until it assumes the familiar pattern of rise, turning-point (or climax), descending struggle, catastrophe, and extinction.

The historians were the great re-shapers, but there was another even more important (because literary) channel through which the Plutarchan idea impressed itself on British history and the history of other nations. Petrarch knew the Greek idea and accepted it. He believed that life takes on the pattern of rise and fall, and that fate can be relied upon to strike down at their very summit all those who rise like tall towers to positions of power, eminence, and happiness. Indeed, the idea had lived on through the Middle Ages. Petrarch wrote *De Casibus Virorum Illustrium,* Chaucer imitated him in *The Monk's Tale,* Lydgate translated him with additions, and in the wake of Lydgate came the famous *Mirror for Magistrates,* the most complete expression of the idea of the fall of princes in the age, a work which afforded subjects for dozens of dramas and had of itself a mood of its own—stories of the downfalls, not only of princes, but of many other men of importance. Patrick Henry had the idea in mind when he said before the House of Burgesses, "Caesar had his Brutus; Charles I his Cromwell; and George III . . . may profit by their example."

Holding in mind Plutarch's rubric, we may begin in Roman history with Caius Marius (we could begin with the Gracchi). Let us imagine a play in which Caius Marius overcomes his enemies. That play would **not** be his tragedy; it would be theirs. Then a play, the tragedy of Caius Marius, in which he is overcome by Sulla. Then a tragedy of Sulla, in which he is overcome by Pompey. Then a tragedy of Pompey, in which he is overcome by Caesar. Then a tragedy of Caesar, in which he is overcome by Brutus and Cassius. Then a tragedy of Brutus, in which he is overcome by Antony. Then a tragedy of Antony, in which he is overthrown by Octavius Caesar. *Cetera desunt*, since Augustus is on the throne and the Roman empire has begun. Shakespeare in *Julius Caesar* has combined on a wide canvas two of these events. In the first Caesar is cadent and Brutus crescent; in the second Brutus is cadent and Antony crescent. Because *Julius Caesar* treats two of these units and covers a long range of events it is natural that its technique should be partly that of tragedy and partly that of history play. There are other resemblances to history plays in *Julius Caesar*, arising no doubt from political parallelism. The Renaissance was opposed to tyrannicide and regarded the populace as a mob. There is no doubt that in the series as a whole Octavius was a sort of Richmond.

It is easy to see why the play is called "Julius Caesar"; for, not only was the fall of Julius Caesar the most important event of the ancient world, but the play in its first major movement is actually his tragedy. Since the play presents the complete story of the rise and fall of Brutus and only the fall of Caesar, certain mistakes have been made in the interpretation of Caesar's rôle, which has been subordinated. Indeed, certain casual details in Plutarch as to the weakness of the falling hero have been exaggerated, and Shakespeare has been thought to have blackened the Caesar of Plutarch and to have made him the victim of these weaknesses rather than the victim of a larger fate. It is said that he has been made deaf, vain, superstitious, and boastful. The truth of the matter is that Caesar was these things and at the same time the greatest man in the world. The effect of vanity and boastfulness is an accidental result of the compression of the characterization. If one considers the Caesar scenes in the light of Antony's "mighty, bold, royal, and loving" (III, i, 127), one will find that they carefully project each of these epithets. The north star-Olympus speech (III, i, 58-74), in view of the fawning behavior of the conspirators and the apparent unreason of the false petition, should be set down as an expression of his masterful pride and of his surprise and disgust. In the circumstances it reveals no weakness and only a towering exaltation of Caesar's own superiority in strength and sincerity. His superstition is less than Calpurnia's, less than Casca's; a great deal less, in point of fact, than was safe for Caesar. So far as the play concerns Caesar, it presents the ancient theme of regicide vs. tyrant; but one looks in vain for any evidence that Shakespeare thought highly of the republicanism of Brutus, and it is pretty plain that Shakespeare's sympathies were on the side of Caesar, whose downfall involved the world in sedition and civil war. Cassius is clearly subversive, and his motives are selfish and personal. The cry for freedom is a fraud, and the accusation of tyranny without "colour."

In the case of Brutus we have another sort of tragedy, largely a tragedy of character. It is a tragedy of mistaken loyalty, of impracticality, of a man too great and good for his age, time, and associates. In so far as Cassius is entitled to be considered a tragic hero, and he is not without his claims, he, an essentially good man, plays the unattractive rôle of the villain-hero (I, ii, 312-26). He starts with cynicism, malice, and jealousy, and his tragedy is that of the practical man who lacks the strength to carry through his efficient ideas. He is in practice constantly thwarted by idealism. To this day in the world the hard-headed practical man is helpless when he opposes theory and idealism. Cassius attempts to wield forbidden and impossible power, but cannot master it because he cannot master Brutus. The two are foils, and one cannot help seeing them in a general figurative sense as well as in a narrow realistic sense. Shakespeare represents Cassius as always right, but Brutus stands over him like the conscience of the world. The heart of the play is made up of their differences, and the momentous issues between theory and practice are dramatized in their famous quarrel (IV, ii, iii).

It is impossible for a conspiracy to thrive and succeed on such a basis as Brutus lays down in his soliloquy (II, i, 10-34), which begins "It must be by his death." Brutus agrees to the destruction of Caesar for strictly theoretical and conjectural reasons. When the conspirators meet in the same scene Brutus makes in noble rhetoric three separate serious errors (ll. 114-183). He prevents the conspirators from binding themselves by an oath. Oaths were important matters in the ancient world, since no man wanted to incur divine vengeance, and Plutarch knew it. Oaths had not lost their spiritual power in Shakespeare's day. Brutus prevents their including Cicero and thus robs them of the greatest voice of the age.

Cicero would have enjoyed debating with Mark Antony. Finally, Brutus refuses to have them include Antony in their attack against Caesar. Cassius knows the danger of letting the versatile Antony live, but Brutus saves him with a sentiment.

Shakespeare seems, as the conspiracy ripens, to be very conscious of Portia. The first scene of the second act depicts her in unforgettable terms and generalizes for all men the bond between husband and wife. She demands the confidence of her husband and seems to get it (ll. 292-308):

> I grant I am a woman; but withal
> A woman that Lord Brutus took to wife: . . .
> *Bru.* All my engagements I will construe to thee,
> All the charactery of my sad brows.

That Brutus had the loyalty of Portia one may be sure; that he proceeded against her advice one may only surmise from her agitation in the last scene of the act.

The next clash between the practical wisdom of Cassius and the ideal sentiment of Brutus is after the assassination (III, i, 143-6). The question at issue is whether they should attempt to win Antony over to their side. Cassius knows it is a matter of self-interest purely. Does he not say to Antony when they meet (ll. 177-8),

> Your voice shall be as strong as any man's
> In the disposing of new dignities?

But the most disastrous of Brutus's victories over Cassius is the permission given Antony to speak at Caesar's funeral. Brutus says (ll. 236-7),

> I will myself into the pulpit first,
> And show the reason for our Caesar's death.

Does he think that truth will be accepted because it ought to be? And what a calamity fell upon them by their permitting an unscrupulous orator to address a mob! The Elizabethans would have made no mistake in this matter. The oration of Brutus is in prose in the best Attic style. It is, as an appeal to reason, a marvel of clarity; but there was no reason in that assembly to appeal to. Antony's style is perhaps Corinthian, and yet it is not so florid as to hinder it from being a perennial model of incitement to action. It is in verse. He avows peaceful intentions and ingratiates himself, according to custom, with undeniable platitudes (III, ii, 80-1).

> The evil that men do lives after them;
> The good is oft interred with their bones.

Then he proceeds, again according to pattern, with definition. Caesar was said to be ambitious; what is ambition? As he destroys the value of the charge he uses ironically the figure of iteration (l. 97).

> Ambition should be made of sterner stuff.

He gains further sympathy by a display of personal emotion. If you wish men to weep, you must weep yourself (l. 111):

> My heart is in the coffin there with Caesar.

Then begin Antony's suggestions for action, a perfect ladder of suspense (ll. 126-49).

> O masters, if I were disposed to stir
> Your hearts and minds to mutiny and rage, . . .
>   I rather choose
> To wrong the dead, to wrong myself and you, . . .
> Let but the commons hear this testament—
> Which, pardon me, I do not mean to read—
> And they would go and kiss dead Caesar's wounds
> And dip their napkins in his sacred blood, . . .
> It is not meet you know how Caesar loved you.
> You are not wood, you are not stones, but men;
> And, being men, hearing the will of Caesar,
> It will inflame you, it will make you mad.

Then comes suggestion by pretended restraint (ll. 156-7):

> I fear I wrong the honourable men
> Whose daggers have stabb'd Caesar; I do fear it.

Then comes the introduction of object and symbol; they will view the body of Caesar (ll. 174-7):

> You all do know this mantle: I remember
> The first time ever Caesar put it on;
> 'Twas on a summer's evening, in his tent,
> The day he overcame the Nervii.

Thus Antony visualizes the scene of Caesar's death for conviction and the heightening of emotion. The bow is well bent. The mob is shouting, "Revenge! About! Seek! Burn! Fire! Kill! Slay!" But he does not let them go. Like a masterly archer he puts his body behind the bow and gives the bowstring those final inches which make for distance and deadliness (ll. 211-14):

> Good friends, sweet friends, let me not stir you up
> To such a flood of mutiny. . . .
> What private griefs they have, alas, I know not,
> That made them do it.

Then with the orator's trick of putting the burden and responsibility on the audience, he, with a final pull at the bowstring, releases the shaft (ll. 221-34):

> I am no orator, as Brutus is;
> But, as you know me all, a plaiŋ blunt man,
> That love my friend; . . .
>   but were I Brutus,
> And Brutus Antony, there were an Antony
> Would ruffle up your spirits and put a tongue
> In every wound of Caesar that should move
> The stones of Rome to rise and mutiny.

He then repeats the terms of the will, an act held skillfully back until that moment. "Now let it work."

The adversaries have taken the field. The armies of Brutus and Cassius are near Sardis, the ancient capital of Lydia in Asia Minor. There is an issue between Brutus and Cassius, and it is a familiar one. Cassius supports his army by extortion; it lives off the land, as many armies have lived before and since. Brutus spares the peasantry and is dependent for his support on the war-chest common to him and Cassius. Cassius has refused to share with Brutus, and Brutus is indignant. They return to Brutus' tent to discuss the matter. Then occurs one of the most famous dialogues in all Shakespeare, admired for its passion, its manliness, its give and take. Cassius is overcome (IV, iii, 86, 110):

> A friend should bear his friend's infirmities. . . .
> O Cassius, you are yoked with a lamb.

The reconciliation is a victory for Brutus, and this appears in the decision to give battle at once to their enemies at Philippi. Cassius is against it, and he is right. He is again beaten down by the high mystery of the idealist (IV, iii, 213-24):

You must note beside,
That we have tried the utmost of our friends,
Our legions are brim-full, our cause is ripe:
The enemy increaseth every day;
We, at the height, are ready to decline.

If the facts conform to these propositions, Brutus is also right; but he shuts out the answer by a noble sentiment that overwhelms Cassius.

There is a tide in the affairs of men,
Which, taken at the flood, leads on to fortune;
Omitted, all the voyage of their life
Is bound in shallows and in miseries.

There is no arguing against such eloquence, but we learn that Brutus has played into the hands of Antony and Octavius.

Brutus is one of the bravest of all men. Where is there such courage as that with which he confronts the ghost of Caesar (IV, iii, 281-87)?

Ghost. To tell thee thou shalt see me at Philippi.
Bru. Well: then I shall see thee again?
Ghost. Ay, at Philippi.
Bru. Why, I will see thee at Philippi, then.

Brutus was a good soldier, and it is a trick of fate that, in spite of the mistake in strategy, Brutus' army is victorious; it is Cassius who is defeated. The battle is presented by a series of crucial scenes, mainly between individuals, and is one of Shakespeare's more successful stage battles. Through it is woven a recognizable thread of fate. The battle is lost, in part at least, by accident, and the scenes seem to say that no plans of man are certain and that no human character is steadfast. Note the discussion by Brutus and Cassius (V, i, 93-126) as to what they will do "with the worst that may befall." The scepticism and realism of Cassius, the Epicurean, break down, and he begins to believe in portents as expressive of the higher divine will; but for once he wins his argument with Brutus. He converts Brutus, a Stoic who believed in bearing the very worst to the very end, to the Epicurean doctrine that, when life no longer has value, it should be ended with suicide.

The farewell speech of Marcus Brutus (V, iv, 31-42) was long a puzzle to me, but ultimately I thought I saw a great vision that had come before the eyes of Shakespeare, a vision such as that which closes *Hamlet*.

Countrymen,
My heart doth joy that yet in all my life
I found no man but he was true to me.
I shall have glory by this losing day
More than Octavius and Mark Antony
By this vile conquest shall attain unto.
So fare you well at once; for Brutus' tongue
Hath almost ended his life's history:
Night hangs upon mine eyes; my bones would rest,
That have but labour'd to attain this hour.

It is an odd saying that Brutus, of all people, has "found no man but he was true to me," until it is remembered that it is the fate of truth on earth that it must be believed. This "noblest Roman of them all" held "in a general honest thought" the "common good to all." Even his enemies believed in him. If we doubt the justice of posterity, let us think of Woodrow Wilson, his general reputation at the present time, and the misfortunes which he encountered after the first World War.

CHAPTER VIII

The Great Trio: Hamlet, Othello, King Lear

SHAKESPEARE established the dominant form of Elizabethan drama. The dominant form in a literary age is normally the one that represents that age most truly and vividly. It was Shakespeare whose presuppositions about life were most probable. What he had to say about man, his nature, and his interests represents the Elizabethan age best and agrees best with the hypotheses about man habitually made by impartial and enlightened humanity, both living and dead. Pleasures and pains, success and failure, aspirations and discouragements, joy and sorrow, righteousness and sin are the things which we believe are correctly conceived of and assessed by Shakespeare. This is not merely a consequence of Shakespeare's genius; it is also a matter of representative quality, culmination of literary trend, and faith in human life. Shakespeare was never diverted from the great probabilities of existence.

In the history of the development of every art form, both before and after the dominant form establishes itself, but usually after it reaches maturity, many sub-species make their appearance. Some of these sub-species, so to speak, outlive the dominant form and in later ages themselves generate new dominant forms, just as the Restoration comedy of wit arose out of the earlier comedy of manners. The Shakespearean type of romantic drama was quickly superseded by variations and new inventions within the general frame. Men like Dekker and Heywood were not caught up in the new current; but younger men of genius somewhat akin to Shakespeare's, like Beaumont and Webster, followed new fashions, and we shall never know what they might have done had they followed the older one.

This theory does not rest, of course, on dramatic talent or other merit.

It rests on the validity of the hypotheses about life which are entertained
by literary men themselves. At the beginning of the seventeenth century
there came into existence a new and less catholic, less broadly probable,
way of looking at life, and at the same time there appeared certain clever
and dominating literary men who saw life in the new way. These men
were innovators, ingenious, often learned and authoritative, and uncompromising from the superiority of their culture. Marston, Chapman, Jonson and his followers, Beaumont and Fletcher, Middleton, and later Webster were critical, worldly, and disillusioned. They were easily able to
modify the dominant type established by Shakespeare, not, of course, completely; but, with equal or superior technical skill, they gave us essentially
different hypotheses about life.

The age had changed with some suddenness. The new generation as
representatives of the new times were not worse dramatists than Shakespeare; in some respects they were better; but, as representatives of the
ages, they were far inferior. They put forward clever, ingenious, often
brilliant and far-reaching propositions about life, not so completely probable as those of Shakespeare. Writers, however great their immediate
success, pay a penalty for their deviations into the realm of the improbable
and the impossible. As Dr. Johnson says, somewhat unfairly, of Gray's
"The Bard,"

> To select a singular event, and swell it to a giant's bulk by fabulous
> appendages of spectres and predictions, has little difficulty, for he
> that forsakes the probable may always find the marvelous. And it has
> little use; we are affected only as we believe; we are improved only
> as we find something to be imitated or declined.

There were reasons, social, political, and philosophical, for the narrowing of the national mind in the early seventeenth century. James I was
on the throne, a moralist without moral character and a learned man
without the humanistic spirit. Elizabeth had been contented to possess
absolute royal power without too much justification. James I was actually
more anxious about the establishment of the theory of divine right than
about the actuality of sovereignty. Elizabeth dominated her court and,
by and large, in accordance with the times, kept it in order. James I's court
quickly became a scandal in an age of growing licentiousness. Elizabeth
ruled even her favorites and was conspicuous for her ability to choose her
ministers and to rule them and rule through them. James I was favorite-

ridden; flattery was the only road to his favor, so that the perniciousness of the flattering courtier and corrupter of princes, preached against in the reign of Queen Elizabeth, became an actuality in the reign of her successor. Partly for these reasons, but also for others, English patriotism waned. Men grew less enamored of the country; many of them no doubt were ashamed of it. Elizabeth had avoided war as a matter of policy, but James truckled in a cowardly way and bargained·unskillfully.

The theater soon began to have a different and a narrower appeal. The Puritans had been subdued, many of them banished, but their morals had been neither subdued nor banished. These were on hand to work havoc in the consciences of those citizens, mainly of the burgher class, who had sympathized with the Puritans often, without joining them. The theater became in the minds of a large part of the population an embodiment of sin and wickedness. It is usually said, and no doubt in part truly, that the theater in which the earlier plays of Shakespeare were performed had all classes of people within it; whereas the theater of Beaumont and Fletcher, Middleton, and Ford, had within it mainly the courtly classes, their hangers-on, and the socially irresponsible part of the population. That the theater became an appendage to the court party and was regarded with more and more aversion by soberer citizens is borne out by the fact that when Parliament rose against the King in the next reign, one of its first acts of reform was to close the playhouses. No doubt the audience, in so far as it was made up of the courtly classes, was far more intelligent than was the audience of the previous generation; but it was less representative, so that the stage spoke, not to all men, but to men with somewhat specialized interests.

An illustration of the fallacy of taking a part for the whole, itself so pervasive as to be a general characteristic of seventeenth-century drama, was a mistaken psychology.[1] If Aristotle wrote a psychology of the passions, it did not come down to posterity except in part in the *Rhetoric*, but Galen had given a full account of the subject and had lent it his authority. His theory of the relation of the bodily humors to the passions and of the passions to morals had been well known in the ancient world, in the Middle Ages, and in the Renaissance and was an established way of thinking and

---

[1] The word "psychology" did not come into use until the end of the seventeenth century. It is, however, convenient to employ it here to designate the mental science of the earlier time.

talking about feelings, desires, and mental states. It had been held that reason could and should control the passions through the will, but the soundness of the theory had never been tested by putting it into close application. Images were yielded by the senses to the imagination and were referred to the heart. The spirits rushed thither or rushed away to the periphery, and motion resulted, but reason sat in his central cell and was the arbiter. For some reason this body of false science, based on a false physiology, suddenly sprang into great popularity just at the end of the Renaissance. It underwent extensive and varied exploitation. The psychology of the passions was a mechanical system, agreeing in its parts and supported by much particular observation, which pretended to explain human action by a formula. Shakespeare himself was affected by the newly revived stoic psychology of the passions, although to him it was mainly a heightened way of talking about feelings and emotions and possibly a means of explanation. Some of the modernists, such as Jonson, Chapman, and Ford, took psychology seriously and used it, mechanical and inadequate as it was, as a guide in the conception of character and action.

Another way of saying this is to declare that satire and criticism superseded moral suasion, exhortation, proverbial wisdom, and faith in example; so that realism displaced romance. This statement can be true only in a general sense, but it has truth in it, and much of the criticism of the morals of the Jacobean and Caroline drama has failed to take account of the important change in ethical theory above described. The ethical field was constantly narrowed until in the Caroline period many dramas actually followed code morals and drew their sanctions from cults and coteries. It is important for the appreciation of the post-Shakespearean drama that justice should be done to its authors, and to such justification as may be derived from a less representative audience and from a narrowing moral code they are entitled. It will be found that aside from these limitations Shakespeare's successors in the drama were for the most part honorable as well as able men.

1. *Hamlet.*

Shakespeare's influence in shaping what we have described as the typical form of Elizabethan drama did not come to an end with the sixteenth century or even with the end of Queen Elizabeth's reign, although by 1600 the forces of satire, science, and criticism were already at work. *Ham-*

let may be regarded as the culmination of Shakespeare's shaping influence. He was to make other great contributions later, but *Hamlet* is central to his achievement as a dramatist. There is reason for thinking that he wrote the play in its final form about the year 1601. The first quarto version, a stage version based on Shakespeare's original and degentrated by acting on the stage, has been possibly revamped from the authorized form, since it has parts derived verbatim from the true text. The first quarto was entered in the Stationer's Register in 1602, and the full version must have been in existence at that time. There is a reference to Shakespeare's *Hamlet* in Gabriel Harvey's *Marginalia*, which is usually thought to have been made between 1598 and 1601, so that *Hamlet* may be taken as a starting point for the new century. The play, it may also be said, shows an awareness on Shakespeare's part of the new way of thinking. The ethical contest in the play is not so much between passion and reason as between passion and a self-mastery which leads to indifference to the blows of fortune. In other words, the contest has a stoical rather than an Aristotelian basis. Shakespeare in *Hamlet* sees man's situation in the broadest possible way, but the remedy for human ills that he proposes and works out triumphantly is stated quite definitely in stoical terms.

The scope of *Hamlet* is very broad. It is a tragedy of the battle of life; of willingness to live; of human affliction, trouble, disgust, and grief; of an individual who is also the prospective head of the state and a member of a family. *Hamlet* therefore appeals to the widest variety of persons, for it lies close to the most general issues of life. Critics have been engaged for generations in plucking the heart out of Hamlet's mystery, in explaining the play away; but they have failed, because they have not been content to rest their case on the simple thesis that *Hamlet* is well nigh universal in its appeal and so continues in the center of human interest. Goethe thought of *Hamlet* as the tragedy of an over-refined nature in a rude generation. Coleridge almost convinced the world that *Hamlet* is a tragedy of weakness of will—a tragedy in which the balance is disturbed between the real and the imaginary worlds. "Hamlet," he says, "is brave and careless of death; but he vacillates from sensibility, and procrastinates from thought, and loses the power of action in the energy of resolve." Some critics have seen in *Hamlet* a tragedy of barbarian power. In its source it is a story of cleverness opposed to armed and oppressive ignorance. Not all of these views can be true. No one of them expresses the whole truth. *Hamlet* seems to be like a fiddle on which every fiddler can play his own tunes, every critic make his own interpretation; and yet these interpretations are not equally true or equally profound.

The problem of *Hamlet* may be thus stated: Man is born to trouble as the sparks fly upward; how shall he triumph over tribulation, the universal enemy? Man's only salvation lies in self-control, control of his mind, since the frame of his being is within his own mind. Hamlet was deeply immersed in trouble, and his tendency, like that of all men, was to sink himself in what seemed to be the mire of eternal woe; but Hamlet knew there was a remedy, and it is he who says, "There's nothing either good or bad but thinking makes it so." He adds significantly the statement that to him Denmark is a prison.

It follows that to achieve happiness, one might say victory, Hamlet, like all men, must control his mind. Control of mind is a goal of the Renaissance, reinforced by stoical teachings. The Renaissance knew that unhappiness ties man's hands and leaves him in impotent misery. Man must arrive at a point where he can calmly meet his fate, no matter what it is. He must be indifferent to consequences, but he must also act. The terms of the good life, as the Renaissance saw it and as we too must see it, are a settled and balanced self-control plus action. The play of *Hamlet* rests on these two fundamentals of individual life, and, in spite of all attempts to explain it away, it continues to speak to the world. *Hamlet* cannot be ignored; it is unforgettable. It is Shakespeare's play of everyman. However much critics may declare they are not as other men, *Hamlet* returns to plague them. To say that Hamlet is troubled and hesitant is merely to say that all men are troubled and hesitant. How erroneous then is the widespread opinion in ill-informed minds that Hamlet is a special sort of person, a horrible example of doubting and hesitation; Hamlet and his solution of life's most fundamental problem are of universal and interminable significance. Shakespeare has told the story with the most perfect clarity, and it is only the preconceptions of critics which have made a mystery of this most universally applicable of Shakespeare's plays.

Some light may come from an examination of the Hamlet theme. It is an old story, and it is an axiom that a theme handed down for centuries, no matter how much its form may from time to time be altered, will retain its integrity. The essential feature of the Hamlet story is a hero beset by very powerful enemies whom he thwarts and conquers by superior shrewdness, specifically by the device of feigned insanity. Hamlet is therefore a success story, and we must grant, to begin with, that Shakespeare's Hamlet succeeds spiritually although he meets his death. The original Hamlet succeeded materially.

A riddle in an Icelandic saga describes the sea as "Hamlet's mill." The sea is the greatest of mills, because it grinds up the rocks into sand. The story of Hamlet is thus ancient and is first told at length by Saxo Grammaticus, who wrote a Latin history of Denmark about 1200 A.D., published at Paris in 1541. It was the practice of the sixteenth century to hunt up good stories and republish them, and the tale of Hamlet was retold in French by Belleforest in *Histoires Tragiques* (third story of the fifth volume) in 1570. An English version of this story, *Historie of Hamblet* (1608), may go back in an edition now lost to a date nearer Belleforest. In this story Fengon murders his brother, the elder Hamlet, having previously seduced his queen, whom he now marries. Hamlet undertakes to revenge his father's murder on the powerful usurper and feigns madness in order to allay suspicion and make his vengeance sure. It is thus a story of delayed and careful revenge. Hamlet is suspected of vengeful intentions, and three separate attempts are made to get him to betray himself. His cunning enables him to defeat each of the three attempts; these three attacks will be recognized as the structural elements of Shakespeare's plot. The first is made by Hamlet's own deceitful companions. He sees through their wiles and makes fools of them (see *Hamlet*, II, ii, 224 and III, ii, 302). The second attempt is made by putting in his way a woman, since it is thought that men under the influence of love betray themselves most readily. Hamlet escapes, but one asks if this feature of the old plot determines in any measure Hamlet's rather cruel attitude toward Ophelia. The third attack is by a clever courtier, who arranges an interview between Hamlet and his mother and hides himself under a pile of straw (evidently the royal couch) in order to overhear the conversation. Hamlet mounts on the straw, crows like a cock, discovers the hidden courtier, and stabs him, crying out "A rat." He disposes of the courtier's body by cutting it into bits and feeding it to swine, a situation which seems to reveal that in mediaeval Denmark the royal palace had a royal pigsty near at hand. These events may do something to account for Hamlet's callousness about the killing of Polonius in Shakespeare. A fourth attack is also provided by Saxo in the sending of Hamlet to England. There is no adventure with pirates, but Hamlet witnesses the death of his deceitful companions, returns to Denmark, and kills, not only Fengon, but all the courtiers by the device of a net let down on them while they are drunk and asleep. It is staked down with certain crooked sticks which Hamlet has been sharpening in the fire. The hall is then burned and Hamlet's enemies perish. Hamlet, now triumphant, returns to England and marries two wives successively. One of them betrays him to his death and marries his slayer.

Before Shakespeare wrote *Hamlet* the story had been reshaped as a tragedy omitting all the latter part. This job was probably done by Thomas Kyd. It is pretty clear from the famous *Epistle to the Gentlemen Students of both Universities*, prefixed to Greene's *Menaphon* (1589), that Kyd was the author of a revenge tragedy, with a ghost in it, on the subject of Hamlet, and such a play is known by several allusions to have been on the boards and to have been notorious for bombast. From Nashe's *Epistle* and from these allusions one can form some idea of what the old play was like, and, if *Der Betraffte Brudermord*, a German *Hamlet* preserved in a late form, is a degenerate version of Kyd's play, one can go still further in determining what had been done to the theme before Shakespeare handled it. It is certain that the Ghost was added by Thomas Kyd and practically certain that so also was a play within the play; probably also the madness of the heroine and the adventure with pirates. The sparing of the King at prayer for the savage reason of slaying his soul as well as his body, the fencing bout with poisoned foils, the poisoned drink, and Hamlet's final achievement of vengeance and death are in the German play; they have a Kyd-like quality in their intrigue. It is certainly highly probable that the German *Hamlet* is descended directly from the old *Hamlet* by Kyd, for it is certainly not descended from Shakespeare's *Hamlet*. It presents the story in more primitive form and is closer to Belleforest's version than is Shakespeare's play. The German versions of English plays of the period were introduced into Germany mainly in the last decade of the sixteenth century by English actors under the patronage of various German princes. Of those which have been preserved no one of them represents a Shakespeare original; most of them are pre-Shakespearean.

It must be admitted that, so far as features of the plot are concerned, Shakespeare's share in *Hamlet* is relatively small, and we must look to spirit and treatment for his real contributions. Into the warp and woof of the drama he wove his brightest threads. Every character, major and minor, has been realized at the height of Shakespeare's great powers, and his style shows nowhere more vigor. To his genius we may attribute specifically the gentle, obedient, sweet-tempered Ophelia; the just, judicious, and courageous Horatio; the valiant and competent Fortinbras; the Gravediggers with their thrill of mortality; the fantastic Osric; and the strangely puzzling, womanly, sinful Queen, who hoped, it will be remembered, to deck Ophelia's bride-bed when she became Hamlet's spouse. From her Shakespeare lifts some part of the black load of guilt she inherited from the source. Above all there is the characterization of Hamlet.

Shakespeare makes clear in many places what kind of man Hamlet is. He has Hamlet comment most wisely on the drunkenness of the court (I, iv, 13-38). Hamlet often speaks with princely wisdom about affairs of state. Ophelia's heartbroken comment beginning, "O, what a noble mind is here o'erthrown!" expresses the Renaissance ideal of noble manhood, and Fortinbras tells us at the end of the play that Hamlet was like to have proved most royally, had he been put on. Shakespeare not only makes clear what kind of man Hamlet was, but takes pains in many places to indicate the kind of man Hamlet would have liked to be. The most remarkable of these passages is the address to Horatio (III, ii, 59 ff.) beginning

> Horatio, thou art e'en as just a man
> As e'er my conversation coped withal.

If Horatio expresses for Hamlet one side of the Renaissance ideal, that of balanced self-control, Fortinbras as clearly expresses the other. Fortinbras is a man of action, and Hamlet emulates him. Few men in the world have both gifts, and all men strive for them, so that in depicting his hero as he has, Shakespeare has delineated the common state of man. The course of Hamlet's struggle can be traced through the soliloquies and the dialogue to the point in the fifth act (V, ii, 230-35) where Hamlet gives expression to the ultimate significance of the play: ". . . we defy augury; there's a special providence in the fall of a sparrow. If it be now, 'tis not to come; if it be not to come, it will be now; if it be not now, yet it will come: the readiness is all."

To trace the steps by which Hamlet arrived at this state of mind is to master the meaning of the play. The terms of the problem of living,

as conceived both by Shakespeare's age and by ours, are two. The first
of these is courage to undertake and to do. All men hesitate to take up
arms against a siege of troubles, and all men are prone to hesitation and
discouragement. All the blame bestowed upon Hamlet as a procrastinator
rests squarely on the shoulders of all men, and they know it. They too,
if they are honest with themselves, must pause and say with Hamlet
(IV, iv, 39-44),

> Now, whether it be
> Bestial oblivion, or some craven scruple
> Of thinking too precisely on the event,
> A thought which, quarter'd, hath but one part wisdom
> And ever three parts coward, I do not know
> Why yet I live to say 'This thing's to do.'

There is also another principle widely recognized by the Renaissance
and, in appropriate form, by us. Before a man can act effectively he must
master his own soul. His hand must be guided by intelligence and his
heart fortified by wisdom. His reason must rule, and he must possess the
calmness which comes with self-knowledge and self-control. He must
learn to be indifferent to what Hamlet calls "the event." No man knows
the future, or the outcome of any moral action, and solicitude for these
unpredictable consequences must not usurp the present. Shakespeare makes
these principles abundantly clear throughout the play of *Hamlet*. The
soliloquies show Hamlet's progression toward both action and peace of
mind. Horatio stands on one side of him as a man who has self-mastery,
and Fortinbras on the other as a man to whom action is instinct.

This struggle to act and to act wisely, to discharge duty with some
indifference to consequences, is man's most typical struggle in the world.
Indeed, it is the typical struggle of the race of man against earthly environment both now and through eons of time. This is the reason why
Hamlet is one of the most significant literary works ever written by the
human hand and also the reason why *Hamlet* inescapably intrudes itself
into the minds of the civilized world. Jerome Cardan, the Milanese
physician of the sixteenth century, suffered so much from the blows of
fortune that he wrote a book *De Consolatione* in order to give himself
the courage to do, to suffer, and to be calm. There is no doubt in my mind
that Shakespeare knew this book and that it aided him in conceiving of
his most typical character.

There is no doubt about the genuineness of the troubles that beset Hamlet. His first soliloquy (I, ii, 129-59) shows him shocked, stupefied, his hand inert.

The exhortation to revenge by his father's ghost plunges Hamlet into a state of bewilderment (I, v, 97-112). He shows conviction and determination to act, but in his speech is no element of reason.

Remember thee!
Yea, from the table of my memory
I'll wipe away all trivial fond records,
All saws of books, all forms, all pressures past,
That youth and observation copied there;
And thy commandment all alone shall live
Within the book and volume of my brain,
Unmix'd with baser matter: yes, by heaven!
O most pernicious woman!
O villain, villain, smiling, damned villain;
My tables,—meet it is I set it down,
That one may smile, and smile, and be a villain;
At least I'm sure it may be so in Denmark:
              [*Writing*
So, uncle, there you are. Now to my word;
It is 'Adieu, adieu! remember me.'
I have sworn 't.

It must be remembered that action alone will not satisfy the demand; it must be wise and fitting action. Hamlet conquers his mood of frenzy, and in the most familiar of the soliloquies (III, i, 56-88) it is plain that he has progressed to a state of balance between action and inaction so typical that the world has learned the expression of it by heart. It is a question whether or not he will do anything at all:

To be, or not to be: that is the question:
Whether 'tis nobler in the mind to suffer
The slings and arrows of outrageous fortune,
Or to take arms against a sea of troubles,
And by opposing end them?

In the most seriously debated soliloquy of the play (III, iii, 73-96) it is plain that Hamlet has studied his part so well that we think him over-scrupulous. The King is at prayer, and Hamlet looks at him:

> Now might I do it pat, now he is praying;
> And now I'll do't.

Then he decides against immediate action, not through cowardice, but through thinking too precisely on the event. He still lacks that indifference to consequences which he must achieve before he becomes the perfect hero:

>   And so he goes to heaven;
> And so am I revenged. That would be scann'd:
> A villain kills my father; and for that,
> I, his sole son, do this same villain send
> To heaven.
> O, this is hire and salary, not revenge.
> He took my father grossly, full of bread;
> With all his crimes broad blown, as flush as May;
> And how his audit stands who knows save heaven?
> But in our circumstance and course of thought,
> 'Tis heavy with him: and am I then revenged,
> To take him in the purging of his soul,
> When he is fit and season'd for his passage?
> No!
> Up, sword; and know thou a more horrid hent. . . .
> Then trip him, that his heels may kick at heaven,
> And that his soul may be as damn'd and black
> As hell, whereto it goes.

Hamlet's failure to act is not due to mere procrastination. It is due to a desire to act too exquisitely, to regulate all the consequences. Coleridge reproves Dr. Johnson for "mistaking of the marks of reluctance and procrastination for impetus, horror-striking fiendishness." Neither of these two great Shakespeareans is entirely right, but of the two Johnson is the more nearly so. The standard of revenge required that the avenger should be completely evened with his victim. Cutwolfe in *Jack Wilton* follows the Italian prescription. Cutwolfe has tracked down his victim and has him at the pistol's point. For the act of revenge to be adequate he must destroy his enemy's soul as well as his body. Cutwolfe accordingly promises to spare his victim's life if the poor wretch will abjure Christ. When his enemy has cursed God and renounced salvation, Cutwolfe fires the pistol into his victim's mouth, so that there may be no recantation. Hamlet is not to blame for not killing the King; he is trying to do the thing properly, and like other human beings merely makes a mistake, which, like most mistakes, results in a greater one—the killing of Polonius behind the arras (III, iv, 31-2):

> Thou wretched, rash, intruding fool, farewell!
> I took thee for thy better.

During the period of inaction brought upon him by his misfortune Hamlet, in a very human way, keeps his courage up by blaming himself, nowhere more obviously than in the soliloquy he utters after he beholds the march of the troops commanded by Fortinbras (IV, iv, 32-66):

> How all occasions do inform against me,
> And spur my dull revenge! What is a man,
> If his chief good and market of his time
> Be but to sleep and feed? a beast, no more.
> Sure, he that made us with such large discourse,
> Looking before and after, gave us not
> That capability and god-like reason
> To fust in us unused. Now, whether it be
> Bestial oblivion, or some craven scruple
> Of thinking too precisely on the event,
> A thought which, quarter'd, hath but one part wisdom
> And ever three parts coward, I do not know
> Why yet I live to say 'This thing's to do';
> Sith I have cause and will and strength and means
> To do't.

If Hamlet is talking solely about the state of his own affairs, there is sufficient reason why he should say what he says. But is he not also talking about the affairs of all men? Is he more cowardly than are all men, and have they any guarantee against making mistakes as serious as he has made? Is it not true that "not to be receives reproach of being"?

That Hamlet has advanced to a more philosophic state of mind with reference to the value of life appears in his conversation with Horatio in the churchyard. But even the stoical conviction of the transitory nature of all things human amounts but to (V, i, 236-7)

> Imperious Caesar, dead and turn'd to clay,
> Might stop a hole to keep the wind away.

This conclusion is an element in the final adjustment, but it is not the ideal. Hard on this scene, as if to sound the warning of action and passion,

comes the great outburst at the grave of Ophelia. Hamlet has suffered
in his heart, and no array of schematic filial or public duty can prevent
all men from suffering the pangs of purely personal grief.

There is no doubt that Shakespeare meant us to understand that Hamlet
loved Ophelia dearly. There is that pitiful scene reported by Ophelia
and misunderstood by her as well as by Polonius (II, i, 75-100):

> He took me by the wrist and held me hard;
> Then goes he to the length of all his arm;
> And, with his other hand thus o'er his brow,
> He falls to such perusal of my face
> As he would draw it. Long stay'd he so;
> At last, a little shaking of mine arm
> And thrice his head thus waving up and down,
> He raised a sigh so piteous and profound
> As it did seem to shatter all his bulk
> And end his being: that done, he lets me go:
> And, with his head over his shoulder turn'd,
> He seem'd to find his way without his eyes;
> For out o' doors he went without their helps,
> And, to the last, bended their light on me.

The source history of Ophelia is very unpromising, but Shakespeare at
least gives her a trial. There is something very terrible in the testing of
that girl. Hamlet is being brought squarely up against the morals of the
Polonius family. Ophelia in obeying her father fails Hamlet both actually
and spiritually. Milton comments in *Areopagitica* on the Polonius system:

> I cannot praise a fugitive and cloistered virtue, unexercised and
> unbreathed, that never sallies out and sees her adversary, but slinks
> out of the race, where that immortal garland is to be run for, not
> without dust and heat.

There was still a chance, for love was still in the heart of Hamlet. There
is no more suggestive scene in the play than that which follows the great
soliloquy (III, i, 88-169). Ophelia has allowed herself to be used as a
decoy. When Hamlet first sees her reading in her book that "show of
such exercise may colour her loneliness," his words are the words of a
lover,

> —Soft you now!
> The fair Ophelia! Nymph, in thy orisons
> Be all my sins remember'd.

Nor does Hamlet speak with unkindness or feigned madness in the earlier part of the interview between them. His decision is against her, and he reproaches himself and fate; but he is not unkind even when he chides her,

> Get thee to a nunnery: why wouldst thou be a breeder of sinners?

But he discovers her father in hiding (an old stage custom, probably valid, has Polonius peeping out between the curtains). When he says to her, "Where is your father?" and she lies to him, his first words are anger, as sane as anything he ever said:

> Let the doors be shut upon him, that he may play the fool no where but in's own house.

After that Hamlet's words are a mixture of personal bitterness and feigned insanity. The moment, though often missed in playing the scene, is clearly marked.

We are therefore not unprepared for Hamlet's outburst at poor Ophelia's grave (V, i, 277-315), than which the passion of utterance can rise no higher. The very verse and language break down in the expression:

> Why, I will fight with him upon this theme
> Until my eyelids will no longer wag. . . .
> I lov'd Ophelia: forty thousand brothers
> Could not, with all their quality of love,
> Make up my sum. . . .
> 'Swounds, show me what thou'lt do:
> Woo't weep? Woo't fight? Woo't fast? Woo't tear thyself?
> Woo't drink up eisel? eat a crocodile?
> I'll do't. Dost thou come here to whine?
> To outface me with leaping in her grave?
> Be buried quick with her, and so will I:
> And, if thou prate of mountains, let them throw
> Millions of acres on us, till our ground,
> Singeing his pate against the burning zone,
> Make Ossa like a wart! Nay, an thou'lt mouth,
> I'll rant as well as thou.

We are therefore prepared to reread the little conversation between Hamlet and Horatio before the duel (V, ii, 219-36):

Hor. You will lose this wager, my lord.

Ham. I do not think so; since he went into France, I have been in continual practise; I shall win at the odds. But thou wouldst not think how ill all's here about my heart; but it is no matter.

Hor. Nay, my good lord,—

Ham. It is but foolery; but it is such a kind of gain-giving, as would perhaps trouble a woman.

Hor. If your mind dislike anything, obey it: I will forestall their repair hither, and say you are not fit.

Ham. Not a whit, we defy augury: there's a special providence in the fall of a sparrow. If it be now, 'tis not to come; if it be not to come, it will be now; if it be not now, yet it will come: the readiness is all: since no man has aught of what he leaves, what is't to leave betimes? Let be.

It is usual to say that a typical tragedy is concerned with a conflict of wills and with a great personality engaged in a struggle that ends disastrously. This definition applies to Œdipus, Agamemnon, Faustus, Othello, and Macbeth. It hardly applies to Hamlet, who was never the minion of fortune. Hamlet struggles through an existence very full of danger and distress and, as regards the future, disastrous. So far as one can see, there is no question of praise or blame. He merely confronts his life as you and I confront ours, and ultimately finds a remedy for its evils. He has never occupied a high position from which he might be cast down by the jealousy of the gods or the Nemesis of his own misconduct. His movement is upward, not downward. Like Prometheus, and like many men and women in the world, Hamlet has a contract which calls for suffering. The same thing seems to be true of Hercules in *Hercules Furens* and *Hercules Œtaeus*. Prometheus and Hercules as well as Hamlet present the case of enforced suffering without surrender.

Does Hamlet not therefore present a different kind of tragedy from that called for in the traditional definition? Distinguished critics have seen in Hamlet a man dominated by fate in the form of extreme weakness of will. To do this is to rob the most representative of all fictional characters of his representative quality. If he is weak in will, or if he is limited by a conflict between his ideals and his realities, these shortcomings are merely those of all men. All men are immersed in difficulties. Most men care, as Hamlet did, too acutely about them and strive not too effectively to cast off the shackles of grief. Hamlet's problem is merely "Who will deliver me from the body of this death?" The representative quality of Hamlet accounts for his never being explained away by the numerous attempts that have been made to account for him as a special sort of character. He remains a hero in whom we recognize our common humanity and whose lot as a human being is perennially significant to each of us.

2. Othello.

Othello is sometimes said to be Shakespeare's most perfect, most typical tragedy. It behooves us to inquire what is meant by this.

In the beginning of such an inquiry certain elementary facts stand out. Shakespeare's tragedy is a tragedy of blood, violence, and revenge. His age called for such a tragedy and his tradition dictated it. In this kind of tragedy death was the only acceptable end. Perhaps this feature was merely Senecan tradition; perhaps it arose from the fear of death entertained in Shakespeare's time and long before. Death was indeed of common occurrence. Man strove not so much to live as to avoid death. The theology of the age held out horrid spectacles of a life of torment after death. There seems little reason to doubt that Shakespeare and his contemporaries believed in the existence of perfect villains, children of the devil, not children of God. This belief underlies the destruction of heretics and witches. In our age we sometimes doubt whether there exists a human being who steadily, persistently, and naturally desires evil. But the villainy of Elizabethan villains was a force in the world.

Such belief in absolute villainy could have been readily enough derived from Seneca but seems to have established itself on the Elizabethan stage with Marlowe's Barabas in *The Jew of Malta*. Plenty of villains had made their appearance in romantic drama before Marlowe, but he introduced the code of complete villainy with his first Machiavel. Kyd's Lorenzo in *The Spanish Tragedy* is also a Machiavel, and he has sometimes been thought earlier than Barabas. The point is that these absolute villains differ from ordinary villains in their lack of any conflict between will and conscience. But they stand somewhat apart from romantic tragedy, and it remains to be decided whether, apart perhaps from Aaron, Shakespeare has any villain of completely evil character.

Again the Elizabethans held traditionally the view that tragedy might achieve sufficient dignity and importance to be worthy of treatment only when it concerned persons of high estate—as kings, princes, great prelates,

noblemen, and heroes. The modern world has learned, in part through
Ibsen, that the mere fact of being a man has in it sufficient import to
achieve a tragic level of dignity and consequence. Modern fiction has
taught the world much about the omnipresent possibility of tragedy.
The Elizabethans probably knew this also, but without realizing it as a
doctrine and practice. There was greatness and breadth in the Elizabethan
point of view. To them, the greatest of them, the phenomenal world
was a small and alien thing, and nature was subject to time and change.
Philosophy could not then be approached through science, since no
reliance was placed on the senses. Philosophy must be sought at the
throne of God, in the stars, or in the pages of the wise men of the ancient
world. Stoicism, which is not so much a philosophy as an exaltation of
fortitude, was resorted to by the later Elizabethans as a sort of insurance
against calamity. A certain haughtiness and sense of superiority to the
multitude mark the Renaissance stoics. The Elizabethans exemplified,
but probably rarely held as a conscious doctrine, the ideal of what we
may call success in failure, although perhaps in true tragedy there is
always a final note of triumph, sometimes of enlightenment, sometimes
of repentance, sometimes of admiration for fortitude and virtue.

As a basis for the study of *Othello*, let us consider the following summary of Shakespearean tragedy, based in part on the work of a distinguished scholar, the late Professor R. M. Alden: Shakespeare inherited
a crude tragedy of blood, but developed through the treatment of such
stories as those of Romeo and Juliet and King Richard II an interest in
the possibly tragic results of character and the inner life. He accepted
the current belief in the possibility of human fiendishness, which he
developed into terrible malignancy; and yet it is an open question whether
he ever goes so far as to rob his villains of their human status. He found
elements of tragedy in weakness, inefficiency, and defect of character as
well as in positive tragic guilt. He made full use of the tragic backgrounds of life which appear in accident, untoward birth, and inescapable
fate; but he never abandoned his faith in the human will, which is always
allowed to play a part. He frequently lifts his defeated characters to a
point where they may be said to defeat defeat. In his later work, as in
Othello, he saw deeply into human nature and in terms of the psychology
of his time presented terrific struggles of man against his own passions.

In *Othello*, a tragedy written probably in 1604, Shakespeare faced the cruelty and mystery of human life—power, passion, craft, elemental forces—greater things than man. Man's orderly habits are seen to be precarious. We even fear that character is not destiny. Othello suffers from his virtues. He is not jealous by nature, and his sudden attack is bolstered up by a psychology which we might call incredible if the news did not give us daily records of just such unexpected obsessions. The Elizabethans plainly believed because of their mechanistic physiological psychology that every man was a potential Othello. Othello is a colossal hero, sure of pre-eminence when in repose, but as terrible as an earthquake when disturbed. He is a romantic hero, a warrior, a traveler, and a leader of men. We see his life crowned with the glory of love. His is an elemental, simple nature. He has lived by faith alone, his faith has eventuated in love, and it is the wreck of the two that is his tragedy. Some critics have thought that his fall is rationally an impossibility and have argued that we have in the play a mere convention of the "calumniator believed," that Iago had to be believed in order that we might have a play. But this view needs qualification by the ancient idea of the effects of the evil counselor. In narrative the prince or high person is set upon a pedestal and glorified. He, as God's vicegerent, is untouchable. As soon as he becomes culpable, he forfeits our sympathy. Blame must be transferred from him to those who mislead him. Othello is presented as a great and good person largely by his wonderful speeches in the senate house and by the respect that is everywhere shown him, so that it is Iago who is to blame. This is true in literary convention and in actuality.

Iago has been selected and constructed for the ruin of Othello. Iago is a soldier with a soldier's discipline and the cunning that comes to a soldier in camp and field in getting the best for himself, in insisting on his rights, and in the manipulation of his superior officers. He has a superficial good nature and is careful of the practical value of reputation. He is possessed of cold selfishness and great powers of intellect and will but not of imagination. His is the creed of the ego. He has unexpectedly little positive ill will. He has spite only against anything that might weaken his self-esteem. His want of passion is horrible. Love of power he has. The fact that he is not deaf to public opinion makes him dangerous when affronted. Dull in many ways, he does not understand love. He is a master in the manipulation of others, but he does not know their motives if these motives are in the realm of the ideal. Coleridge spoke of Iago's casuistry as "the motive hunting of a motiveless malignity." That fine phrase has almost wrecked the dramatic interpretation of Iago.

We know there are persons who get a certain satisfaction out of torturing people who are in their power; we call them sadists. But Iago is not like that. In the sixteenth century as well as today there was a relentless struggle for survival. Shakespeare must have been aware of this struggle and must have known participants in it. He may have seen persons ruined by ambition or made ruthless by disappointment or injustice. Iago is no stranger than is any such man. Disappointment over military promotion may well have started him on his cruel path. It is doubtful if he ever dreamed of the real end of his efforts. Used to the gains to be made from the stupid Roderigo, Iago never in his wildest fancy caught sight of the ruin to be accomplished by the innocence of Desdemona. Good women, ignorant and innocent of the world, may, in certain circumstances, be like dynamite. It is because evil makes tools of such as they that its sinister power awes us. Evil also uses incapable people in high places, like Othello, makes them commit blunders, which in turn may be used to generate other evils. Thus horror piles on horror, and evil adds deed to deed.

With reference to Iago, it should also be added that he has a method perfectly appropriate to him and his calling and especially effective for the task he has before him. Iago is a master opportunist. Could such a man as Iago drive such a man as Othello into jealousy and murderous frenzy? Shakespeare thought that he could. Something must of course be written off for histrionic power. There would be something added to our sense of plausibility if we saw Lawrence Barrett in the rôle of Othello and Edwin Booth in that of Iago, but, in any case, Shakespeare's art seems adequate without any factitious circumstances. Perhaps the central, the greatest, quality of drama is dramatic suspense, and we find in this play one of the greatest achievements of that kind. Let us see how it operates, how a good man at the very acme of happiness and contentment may step by step be driven to the uttermost extreme of wretchedness. Let us remember also that in order to accomplish this, Shakespeare, before the trial begins, has thought it wise to shift his scene to Cyprus. These things could hardly have happened in Venice, where the unity of the action could not have been so intensified.

The first act of *Othello*, and to a certain extent every other part of the play, has a decidedly realistic quality. The first scene serves to characterize Iago as a professional soldier. He is sure of his own deserts. He is a practical soldier and has all the contempt of the veteran for Cassio, "that never set a squadron in the field" (I, i, 26-7, 36-8).

> Mere prattle, without practice,
> Is all his soldiership. . . .

The command is to blame.

> 'Tis the curse of service,
> Preferment goes by letter and affection,
> And not by old gradation, where each second
> Stood heir to the first.

Iago has not only been wronged, he has been insulted. He is not a nobody; he has influence with the great ones of the city; but he has been nonsuited. What is worse, Othello has evaded Iago's backers "with a bombast circumstance horribly stuffed with epithets of war"; and, when it came to the soldier-to-soldier meeting, Othello has bluntly said, "I have already chose my officer." By nature and long training Iago does not admit any motive of an idealistic nature. Othello has seen him in action "at Rhodes, at Cyprus, and on other grounds." Othello simply has lost his own pride and purposes and has turned his back on justice. A situation exists, Othello wedded to Desdemona without her father's consent, and Iago goes to work on what he has. Iago raises an outcry and shouts vulgarities in the street. What he does is calculated to confirm the aristocratic Brabantio in his sense of disgrace. Iago renders the marriage preposterous in the old man's eyes. With reference to Iago's revelation of his hatred of Othello and of his temporizing, opportunistic method, it may be noted that he usually speaks truth to Roderigo. In the second scene Othello is summoned to the senate house, and modern stage-craft has almost bettered Shakespeare in delaying Othello's entry until line 59 in the second scene. Salvini's

> Keep up your bright swords, for the dew will rust them

was said to be magnificent. The second and third scenes build Othello up to a towering height. His description of his courtship is one of the most winning speeches in all Shakespeare, although a tragic premonition lurks in Brabantio's obduracy (I, iii, 193-8, 293-4):

I here do give thee that with all my heart
Which, but thou hast already, with all my heart
I would keep from thee. . . .
Look to her, Moor, if thou hast eyes to see:
She has deceived her father, and may thee.

At line 260 one notes that Desdemona wishes to accompany Othello to
Cyprus, a desire which is set down to her as a fault in Cinthio's story. A
fair interpretation of the long and twisted interview between Iago and
his dupe (ll. 302-88) would be to see in it, in addition to Iago's skill
in manipulating Roderigo to his purpose, certain qualities in Iago. He is
not only cynical but wrong-headed. He actually does not know the higher
nature in man or woman. After he has given his convincing picture of
the doctrine of self-seeking, beginning "Our bodies are our gardens," he
goes on to tell Roderigo that it "cannot be that Desdemona should long
continue her love to the Moor."

> If sanctimony and a frail vow betwixt an erring barbarian and a super-
> subtle Venetian be not too hard for my wits and all the tribe of hell,
> thou shalt enjoy her.

"I cannot believe that in her; she's full of most blessed condition,"
says Roderigo in a later similar scene (II, i, 254-8). "Blessed fig's-end!"
says Iago, "The wine she drinks is made of grapes: if she had been blessed,
she would never have loved the Moor." It is natural to think that these
things are only lies told to deceive Roderigo, but the matter is not so
simple as that. Iago actually does not comprehend virtue or believe in
its existence. How else explain the later soliloquy (ll. 295-6):

> That Cassio loves her, I do well ·believe it;
> That she loves him, 'tis apt and of great credit.

He is very primitive in his knowledge of people, knows behavior not
character. He knows that (I, iii, 405-8)

> The Moor is of a free and open nature,
> That thinks men honest that but seem to be so,
> And will as tenderly be led by the nose
> As asses are.

He knows that because he has tried it out, but he suspects Othello and
Emilia of incontinency and does not know in any honest inferential judg-

ment that his suspicions are groundless. Iago's final soliloquies in both
Act I, scene iii, and Act II, scene i, are very perfect in their depiction of
the opportunist attitude. One sees him poised and waiting, ready to strike
when opportunity offers. It is indeed very doubtful whether Othello did
not make a great mistake in not placing this perfect tactician in high military
command. As a strategist he is nothing; his plots are at once vague and
limited, but his actions are unerring.

In the third scene of the second act we draw nearer to the great action.
We see Iago in the rôle of the good fellow, a rôle which for his own
interests army life would have taught him. He skillfully contrives to have
Cassio provoked to a drunken rage and in the midst of the brawl know-
ingly has the alarm sounded. He understands the methods of enraging a
commanding officer, and his plan works. We see Othello's capacity for
passion in his ominous speech (II, iii, 204-17).

> Now, by heaven,
> My blood begins my safer guides to rule;
> And passion, having my best judgement collied,
> Assays to lead the way: if I once stir,
> Or do but lift this arm, the best of you
> Shall sink in my rebuke. Give me to know
> How this foul rout began, who set it on;
> And he that is approved in this offence,
> Though he had twinn'd with me, both at a birth,
> Shall lose me. What! in a town of war,
> Yet wild, the people's hearts brimful of fear,
> To manage private and domestic quarrel,
> In night, and on the court and guard of safety!
> 'Tis monstrous.

With the end of the second act, Iago's wits quickened to rapid action,
the arrangements for his deceit are complete. The great example of
dramatic suspense, where one thought or one act grows naturally out of
its predecessor, begins with the third scene. One will note that Iago's
hands are bare. He has nothing but an evil intention; for, though he does
bring in Othello "jump" when he may find Cassio soliciting Desdemona's
aid, nothing seems to come of it. Iago sows his first little seed in the soil,
"Ha! I like not that," and hears the tender Desdemona say,

> What! Michael Cassio,
> That came a-wooing with you, and so many a time.

But when Desdemona leaves the stage Othello˙marks his love, his faith, and his happiness (ll. 90-92):

> Excellent wretch! Perdition catch my soul,
> But I do love thee! And when I love thee not,
> Chaos is come again.

Starting from this high point of Othello's love and confidence, Iago batters him down by one stroke after another. One may count more than a score of varied attacks. Iago's main weapon is false interpretation (ll. 38-9):

> That he would steal away so guilty-like,
> Seeing you coming.

He makes use of what he has (ll. 95-6):

> Did Michael Cassio, when you woo'd my lady,
> Know of your love?

He uses also the direct provocation to inquiry (ll. 97-8):

> But for a satisfaction of my thought;
> No further harm.

He resorts to platitudes as bases for procedure and for provocation to further question (l. 125):

> Men should be what they seem.

He establishes the state of mind he desires to create by declaring or inferring that it already exists (ll. 165-7):

> O, beware, my lord, of jealousy;
> It is the green-eyed monster which doth mock
> The meat it feeds on.

Or consider line 214:

> I see this hath a little dash'd your spirits.

He recommends delay and espial, not only an excellent method of villainy to prevent face-to-face settlement, but a course peculiarly difficult for Othello (ll. 247-50):

> For, sure, he fills it up with great ability,
> Yet, if you please to hold him off awhile,
> You shall by that perceive him and his means.

He reinforces his carefully established reputation for innocence and honesty, does not forget that it is the main base from which he operates (III, iii, 375-6):

> O wretched fool,
> That livest to make thine honesty a vice!

He works from within and cuts down Othello's will to resist (ll. 395-6):

> Would you, the supervisor, grossly gape on—
> Behold her topp'd?

In lines 413-26 he launches his first great palpable lie. He has prepared Othello to swallow it. All the way through, we must remember, his task has been easy. Hamlet would have torn Iago's stratagems to tatters; Othello cannot.

> In sleep I heard him say 'Sweet Desdemona,
> Let us be wary, let us hide our loves.'

Iago next resorts to a device provided for in the source (ll. 434-5):

> Have you not sometimes seen a handkerchief
> Spotted with strawberries in your wife's hand?

Iago has got possession of the handkerchief and by the agency of the loyal Emilia. She is doubtful about letting him have it, because she knows his villainous practices, but he snatches it and gives her no satisfaction. As to the stealing of it, it is a simple matter. The Elizabethans were great pilferers. When Elizabeth was on her progresses and entertained at noblemen's houses, her entourage stole spoons and everything that they could lay their hands on from her hosts. The lie about the handkerchief's being in Cassio's possession produces what is perhaps the turning point of the tragedy. Othello is convinced and his passion is stirred. He himself knows its power (ll. 451-60).

From this time on Iago's task is confirmation; he has only to secure his case. In the presence of violent enactments of rage he shows an increasing uneasiness, as if he has let loose forces he does not know how to control. His activity still continues and he not only maintains in Othello a head of dangerous passion but, willingly or unwillingly, increases it. His greatest trial comes in the first scene of the fourth act when Othello demands that Iago shall make good his charges. The handkerchief then

becomes the chief device by which Iago operates. Othello's description
of it (III, iv, 55-75) elevates it into a mighty symbol, and Desdemona's
lie makes of it a tragic instrument. Why did Desdemona lie? Why do the
weak lie? And with the terrible Othello storming over her, is she more
to blame than are the weak? The truth, to be sure, would have saved her,
but paradoxically it is he and not she who kills the truth.

A fourth act normally shows the working out of the central action or
motive of a tragedy, and the fourth act of *Othello* observes this principle
in many interesting ways. It shows the depths to which Othello has already
fallen in his degeneration. Iago can now be crude: there is no longer
occasion for finesse. When the fourth act opens, Iago is conducting a
pseudo-argument that to kiss in private is no matter,

> Or to be naked with her friend in bed.

Othello is not without some incredulity, but Iago's defence is as clever
as his offence (ll. 30-1):

> He [Cassio] hath, my lord; but be you well assured,
> No more than he'll unswear.

Lines 66-8 present the ancient insulting consolation for the cuckold:

> Good sir, be a man;
> Think every bearded fellow that's but yoked
> May draw with you.

The double scenes of this act are marvels of clever intrigue; for example,
in lines 107-8,

> Now, if this suit lay in Bianca's power,
> How quickly should you speed!

Iago speaks to Cassio about Bianca, but leads Othello to believe he is
speaking of Desdemona (l. 180):

> Did you perceive how he laugh'd at his vice?

Here Iago says "his vice." Up to this point he has not directly maligned
Desdemona; but, when he decides that she must go and go without a
chance to speak, he lays blame on her (ll. 220-1):

> Do it not with poison, strangle her in her bed, even the bed she hath
> contaminated.

Observe that Othello calls Desdemona "whore" and "devil," and that this noble warrior strikes a woman.

There are other points of fourth-act interest. The second scene furnishes a perfect example of a moment of final suspense. Words are the deeds of drama, and Emilia is eloquent in defense of Desdemona. Incidentally her defense of women (IV, iii, 68-104) is a brilliant exaltation of the ordinary and a convincing evidence of Shakespeare's almost illimitable breadth of mind. It is perhaps a feature of a fourth act also that one should find a revelation of emotional tone, and in Desdemona's mention of her mother's maid called Barbara and her singing of the song of "Willow" our expectations are confirmed.

Shakespeare seems to have known that he was dealing with a tragic hero with his fatal pride. Othello assumes the rôle of eternal righteousness. Shakespeare could hardly have been unconscious of the thing he is having his hero do (V, ii, 1-22):

> It is the cause, it is the cause, my soul. . . .
> this sorrow's heavenly.

Later (ll. 294-5) he says of himself,

> An honourable murderer, if you will;
> For nought I did in hate, but all in honour.

Othello, like all such tragic heroes, suffers or is blessed with a revelation of himself to himself. He comes to himself too late. Iago has fooled him to the top of his bent and has built up in Othello such a fortress of passion that Othello rejects both his own better judgment and nature together with all normal testimony to the truth. He is deaf to the importunity of Desdemona herself. Nobody has ever known better than Shakespeare the passion of one who pleads for his life. Othello, taking on himself the justice of God, the acme of tragic madness in both ancient and modern drama, destroys Desdemona. Then the calm floods of a sane objective world overwhelm him, and he sees what he has done. It is then that he says (V, ii, 259-81):

> Behold, I have a weapon;
> A better never did itself sustain
> Upon a soldier's thigh: I have seen the day,
> That, with this little arm and this good sword,
> I have made my way through more impediments

Than twenty times your stop: but, O vain boast!
Who can control his fate? 'tis not so now.
Be not afraid, though you do see me weapon'd;
Here is my journey's end, here is my butt,
And very sea-mark of my utmost sail.
Do you go back dismay'd? 'tis a lost fear;
Man but a rush against Othello's breast,
And he retires. Where should Othello go?
Now, how dost thou look now? O ill-starr'd wench!
Pale as thy smock! when we shall meet at compt,
This look of thine will hurl my soul from heaven,
And fiends will snatch at it. Cold, cold, my girl!
Even like thy chastity. O cursed slave!
Whip me, ye devils,
From the possession of this heavenly sight!
Blow me about in winds! roast me in sulphur!
Wash me in steep-down gulfs of liquid fire!
O Desdemona! Desdemona! dead!

From this and from his last great speech one knows that Othello has,
as E. A. Robinson has it in his poem, looked into the eyes of Amaranth
and seen himself as he is.

There is one other important question to be asked. Does Shakespeare
in *Othello*, perhaps for the first time, develop the notion that, not a
man's faults only, but his virtues may involve him in tragic consequences?
He seems to do so, and it is a cruel idea, for it makes of human life a
fearful thing. We shall encounter the thought again in connection with
Coriolanus, where the case seems to be still clearer. Perhaps Brutus's
virtues caused him to mismanage the conspiracy and the war which his
patriotism had led him to enter. It is perhaps nothing unusual for good
men and women to be destroyed in literature and life because of their
goodness, but the spectacle is always shocking. It would make this a
perilous world if we should train ourselves in virtuous living only to
find that our arduously acquired merits may themselves lead us into
tragic error and tragic guilt. Of course this calamity often befalls minor
and dependent characters in Shakespeare. Ophelia, in her gentle obedience
to her father and brother, was an example of Elizabethan womanhood
and is to this day an admirable and recognized type. Her very virtues
prevent her from understanding and supporting Hamlet. Cordelia might
be another case. Desdemona's sweetness and mercy help to bring about

her own destruction. But here we have a hero, a man of impeccable justice, courage, and efficiency—virtues he needed in order to be a soldier and a leader of men—indeed, to be Othello—and yet that irresistible drive of passionate rectitude makes of him the victim of deceit and the architect of ruin.

3. King Lear.

King Lear seems to have been written about 1605. It is known from an entry in the Stationers' Register to have been acted before King James I on St. Stephen's Day (December 26) in 1606. It could not have been written before 1603, since in that year was published Harsnet's *Declaration of Egregious Popish Impostures*, a book from which Shakespeare borrowed the names of the fiends who are supposed to torment the Bedlam Beggar. Moreover, the rather fine old play, *The True Chronicle History of King Leir, and his three daughters, Gonerill, Ragan, and Cordella*, which Shakespeare used as a source, was published in 1605, as if in response to the popularity of Shakespeare's play on the stage. *King Lear* itself appears in two forms, and the textual problem of the relation of these versions has long been a puzzle to critics. There is the edition in quarto "printed for Nathanial Butter, and are to be sold at his shop in Pauls Church-yard at the signe of the Pide Bull," issued in 1608 and reprinted in 1619, and also the version which appears among the "Tragedies" in the First Folio of 1623. The quarto, which is rather incorrectly reproduced, is a fuller and in many respects a better version than that of the Folio. Many hypotheses have been advanced to account for the relationship, and we need not take them up in detail. It has always seemed to the present writer pretty obvious that the so-called "Pide Bull" edition was printed from Shakespeare's "foul papers" and that the Folio version was printed from Shakespeare's "fair copy," which had undergone some modifications in the theater. There has been a good deal of ill-based talk about the "piracy" of printers and their anxiety to lay their hands on plays which belonged to acting companies. Plays were hardly worth the expense of making stenographic copies or transcripts in long hand, and a large majority of the quartos we have seem to have been published because there were superfluous copies available. The late R. B. McKerrow has thrown light on this question in his article "Elizabethan Printers and Dramatic Manuscripts" (*Library*, 4 ser., XII, 253-75).

King Lear, in spite of its intensity, is a less individual tragedy than is *Othello*. Indeed, although it starts with the family and the innermost circle of human relations, it ranges out through the state and through nature itself to the ultimate and unchangeable aspects of man's life on earth. Lear is at the opposite pole from Hamlet. If a man will not or cannot enter into the solution of his own problem, nature can be counted on to solve it for him. In *King Lear* nature is seen as power, generation, and cohesion. Left alone, it is chaos; subdued and shaped by God's law and man's law, it is order, civilization, justice, and mercy. When Lear gives over his kingdom, he commits a sin against nature and the law of God. Lear's behavior as a father is equally subversive, and throughout the play appear the consequences of the violation of fundamental laws of nature. The stresses and strains of the natural world which Lear has offended finally destroy his sanity, and, as we shall see, the moment can be marked exactly. Thus with the wreck of all ordered systems and the wreck of mind itself *King Lear* becomes perhaps the most far-reaching of all tragedies. It displays the ultimate idea of calamity in the ethics of the Renaissance. In universality *King Lear* rivals *Hamlet*, although the two plays occupy different fields. Hamlet represents the innermost life of all men; Lear, man's life in its social relations.

Dramatically the play is notable for its perfect handling of two plots. Shakespeare had had from the beginning a remarkable power of uniting component plots into unified wholes. Nowhere does he show greater skill than in *King Lear*. For his major plot he went to an anonymous play, a very good one, the old *King Leir*, but seems also characteristically to have read up the Lear story in Geoffrey of Monmouth's *Historia Regum Britonum* and in all available sources. Wilfred Perrett in his *Story of King Lear from Geoffrey of Monmouth to Shakespeare* (Berlin, 1904) makes these facts pretty clear. The most important alteration Shakespeare made in the old plot was to give it a tragic ending, an ending clearly called for in the thought and temper of the Renaissance. The minor plot of Gloucester and his two sons Shakespeare borrowed from Sidney's story of the blind King of Paphlagonia in *Arcadia*. Of the nefarious intrigue between Edmund and the two wicked daughters of Lear and of the belated repentance of the wicked brother there is no trace in Sidney. These features seem brilliantly consequential, and Shakespeare probably invented them. The minor plot itself is an obvious counterpart of the major plot. What then is the major theme of the play?

King Lear says to Kent, disguised as Caius (I, iv, 28-32),

> Dost thou know me, fellow?

And Kent replies,

> No, sir, but you have that in your countenance which I would fain call master.
> *Lear.* What's that?
> *Kent.* Authority.

The underlying concept of *King Lear*, one of those great moral, meaningful themes which Shakespeare often embodies in current thought, is not ingratitude as many have said. It is authority. *King Lear* is, first of all, a play about kingship; about a trustful old king, every inch a king, who in old age brings destruction to himself, and to certain persons in his own circle, and to his country. It is a play which tears off the outer coverings. Pious and innocent-seeming people who are villainous, are revealed in their true natures, and the "simular" is disclosed for what it is, as it works destruction. This is done in a world in which most men are constantly seeking their own advancement, in a court in which flatterers are always lurking, and in which a king should be constantly wary and constantly careful to follow the advice of such practical honest men as Kent. It is a courtly situation, and Elizabeth herself has gone down in history as one who did, although often suspected of heeding flatterers, usually follow the counsels of the wise. The basis of *King Lear* is belief in authority, in a strong single rule.

In order to make this theme a tangible thing, or as we say, to give it artistic embodiment, Shakespeare has used various patterns of thought, themselves embodied in character, scene, and action, and has delineated them by these means. There are various structural devices by the use of which the form of the great concept is rounded out and completed, voiced and made luminous. The most conspicuous of these is the plot of Gloucester and his two sons, which parallels closely the plot of Lear and his three daughters. One may perhaps say that Gloucester's blinding is symbolic of the destruction of true authority at the hands of the great social sins of flattery, ambition, sedition, and usurpation. Ingratitude is King Lear's main plea and it saves him from the censure which might fall upon him as a consequence of his naked folly. It is a conventional and expected element in the portrayal of the suffering, the personal tragedy, of the hero. Ingratitude has somewhat the same relation to *King Lear* that the motive of fear has to *Macbeth*.

Yet "Monster ingratitude!" and "Ingratitude, . . . marble-hearted fiend" are less fundamental to the play than are Regan's saying,

> he hath ever but slenderly known himself,

and Goneril's reply (I, i, 296-9),

> The best and soundest of his time hath been but rash.

In Renaissance thought, as in ours and in that of the early Greeks, it was important to know oneself, and yet the issue of the play does not turn on the errors of this king. Lear himself defines the issue by suggestion when he protests against the loss of his knights to Goneril and Regan, who have said respectively, "What need you five and twenty, ten, or five?" and "What need one?" (II, iv, 264-86):

> O, reason not the need: our basest beggars
> Are in the poorest thing superfluous:
> Allow not nature more than nature needs,
> Man's life's as cheap as beast's: thou art a lady;
> If only to go warm were gorgeous,
> Why, nature needs not what thou gorgeous wear'st,
> Which scarcely keeps thee warm. But, for true need,—

And again, most truly and suggestively, when he says (IV, vi, 97-107):

> They flattered me like a dog; and told me I had white hairs in my beard ere the black ones were there. To say 'ay' and 'no' to everything that I said!—'Ay' and 'no' too was no good divinity. When the rain came to wet me once, and the wind to make me chatter; when the thunder would not peace at my bidding; there I found 'em, there I smelt 'em out. Go to, they are not men o' their words: they told me I was every thing; 'tis a lie, I am not ague-proof.

Kingship in *King Lear* is not conceived of as sovereignty of a political body only, not as an office only, but as a divine institution, the king being the voice of God and the embodiment of God's will. It follows that God installs a king, determines the length of his reign, and makes of loyalty or treason to a king loyalty or treason to God. A king is part of the grand structural unity of the universe, and there is nowhere in

Shakespeare such an elaborate use of the microcosmic theory. The whole notion of order and chaos in the universe is involved, and the happenings in this play illustrate the doctrine of Ulysses when he says (*Troilus and Cressida*, I, iii, 108-24):

> Take but degree away, untune that string,
> And, hark, what discord follows! each thing meets
> In mere oppugnancy: the bounded waters
> Should lift their bosoms higher than the shores
> And make a sop of all this solid globe:
> Strength should be lord of imbecility,
> And the rude son should strike his father dead:
> Force should be right; or rather, right and wrong,
> Between whose endless jar justice resides,
> Should lose their names, and so should justice too.
> Then every thing includes itself in power,
> Power into will, will into appetite;
> And appetite, an universal wolf,
> So doubly seconded with will and power,
> Must make perforce an universal prey,
> And last eat up himself.

And so the wreck begins. No sooner does King Lear hearken to his flattering daughters than he yields to injustice, injures the frank and innocent Cordelia, and according to the convention observed in *Gorboduc* and everywhere else, banishes the honest courtier Kent. Passion makes him deaf (I, i, 124-54).

Here starts an under-current in the cosmical structure of this drama which must not remain unobserved, namely, that the ministers of God will ultimately restore the right. Righteous forces are not weaker than those of malignancy but stronger. The suffering of the hero is portrayed in terms of the shifting of grief to anger, righteous anger. Kent stands for the resistance to evil wherever it appears. In Lear there is a long battle between grief and anger, and, when grief wins, insanity results. Gloucester lacks resistance, and the elaborately attempted suicide over the imaginary cliff and many ministrations of his son Edgar are necessary before he accepts salvation in the doctrine (V, ii, 9-11),

> **Men must endure**
> Their going hence, even as their coming hither:
> **Ripeness is all.**

Lear never completely weakens (IV, vi, 188-91),

> It were a delicate stratagem, to shoe
> A troop of horse with felt: I'll put't in proof;
> And when I have stolen upon these sons-in-law,
> Then, kill, kill, kill, kill, kill, kill!

When Goneril asserts authority over him (I, iv) his indignation blazes out in

> The untented woundings of a father's curse.

To read his curses is to understand why curses had validity in Renaissance thought. They are in terms of generic nature, of which Lear is a part (ll. 297-311). One passage begins:

> Hear, nature, hear; dear goddess, hear!

and ends:

> How sharper than a serpent's tooth it is
> To have a thankless child!

The first of the natural units to be disrupted is that of the family, the family of Lear and that of Gloucester. In Edmund's attack on Edgar is much of the technique of Iago—hypocrisy, apparent reluctance, delay, opportunism, and the taking advantage of those whose natures are so far from doing harm that they suspect none. There is also use of general and portentous matters to cover up particular chicanery. In one scene (V, ii) there is a conversation, often misunderstood, between Gloucester and Edmund. The religion of *King Lear* is pagan, a sort of nature worship, and it is piety on Gloucester's part for him to say (I, ii, 112-27):

> These late eclipses in the sun and moon portend no good to us: though the wisdom of nature can reason it thus and thus, yet nature finds itself scourged by the sequent effects.

He goes on to cite evidence of the disturbance of the natural order, and when he withdraws from the scene, Edmund takes up the theme in a spirit of pure infidelity. Because his rejection of signs and portents is ultra-modern, he has been admired for his realistic stand and has been thought to speak with the voice of Shakespeare. Nothing could be further from the truth; the facts are all against such an opinion, and in the play there is nothing to support it. Gloucester has looked into the future and told us what is about to happen and what does happen. Edmund's words are clever, but they reveal him as a villain and not as a scientist (ll. 128-45):

> This is the excellent foppery of the world, that, when we are sick in fortune,—often the surfeit of our own behaviour,—we make guilty of our disasters the sun, the moon, and the stars: as if we were villains by necessity; fools by heavenly compulsion; knaves, thieves, and treachers, by spherical predominance; drunkards, liars, and adulterers, by an enforced obedience of planetary influence; and all that we are evil in, by a divine thrusting on: an admirable evasion of whoremaster man, to lay his goatish disposition to the charge of a star! My father compounded with my mother under the dragon's tail; and my nativity was under Ursa major; so that it follows, I am rough and lecherous. Tut, I should have been that I am, had the maidenliest star in the firmament twinkled on my bastardizing.

Quite apart from the dramatic situation, it is altogether probable that Shakespeare, like other Elizabethans, believed that nature acted in sympathy with man and that event was written in the stars.

The play moves rapidly in the first two acts of *King Lear*. Edgar, betrayed by Edmund and banished, conceals himself in the disguise of a Bedlam beggar. Lear makes a stalwart fight broken now and then with threats of approaching madness, and in the last scene is turned out into the storm. The first scene of the third act gives news of forces gathering in France for his succor. There are hints of sedition and civil war, and we see that the state is suffering disintegration. Then comes the storm in *King Lear*. It is not improbable to our thinking and must have been most probable in the thought of Shakespeare that the indifferent elements themselves would at such a time have been mingled as in primordial chaos. To us it is a tempest of words. The dramatist has mainly words to serve his turn, and there is nothing quite like this in literature (III, ii, 1-9):

> Blow, winds, and crack your cheeks! rage! blow!
> You cataracts and hurricanoes, spout
> Till you have drench'd our steeples, drown'd the cocks!
> You sulphurous and thought-executing fires,
> Vaunt-couriers to oak-cleaving thunderbolts,
> Singe my white head! And thou, all-shaking thunder,
> Strike flat the thick rotundity o' the world!
> Crack nature's moulds, all germens spill at once,
> That make ingrateful man!

This aged man has gone to school, and not the least interesting things to be observed are Lear's own reflections (ll. 49-60):

> Let the great gods,
> That keep this dreadful pother o'er our heads,
> Find out their enemies now. Tremble, thou wretch,
> That hast within thee undivulged crimes,
> Unwhipp'd of justice: hide thee, thou bloody hand;
> Thou perjured, and thou simular man of virtue
> That art incestuous: caitiff, to pieces shake,
> That under covert and convenient seeming
> Hast practised on man's life: close pent-up guilts,
> Rive your concealing continents, and cry
> These dreadful summoners grace. I am a man
> More sinn'd against than sinning.

And in scene four (ll. 28-36) in a moment of convincing sanity preceding his own mental break-down Lear says,

> Poor naked wretches, whereso'er you are,
> That bide the pelting of this pitiless storm,
> How shall your houseless heads and unfed sides,
> Your loop'd and window'd raggedness, defend you
> From seasons such as these? O, I have ta'en
> Too little care of this! Take physic, pomp;
> Expose thyself to feel what wretches feel,
> That thou mayst shake the superflux to them,
> And show the heavens more just.

But the spectacle of devastation is too much for Lear when he sees the Bedlam beggar. We know it is Edgar in disguise, but to the Elizabethan a man's nature was permeated by a disguise and he became the thing he imitated. When Lear sees him naked and miserable, Edgar becomes a symbol of ultimate destitution, without a trace of what we call civilization, the world that man under the eye of God has built. There is already present the natural imbecile and the Bedlam beggar, and Lear completes the trio by becoming a madman. Perhaps there is no greater climax in Shakespeare (III, iv, 105-40):

> Why, thou wert better in thy grave than to answer with thy uncovered body this extremity of the skies. Is man no more than this? Consider him well. Thou owest the worm no silk, the beast no hide, the sheep no wool, the cat no perfume. Ha! here's three on's are sophisticated!

Thou art the thing itself: unaccommodated man is no more but such
a poor, bare, forked animal as thou art. Off, off, you lendings! come,
unbutton here. *[Tearing off his clothes.*

Thus the ruin of the family, the kingdom, and the natures of men
culminates in the ruin of the mind. After this point the theme of ruin
appears mainly in the mad talk of Lear in the sixth scene of the fourth
act where, in matter and impertinency mixed, is some of the bitterest of
pessimism (ll. 168-74):

> Through tatter'd clothes small vices do appear;
> Robes and furr'd gowns hide all. Plate sin with gold,
> And the strong lance of justice hurtless breaks;
> Arm it in rags, a pigmy's straw does pierce it.
> None does offend, none, I say, none; I'll able 'em:
> Take that of me, my friend, who have the power
> To seal the accuser's lips.

The saner passages appear in a little oasis in Lear's madness created
by Gloucester's question, "Is't not the king?" "Ay, every inch a king" is
Lear's reply, and as his sanity returns he speaks in blank verse more
regular as his thought gains in clarity. One interest of the passage is the
expression in detail of the vision of disorder set forth by Ulysses in
Troilus and Cressida (I, iii, 94-134).

Meantime, in the last scene of the third act, occurs the blinding of
Gloucester. Shakespeare had found this horror in Sidney's story of the
blind King of Paphlagonia in *Arcadia*. Shakespeare ironically has Gloucester suggest his fate in the words (ll. 56-7):

> Because I would not see thy cruel nails
> Pluck out his poor old eyes.

The event is outrageous, and no glib words about Elizabethan love of
violence will justify it. Shakespeare has, however, with his usual tact done
something to redeem it. He, long before Ibsen, saw his ordinary people
as human beings, so much so that he has been mistakenly called democratic. What he saw was not that all men have an equal right to rule in
the state—a later idea—but that even common people are human beings,
capable of love, wisdom, bravery, self-sacrifice, and shrewd good sense,
each with a feeling of personal pride as true as that of any king or any
modern man in a free country. That mere First Servant in *King Lear*, a

man without a name, revolts in behalf of humanity. He fights with Cornwall and kills him (l. 79):

> Nay, then, come on, and take the chance of anger.

Not less striking in its recoil to nature is the later history of the old King. How intentionally it was done one does not know, but Shakespeare has given us a picture of Lear restored to sanity, chastened, wise, and at peace with all the world, as serene almost as the king Pippa sings about in *Pippa Passes*:

> A King lived long ago,
> In the morning of the world,
> When earth was nigher heaven than now.

When Lear and Cordelia are captured and carried off he says in idyllic terms (V, iii, 7-21):

> Come, let's away to prison:
> We two alone will sing like birds i' the cage:
> When thou dost ask me blessing, I'll kneel down,
> And ask of thee forgiveness: so we'll live,
> And pray, and sing, and tell old tales, and laugh
> At gilded butterflies, and hear poor rogues
> Talk of court news; and we'll talk with them too,
> Who loses and who wins; who's in, who's out,
> And take upon's the mystery of things,
> As if we were God's spies.

He has arrived at the point where he believes in the existence of love, and love is enough to restore the shattered world.

But rest and peace on earth were not for him. His mighty passion must once more flame through the ages. The quality of that last scene in *King Lear* is suggested by a story told of Edmund Kean. Kean had at last got his opportunity and gained fame as the greatest exponent of human passion who had appeared on the English stage. When his Othello had been proclaimed as a sublime and moving spectacle, he remarked, "The London audience have no idea what I can do until they see me over the dead body of Cordelia."

The staunch old Lear was never more masterly, more practical than at the end of his life (V, iii, 257 ff.):

She's gone for ever!

I know when one is dead, and when one lives;
She's dead as earth. Lend me a looking-glass;
If that her breath will mist or stain the stone,
Why, then she lives. . . .
This feather stirs; she lives! If it be so
It is a chance which does redeem all sorrows
That ever I have felt. . . .
I might have sav'd her; now she's gone forever!
Cordelia, Cordelia! stay a little. Ha!
What is't thou say'st? Her voice was ever soft,
Gentle, and low; an excellent thing in woman.
I kill'd the slave that was a-hanging thee.
Capt. 'Tis true, my lords, he did.
Lear.   Did I not, fellow?
I have seen the day, with my good biting falchion
I would have made them skip.

It was Lamb who said "the Lear of Shakespeare cannot be acted." That is true to this extent, that it requires a genius to do the part full justice. There is much that is disappointing in the early Lear. He is so wise, so observant, so experienced that he ought not, for example, to have failed to see the difference between Cordelia and his other daughters. Being the man he is, he should have seen that Cordelia was ashamed to display her tenderness before the world and too proud to buy a dowry with it. Lear's mind and heart must have been asleep, perhaps partly never awakened, until fate issued its writ and put him on trial. Thus an old story of kingship becomes a play about kingship, although the suffering of Lear, embodying much of the poetry, learning, and humanity of Shakespeare, at times overshadows everything else. It was not only a Renaissance characteristic, but particularly a characteristic of Shakespeare, to look beyond the sufferings of men and endeavor to discover the larger forces at work as causes and concomitants. By this means emotional strength and artistic validity are established.

Lear is thus the tragedy not of a single individual, but of society, Lear being the symbol as well as the chief protagonist. As might be expected in the treatment of such a theme, all the participants are fully realized. Lear in his troubles is not without supporters and advocates—men of justice, courage, and wisdom. The honest, loyal, and intelligent Kent has been the theme of much praise. His humor, his realism, his vigorous action are irresistible. His philosophical acceptance of the stocks, his natural antipathy to Oswald the sycophant, and his persistent care of Lear seem crowned in his great speech (V, iii, 313-15):

> Vex not his ghost: O, let him pass! he hates him much
> That would upon the rack of this tough world
> Stretch him out longer.

Edgar is something of a hero of romance, has in him some flavor of *Arcadia*; and, if one must see virtue in the miserable Restoration version of *King Lear*, which gave the play a happy ending, one might say that Tate did well in marrying Cordelia off to Edgar. He is a clever, resourceful man of tender heart. It was he who saved old Gloucester's soul with the elaborate counterfeiting of suicide, and, in that connection, we owe to Edgar, whose motives were purely filial, one of the most perfect bits of descriptive literature in the language (IV, vi, 11-24):

> How fearful
> And dizzy 'tis, to cast one's eyes so low!
> The crows and choughs that wing the midway air
> Show scarce so gross as beetles: half way down
> Hangs one that gathers samphire, dreadful trade!
> Methinks he seems no bigger than his head:
> The fishermen, that walk upon the beach,
> Appear like mice; and yond tall anchoring bark,
> Diminish'd to her cock; her cock, a buoy
> Almost too small for sight: the murmuring surge,
> That on the unnumbered idle pebbles chafes,
> Cannot be heard so high. I'll look no more;
> Lest my brain turn, and the deficient sight
> Topple down headlong.

And it is Edgar who utters the thought, congenial to Shakespeare and the Renaissance, which sums up the lesson poor Gloucester has learned (V, ii, 9-11):

> Men must endure
> Their going hence, even as their coming hither:
> Ripeness is all.

In this play old men are put to school, and the pathos of Gloucester, less obvious, is deeper than that of Lear. It is his pity for Lear that brings upon him his calamity and later affords a means by which Edgar may rescue him body and soul.

Edmund is a striking character, a man who, like Iago and Richard III, chooses villainy as his part. He is the most varied and perhaps the most interesting of Shakespeare's studies of evil men. Edmund is a bastard and, according to current belief, is born outside the framework of social and moral conformity. He shows great intelligence in making his way, and, although abominable in his actions, he is not at bottom devoid of humanity. There is something open and brilliant about his downfall; he is neither dour, silent, and obdurate like Iago nor swept away in a tempest of passion like Richard and Macbeth. He confesses and, to some degree, repents, saying significantly (V, iii, 243-4):

> I pant for life: some good I mean to do
> Despite of mine own nature.

It is in conformity with Edmund's nature and situation that he should find the stepping-stones of his rise to power in unsanctioned relations with the unnatural women who have wronged their father. The passion that they both entertain for him brings a threefold destruction in its wake, since it is the inciting force for Goneril's murder of Regan, Goneril's suicide, and Edmund's destruction in combat. The rôles of the two wicked sisters are parallel, and it is not easy to discriminate between them. Dowden calls Goneril "the calm wielder of a pitiless force, the resolute initiator of cruelty," who knows that a helpless old man is merely a helpless old man and that words are only words. Dowden thinks Regan "more unmeasured in her ferocity" and "a smaller, shriller, fiercer, more eager piece of malice."

Cordelia is undoubtedly one of the finer women in Shakespeare's gallery of portraits. The tests with which she is confronted are masculine. She is too honorable to flatter or to lie or to remain silent in the presence of dishonesty. She goes forth to France unsupported and there bends her efforts to the attack on evil. Perhaps Shakespeare could not permit a French army to make conquests in England, or, more probably, he borrowed from the sources the story of her later defeat at the hands of her rebellious nephews; but, in any case, Cordelia suffers defeat. It is on her return to England that Shakespeare makes his perfect depiction of womanly tenderness. The scene of Lear's restoration to sanity (IV, vii) and of the capture (V, iii) are great in their revelation of Cordelia's noble spirit. Her one remark in the latter scene seems to characterize her to perfection and to set her apart from other women in the plays (ll. 3-6):

> We are not the first
> Who, with best meaning, have incurr'd the worst,
> For thee, oppressed king, am I cast down;
> Myself could else out-frown false fortune's frown.

The Fool has puzzled the world, as simplicity, innocence, and helplessness will always puzzle it. He illuminates all the earlier part of the play with that wisdom which issues from the mouths of babes and sucklings. After the sixth scene of the third act he strangely disappears. What, if any, exigencies of casting characters may have caused this we do not know.

CHAPTER IX

Four Plays of Doubtful Interpretation

ALL'S WELL THAT ENDS WELL
MEASURE FOR MEASURE
TROILUS AND CRESSIDA
TIMON OF ATHENS

MOST writers on Shakespeare have said that after Shakespeare had written *Twelfth Night* the "genial spirit of comedy," as Dowden puts it, deserted him. *All's Well that Ends Well* Dowden regarded as "grave and earnest," *Measure for Measure* as "dark and bitter." About the same time, most critics think, Shakespeare told in *Troilus and Cressida* the story of how the young love and faith of Troilus were wrecked in disillusionment by the falsity and fickleness of Cressida. After that, according to this theory, Shakespeare turned to tragedy and produced his great masterpieces in that form—*Othello*, *King Lear*, *Macbeth*, *Antony and Cleopatra*, and *Coriolanus*—and somewhere on the road actually bogged down in the pessimism and misanthropy of *Timon of Athens*. It has been inferred that something sad and cruel must have happened to Shakespeare himself, and there have been various speculations as to what it might have been. It has been suggested that there were family troubles and bereavements and also that, since Shakespeare's patron, the Earl of Southampton, was thrown into prison at the time of the execution of the Earl of Essex for treason, the misfortunes of Shakespeare's great friends had caused him to lose his joy in life, so that he wrote bitter comedies and world-shaking tragedies. Dowden and his followers believed this. George Brandes, the great Danish critic, gave it world-wide currency, and Frank Harris made it the basis of a largely conjectural biographical and critical book on Shakespeare. The idea was that Shakespeare had written himself into plays. The characters, such as

Hamlet, whom he treats most sympathetically, were thought best to embody his mind, his heart, and his view of human life.

There is nothing preposterous in this idea. Most creative artists have made up their works out of themselves; indeed, they have nothing else out of which to make them up. The trouble therefore with this widely accepted theory is that there is so little tangible evidence for it. Shakespeare did no doubt have his share of the world's sorrows as well as its joys, but how can we know that he was personally sorrowful and discouraged about life just at the time selected and that his gloomier views are to be interpreted in terms of his own state of mind? What reason have we to think that a man must feel tragic as regards his private experience when he writes tragedy? Much of Shakespeare's tragic thinking may have come vicariously, and the bitterness about human conduct apparent in certain plays may be the result of observation and reflection at any time from his youth onward. It seems a rather narrow view to believe that a great dramatic genius would be limited to the events of the day or the year, or that his personal feelings must be brought in to reinforce his psychological and dramatic insight. Besides, it has been argued quite simply that Shakespeare was not the only dramatist who turned to the writing of tragedy in the early years of the seventeenth century in England. Chapman, Jonson, Webster, Middleton, Tourneur, Beaumont and Fletcher, and others also wrote tragedies and bitter comedies. Are we to believe that they also had personal experience such as to make them gloomy and pessimistic? Still the idea of the "bitter years," to which Dowden applied the words *de profundis*, has much authority back of it and deserves respectful consideration. *All's Well that Ends Well* and *Measure for Measure*, and, by implication, *Troilus and Cressida*, have been called "problem plays" by Bernard Shaw and many others since, because these critics thought wrongly that Shakespeare was embodying in these plays questions regarded as morally unsolvable. We have been asked to believe that Shakespeare had seen, long before Ibsen, the relative nature of social ethics, a thing which Shakespeare or any other Elizabethan could not possibly have perceived.

The best way to treat the conception of the so-called "dark comedies" is to explain it away. *All's Well that Ends Well* is obviously an early comedy revised and largely rewritten at a later time in Shakespeare's career. Perhaps it is *Love's Labour's Won*, mentioned by Francis Meres, worked over not too carefully, but in a more mature style. The reworking was probably done before *Measure for Measure* was written. *All's Well* is not a dark comedy except to the refined taste of the modern world. To Shakespeare and his age the device by which Helena consummates her marriage with Bertram and thus fulfills the seemingly impossible conditions he has laid upon her was merely ingenious and rather cheerful. *Measure for Measure* retells the cruel story of George Whetstone's *Promos and Cassandra* and in the retelling alleviates it almost beyond recognition. One must remember that in Whetstone's story Cassandra, in order to save her brother's life, yields to Promos, who, nevertheless, destroys her brother, and that she marries Promos in the end. Surely the noble chastity of Isabella, backed by her energy and will and sustained by the wisdom and justice of the Duke, is not darkness, but almost unparalleled illumination. The play seems by its style to belong to the period of *Hamlet* and *Othello*. As to *Troilus and Cressida* the play is not a comedy at all. Even the editors of the First Folio seem to have decided that *Troilus and Cressida* was a tragedy. They originally planned to print the play so that it would follow *Romeo and Juliet*; then some difficulty, possibly in the matter of ownership, caused them to withdraw the play, only to insert it later without pagination between the histories and the tragedies. They might have thought of it as a history, certainly never as a comedy. The death of Hector, who was regarded almost as an ancestor of the British, could never have appeared in a comedy. As to Troilus, he was doomed to death in the impending fall of Troy. Shakespeare was not in the least responsible for the picture of Cressida's infidelity. Henryson's *Testament of Cresseid* and Caxton's *Recuyell* had supplied that. There is little evidence that Shakespeare actually worked from Chaucer's *Troilus and Criseyde*, the facts of which, however, do not differ greatly from those of other versions. Chaucer's sympathy for Criseyde, had Shakespeare accepted it, might have softened his harshness. *Troilus and Cressida* has in it some of Shakespeare's greatest and most constructive writing, and the characters of the sagacious Ulysses, the noble Hector, and the no less noble Troilus, are not the expressions of gloom and satire but, in a tragedy dealing with the ancestors of the British, of wisdom, chivalry, and courage. The quality of Thersites, along with that of Lavache in *All's Well that Ends Well* and of Pompey in *Measure for Measure*, is possibly due to Shakespeare's providing a part for Robert Armin.

1. *All's Well that Ends Well.*

All's Well that Ends Well was published in the First Folio in 1623 and entered in the Stationers' Register for that publication, a thing which indicates that it had never been published as a separate play. *All's Well* is not mentioned by Francis Meres in *Palladis Tamia*, or *Wit's Treasury* (1598) in his famous mention of six comedies and six tragedies by Shakespeare:

> As *Plautus* and *Seneca* are accounted the best for Comedy and Tragedy among the Latines: so *Shakespeare* among the English is the most excellent in both kinds for the stage; for Comedy, witnes his *Gentlemen of Verona*, his *Errors*, his *Love labors lost*, his *Love labours Wonne*, his *Midsummers night dream*, and his *Merchant of Venice*: for Tragedy his *Richard the 2*, *Richard the 3*, *Henry the 4*, *King John*, *Titus Andronicus* and his *Romeo and Juliet*.

The source of *All's Well that Ends Well* is the ninth novel of the third day of Boccaccio's *Decameron*. The novels of this day tell about difficulties, many of them apparently insurmountable, which lovers have overcome in achieving their objects. They are thus stories of love's labor won. It may be that we have in *All's Well* a version, with a new title, of Shakespeare's lost *Love's Labour's Won*, a play which would conceivably be written early to serve as a companion-piece to *Love's Labour's Lost*. It might even have been written earlier than the latter play, since *All's Well* is to a far greater degree a play of the winning of love's labor than the other is of the losing of it. There are certain circumstances which seem to confirm the theory that *All's Well that Ends Well* is a version of *Love's Labour's Won*. We must not forget, however, that arguments have been put forward by scholars to show that *Much Ado about Nothing* and *The Taming of the Shrew* are renamed and revised versions of the lost play. It is thus possible that *Love's Labour's Won* is completely lost.

One little passage that gives some confirmation to the belief that *All's Well* is a version of the lost comedy is in the third scene of the fifth act, lines 314-15, in which Helena says to Bertram,

> This is done:
> Will you be mine, now you are doubly won?

A greater general confirmation comes from the fact that *All's Well* is written in two widely divergent styles, the one style characteristic of

Shakespeare's early plays such as *Love's Labour's Lost* and *The Comedy of Errors*. A large part of the major plot appears in rhymed couplets, such as were used in the sonnet form, and there are lyrical dialogues, puns, conceits, and a certain amount of formal balance and contrast in construction. The other style is mature like that written by Shakespeare in plays after 1600: blank verse characterized by run-on lines, abundant feminine endings, and closely packed expression. The only reasonable explanation of this stylistic situation is to say that Shakespeare wrote a play in the early 1590's and rewrote it after the year 1600. There is no question of any other hand than Shakespeare's in the play. *All's Well that Ends Well* in its major plot follows Boccaccio's story of the physician's daughter, Gilletta de Narbonne, very closely, and most of the evidences of early style appear in this main story.

In it Helena (Gilletta), orphaned daughter of the great physician Gerard of Narbonne, has been brought up in the household of the wise and kindly Countess of Rousillon. Helena falls in love with Bertram, the Countess's son. Her love is of course hopeless because of the differences in birth and fortune between her and the man she loves, but she reflects the very spirit of Boccaccio's laboring lovers; for she adopts the doctrine made familiar in her words,

> Our remedies oft in ourselves do lie,
> Which we ascribe to heaven.

Normally she would never have been chosen, but she earns a chance to choose her husband. Her opportunity comes in the illness of the French king. He has what is described as a fistula. It has been the despair of all the learned medical men of France, but Helena has a prescription of her dead father's which effects a cure. She asks as her reward that she be permitted to select a husband, and her request is granted. Bertram is at court, and she chooses him. So formal and conventional was the choosing of wives and husbands in those days that the French king is surprised at Bertram's reluctance. Of course Bertram was properly snobbish about marrying beneath his station, but the king answers this objection by the bestowal of rank and wealth upon Helena. Shakespeare is even clever enough to suggest that Bertram also objects to Helena because he has grown up in the household with her and has no romantic interest in her whatever. He is anxious for a career in court and in war and feels that a wife will be a burden. These are motives of a sort, and they are all that Boccaccio uses. But we must remember that we have to do with the rule of lifting blame from the shoulders of the hero. Shakespeare therefore makes Bertram young and impulsive, but that is not enough. So in order to strengthen the case for his hero Shakespeare resorts to the device of the evil counselor—a person who may serve as whipping-boy for the young nobleman—brings in a boaster, coward, and flatterer named Parolles, who persuades Bertram to desert his wife immediately after marriage and to put upon her two terrible obstacles to be overcome. She must get a ring from his finger and she must show herself with child by him. Now, whether Shakespeare introduced Parolles in this rôle of misleader of princes in his first draft or in his revision is a matter of some doubt. The solution of Helena's problem is a clever piece of Italian intrigue rather shocking to modern taste. It is a device spoken of as the "bed trick," by which she gets herself substituted for a woman whom Bertram thinks he has seduced. There are in the modern world scruples on both sides of this matter which Shakespeare's age probably did not feel. They were quite formal in the matter of a woman's yielding herself to an unwilling man to whom she was married or betrothed. To us it is a thing a self-respecting woman would hardly do, marriage or no marriage. Then again, it must be confessed that Bertram's intended seduction and adultery, since he was a young nobleman in a free age and situation, carried little stain and disgrace with them. It must be said, however, that Shakespeare carries through this obnoxious intrigue with as great delicacy as it could possibly be done. Bertram returns home when it has been falsely reported to him that Helena is dead, only to find himself confronted by his wife, who has fully complied with his hard conditions. In order to make his defeat into a conquest Shakespeare contrives to get him into hot water because of evidence that he has murdered Helena, so that he will be glad to see her living and to accept her as his wife. There is cruelty in the old story, and Bertram cuts at best a sorry figure. How much of the intricate intrigue designed to conquer Bertram is old and how much is new it is difficult to say. Boccaccio has but little of it. The matter is worth looking into.

With the idea in mind that *All's Well that Ends Well* as originally written by Shakespeare was closer to Boccaccio than is the present play and that those parts of the play which agree with the source show the earlier style, one would decide that Lavache, the clown, is new. His part is dispensable, and it is a part, such as Touchstone in *As You Like It*, Feste in *Twelfth Night*, and the Fool in *King Lear*, for the great comic actor Robert Armin, who entered Shakespeare's company about 1599. Lafeu must also be largely an addition. His speeches are mainly in prose and often serve to interrupt verse dialogue. There have also been very serious changes in the part of Parolles, the most plausible explanation of which is that he was the clown in the earlier version. The inconsistent and surprisingly vulgar dialogue between Helena and him (I, i, 117-178) is in the prose style of the early clowns; so also is Parolles's part in the trial (V, iii); whereas much of his talk (III, vi; IV, iii; V, ii) is in prose style at least as late as Falstaff. It is pretty clear that Jack Drum's entertainment (IV, i, iii) and perhaps some other slight episodes are additions. Nearly all changes are concerned with the white-washing of Bertram, and the job is none too well done in the end.

Otherwise in general the old plot stands. In content the play adheres pretty closely to Boccaccio. Rhyme employed for organic purposes appears sporadically or continuously in all episodes of the main plot except the Jack Drum trick on Parolles. Along with the rhyme there are some passages in fairly simple blank verse which may well have belonged to the early play. The point is hard to determine; but it seems that prose for serious dramatic purposes and closely compacted blank verse in Shakespeare's later manner are characteristic of Shakespeare's revisions. They are likely to appear in patches everywhere throughout the play. The longest prose passages are in Jack Drum's entertainment. The mature blank verse passages mainly serve to lend weight and significance to situations. They carry no single episode of the plot. The Fool's part has the morbid quality that Armin admired and is written in the whimsical style of Touchstone and Feste but with much less gaiety.

Shakespeare inferred the nature of his characters from situations, and almost nowhere is there more exquisite skill in doing this than in the case of Helena. He saw that her situation demanded sincerity, determination, and the ability to undergo tribulation with a stout heart. The cards were stacked against her, but she makes a bold attempt to satisfy her love. She wins and finds that she has won a pyrrhic victory. She finds herself despised by the man she loves and has secured, a terrible test of her patience and the validity of her character. She understands and sympathizes with Bertram, but there is no sentimentality in her sweet and simple character, no disposition to cease her effort or to feel sorry for herself. She has, however, what Boas calls "a few sharp twitches of pain": "This is a dreadful sentence," "'Tis bitter." She has just the qualities to carry her through the ordeal of the horribly ingenious intrigue laid upon her by the plot of Boccaccio's story.

The very thought of the learned father whom she also mourns and the idea of travail vivified by her dialogue with Parolles bring her to her great resolution (I, i, 231-44):

> Our remedies oft in ourselves do lie,
> Which we ascribe to heaven: the fated sky
> Gives us free scope, only doth backward pull
> Our slow designs when we ourselves are dull. . . .
>   Who ever strove
> To show her merit, that did miss her love?
> The king's disease—my project may deceive me,
> But my intents are fix'd and will not leave me.

In Italy Helena watches the current of circumstances as sharply as Iago himself, and Bertram weaves the net for his own recapture. Shakespeare seems to tell us that accomplishment in this world is a matter of making use of casual opportunity, for

> The web of our life is a mingled yarn, good and ill together.

There is no time, however, when Helena does not say and believe that

> No legacy is so rich as honesty.

Characterization in drama is not merely what characters do and say. It is also a matter of how these things are accomplished and what other characters say of them and think of them. Helena is beautifully attended and vouched for, largely by elderly people. Nothing graces youth more than the friendship of the old. The wise, kindly, clear-eyed Countess of Rousillon loves her as a daughter and knows her heart. She backs Helena up even in the extraordinary enterprise of gaining Bertram, the son of the Countess, as her husband. Cynics might tell us that that is the last thing you might expect a mother to do, and yet it is convincing. Lafeu, possibly invented to ease Helena's way at court and to help her in the end, is also, in his way, a triumph. Sharp-sighted, rather crusty, he is valuable to Shakespeare as a means of making actual truth known to the audience.

He is an early member of that group of plain-speaking elderly characters, which includes Enobarbus, Menenius Agrippa, and Gonzalo, that characterize Shakespeare's later plays. The King trusts Helena against all advice and normal prudence, and the Florentine Widow knows that she and her daughter are safe in Helena's hands. As to the modern bit of smart anachronism which discovered that Helena was a huntress in quest of her prey, it is inconsiderable. When has such pursuit been anything extraordinary in the great enterprise of courtship and marriage? It is as old as Ruth and Naomi.

As to Parolles, he is not worth the trouble it takes to disgrace him and expose his impostures to Bertram. Bertram inevitably suffers in our estimation by being taken in by such a clown. The elaborate trick of sending Parolles out to pretend to recover his drum is funny in a few places— as where the French soldiers speak to each other and to Parolles in dog Latin—but as a whole it is overdone and a bore. The finest thing in the whole part of Parolles is the scene at the end between him and Lafeu in which justice is shown to be capable of mercy (V, ii, 28-59):

> *Par.* My lord, I am a man whom fortune hath cruelly scratched.
> *Laf.* And what would you have me to do? 'Tis too late to pare her nails now. . . .
> Sirrah, inquire further after me; I had talk of you last night: though you are a fool and a knave, you shall eat; go to, follow.
> *Par.* I praise God for you.

All's Well that Ends Well is not a successful play or a very pleasant one, but it is no problem play in the modern sense. "The inaudible and noiseless foot of Time" has worked against it. It was unquestionably agreeable to Elizabethan taste and was successful. Shakespeare shows no reluctance about handling the theme and no self-consciousness about it. *All's Well* was to its age a bright and active comedy with, however, an element of danger and distress within it. Helena's task is indeed bitter. The events are displeasing to us and were probably not altogether pleasing to the Elizabethans, who, however, would have minded them less than we do.

2. *Measure for Measure.*

King James VI of Scotland arrived in London on May 7, 1603, to succeed Queen Elizabeth on the throne of England. Plays had been inhibited at the Queen's death on March 24, but were allowed on May 9. On May 19, the Lord Chamberlain's Company was licensed as the King's Company and placed under royal patronage. The plague raged in the city and the theaters were closed on May 26, so that Shakespeare's company traveled in the country. King James made a long stay first at Wilton and then at Hampton Court, delaying his royal entry until March 15, 1604. On that occasion the leading members of the King's Company, as grooms of the royal chamber, received liveries and took part in the ceremony. When the theaters opened on April 9, 1604, Shakespeare's company had probably its first great opportunity to win the new King's favor. A Revels Office account, the authenticity of which has long been debated but is now generally admitted, has been preserved which gives a list of plays presented before and after Christmas of that year. "John Heminges one of His Majesties players" was paid for plays performed by the King's Company. They included "Mesure for Mesure by Shaxberd."

If *Measure for Measure* was not written for this occasion, it may have been revised. In Act I, scene i, ll. 67-72, is a possible allusion to King James's well advertised modesty, for the Duke remarks that though he loves the people, he does not "like to stage me before their eyes." Malone saw in the use of the word "sweat" (I, ii, 84) an allusion to the recent plague; and Pompey's speech, at the beginning of scene iii, Act IV, seems to refer to the recently proclaimed "statute of stabbing." Parts of the play at least and its general temper and style associate it with *Othello*. Everything seems to point to 1604.

The play is very irregular, almost as much so as *All's Well that Ends Well*, and one is tempted to see in it a hasty composition. In the matter of sources Shakespeare seems to have taken his characteristic pains. It used to be said that *Measure for Measure* rests solely on a play called *Promos and Cassandra* by George Whetstone (1578), but more recent and more careful studies indicate that Shakespeare in writing *Measure for Measure* consulted not only Whetstone's play but Whetstone's translation in prose of the same narrative from Geraldi Cinthio's *Hecatommithi*, the story in the *Hecatommithi* itself, and even *Epitia*, a Latin play by Geraldi. *Measure for Measure* is a poor play from the points of view of structure, subject matter, dramatic consistency, and the characterization of minor figures. On the other hand, it contains some of Shakespeare's finest dramatic poetry and Isabella is one of Shakespeare's greatest women. Angelo too is extremely well done, and the Duke, although suffering much by an anachronistic denunciation, becomes, if seen with the eyes of Shakespeare's age, a character of poise and wisdom.

The scene is laid in Vienna and is so marked in the Folio. That city is suffering greatly from lawlessness, particularly sexual vice. The Duke, who is the governor of the city, apparently despairs of enforcing the laws himself. He, therefore, turns over the government of the city to a deputy, one Angelo, a severe moralist with a great reputation for uprightness, but with at least one breach of promise in his own past. It is sometimes thought that the Duke gave up his government in order to expose the professional reformer and to indicate that reforming a city by cruel exaction of penalties is not a proper thing. The Duke goes away on a pretended journey and presently returns disguised as a friar to correct the injuries done by his pious substitute.

The story of the play, widely known over Europe for at least two centuries, arises out of Angelo's rigid enforcement of a law which makes it a capital offense to beget an illegitimate child. Claudio has offended with his sweetheart Juliet. His chaste and beautiful sister Isabella goes to Angelo to plead for her brother's life. Angelo, who prided himself in being above all temptation, makes to Isabella the base proposal that he will spare Claudio's life if she will yield to his lust. She scorns him, then visits her brother in prison, feeling sure that Claudio will die rather than see her sacrifice her honor. This gives occasion for one of Shakespeare's famous scenes, albeit a somewhat pessimistic one. At first Claudio declares he will "encounter darkness as a bride" and hug it in his arms; but later he sees it differently and makes his cringing, eloquent speech (III, i, 118-32):

> Ay, but to die, and go we know not where;
> To lie in cold obstruction and to rot.

He desires her sacrifice, but she bids him perish in his ignominy. At this point the Duke, who knows what has happened, begins to operate the machine, and the consistency of the major plot suffers. He arranges to have Isabella pretend to consent to Angelo's proposal, but in the assignation substitutes for her Mariana, a former betrothed of Angelo, rejected by him because she had lost her fortune. Angelo thus consummates his marriage with Mariana. It helps this bad plot to remember that a betrothal had the validity of a marriage, but nothing can save it from its ingrained unpleasantness. Angelo decrees, in spite of his apparent victory, that Claudio shall die. Before, however, the execution can be carried out, the Duke reveals himself, resumes his authority, and proceeds to arrange everything. Claudio is forgiven and marries Juliet. Angelo marries Mariana. The Duke marries Isabella. The immoral people in the underplot, whom Claudio's imprisonment has brought into the story, are also all forgiven.

Measure for Measure remains one of Shakespeare's worst plays in spite of its touches of beauty. Its badness, however, has not prevented it from having great popularity on the stage. It was acted often in modified form in the late seventeenth century and was extremely popular with the great actors of the eighteenth and earlier nineteenth centuries: Colley Cibber, Garrick, Mrs. Siddons, Miss O'Neill, John Philip Kemble, and Macready. Miss Neilson revived it in London and New York in 1876 and 1880 respectively, and there are persons still living who have seen one or more of Madame Modjeska's revivals in New York or some other American city. It was played with great skill by the Stratford players in the thirties of this century and was brought on tour to the United States. *Measure for Measure* is usually played on a darkened stage, and its meaning often remains dark.

Our purpose is to arrive at a unified conception of Shakespeare as a dramatist, and in order to do this we must put ourselves in a position to know what Shakespeare meant by each of his plays. We arrive at that position most naturally and easily by finding out how each play came to be what it is and what it is not. *Measure for Measure* presents many problems. It is almost always regarded as a difficult play, usually as an unpleasant play. Even on the stage the play is rather dismal. The scenes are indoors, a number of them in prison. The major plot is objectionable to modern taste and is solved by the repetition of the objectionable "bed-trick" which belongs to *All's Well that Ends Well*. The behavior of Angelo is almost unbelievably vile, and it cannot be said that Shakespeare is successful in his effort to win back favor for him, or even tolerance. Shakespeare does, however, permit him to repent, and his words have the ring of sincerity (V, i, 371-8).

In *Measure for Measure* Shakespeare undertook to make a comedy out

of most unpromising materials. George Whetstone wrote a drama, supposed to be a comedy, *Promos and Cassandra*, and based it on a novella by
Geraldi Cinthio in *Hecatommithi*. Whetstone's play was perhaps never
acted; at least it had not been in 1578, and one rejoices in that fact. Cassandra yields to the wickedness of Promos; her brother Andrugio is nevertheless put to death by Promos, and Cassandra undergoes by way of reward
the unspeakable fate of marrying Promos. To the very objectionable major
plot Whetstone added a great deal of objectionable comedy of low life,
which makes very bad reading and serves to string out the wretched drama
into two·five-act parts. Shakespeare's comic scenes are almost universally
regarded as bad, but, whether that is true or not, they are a thousand times
better than Whetstone's. The story as told by Whetstone is from an
ethical point of view thoroughly bad. The question is as to what Shakespeare did to salvage or sterilize this plot.

Shakespeare's means of saving the heroine and of exposing Angelo is
the introduction of Mariana and the rectification of the wrong Angelo has
done her. It is not our way of saving her, because we demand freedom of
action or nothing. To Shakespeare and his age marriage was a sacrament
and a cure-all. Shakespeare presents her sympathetically, and the youthful
Tennyson was right in his interpretation of our feeling for her when he
wrote "Mariana in the Moated Grange." Shakespeare has thus done something to lend variety to the device of the substituted woman which he had
already used in *All's Well*. That he did borrow from himself there is no
doubt. There are verbal parallels to prove it, and we see the use he made
of this piece of detail in the manipulation of his major plot.

J. Dover Wilson in his edition of the play finds a great deal of un-
Shakespearean verse in *Measure for Measure*. These faults are admitted,
in part at least, by Sir Edmund Chambers. The blank verse of the play
as a whole is uniform, with considerable numbers of run-on lines, pauses
in the midst of lines, and light and weak endings; but these stylistic features are not more conspicuous than in other plays of the late middle
period, such as *Othello* and *King Lear*. The prose too is, for the most part,
late dramatic prose such as appears freely after the Henry IV plays and
Much Ado about Nothing. There is little of the early prose of clownage,
such as that of Launcelot Gobbo in *The Merchant of Venice*. There is
some bad verse in the play, but not enough and not sufficiently unusual to
serve as a reason for believing that there were two hands in the composi-

tion of *Measure for Measure*. Shakespeare did sometimes write bad verse, worse, no doubt, if he was hurried; and acted plays suffered corruption by actors and prompters, and, when such plays were printed, by copyists, editors, and compositors.

The Tudor editor points out a puzzling fact which falls in with Shakespeare's borrowing from *All's Well* and also suggests hasty composition. "Elbow," he says, "is a sketch of Dogberry, who is a finished portrait. Froth bears a similar relation to Slender; the Justice to Justice Shallow. Lucio is a debauched Mercutio combined with Gratiano." Why should Shakespeare, unless he was hurried, have done over less well a lot of his earlier characters?

It seems likely that Shakespeare undertook to rewrite Whetstone's *Promos and Cassandra* because of his interest in the situation and fate of Cassandra. He must here have seen an opportunity to depict a model of female chastity. He never lost his belief in the chastity of women, and he regarded the heroine of this play sympathetically. He no doubt believed in moral virtue, vestal dignity, and perfect purity as within the grasp of noble womanhood. To stress these things is to enter the realm, as Mrs. Jameson does, of precepts for young ladies' seminaries; but, if we must choose between that and the opposite point of view, we shall have to agree with Mrs. Jameson. We cannot, in all conscience, agree with Sir Arthur Quiller-Couch when he says of Isabella,

> She is something rancid in her chastity, and, on top of this, not by any means such a saint as she looks. To put it nakedly, she is all for saving her own soul, and she saves it by turning, of a sudden, into a bare procuress.

This is anachronism with a vengeance. Whetstone had said the woman would yield to the entreaty of her brother; Shakespeare said she would not, and the question remains.

The story of Isabella and Angelo has been looked at as an apologue of puritanism, Isabella presenting puritanism in its most favorable aspect and Angelo presenting its breakdown before the temptations of life and the weakness of character. Aside from the fact that Shakespeare does not elsewhere manifest an interest in such matters, to make of *Measure for Measure* a social document is to put an unwarranted weight upon the play. It is merely a Renaissance story embodying a moral issue. In so far as it deals with wrong and right it may be used to illustrate puritanism, and there is no error in doing so provided one does not involve Shakespeare in the solution of social and political issues of which he was unaware. A recent writer has seen in *Measure for Measure* a critique of puritanism, which is certainly not there:

> In Isabella and Angelo Shakespeare not only embodies the two main types of Puritan, but sets forth all the advantages and defects of Puritan training. He does full justice to its abstract loftiness of principle, to its power of resistance, its strength in warding off evil, its straightforward language, its uncompromising divisions between right and wrong, its freedom from all the sophistries of a more indulgent morality. But his praise is emphatically confined to Puritanism in the abstract. Both Isabella and Angelo are found wanting when they come into contact with real life. Shakespeare points to the conclusion: "Puritanism, in its present state, unmodified, is unfit to come into contact with society."

Shakespeare was greatly interested in the character of Isabella and her problem, not in general morals. He was less interested in Angelo and has left him inconsistent and puzzling. Indeed, there are two Angelos—the good man gone wrong and the hypocrite, and the hypocrite prevails. The first scene of the second act is certainly too pointed not to be an intentional representation of Angelo's insincerity. Angelo walks out of hearing of the flagrantly bad people and leaves their case to his subordinate with the wish that he "find good cause to whip them all."

Considering this scene, one cannot call Angelo at the outset a good man. He may have just cause for priding himself on his personal purity; that is, he may never have been tempted or have succumbed to passion. But his is the Pharisee's character—he is better than the other men of his own rank—the Claudios. He isn't interested in professional vice-mongers, their existence, and their punishment. The potentialities of the hypocrite are in Angelo from the first. A sensitive actor could depict such a person in the first scene; the lines will yield to an unctuous interpretation of a sort. One has no awareness of having been tricked when Angelo's previous relation to Mariana is related. This is not character inconsistency so much as a shortcoming in the plot. The inconsistency—if it may be so called—is in the suddenness of its introduction. The plot would have been strengthened had we known this detail earlier. It probably did occur to Shakespeare late —most likely in the revision stage—but it certainly does not contradict any impression one has of Angelo prior to its introduction. Shakespeare has not, however, made himself entirely clear, and there is little evidence that he took the trouble to see inside Angelo.

He was, on the other hand, certainly interested in the figure of the Duke. Royal and noble characters always appealed to him, and he saw in the Duke a chance to depict a wise and temperate ruler who understood the difficulties of the reformation of vice and who showed, like King James, a tolerant and supposedly wise attitude toward vice and sin among his subjects. It was a vicious age in England and worse throughout Europe, so that Shakespeare's treatment of the Duke would suggest that the handling of vice, as well as other governmental matters, are better left in the hands of a ruler divinely appointed and sustained. This offers the best solution of the problem of the Duke.

The comic parts interested Shakespeare less than any others, and he did the comic scenes rather perfunctorily. His imagination was somewhat stirred by Lucio in his ironic relation to the Duke, and Pompey, a character perhaps intended to be acted by Armin, is a repulsive, although rather striking, study of degeneracy. Other comic parts seem to be hastily done according to older forms. Perhaps Mistress Overdone is the best of the lot, and there is a touch of genius in Barnardine's interview with the Duke disguised as a friar (IV, iii, 53-66):

> *Duke.* Sir, induced by my charity, and hearing how hastily you are to depart, I am come to advise you, comfort you and pray with you.
> *Bar.* Friar, not I: I have been drinking hard all night, and I will have more time to prepare me, or they shall beat out my brains with billets: I will not consent to die this day, that's certain.

The thing above all that Shakespeare did was to contrive a plot which would rescue Isabella from the fate awarded Cassandra by Whetstone and Cinthio, rescue her from the staining of her honor, from the breaking of her will, and from marriage to the villain who had plotted against her. In contriving this device Shakespeare displayed no great originality, but repeated from *All's Well* and Boccaccio the "bed trick." He did it more skillfully and improved upon it by the introduction of a greater sense of justice. The presentation is also more vague and distant than in *All's Well*, and this feature must be regarded as a refinement. When Shakespeare introduced the Mariana episode there are no means of telling. One can hardly agree with Robert H. Wilson that Shakespeare first wrote a play with the mere plot of *Promos and Cassandra* and at a later time revised it by the introduction of Mariana. It seems more likely that the employment of Mariana and her story occurred to Shakespeare while he was writing the play and that he never gave to the work any great perfection. There is some reason to believe that Shakespeare's habit was not always to write his plays straight through, but to write scenes here and there. In such a method inconsistencies might occur, and certain parts might be hastily, if not carelessly, done. Some inevitable roughnesses of composition may have been left standing in Shakespeare's play, which was hastily finished if not hastily composed.

3. *Troilus and Cressida.*

An entry in the Stationers' Register for February 7, 1603, gives an approximate date for *Troilus and Cressida*. A publisher named James Roberts entered his copy to print, "when he hath gotten sufficient authority for it, the book of *Troilus and Cressida* as it is acted by my Lord Chamberlain's men." One does not know why he lacked authority. Perhaps he was acting in behalf of the players and in order to prevent the piracy of the play. It was re-entered to R. Bonian and H. Walley on January 28, 1609, and was first printed that year. It seems almost certain that the printing was unauthorized, for the edition appears in two forms. The texts are in all particulars the same, but what appears to be the earlier has a title page: *The Historie of Troylus and Cresseida. As it was acted by the Kings Maiesties seruants at the Globe.* The second issue has: *The Famous Historie of Troylus and Cresseid. Excellently expressing the beginning of their loues, with the conceited wooing of Pandarus Prince of Licia.* Both title-pages contain the statement "Written by William Shakespeare." The second has also a thing unique among Shakespearean quartos, namely, a preface or epistle to the reader beginning "A Neuer writer, to an euer reader. Newes." It declares that the play is new, "neuer stal'd with the Stage, neuer clapper-clawd with the palmes of the vulgar." It also declares that the play is published against "the grand possessors wills." The new title-page and the epistle seem, therefore, to evade the consequences of publishing a play to which the publishers had no proper title, for, as the earlier entry in the Stationers' Register shows, the play had been acted on the stage.

A reference in the anonymous play *Histriomastix* to "Cressida" and to the knight "shaking" his furious "spear" seems to indicate that Shakespeare

had written a play on the subject by about 1599. The prologue to the play
as given in the Folio version alludes unmistakably to Jonson's *Poetaster*,
which appeared in the summer of 1601. In the light of this and of the
first entry in the Stationers' Register, the play in its final form was written
about 1602. Fleay's attempt to connect it with the war of the theatres, by
identifying Jonson with Ajax and Marston with Thersites, is not regarded
as successful, although it still has its advocates. When the Folio was printed
the text used was a different one from that of the quarto of 1609, probably
the playhouse manuscript in possession of the King's company.

No play in Shakespeare has perhaps been more misunderstood than has
Troilus and Cressida. Critics have been perplexed by it, and it has had no
stage career, although the performance by Cambridge students in 1922
indicated that the play has decided dramatic value and charm. Dowden
was so uncertain as to the significance of *Troilus and Cressida* that he
declined to discuss it in the first edition of *Shakspere, His Mind and Art*.
Later, in the preface to the third edition, he wrote, "I now believe this
strange and difficult play was a last attempt to continue comedy, made
when Shakespeare had ceased to smile genially and when he must be either
ironical or take a deep, passionate, and tragical view of life." "It is," he
says, "the comedy of disillusion." From a point of view which insists on
interpreting Shakespeare's plays as reflections of his private life and of his
attitude toward the world, this is no doubt inescapable: *Troilus and Cressida* could have arisen only from an embitterea mind. But whatever the
truth of the matter may be, it is by no means necessary to mistake our
conception of the story for Shakespeare's.

The tale of Troilus and his love Cressida is the proverbial case of the
fickle woman who deserts a faithful lover. It came originally as an offshoot
of the tale of Troy, not as told by Homer in the *Iliad*, but as invented
by Benoit de Ste. Maure in *Le Roman de Troie* in the eleventh century
and amplified into a long poem, *Il Filostrato*, by Boccaccio before the
middle of the fourteenth century and by Chaucer in *Troilus and Criseyde*
later in the same century. Chaucer told the story sympathetically. His
Criseyde is something more than a faithless woman. But Chaucer's treatment is only one of many and by no means the most influential of the
group. Shakespeare seems to have done in this case what he also did in
the characterization of Julius Caesar and of Cleopatra. He interpreted his
character in line with the current tradition and not according to his source.

He may have taken his material in part from *Troilus and Criseyde*, but he followed Chaucer in substance, not at all in spirit. This mediaeval love story Shakespeare retold with a frankness and cynicism no greater than the events justify and no more realistically than it had been told before. He placed it against a background of the siege of Troy, and here again he is baffling and unsatisfactory to modern taste. We draw our conceptions of the Trojan War from Homer. Shakespeare probably knew some part of Chapman's translation of the *Iliad* and made some use of it, particularly in the characterization of Thersites; but what he really followed in both event and sympathy was the mediaeval romance of Troy. He followed Raoul le Fevre's *Recueil des Histoires de Troyes* as translated and published by Caxton, and probably also Lydgate's *Troy Book*, translated from Guido della Colonna's *Historia Trojana*. These romances do not present the fall of Troy as a neutral war of antiquity. They render it personal and immediate. They sympathize with the Trojans. The English, the Italians, the French, and even the Scandinavians, regarded the Trojans as their ancestors and conceived of the Greeks as crafty, cowardly, and brutal. Hence it is easy to see that Shakespeare and his audience sided with the Trojans. Shakespeare serves the Greeks much better than the tradition warranted. Thersites is a "deformed and scurrilous Greek," Ajax a stupid bully, Achilles a selfish coward, and Menelaus a somewhat ignoble figure. But, on the other hand, Agamemnon is a sagacious and dignified commander of troops, Nestor a sage, and Ulysses one of Shakespeare's real triumphs in the creation of character. Ulysses is so statesmanlike, so shrewd, so wise, and withal so kindly that he suggests one of the great statesmen for whom Elizabeth's reign was celebrated. Among the Trojans, who are as a whole much more admirable, Hector is a truly noble figure offsetting Ulysses on the Greek side, and Troilus a model of love and courage suggesting Romeo. The play presents a wealth of Renaissance learning.

Troilus loves Cressida with a deep and unselfish love. He wins her through the despicable services of her uncle Pandarus, not, however, until she has displayed the arts of the coquette in order to inflame his love. This tale of illicit love is set over against the love of Paris for Helen, stolen wife of the Greek Menelaus. As the play opens, the Greeks lack unity and quarrel among themselves, so that they cannot succeed in capturing Troy. Achilles is enraged at Agamemnon, the Greek general, and is sulking in his tent in company with his beloved Patroclus, as in the *Iliad*. Ulysses tries with all his wisdom and eloquence to heal the breach. The issue arises when Hector, the principal warrior among the Trojans, challenges a Grecian to single combat. The Greeks select Ajax as their representative in the hope of arousing Achilles to action by appealing to his jealousy of Ajax; it is in vain. The Trojan leaders debate on the propriety of returning Helen to her former husband and thus ending the war. Hector wishes to do this, but Troilus stands out against it; so that in spite of the warnings of their sister Cassandra, a prophetess whose fate it is to have her prophecies disregarded, Hector yields and the war goes on. Calchas, the father of Cressida, a Trojan renegade to the Greeks, provides for an exchange of prisoners, so that he may regain his daughter Cressida in exchange for the Trojan Antenor. Diomed has charge of the exchange. Cressida parts from Troilus with renewed oaths of everlasting love and accompanies Diomed. When she arrives in the Grecian camp, she kisses the Greeks all round, except Ulysses, who sees her for what she is. Diomed, breaking through the veneer of her coquetry, takes Cressida for his mistress. Then occur feastings between Greeks and Trojans in the Greek camp. Ulysses accompanies Troilus to Calchas's tent where Troilus overhears Cressida's carryings on with Diomed. Troilus returns to Troy disillusioned and bitter, and on the next morning Hector slays Patroclus, who is wearing the armor of Achilles. On this provocation Achilles goes to battle. He does not, however, meet Hector in fair fight, but surrounds him with the Myrmidons and murders him; then he ties the body to the tail of his horse and drags it about the walls of Troy. The play ends with a curse delivered by Troilus against Pandarus, the go-between. On the basis of this sorry tale critics have been led to believe that Shakespeare was satirizing the heroes of antiquity, pricked on thereto by his jealousy of Chapman, the translator of Homer; but the idea is absurd. Shakespeare has merely put on the stage the mediaeval Troy story, and has elevated rather than debased the tale in so doing. The point is that the tale was ready-made. Shakespeare had no choice, no latitude for manipulation. The story has been a puzzle for generations and is still a puzzle. The editors of the First Folio regarded *Troilus and Cressida* as a tragedy. Dowden and many modern critics have regarded it as a "bitter" comedy. A distinguished scholar has decided that Shakespeare's play is a satire against the sentimental infatuation of Troilus, a conclusion which is perhaps too sophisticated for the age that produced the play. As a drama *Troilus and Cressida* belongs to the romantic tradition and, as such, is not necessarily either a comedy or a tragedy; and as to the making of it into a satire, that could hardly have been done when the unalterable tale was faithfully told by Shakespeare with obvious sincerity.

It is doubtful whether any unity of purpose or mood can be discovered in *Troilus and Cressida*. The play would seem to have been altered by at least two revisions. Perhaps the latest concerned itself with the infatuated Troilus, the flippant Cressida, and the silly Pandarus. The older idea was that Shakespeare may have written a play bearing on the war of the theatres, the rivalry between the regular companies of actors and the children's companies, and later revised it in such a way as to obliterate the traces of the conflict. We know from *Hamlet* that Shakespeare deprecated the quarrel; it would have been like him, if he did participate in it, to withdraw his part, but there are so far no clues by which the mystery can be solved. What we have is a play hard to interpret as a whole. There is the Trojan war on the one side, with its leaders, its politics, and its disaster, and, on the other, the rather gaily and cynically told love story of Troilus and Cressida. Although this story is told in a style which makes light of it, this treatment is not out of line with the tradition. Even Chaucer is not free from a disposition to regard coolly the infidelity of the pattern of feminine fickleness and the easy gullibility of masculine faithfulness; yet neither Troilus nor Cressida is a caricature. It is doubtful whether a case for deliberate satire on Shakespeare's part can be made out. In the Greek plot there is definite condemnation of satire as practised by Patroclus and Thersites, which is harmful to the state and destructive of the specialty of rule.

All this is not the play. Indeed, it seems to say that the play lacks interest and importance; whereas exactly the opposite is true. *Troilus and Cressida* is full of interest. The first two scenes are devoted to the love story, and the second ends in a soliloquy by Cressida that is worth considering. Soliloquies usually inform the audience of the character and intentions of the speaker or of the purpose of the dramatist. Cressida simply says that she loves Troilus, but that she will hold off (I, ii, 314-15):

> That she beloved knows nought that knows not this:
> Men prize the thing ungain'd more than it is.

The lady is too prudent; she endeavors to love and be wise, which the maxim tells us is not possible. We do not see her again until the second

scene of the third act, although we have felt her influence when Troilus
throws in his voice with Paris against returning Helen to her husband,
Menelaus, and thus ending the war (II, ii). The second scene of the third
act is the scene of the assignation, and here Cressida binds herself, as she
was compelled to do by the traditional story, in such a way that if she
proved untrue, she would be forever the pattern of infidelity in love (III,
ii, 190-203):

> If I be false, or swerve a hair from truth,
> When time is old and hath forgot itself,
> When waterdrops have worn the stones of Troy,
> And blind oblivion swallow'd cities up,
> And mighty states characterless are grated
> To dusty nothing, yet let memory,
> From false to false, among false maids in love,
> Upbraid my falsehood! When they've said 'as false
> As air, as water, wind, or sandy earth,
> As fox to lamb, as wolf to heifer's calf,
> Pard to the hind, or stepdame to her son,'
> 'Yea,' let them say, to stick the heart of falsehood,
> 'As false as Cressid.'

These eloquent words are not Cressida's; they are the words of tradition.
In the second scene of the fourth act Cressida speaks again. It is to swear
allegiance to Troilus and to Troy (IV, ii, 113-15):

> Tear my bright hair and scratch my praised cheeks,
> Crack my clear voice with sobs and break my heart
> With sounding Troilus. I will not go from Troy.

But she does go, and in the scene of parting there is nothing to indicate
a double rôle. Her grief at parting seems as genuine as that of Troilus
(IV, iv, 26-9):

> Cressid, I love thee in so strain'd a purity,
> That the bless'd gods, as angry with my fancy,
> More bright in zeal than the devotion which
> Cold lips blow to their deities, take thee from me.

She meditates no treachery, is not covertly glad to leave for the Grecian
camp. When she gets there her behavior is entirely different. Shakespeare
makes no apology or explanation. Chaucer was sorry for her as a weak

woman, but in Shakespeare we have merely the harsh words of Ulysses
(IV, v, 54-63):

> Fie, fie upon her!
> There's language in her eye, her cheek, her lip,
> Nay, her foot speaks; her wanton spirits look out
> At every joint and motive of her body. . . .
>   set them down
> For sluttish spoils of opportunity
> And daughters of the game.

What is one to think of speeches like these (V, ii, 77-82; 107-12)?

> O, all you gods! O pretty, pretty pledge!
> Thy master now lies thinking in his bed
> Of thee and me, and sighs, and takes my glove,
> And gives memorial dainty kisses to it,
> As I kiss thee. Nay, do not snatch it from me;
> He that takes that doth take my heart withal. . . .
> Troilus, farewell! One eye yet looks on thee;
> But with my heart the other eye doth see.
> Ah, poor our sex! this fault in us I find,
> The error of our eye directs our mind:
> What error leads must err; O, then conclude
> Minds sway'd by eyes are full of turpitude.

Cressida is a mere puppet, the impersonalized voice of a tradition, and yet
there seems to gleam faintly through her the trace of Chaucer's more
human Criseyde.

Why the words and actions of Troilus should be thought subject to
ridicule is hard to see. Of course he is unnecessarily burdened with the
tradition that he is the pattern of faithful love, and that fact causes him
to be formalized; but on the stage he makes the impression of a brave
youth, and his words are of the same character as those spoken by Shakespeare's lovers from Romeo to Florizel. Shakespeare has provided him
with a disillusionment, and his reaction is one of manliness (V, ii, 163-76):

> Ay, Greek; and that shall be divulged well
> In characters as red as Mars his heart
> Inflamed with Venus: never did young man fancy
> With so eternal and so fix'd a soul.
> Hark, Greek: as much as I do Cressid love,
> So much by weight hate I her Diomed:

That sleeve is mine that he'll bear on his helm;
Were it a casque composed by Vulcan's skill,
My sword should bite it: not the dreadful spout
Which shipmen do the hurricano call,
Constringed in mass by the almighty sun,
Shall dizzy with more clamour Neptune's ear
In his descent than shall my prompted sword
Falling on Diomed.

The love plot in *Troilus and Cressida* is a thin line not properly specialized, and not given proper general value as it belonged to romantic tradition, but the plot of war and politics is weighty in both political and social significance. We are apt to forget that drama is a speech art to be judged by the greatness of its expression. It is for the dramatist to supply the occasion for significant utterances and to be able to utter thoughts and feeling greatly and appropriately through his characters. *Troilus and Cressida*, in so far as it deals with the Trojan War, treats of the wrath of Achilles. Vastly inferior as a whole to the *Iliad*, it nevertheless rises in certain places to an otherwise unequalled height. As the theme begins (I, iii) Achilles is sulking in his tent, angry at Agamemnon, the Greek commander, on a private count. The other Grecian leaders discuss the situation and agree that until their forces can be united they are doomed to failure.

In this discussion Ulysses delivers what is one of the best known and politically most significant speeches in all Shakespeare. It is the discursus on order and degree (ll. 78-137), which begins,

The specialty of rule hath been neglected.

It is certainly the political creed of Shakespeare and of the Renaissance. It is exemplified in Shakespeare's history plays and is in line with that fundamental document Sir John Cheke's *The Hurt of Sedition*. See lines 85-8, 101-3, 116-24:

The heavens themselves, the planets and this centre
Observe degree, priority and place,
Insisture, course, proportion, season, form,
Office and custom, in all line of order; . . .
        O, when degree is shaked,
Which is the ladder to all high designs,
The enterprise is sick! . . .

> Force should be right; or rather, right and wrong,
> Between whose endless jar justice resides,
> Should lose their names, and so should justice too.
> Then everything includes itself in power,
> Power into will, will into appetite;
> And appetite, an universal wolf,
> So doubly seconded with will and power,
> Must make perforce an universal prey,
> And last eat up himself.

Nestor and Ulysses decide to visit Achilles and remonstrate with him. Before that interview takes place we get (II, i) a view of the behavior of Achilles through the words of the foul cynic Thersites, of Ajax, and of Achilles himself; also a momentous discussion among the Trojan leaders of the question of ending the war by returning the stolen Helen to the Greeks. Paris and Troilus oppose the action, and we have the famous reasonable words of Hector, who nevertheless fails to carry his point. It is fatal to neglect the words of wisdom (II, ii, 163-82):

> Paris and Troilus, you have both said well,
> And on the cause and question now in hand
> Have glozed, but superficially; not much
> Unlike young men, whom Aristotle thought
> Unfit to hear moral philosophy:
> The reasons you allege do more conduce
> To the hot passion of distemper'd blood
> Than to make up a free determination
> 'Twixt right and wrong, for pleasure and revenge
> Have ears more deaf than adders to the voice
> Of any true decision. Nature craves
> All dues to be render'd to their owners: now,
> What nearer debt in all humanity
> Than wife is to the husband? If this law
> Of nature be corrupted through affection,
> And that great minds, of partial indulgence
> To their benumbed wills, resist the same,
> There is a law in each well-order'd nation
> To curb those raging appetites that are
> Most disobedient and refractory.

The scene of the interview with Achilles (sc. iii) begins with the abusive household of Achilles—Thersites, Patroclus, and Ajax. Nestor and Ulysses may not see Achilles, who is indifferently asleep. But a time occurs (III, iii) when Ulysses, pocketing his dignity, forces Achilles to hear him. For

this meeting Shakespeare writes one of the greatest of all dramatic utterances of its kind (ll. 145-90). Not Bacon himself ever spoke more point-
edly or so eloquently.

> *Ulyss.* Time hath, my lord, a wallet at his back,
> Wherein he puts alms for oblivion,
> A great-sized monster of ingratitudes:
> Those scraps are good deeds past; which are devour'd
> As fast as they are made, forgot as soon
> As done: perseverance, dear my lord,
> Keeps honour bright: to have done is to hang
> Quite out of fashion, like a rusty mail
> In monumental mockery. . . .
> One touch of nature makes the whole world kin,
> That all with one consent praise new-born gawds,
> Though they are made and moulded of things past,
> And give to dust that is a little gilt
> More laud than gilt o'er-dusted.
> The present eye praises the present object:
> Then marvel not, thou great and complete man,
> That all the Greeks begin to worship Ajax;
> Since things in motion sooner catch the eye
> Than what not stirs. The cry went once on thee,
> And still it might, and yet it may again,
> If thou wouldst not entomb thyself alive
> And case thy reputation in thy tent;
> Whose glorious deeds, but in these fields of late,
> Made emulous missions 'mongst the gods themselves
> And drave great Mars to faction.

The play ends, like the *Iliad* itself, with the death of Hector. The colossal ferocity of Achilles, which expresses itself in such words as these (IV,
v, 242-6),

> Tell me, you heavens, in which part of his body
> Shall I destroy him? whether there, or there, or there?
> That I may give the local wound a name
> And make distinct the very breach whereout
> Hector's great spirit flew: answer me, heavens!

comes but lamely off in the mere murder of Hector by the Myrmidons
(V, viii). The play ends with Troilus going off to meet his death in battle
and cursing Pandarus as he departs. Almost any fair judgment would
pronounce his last long speech (V, x, 11-31) the speech of a hero,

I do not speak of flight, of fear, of death,
But dare all imminence that gods and men
Address their dangers in. Hector is gone:
Who shall tell Priam so, or Hecuba?

4. *Timon of Athens.*

It is difficult to agree with those critics who find in *Troilus and Cressida* only a hopeless pessimism. It is, after all, but a version of the dark and dreadful story of the Wrath of Achilles, which ended in the death of Hector, intertwined with the discouraging tale of the fickleness of Cressida whose victim was the faithful lover Troilus. Shakespeare could not have made these stories other than they are. No such pessimism hangs over the play as over *Timon of Athens.* In *Troilus and Cressida* Shakespeare has brightened the picture with noble actions, noble purposes, and eloquent words—all he could do. But in *Timon of Athens* pessimism runs into misanthropy, and the story is but scantily relieved by action or idealism.

There is no drama in mere non-participation, where it arises from avoidance of the conflict or from definite refusal to participate. There is also no drama in the possession of complete power, without struggle to exercise it or opposition to its exertions. Neither Prospero in *The Tempest,* who has complete command, nor Timon in *Timon of Athens,* who refuses to act or to resist, is truly dramatic. We must find our drama in heroes like Hamlet, for the field of dramatic action lies in the territory between Prospero and Timon. Timon of Athens, having been deceived and cheated by his fellowmen, becomes a complete and actionless misanthrope. He denounces the sycophants who have abused his generosity, retires to the seashore, and dies there after having written an epitaph in which he curses mankind. Shakespeare's *Timon of Athens* is a play which contains some of the best of Shakespeare's writing but, on the most probable hypothesis, was left by its author incomplete. Shakespeare apparently enjoyed doing certain parts of the play. There is gusto in his presentation of the roguelike crookedness of Timon's flatterers and in Timon's curses against mankind. But it is possible that Shakespeare sickened of the dramatically unworkable subject and never finished it in detail. It has been plausibly argued that Shakespeare wrote only certain scenes and that Chapman, or another dramatist, finished it sufficiently for the stage; but agreement is forestalled by the thought that Chapman, or any competent dramatist of the time, would have done better work. The finer passages, such as one would regard as Shakespearean, occur pretty well scattered through the play rather than in any one part or on any one theme. The play resembles nothing so much as a first draft with certain sections well done and others hardly more than the raw materials written hastily.

It is not even clear what Shakespeare's plan was..He might, for example, have meant it for a play showing three different reactions against the cruelties and injustices of the world. There was Timon, born for magnificence, a practitioner of magnificence in all its minor branches, such as charity, hospitality, and generosity. It is wrong to think of him as a wastrel and spendthrift, for, had the world been as fine in character as Timon was, there would have been no disaster. Timon's spending was set down as a mark of his nobility in the ancient world and was so understood in the Renaissance. Let us not intrude any bourgeois parsimony into the tale of Timon of Athens. It was noble to spend, and Timon was a spender. When the blow fell upon him, he was stricken to the heart, incapable of action, and given over to magnificent railing. There was also Alcibiades, an Athenian soldier, who was betrayed by time-serving politicians in his own country and vilely misused. Later he was needed by the city, sent for, and made much of. Alcibiades' reception of public ingratitude was very different from that of Timon. At the head of his troops he made himself feared and at least professed the intention of overthrowing and punishing his enemies. But the story of Alcibiades is hardly developed at all, and, if Shakespeare had any plans with reference to it, they were never realized. The play also affords another type of man-hater in Apemantus, described as a "churlish philosopher." He has known all his life that men are a sorry lot and has devoted himself on principle to hating them. Little use is made of him. He merely visits Timon in his prosperous days to tell Timon he is making a mistake and later returns to say, "I told you so." Even the theme of misanthropy is not fully worked out in *Timon of Athens*, although the elements of it are present. Shakespeare agreed with Milton, who says in *Areopagitica*, "I cannot praise a fugitive and cloister'd virtue, unexercis'd and unbreath'd, that never sallies out and sees her adversary, but slinks out of the race, where that immortal garland is to be run for, not without dust and heat." Apemantus is one of those who slinks out of the race; Alcibiades had it in him to compete for the immortal garland, and Timon belongs, according to species, to a third class. He does not know about the race, mistakes a part for the whole, wakes up too late, and gets out of bed on the wrong side. He is a sentimentalist by nature and to that extent is a tragic figure. But Shakespeare unfortunately does not bring these things out. If he really understood Timon, he hardly makes his conception clear. Timon is the completely fine gentleman of antiquity who suffers a destructive shock when he finds out what his beloved fellowmen are really like. He cannot make terms with the truth, and it seems to be made a point of honor with him that he cannot. *Timon of Athens* might thus be regarded as the tragedy of a virtue in excess; the tragedy of unwillingness to live in a world of injustice, vice, and ingratitude; possibly as the tragedy of a lack of fortitude. But Shakespeare gives us little to guide us.

When Shakespeare wrote *Timon of Athens* is a difficult matter to determine. It appeared in the First Folio of 1623; there is no contemporary mention of it or its presentation, and allusions to Timon of Athens are so numerous in the literature of the time that no one of them can be taken as a reference to Shakespeare's play. In style the play is late, but possibly not much later than *King Lear*. The unevenness of the workmanship makes the relative position of the play hard to determine. There were two main sources for the Timon story: *Timon the Misanthrope*, a witty dialogue by the Greek satirist Lucian, and Plutarch's *Life of Mark Antony*, which repeats the Timon story. Shakespeare seems to have used both of these, but relied most heavily on Plutarch. He also derived bits from Plutarch's *Life of Alcibiades*. Perhaps there is significance in the fact that Shakespeare used Plutarch's *Life of Mark Antony* in his composition of *Antony and Cleopatra* about 1607 or 1608. It would be natural to think that he may have become interested in the theme when he was writing that play, but this is rather specious, since Shakespeare had probably owned for a long time a copy of North's translation of Amyot's French version of Plutarch's *Lives*. Since the bitter pessimism of *Timon of Athens* bears so strong a resemblance to the insane railings of King Lear (IV, vi) and since the play is a sort of orphan not fitting in with any groupings of plays, it seems just as well to treat it here. There was disillusionment in the mind of Shakespeare when he wrote *King Lear*. It is just possible that it carried over into *Timon of Athens*.

There is a formal as well as a static quality in the conception of Timon's character. Timon is not quite humanized, and the same mechanical quality appears in nearly all the minor characters of the play. *Timon of Athens* is a sort of morality play. There are few human situations and relations in it. Flavius, Timon's steward, is almost the only natural-seeming person in the drama. There are no domestic relationships as in *Othello* and *King Lear*, no emotional conflicts as in *Romeo and Juliet* and *Antony and Cleopatra*, no perplexing struggle as in *Hamlet* and *Measure for Measure*, no moral conflict as in *Macbeth*, no passionate idealism as in *Julius Caesar* and *Henry V*. In other words, *Timon of Athens* lacks the element of struggle. Elsewhere men have to make choices which touch their inmost hearts or their loyalties to wives, children, sweethearts, friends, or sovereigns. Timon makes no choice of this kind. He has no human ties and no involvements of personality. There is thus little individuality in the characterization. He is a moral voice censuring humanity. And the other characters in this play are types. Apemantus is a cynic. Alcibiades is an unreflective doer. The Poet and the Painter are professionals who speak well about their arts. They are intellectuals who wish to make the most of their endowments. The rest are practical men out for Number One, parasites, flatterers, thieves, and prostitutes—all typical. Perhaps Timon is meant to represent the unbiased individual, like the consumer in the modern cartoon, preyed upon by all classes including his own and recognized sympathetically as a mere Citizen.

From the terms of the traditional plot, *Timon of Athens* would seem to develop the theme of the fickleness of fortune with the consequent withdrawal of all his fair-weather friends from Timon, on whom the blow has fallen; but, if this were all, the rôle of the faithful steward would certainly have been exalted. As it is, he is merely a reporter of the woeful conditions of Timon's estate, and later he is dismissed because Timon does not wish to be disturbed in his misanthropy by the companionship of a kindly man. The conduct of Timon becomes the theme of the play. In the first part of the drama he dispays the extreme of prodigality. This prodigality is to be regarded as folly perhaps but not as vice. It is plainly a fault which leans to virtue's side. It is something like the folly of Lear, but the shock of disillusionment brings different effects. Lear's suffering is not the loss of his hundred or his fifty knights, but the loss of the devotion which was due him as a father and a benefactor. He says (II, iv, 266-70):

> O, reason not the need! Our basest beggars
> Are in the poorest thing superfluous:
> Allow not nature more than nature needs,
> Man's life is cheap as beast's.

There is a sense of justice in Lear's pessimism which must also be present in Timon's pessimism; and Lear ultimately finds a mean of behavior, he learns about himself, and the world adjusts itself to him. But when the shock comes to Timon, he does not find salvation in any mean; he flies to another and a worse extreme. Lear's misanthropy refers to the family and the state. Timon expresses himself in cosmic terms. The ethical principles by which Renaissance moralists measured life Timon reinterprets in terms of the villainy of all human kind. His pessimism extends to the macrocosm. As the first senator says of him when he withdraws from the scene (V, i, 227-8):

> His discontents are unremoveably
> Coupled to nature.

In spite, however, of deprecations and dissatisfactions there are fascinations about *Timon of Athens*. For example, it begins with the Poet and the Painter and these puppets talk about their art. One can almost tell from what they say how the master artist conceived of art. The Poet talks most, and we learn from him that poetry flows in easy numbers (I, i, 22-5):

> The fire i' the flint
> Shows not till it be struck; our gentle flame
> Provokes itself and like the current flies
> Each bound it chafes.

His criticism of the Painter's work tells us that the basis of art is suggestion and that art is livelier than life (ll. 30-8):

> How this grace
> Speaks his own standing! what a mental power
> This eye shoots forth! how big imagination
> Moves in this lip! to the dumbness of the gesture
> One might interpret. . . .
> I will say of it,
> It tutors nature: artificial strife
> Lives in these touches, livelier than life.

Poetry, he says, must be plastic, universal, and free from temporal bondage (ll. 45-50). The Poet has written a moral apologue, which is itself characteristic of the Renaissance view that poetry existed to give pleasure while it taught virtue. The idea is commonplace enough, and the Painter says (ll. 90-4):

A thousand moral paintings I can show
That shall demonstrate these quick blows of Fortune's
More pregnantly than words. Yet you do well
To show Lord Timon that mean eyes have seen
The foot above the head.

The first two acts of *Timon of Athens* are somewhat broken, irregular, and imperfect. They show evidence of artistic planning rather than artistry. There is, for example, in the second scene of the first act a tiny masque of Cupid and Amazons with lutes in their hands. Timon and Apemantus make clear their points of view, Timon infatuated with hospitality and friendship, Apemantus bitterly disdainful yet willing, all the same, to eat Timon's food. In the same scene one hears the warning voice of Flavius, the faithful steward, telling the audience in an aside in what parlous shape Timon's affairs are. One feels that the first act might have been and should have been a more sumptuous picture, and the same is true of the abbreviated second act, which is also rather confused with Senators, Apemantus, and an uncalled-for Fool. The act concerns the news of Timon's financial disasters. His creditors display a typical uneasiness; but, when Timon is confronted by them and the report of his ruin is confirmed by Flavius, he is not in the least put out. He has faith in the investment he has made in the friendship and good will of men (II, ii, 239-40):

Ne'er speak, or think,
That Timon's fortunes 'mong his friends can sink.

There is some lively, subtle comedy in the third act in the various refusals of Timon's false friends to aid him. This rises to no mean height in the brilliant execution of Timon's famous last banquet, the grace he says before it, and his resolution to hate the world. The crowd of sycophants, thinking Timon's wealth regained, assemble, licking their lips (III, vi, 78-105):

You great benefactors, sprinkle our society with thankfulness. For your own gifts, make yourselves praised: but reserve still to give, lest your deities be despised. Lend to each man enough, that one need not lend to another; for, were your godheads to borrow of men, men would forsake the gods. Make the meat be beloved more than the man that gives it. Let no assembly of twenty be without a score of villains: if there sit twelve women at the table, let a dozen of them be—as they are. The rest of your fees, O gods—the senators of Athens, together with the common lag of people—what is amiss in them, you gods, make suitable for destruction. For these my present friends, as they are to me nothing, so in nothing bless them, and to nothing they are welcome.

Uncover, dogs, and lap!

The dishes are uncovered and found to be full of warm water. Timon speaks again:

> May you a better feast never behold,
> You knot of mouth-friends! smoke and lukewarm water
> Is your perfection. This is Timon's last;
> Who, stuck and spangled you with flatteries,
> Washes it off, and sprinkles in your faces
> Your reeking villany.

He throws the water in their faces, the dishes after it, and drives them out.

> What, all in motion? Henceforth be no feast,
> Whereat a villain's not a welcome guest.
> Burn, house! Sink, Athens! henceforth hated be
> Of Timon man and all humanity!

This strikes the characteristic note of the play. After it until his death Timon is like a man armed with a machine gun with which he mows down all who approach his cave. The lure is the pot of gold which Timon finds in the fields while he is digging roots to serve as food. The Poet and the Painter reappear and go limping off. There is a scornful rejection of Alcibiades and an emptying of filth upon his fine ladies. Alcibiades is not hostile to Timon, but he appears here in a bad light. Timon's brawl with Apemantus (IV, iii, 197-398) strikes new heights in the flyting or tirade (ll. 374-7). Just why Timon reserves his special hatred for Apemantus is not clear unless it be that Apemantus, who has no cause for misanthropy, parodies Timon, who has.

Timon gives gold to the banditti (IV, iii, 438-53):

> I'll example you with thievery:
> The sun's a thief, and with his great attraction
> Robs the vast sea: the moon's an arrant thief,
> And her pale fire she snatches from the sun:
> The sea's a thief, whose liquid surge resolves
> The moon into salt tears: the earth's a thief,
> That feeds and breeds by a composture stolen

From general excrement: each thing's a thief:
The laws, your curb and whip, in their rough power
Have uncheck'd theft. Love not yourselves: away,
Rob one another. There's more gold. Cut throats:
All that you meet are thieves: to Athens go,
Break open shops; nothing can you steal,
But thieves do lose it: steal no less for this
I give you; and gold confound you howsoe'er!
Amen.

The Third Bandit remarks that Timon

Has almost charmed me from my profession, by persuading me to it.

Timon writes his famous epitaph and disappears in the second scene of
the fifth act. His interview with Flavius and the re-appearance of that
character is puzzling. The speeches of Flavius are unmarked in the Folio
text, and his appearance here may be an afterthought. He introduces a
positive element of redemption and consolation opposed to the bitterness
of Timon. It looks as if Shakespeare or another had tried to make the play
assume the conventional form of tragedy. This seems borne out also in the
last three scenes of the play, in which the rather inconsistent Alcibiades
appears as a restorer of normal social life—a sort of Richmond or Octavius.
He will apparently work out a belated rectification of his own and Timon's
wrongs (V, iv, 81-4):

Bring me into your city,
And I will use the olive with my sword,
Make war breed peace, make peace stint war, make each
Prescribe to other as each other's leech.

The stuff from Plutarch's *Life of Alcibiades* is somehow used as patchwork.
It is not clear why such a burden of guilt is placed upon Athens. To be
sure, the Senators refuse to assist Timon and later, when they need him,
come to win his help. They behave on that occasion rather well and take
his rebukes in good part; but they have little organic connection with the
story of Timon. The part of Alcibiades is downright inconsistent. Someone,
Shakespeare probably, has worked hastily to make a general tragedy on
the basis of a brilliant and sympathetic treatment of Timon himself.

CHAPTER X

Three Great Political Tragedies

MACBETH

ANTONY AND CLEOPATRA

CORIOLANUS

1. Macbeth.

THE fourth of Shakespeare's greatest tragedies, *Macbeth*, has taken rank with many critics as the greatest of his dramatic achievements. In *Macbeth* one finds a sinewy strength, a unity, a depth of passion, and a loftiness of style comparable to those of *Agamemnon, Prometheus Bound*, and other plays of Aeschylus, for *Macbeth* is in the tradition of the greatest tragedy. Again in *Macbeth* one sees an example of Shakespeare's perfect joinery in the handling of his sources. The events of the tragedy came from various parts of Holinshed's *Chronicles*, all from the chronicles of Scotland except two episodes from the story of Edward the Confessor, which came from the Chronicles of England. The latter describe how that sainted monarch cured the King's evil by his touch and also set forth the invasion of Scotland by Siward, who overthrew Macbeth. From the account of the reign of King Duff comes a story of how Donwald, a man whom King Duff never suspected, murdered Duff in the castle of Forres, and subsequently cleared himself of the crime, but not of suspicion, by killing the servants whom he had induced to commit the deed. The moving forest and the man not born of woman, two bits of folklore, came from the chronicle of Macbeth, which is the main source of the account of that King's reign and carries with it the story of Macduff and his family. The chronicle of King Kenneth furnishes the voice which cried out, "Sleep no more." The witches came from Holinshed, who speaks of them as "goddesses of destiny." Shakespeare himself calls them the "weird sisters," and yet they are probably not to be thought of as such compelling forces that Macbeth's will might fairly be said to be wrenched from its true purpose by "supernatural soliciting" and Macbeth thus relieved of moral responsibility. The "weird sisters" in *Macbeth* are certainly emissaries of the devil, but Shakespeare has lowered their status by giving them the tricks of Scottish witches.

Indeed, the chief means by which Shakespeare unifies his tragedy is by placing responsibility squarely on Macbeth. Macbeth commits a great crime with his eyes open. Lady Macbeth's responsibility is less. Ambition, to the people of the time, was fundamentally a sin, and the idea of surrendering one's soul to the evil one was immediately and horribly possible. The persons of a king and a guest had about them an especial sanctity, and Macbeth murders his king, who is also his guest. He acknowledges his league with evil when he speaks of (III, i, 68-9)

> mine eternal jewel
> Given to the common enemy of man.

The consequences of the compact are broadened and deepened in Macbeth's realization that his punishment cannot be postponed until after death. He wishes that (I, vii, 4-7)

> this blow
> Might be the be-all and the end-all here,
> But here, upon this bank and shoal of time,
> We'ld jump the life to come.

He cannot rid himself of the fear of human justice, so that his tragedy becomes that of the criminal as well as the sinner. *Macbeth* thus becomes a drama of fear, of the most perturbing terror. Macbeth is himself not particularly skillful in controlling his perturbations, a thing necessary if he is to escape anguish and if his actions are to be efficient and successful. Lady Macbeth, having a livelier sense of the present, is better able to dominate her feelings, so that her breakdown comes when the load has grown too heavy for her body and her mind to bear. She fully understands that emotional control rests on corporeal control, as when she says (III, iv, 63-7),

> O, these flaws and starts,
> Impostors to true fear, would well become
> A woman's story at a winter's fire,
> Authorized by her grandam. Shame itself!
> Why do you make such faces?

Renaissance psychology, based originally on observation, is usually sound in its normal applications, and in the principle just described agrees with the most recent theories. Shakespeare, although no doubt aware of current learning in the field of psychological theory, nevertheless places his characters in the high road of human nature as he knew it.

Macbeth is probably the best known and certainly the most perfectly unified of Shakespeare's tragedies. There is perhaps no Shakespearean play, unless it be *Romeo and Juliet*, of which the mere enumeration of its events is so significant, so impressive. On the ground of this universal application, it presents the spectacle of a representative man and woman embarking on a sea of sin and error and encountering a shipwreck, not only as individuals, but as husband and wife. *Macbeth* is thus a tragedy of the marriage relation as well as of the state. The joint guilt of Macbeth and Lady Macbeth ultimately separates them, and they perish as individuals, each alone.

The account of Macbeth before he undertook the murder of his kinsman, his guest, and his king, the "gracious Duncan," is so brief and Macbeth's ambition leads him so quickly to such violent crime that we are apt to forget that he was originally a good man and that it is a mistake to play his part, as has sometimes been done, as if he were naturally a villain. That he was a brave soldier and a loyal subject of King Duncan of Scotland is witnessed by "the bleeding Sergeant," who describes Macbeth's battle against the rebellious Macdonwald and the Norwegian invader Sweyn (I, ii, 7-23, 35-44):

> *Dun.*   Dismay'd not this
> Our captains, Macbeth and Banquo?
> *Cap.*   Yes;
> As sparrows eagles, or the hare the lion.
> If I say sooth, I must report they were
> As cannons overcharged with double cracks, so they
> Doubly redoubled strokes upon the foe:
> Except they meant to bathe in reeking wounds,
> Or memorize another Golgotha,
> I cannot tell.

Yet Macbeth, in spite of his virtue, was tempted to commit a great crime.

To understand Macbeth's temptation we must realize what an overpowering, all-embracing prize kingship offered to the men of the day. As Macbeth and Banquo were returning from the war, they were greeted by the "weird sisters," witches and agents of the Evil One, who promise that Macbeth shall be king hereafter (I, iii, 48-88).

Perhaps their "supernatural soliciting" is merely the utterance of the ambitious longings of Macbeth's own heart (I, iii, 128-142):

> *Macb.*   (*Aside*) Two truths are told,
> As happy prologues to the swelling act
> Of the imperial theme. . . .
> (*Aside*) This supernatural soliciting
> Cannot be ill, cannot be good: if ill,
> Why hath it given me earnest of success,
> Commencing in a truth? I am thane of Cawdor:
> If good, why do I yield to that suggestion
> Whose horrid image doth unfix my hair
> And make my seated heart knock at my ribs,
> Against the use of nature? Present fears
> Are less than horrible imaginings:
> My thought, whose murder yet is but fantastical,
> Shakes so my single state of man that function
> Is smother'd in surmise, and nothing is
> But what is not.

Macbeth was the savior of his country. He was of royal blood, and, in accordance with the customs of the time, might properly have been chosen to succeed Duncan on the throne of Scotland. But Duncan destroys Macbeth's hopes by appointing his own son Malcolm to be Prince of Cumberland, thus designating Malcolm as his heir (I, iv, 35-53). Macbeth had loyally said (I, iii, 143-4)

> If chance will make me king, why, chance may crown me.

But will he suffer himself to be barred by Duncan's order from the crown which he covets?

Macbeth was infatuated with the glory of an earthly crown, but, even so, why did he consent to commit a crime, not a crime only, but an act of profanation? Duncan was Macbeth's king, God's anointed, and was Macbeth's guest, being thus protected by the sanctities of hospitality as well as of fealty and religion. Lady Macbeth had a large share in the motives of the deed. Her comments after she has read Macbeth's letter show this (I, v, 17-31), and she speaks out with a resolution so black that it still has power to fill the mind with horror (ll. 39-55):

Glamis thou art, and Cawdor; and shalt be
What thou art promised: yet do I fear thy nature;
It is too full o' the milk of human kindness
To catch the nearest way: thou wouldst be great;
Art not without ambition, but without
The illness should attend it: what thou wouldst highly,
That wouldst thou holily; wouldst not play false,
And yet wouldst wrongly win: . . .
                              Hie thee hither,
That I may pour my spirits in thine ear;
And chastise with the valour of my tongue
All that impedes thee from the golden round,
Which fate and metaphysical aid doth seem
To have thee crown'd withal. . . .
                    The raven himself is hoarse
That croaks the fatal entrance of Duncan
Under my battlements. Come you spirits
That tend on mortal thoughts, unsex me here,
And fill me from the crown to the toe top-full
Of direst cruelty! make thick my blood;
Stop up the access and passage to remorse,
That no compunctious visitings of nature
Shake my fell purpose, nor keep peace between
The effect and it! Come to my woman's breasts,
And take my milk for gall, you murdering ministers,
Wherever in your sightless substances
You wait on nature's mischief!

Lady Macbeth is the aggressor and yet in the enacting of the crime is no more to blame than Macbeth. He knew the nature of the enterprise; she did not. This relation between man and woman is as old as Adam and Eve. Adam was tempted as well as Eve, but Adam lacked the blind courage of ignorance to make him sin. Lady Macbeth urges her husband on by every wile known to woman: you said you would; you are a coward if you don't; you will do it if you love me ("Thus I account your love"); if you don't, I will do it myself ("Infirm of purpose, give me the daggers"). Women often want their men to do unwise and desperate things. They are most successful when their men really wish to do them. Macbeth, soldier and statesman that he is, is much to blame for involving his delicately nurtured wife in such an enterprise, but this aspect of the matter does not appear in the play.

Macbeth realizes fully the nature of the crime. His hesitation is emphatic and natural. He reveals the fact that his final fear is that of earthly consequences; for he knew, as we do, that human justice does not sleep (I, vii, 1-27).

The consequence of Macbeth's fears and scruples is that, when Lady Macbeth enters, he definitely refuses to proceed further with the bloody business. She rises to the occasion and so dominates and fascinates him that he holds on his fatal course (I, vii, 31-73):

> *Macb.* We will proceed no further in this business:
> He hath honour'd me of late; and I have bought
> Golden opinions from all sorts of people,
> Which would be worn now in their newest gloss,
> Not cast aside so soon. . . .
> *Lady M.*   What beast was't, then,
> That made you break this enterprise to me?
> When you durst do it, then you were a man;
> And, to be more than what you were, you would
> Be so much more the man. Nor time nor place
> Did then adhere, and yet you would make both:
> They have made themselves, and that their fitness now
> Does unmake you. I have given suck, and know
> How tender 'tis to love the babe that milks me:
> I would, while it was smiling in my face,
> Have pluck'd my nipple from his boneless gums,
> And dash'd the brains out, had I so sworn as you
> Have done to this.
> *Macb.*   If we should fail?
> *Lady M.*   We fail!
> But screw your courage to the sticking-place,
> And we'll not fail. . . .
> *Macb.*   Bring forth men-children only;
> For thy undaunted mettle should compose
> Nothing but males. . . .

Duncan approaches the castle at Forres and, as he does so, there occurs a passage of such lyrical beauty that it serves to set off the horror of the impending crime (I, vi, 1-10):

> *Dun.* This castle hath a pleasant seat; the air
> Nimbly and sweetly recommends itself
> Unto our gentle senses.

Ban.   This guest of summer,
The temple-haunting martlet, does approve,
By his loved mansionry, that the heaven's breath
Smells wooingly here: no jutty, frieze,
Buttress, nor coign of vantage, but this bird
Hath made his pendent bed and procreant cradle:
Where they most breed and haunt, I have observed,
The air is delicate.

Murder plays were not uncommon in Elizabethan drama, and from one of these, *Arden of Feversham*, Shakespeare may have learned something of the dramatic realization of murder. Another, *The Yorkshire Tragedy*, was published with Shakespeare's name and has psychological features not unworthy of him. There are few scenes, even in Shakespeare, of such penetrating and suggestive realism as the murder of Duncan in *Macbeth*. To find its equal we must go to the *Agamemnon* of Aeschylus. Let us begin with the "air-drawn dagger" (II, i, 33-60; ii, 10-33, 46-63):

Is this a dagger which I see before me,
The handle toward my hand? Come, let me clutch thee.
I have thee not, and yet I see thee still.
Art thou not, fatal vision, sensible
To feeling as to sight? or art thou but
A dagger of the mind, a false creation,
Proceeding from the heat-oppressed brain?
I see thee yet, in form as palpable
As this which now I draw. . . .
.   There's no such thing?
It is the bloody business which informs
Thus to mine eyes. . . .
Lady M. Alack, I am afraid they have awaked,
And 'tis not done. The attempt and not the deed
Confounds us. Hark! I laid their daggers ready;
He could not miss 'em. Had he not resembled
My father as he slept, I had done't. [*Enter Macbeth.*]
                    My husband!
Macb. I have done the deed. Didst thou not hear a noise?
Lady M. I heard the owl scream and the crickets cry.
Did not you speak?
Macb.   When?
Lady M.   Now.
Macb.   As I descended?

Lady M. Ay.

Macb. Hark!

Who lies i' the second chamber?

Lady M.   Donalbain.

Macb. [*Looking on his hands*] This is a sorry sight.

Lady M. A foolish thought, to say a sorry sight.

Macb. There's one did laugh in's sleep, and one cried 'Murder!'

That they did wake each other: I stood and heard them:

But they did say their prayers, and address'd them

Again to sleep.

Lady M. There are two lodged together.

Macb. One cried 'God bless us!' and 'Amen' the other;

As they had seen me with these hangman's hands.

Listening their fear, I could not say 'Amen,' . . .

Lady M.   Consider it not so deeply.

Macb. But wherefore could I not pronounce 'Amen'?

I had most need of blessing, and 'Amen'

Stuck in my throat.

What we have just overheard is the secret and personal side of murder, but there is another aspect also. The outside world has an interest in it. To Forres Castle and its silence there comes an inevitable, symbolic "knocking at the gates" with a contrast between the secret and the open so vivid that it always seems to be new. The knocking wakes the sleepy Porter, who ironically fancies himself the Porter of Hell-Gate, a character made familiar to the audience in the mystery play *The Harrowing of Hell* (II, iii, 1-25):

Here's a knocking indeed! If a man were porter of hell-gate, he should have old turning the key. Knock, knock, knock! Who's there, i' the name of Beelzebub? Here's a farmer that hanged himself on the expectation of plenty: . . . Who's there, in the other devil's name? Faith, here's an equivocator, that could swear in both the scales against either scale; . . . O, come in, equivocator. Knock, knock, knock! Who's there? Faith, here's an English tailor come hither, for stealing out of a French hose: come in, tailor; here you may roast your goose. Knock, knock; never at quiet! What are you? But this place is too cold for hell. I'll devil-porter it no further: I had thought to have let in some of all professions that go the primrose way to the everlasting bonfire.

More significant for the future is the horror-stricken voice of Macduff as he arouses the castle to a knowledge of what has been done (ll. 68-85):

O horror, horror, horror! Tongue nor heart
Cannot conceive nor name thee! . . .
                    Awake, awake!
Ring the alarum-bell. Murder and treason!
Banquo and Donalbain! Malcolm! awake!
Shake off this downy sleep, death's counterfeit,
And look on death itself! up, up, and see
The great doom's image! Malcolm! Banquo!
As from your graves rise up, and walk like sprites,
To countenance this horror! Ring the bell.

In the midst of confusion comes action of lightning-like rapidity. Note the whispered words of Malcolm and Donalbain (II, iii, 126-31):

Mal. Why do we hold our tongues,
That most may claim this argument for ours?
Don. What should be spoken here, where our fate,
Hid in an auger-hole may rush, and seize us?
Let's away;
Our tears are not yet brew'd.
Mal.   Nor our strong sorrow
Upon the foot of motion.

Banquo is the first proponent of loyalty and justice against the criminal usurpation of Macbeth, Macduff the second. After the murder of Duncan and the coronation of Macbeth there were many persons in the Scottish court who suspected the indirect and crooked means by which Macbeth had gained the crown. With Banquo it is more than suspicion (III, i, 1-10). Macbeth on his part is not unaware of his danger; his fears in Banquo "stick deep." He has already learned the lesson of crime, namely, that crime plucks on crime and that he himself is in blood stepped in so far that "should he wade no more, returning were as tedious as go o'er." He accordingly plots the murder of Banquo (III, i, 48-72). Macbeth is perturbed and uncertain in his movements, and the spectacle of the refined lady lending him strength to go on is at once baleful and pathetic (III, ii, 7-55):

Lady M. How now, my lord! why do you keep alone,
Of sorriest fancies your companions making,
Using those thoughts which should indeed have died
With them they think on? Things without all remedy
Should be without regard: what's done is done.
Macb. We have scotch'd the snake, not kill'd it:

She'll close and be herself, whilst our poor malice
Remains in danger of her former tooth. . . .
O, full of scorpions is my mind, dear wife!
Thou know'st that Banquo, and his Fleance, lives.
Lady M. But in them nature's copy's not eterne.
Macb. There's comfort yet; they are assailable;
Then be thou jocund: ere the bat hath flown
His cloister'd flight, ere to black Hecate's summons
The shard-borne beetle with his drowsy hums
Hath rung night's yawning peal, there shall·be done
A·deed of dreadful note.

In the scene of the murder Fleance, the son of Banquo, escapes. This
is the turning-point of the tragedy, Macbeth's first failure. Eternal rectitude or fate or nature has barred his course. The child goes screaming
through the woods (III, iii, 17-18):

O, treachery! Fly, good Fleance, fly, fly, fly!
Thou mayst revenge.

So far as we know, ghosts were actual and material persons on the
Elizabethan stage, and in *Macbeth* it is said quite definitely in a stage
direction at the beginning of the scene of the feast, "Banquo prepar'd,"
and later "Enter the Ghost of Banquo, and sits in Macbeth's place." And
yet there is something psychologically appropriate in the practice begun
by John Philip Kemble and continued by Macready, Booth, and Irving of
having no actor enter as the Ghost of Banquo, thus making of it a ghost
within the mind of Macbeth. When Macbeth enters he quite casually
observes that there is no vacant place (III, iv, 50-109):

Macb. Thou canst not say I did it: never shake
Thy gory locks at me. . . .
Lady M. Sit, worthy friends: my lord is often thus,
And hath been from his youth: pray you, keep seat;
This fit is momentary; upon a thought
He will again be well: if much you note him,
You shall offend him and extend his passion:
Feed, and regard him not. Are you a man?
Macb. Ay, and a bold one, that dare look on that
Which might appal the devil.
Lady M.   O proper stuff!
This is the very painting of your fear:
This is the air-drawn dagger which, you said,

Led you to Duncan. O, these flaws and starts,
Impostors to true fear, would well become
A woman's story at a winter's fire,
Authorized by her grandam. Shame itself!
Why do you make such faces? When all's done,
You look but on a stool. . . .
Macb. Blood hath been shed ere now, i' the olden time,
Ere humane statute purged the gentle weal;
Ay, and since too, murders have been perform'd
Too terrible for the ear: the time has been,
That, when the brains were out, the man would die,
And there an end; but now they rise again,
With twenty mortal murders on their crowns,
And push us from our stools; this is more strange
Than such a murder is.

Macbeth's uncertainty causes him to consult the witches. They are ready for him with their diabolical conceits, and it is a strange pageant that they show him. There is an "armed head," which symbolizes Macbeth's own head cut off in the last scene and presented by Macduff to Malcolm. There is also a "bloody child," who symbolizes Macduff, not born of woman, "but from his mother's womb untimely ripped"; finally, a "child crowned, with a tree in his hand," by whom is meant the royal heir, Malcolm, advancing from Birnam wood on Dunsinane. Note that these spirits are genuine. They tell truth about the future; but, since they are of and from the Evil One, their revelations are for purposes of deception (IV, i, 48-61, 68-72, 79, 90-105).

Be bloody, bold and resolute

they say, and

Be lion-mettled, proud; and take no care
Who chafes, who frets, or where conspirers are.

Macbeth's new devilish resolution is (ll. 146-8),

from this moment
The very firstlings of my heart shall be
The firstlings of my hand.

"Macduff is fled to England!" He had not reckoned on the cruelty of Macbeth, although there is nothing new in the behavior of tyrants (ll. 150-4). Lady Macduff laments her husband's absence and blames him for leaving her unprotected. Out of the dark scene of murder the courage of Macduff's little son shines forth like a gleam of light (IV, ii, 73-85):

> *L. Macd.* What are these faces?
> *First Mur.* Where is your husband?
> *L. Macd.* I hope, in no place so unsanctified
> Where such as thou mayst find him.
> *First Mur.*   He's a traitor.
> *Son.* Thou liest, thou shag-hair'd villain!
> *First Mur.*   What, you egg! (*Stabbing him.*)
> Young fry of treachery!
> *Son.*   He has kill'd me, mother:
> Run·away, I pray you!

Macduff in England has just had an interview with Malcolm, then in exile at the English court. Malcolm has had many plots laid against his life by Macbeth, and, before he is willing to trust Macduff, Malcolm subjects him to an elaborate test. Just as he has become satisfied of Macduff's sincerity, Ross enters and reports the murder of Macduff's wife and children. Macduff is crushed, but Malcolm rallies him with the thought of revenge. We have another of the many cases in which in Shakespeare grief must be converted into anger. Even as the thought of revenge comes to Macduff he realizes that he can never be evened with Macbeth. The first words that he says, "He has no children," exemplify that penetrative imagination in which no writer has ever equaled Shakespeare.

As a soldier and a man of the world, Macbeth is aware of consequences and prepared for them. Lady Macbeth is harder, more resilient, more bent on the immediate object than is Macbeth. She too has a conscience, and when she yields to it, she breaks with a sudden snap. It is she, and not Macbeth, who is slain by remorse. Shakespeare's way of showing this is the famous sleep-walking scene, movingly enacted by Sarah Siddons, by Modjeska, and by others (V, i, 38-59).

Macbeth, although life has become a bitter thing to him, yet clings to life. That which should accompany old age, "as honour, love, obedience, troops of friends," he may not look to have; and yet, so callous to the blows of fate has he become, that even the death of the wife bound to him in virtue and in crime moves him scarcely more than any casual, dark event (V, iii, 37-56). Soon there comes a cry of women, a keening, which is followed by the announcement that Lady Macbeth is dead (V, v, 16-28):

Macb. Wherefore was that cry?
Sey. The queen, my lord, is dead.
Macb. She should have died hereafter;
There would have been a time for such a word.
Tomorrow, and tomorrow, and tomorrow,
Creeps in this petty pace from day to day
To the last syllable of recorded time,
And all our yesterdays have lighted fools
The way to dusty death. Out, out, brief candle!
Life's but a walking shadow, a poor player
That struts and frets his hour upon the stage
And then is heard no more: it is a tale
Told by an idiot, full of sound and fury,
Signifying nothing.

Macbeth, however, still goes on relying on the deceitful promises of the witches, and, as one after another these prophecies fail, they form dramatically perfect examples of what are called "moments of final suspense," or situations which seem for the time to contradict the trend of the drama. The wood moves (V, v, 33-46):

Mess. As I did stand my watch upon the hill,
I look'd toward Birnam, and anon, methought,
The wood began to move.
Macb.   Liar and slave! . . .
                        If thou speak'st false,
Upon the next tree shalt thou hang alive,
Till famine cling thee: if thy speech be sooth,
I care not if thou dost for me as much.
I pull in resolution, and begin
To doubt the equivocation of the fiend
That lies like truth: 'Fear not, till Birnam wood
Do come to Dunsinane:' and now a wood
Comes toward Dunsinane.

The last prop and stay of Macbeth's hope is the prophecy that his life will never yield to one of woman born. Confident in his invulnerability, he meets and slays the Young Siward. The Elder Siward's words are all too familiar (V, viii, 39-53):

Why then, God's soldier be he!

Macduff comes in, questing for his mortal foe (V, viii, 3-34):

Macd.   Despair thy charm;
And let the angel whom thou still hast served
Tell thee, Macduff was from his mother's womb
Untimely ripp'd. . . .
Macb.   I will not yield,
To kiss the ground before young Malcolm's feet,
And to be baited with the rabble's curse.
Though Birnam wood be come to Dunsinane,
And thou opposed, being of no woman born,
Yet I will try the last. Before my body
I throw my warlike shield. Lay on, Macduff,
And damn'd be him that first cries 'Hold, enough!'

The soul of Macbeth while he lives never completely disappears into the dark, and it heightens his tragedy to realize that, robbed of every reliance, he is still "Bellona's bridegroom lapp'd in proof." Like Richard Crookback he goes out in a burst of immortal bravery. Fear and despair convert to anger and pride, and anger and pride into fearlessness. This is perhaps the explanation yielded by the old psychology and it is not contradicted by the new. But the nature of courage is still puzzling, and its sources are many and diverse. Courage is will-power, says Lord Moran; courage is moral character; courage is lack of imagination; it comes, he says, from discipline and habit and from a sense of fellowship; it comes from an idea greater than fear, from the spirit of revenge, from the love of sport; it comes from pride, desperation, loyalty, religion. It is, says Lord Moran, always admirable.

The Elizabethan stage was open, and plays never ended with the drop of a curtain. Shakespeare characteristically made use of this defect, if it be a defect, and used it to express his faith in the future, his belief that this is God's world and that human life is an endurable enterprise. After Macduff brings in the head of the slain Macbeth, we get a prospect of a normal, peaceful Scotland under the sovereignty of King Malcolm (V, viii, 62-77).

2. *Antony and Cleopatra.*

Plutarch's *Life of Antony*, on which Shakespeare based his *Antony and Cleopatra*, differs from the other lives in the great biographical work in being a sort of historical novel. *Antony and Cleopatra* reflects this discursiveness, for, great as it is, it is in part roughly dramatized. It has too many scenes, although the stylistic effect of its variety is like that of rich tapestry. Nowhere does Shakespeare grasp more fully the real nature of tragedy than in the story of Antony, the man who with his sword "quartered the world" and then gave it away in the infatuation of love. Before this spectacle the ancient world stood in awe, and the story is still both perplexing and momentous. The case of Antony is clear, but that of Cleopatra is more difficult to describe. Shakespeare found in his source two Cleopatras, the one licentious, self-willed, completely incorrigible; the other a perfect lover and a woman moved to heroic death by her love. Shakespeare told the story as he found it, and some critics declare that these qualities could never co-exist in the same woman. Whether or not that is true does not concern us. Evidently Shakespeare thought they could, and it is perhaps best to accept what, in spite of some inconsistencies, seems to have been Shakespeare's simple intention. He was content to depict Cleopatra as utterly fickle, vain, unscrupulous, and sensual as far as the thirteenth scene of the third act; and beyond that point to show her possessed of womanly fidelity, steadfastness, and resolution.

The question is anachronistic. Conversion was a sudden matter with Shakespeare and the Elizabethans, and nobody in that age would have wondered at the change. Certainly Cleopatra becomes a tragic figure in the fifth act when she, after the death of Antony, occupies the stage. One would not claim that the play was carefully planned as compared with *Macbeth* and *Coriolanus*, but, so far as the general conception is concerned, we may take it at the face value given it by the master dramatist.

Shakespeare's minor characters are always convincing, and none more so than Enobarbus in *Antony and Cleopatra*. In him one sees a tragedy within the tragedy. There is an array of convincingly depicted Roman soldiers, such as Ventidius, Eros, Agrippa, Dolabella, and Menas, as well as that brave man Scarus, who, when Antony says (IV, vii, 6-8)

> Thou bleed'st apace,

replies,

> I had a wound here that was like a T,
> But now 'tis made an H.

There is also that mere puppet Charmian, whom Shakespeare endows at the end of the play with such noble eloquence (V, ii, 316-31). Cleopatra's last words are, "What should I stay—"

Char. In this vile world? So, fare thee well.
Now boast thee, death, in thy possession lies
A lass unparallel'd. Downy windows, close;
And golden Phoebus never be beheld
Of eyes again so royal! Your crown's awry;
I'll mend it, and then play. [*Enter the* Guard *rushing in.*
First Guard. Where is the queen?
Char.   Speak softly, wake her not.
First Guard. Caesar hath sent.—
Char.   Too slow a messenger. [*Applies an asp.*
O, come apace, dispatch! I partly feel thee. . . .
It is well done, and fitting for a princess
Descended of so many royal kings.
Ah, soldier!   [*Dies.*

Characterization is a relatively new conception in the world of criticism, and we seem to owe our whole theory of it, as we do so much else, to the critics of the Romantic generation. The conception of character, as distinct from the depiction of persons, seems to have had, as it rose to its present critical importance, two lines of development. One of these was the idea of that which was marked with the external manifestations of inward peculiarity or speciality. This was the "character" as a technical literary form, which was followed later on in the seventeenth century in the drawing (they used that word) of characters. This phase will be seen in Clarendon, Shaftesbury, Pope, and Swift, and among the eighteenth century historians. It was simply a fixed attempt to analyze. It proceeded from the type to the individual and for the most part contented itself with the discovery of the type in the individual. The other line of development was the enacting and presentation of characters on the stage. This is probably the line from which the Romantic critics got their conception of the technique of character depiction. Lamb and Hazlitt knew a great deal about the stage, and Coleridge was by no means ignorant of it.

All of this is far later than Shakespeare, and to examine Shakespeare's works by any such devices is to lay oneself liable to error, since Shakespeare, not knowing the law, was in some measure above the law. In other words, when one talks about consistency of characterization within the character itself, within the different parts of the play, and with relation to the action in which the character is obliged to participate, there is a sort of anachronism in the process. Our current talk about plot, setting, and character is later than Shakespeare—sometimes by more than two hundred years. This fact may not destroy the utility of such rubrics of study, but to some extent it changes their bases.

Evidently Shakespeare was telling stories by means of the stage and putting up actors to represent people without asking himself anything about the characters he was creating. We cannot tell with certainty that he had any conception of character as an abstraction. If he had, he did not reveal it. He merely inferred character from action and let it go at that. His depiction of character was therefore objective, unconscious, and spontaneous. We cannot ascertain surely whether Shakespeare intended to create any character of any particular pattern. He had no thought for such an exercise and no technology in which to think of it. As a sane man, he made people do things which it was natural for such people to do. In practice, this, in some respects, comes to pretty much the same thing as the products of conscious, modern art, but not absolutely. We may ask then if Shakespeare forgot while he was writing the latter part of a play what he had put down in the first part. Did he, as Professor Schücking thinks, first put Polonius down as a dignified and responsible minister of state, and later unconsciously degrade him into a clown? If so, he must have been so carried away by the enticements of comic creation that he forgot his first conception. We may ask then if Shakespeare merely forgot, if he was careless, and if in writing on a certain theme he was so absorbed by the immediate situation that he put into the mouth of his character words inappropriate to that character when looked at from the point of view of the story as a whole. Shakespeare may sometimes have been deflected from the main intention of his tale, but in general he was not prone to such obliviousness.

In *Character Problems in Shakespeare's Plays* (New York, 1922) Professor Schücking advances the hypothesis that Shakespeare had "different conceptions of the same character in different scenes." He illustrates this specifically from the part of Cleopatra in *Antony and Cleopatra*. Professor Schücking thinks it possible that sometimes in the working out of a complex character Shakespeare may have introduced features in certain scenes which are contradictory to features depicted in other scenes. He admits that Plutarch as translated by North throws a favorable light on Cleopatra as a woman of culture, stressing her knowledge of languages, the charm of her conversation, and the "infinite agility of her mind," which "is shown by her love of adventures." She infatuates Antony by these qualities and by her ability and willingness to share in all his occupations.

The Cleopatra of Shakespeare's drama, says Professor Schücking, is inferior to the original. She gives no audiences to ambassadors and exercises none of the higher functions of state. She lives for love and reclines lazily on her couch in voluptuousness and sensuality. When her lover is away she has no occupation. She is described as a gypsy and a strumpet. When she hears of the marriage of Antony and Octavia she rises to the hysterics of a harlot, loses all self-control, beats and stabs the helpless messenger who had brought the news. This beating of the messenger is Shakespeare's own peculiar development and ought, therefore, to be regarded as an evidence of the conception of Cleopatra's character in Shakespeare's mind at the time he wrote that particular scene. Essentially Cleopatra's character has the pride of the courtesan in the number of distinguished lovers she has had. More than that, her treatment of Antony is dominated by an element of calculation. "She is cunning past man's thought" (I, ii, 150). She deliberately wards off satiety; she is always the wronged one, and understands how to turn the tide against Antony. So much for Cleopatra in the first three acts.

In the last two acts we have, according to the same writer, a very different Cleopatra. In conformity with the characterization of the early Cleopatra, she should, in the last two acts, have been solicitous only for her own safety, but she makes no effort to secure it, except only in the insignificant flirtation with Thyreus. It is not her fault that her ships go over to the enemy. Antony wrongs her by his suspicion. When he levels at her the devastating reproaches of the end of the fourth act, she bears them with the utmost meekness and humility. She shows actual fear in the particular pretense of being dead, for Antony is represented as actually dangerous. After Antony inflicts upon himself the mortal wound, "there is a touch of soft conjugal tenderness in all that she says or does." Before that she arms him for the fight and parts with him as Andromache parts with Hector. When Antony bids her seek her honor with her safety, she nobly replies, "They do not go together." In IV, xiii and V, ii, she is like Portia in her Roman nobleness. And, says Professor Schücking, it cannot well be doubted that this woman, who now is inwardly as well as outwardly a queen, has but little in common with the harlot of the first acts.

For the most part this is a true enough observation, but Professor Schücking would account for the inconsistency by the suggestions (1) that Shakespeare follows the older form of the primitive epic drama and isolates his scene in a way resulting in intentional dramatic formlessness, analogous to baroque art; (2) that some careless and hasty work is also involved; and (3) that Shakespeare, influenced by the popular reputation of Cleopatra as the typical courtesan, gave her in the first acts a character inferior to that attributed to her by Plutarch. If Shakespeare had intended us to believe that Cleopatra is reformed by her experiences—for example, by Antony's disgust—there would have been some trace of his intent. There is none. The late Cleopatra is not foreshadowed in the early.

The one thing that Professor Schücking fails to do is to observe that Shakespeare's Cleopatra is merely Plutarch's Cleopatra put on the stage. There is no point in Shakespeare's characterization which is not provided for in Plutarch, and, one may say, in the general romance of Cleopatra.

There were dramas of Marcus Antonius, also of Cleopatra. We do not know how many there may have been of each. Garnier's *Marc Antoine* was translated by the Countess of Pembroke. Estienne Jodelle's *Cléopâtre Captive* was published in 1552 and had a wide influence over drama both French and English. It contained the same dramatic struggle which occupies the fifth act of *Antony and Cleopatra*. Giraldi Cinthio wrote a tragedy of Cleopatra, and Samuel Daniel in 1594 produced his *Tragedie of Cleopatra*. The fifth act in *Antony and Cleopatra* corresponds in contents roughly to Daniel's whole play and has the same dramatic theme. This might be stated as follows: Will Cleopatra yield to her fear, her greed, and the clever deceptions of Octavius, and grace his triumph in Rome, or will she play a noble Roman part and take her own life, shrewd enough to find death in spite of the subtle Octavius? There seems nothing out of place or disjointed in this theme.

The tragedy of Antony is the tragedy of the fallen man. He staggers to his end. Cleopatra has her colossal part in ruining him, bringing on his downfall. He becomes a spectacle for gods and men; reason deserts him, and so does soldiership. He rides his course to destruction as Caesar and Pompey rode theirs before him, and as such tragic heroes must. Whereas in the Brutus play Antony was still on the crest of his fate, in his own play he is fallen into the sere, the yellow leaf. Now, with reference to Cleopatra, one finds Antony's situation exactly paralleled. In the

Antony play Cleopatra is on the upward trend, doing and destroying. In the Cleopatra tragedy she is beaten and fighting, only for a noble death. Perhaps these things do not jibe; but the fault is not Shakespeare's. They are written in the bond, in its very terms, and are all provided for by Plutarch in the *Life of Antony*. Plutarch filled a storehouse with tragic tales. He made them, shaped them by his pattern into the form of tragic thought. In doing this he was an inventor and reshaper, a writer of fiction who was none the less a writer of history; for fiction had not yet been invented, or at least was not as yet a fully recognized form. Poetry, it was thought, might invent (a sort of invention), but prose was devoted to truth.

There remains then this criticism of Professor Schücking's widely accepted theory. He says that Shakespeare did not follow Plutarch, whereas it seems that Shakespeare did in fact follow Plutarch with the greatest and most surprising fidelity. Professor Schücking states that Shakespeare's Cleopatra is something worse and lower than Plutarch's and that there are no traces in Shakespeare's figure of the accomplishments mentioned by Plutarch. There is, of course, no very insistent dramatic reason why these qualities should have been recorded, and yet they are not absent from the play. Cleopatra's speech is for the most part elevated in style and often very gracious, as when she bids Antony goodbye when he sets out for Rome (I, iii). She is the "enchanting queen." To Enobarbus Cleopatra is the marvel, the woman who carries all before her (II, ii, 228 ff). Even her methods of coquetry, clearly laid down in Plutarch, are presented in the play. As to her soft and conjugal ways, also perfectly described in Plutarch, one wonders how it could be claimed that Shakespeare was in any sense involved in their invention.

A possibly hitherto not wholly exploited source of knowledge of Shakespeare's characterization is to be found in descriptions of characters in his sources. He would seem, where he can be traced, to have heeded such pointers very simply, as for example, in the characterization of Antony in *Antony and Cleopatra*, in which Shakespeare has embodied Plutarch in an almost naïve way.

In any case, characterization in Shakespeare's age was by no means the fixed and consistent matter which it is in the minds of modern critics. The psychology of the time did not admit of it. If a given passion occupied the heart of a man, it might be quickly displaced by another with only a brief period of confusion and hesitation between the two. Almost any man was liable to be obsessed by almost any passion. The matter was as simple as emptying one liquid from a cup and filling it with another. This physiological psychology seems very crude, and yet, when one appeals to life, one finds everywhere sudden, unexpected, violent actions. Newspapers are full of such cases, and one must conclude that the old psychology, in practice, although not in theory, was not totally wrong in its provision for the vagaries of the human mind. The conversion of Cleopatra to a nobler state of mind would not have seemed implausible to the Elizabethans, and it is doubtful if it ought to seem so to us. What we know of the Elizabethan mind bears this out. At a distance the age presents the spectacle of a series of disasters and fulminations. Vividness of existence, contrasts in daily life, sudden joy and sorrow, sudden hope and despair, sudden love and hatred are part of the temper of the time, which was indeed a time of sudden reversions, enduring conflicts, fierce duels, impossible conspiracies, and killings in the heat of passion. All in all, it seems that life in Elizabethan England was, relatively to our own, more hectic in religion, politics, the family, love, and friendship. Not only would the conversion of Cleopatra have seemed more natural to the Elizabethans than it does to us, but so also would the calamitous willfulness of Antony.

There is no known text of *Antony and Cleopatra* earlier than that which appears in the First Folio of 1623. "A booke Called: Anthony and Cleopatra" was entered in the Stationers' Register to Edward Blount on May 20, 1608. It is generally believed that this was Shakespeare's play and that Blount's was possibly a "staying" entry or entry designed to prevent issue by another publisher. The suggested date, 1607-1608, is universally accepted as appropriate to the style of the play, which is a continuation of the compressed and flashing tragic style appearing in *Macbeth*, and there are other considerations which look to the date indicated.

Antony and Cleopatra makes full use of the rapidly and easily changing scenes of the Elizabethan stage. Whether this was intentional or not, one does not know. The fact that there are forty-two different scenes within the five acts has caused some critics to surmise that Shakespeare was working hastily. There is no great deal of evidence for this, since the stories of Antony and of Cleopatra are told with great completeness and with few inconsistencies. In one place (IV, xii, 3-6) we are told that

Swallows have built
In Cleopatra's sails their nests: the augurers
Say they know not, they cannot tell; look grimly,
And dare not speak their knowledge.

This Shakespeare took from a marginal note in North's *Plutarch* and
not from the text, a circumstance which may indicate hasty workmanship;
but, in general, *Antony and Cleopatra* attempts to do a different thing
from what is done in *Macbeth*. Shakespeare's method here is more like
that of the history plays. He takes time to present picturesque details as
he goes along, so that the play is like a beautiful tapestry. His poetic
style is not only brilliant in the extreme, but is carefully wrought. Nowhere else, except perhaps in *Macbeth*, do we find such force, such
pregnancy, and such condensed immediacy in imagery and in syntax.

Both Antony and Cleopatra are tragic figures and yet they differ very
greatly from each other, in fact may be said to exemplify two kinds of
tragedy. Antony is the traditional tragic hero—the man who stood in
high estate and was cast down by envious fate. Tragedy has always been
aware that character is destiny. Cleopatra, on the other hand, is a character
who, like Hamlet, achieves victory when she meets death. She triumphs
in the end and saves herself, by her death, from shame and degradation.
Her death is a symbol of nobility. Both of these cases are worth looking
into.

That Antony is a hero is manifest in his career. As the play opens he
is still capable of realizing his own state (I, ii, 120-1):

These strong Egyptian fetters I must break,
Or lose myself in dotage.

He is capable of justice, for he says of Fulvia (ll. 126-34):

There's a great spirit gone! Thus did I desire it:
What our contempt doth often hurl from us,
We wish it ours again.

He is capable of resisting the ridicule of Enobarbus (ll. 183-203). He
is, as Cleopatra says, capable of being struck by "a Roman thought" and,
to do her justice, she honors him for his manliness (I, iii, 83-5). And she
lets him depart with some show of graciousness. Caesar, bitterly censorious,
knows what Antony is like (I, iv, 55-71):

> Antony,
> Leave thy lascivious wassails. When thou once
> Wast beaten from Modena, where thou slew'st
> Hirtius and Pansa, consuls, at thy heel
> Did famine follow; whom thou fought'st against,
> Though daintily brought up, with patience more
> Than savages could suffer: . . .
>   on the Alps
> It is reported thou didst eat strange flesh,
> Which some did die to look on: and all this—
> It wounds thine honour that I speak it now—
> Was borne so like a soldier, that thy cheek
> So much as lank'd not.

It breaks Pompey's hope when he learns of Antony's return to Rome
(II, i, 31-5):

>   his soldiership
> Is twice the other twain.

Enobarbus boasts of Antony's indomitability, but Antony meets men well
in counsel and within the limits of dignity plays the penitent in Rome.
When the shrewd Agrippa suggests the marriage of Octavia to Antony,
Antony sees the advantage of the union, and it is at least probable that
his honor went with his pledge. Two things seem significant about the
breaking of his faith. The first is the odd passage with the Soothsayer,
which Shakespeare took over unchanged from Plutarch (II, iii, 15-40):

> *Ant.*   Say to me,
> Whose fortunes shall rise higher, Caesar's or mine?
> *Sooth.* Caesar's.
> Therefore, O Antony, stay not by his side:
> Thy demon, that's thy spirit which keeps thee, is
> Noble, courageous, high, unmatchable,
> Where Caesar's is not; but, near him, thy angel
> Becomes a fear, as being o'erpower'd. . . .
> *Ant.*   Be it art or hap,
> He hath spoken true: the very dice obey him;
> And in our sports my better cunning faints
> Under his chance: if we draw lots, he speeds;
> His cocks do win the battle still of mine,
> When it is all to nought; and his quails ever
> Beat mine, inhoop'd, at odds. I will to Egypt.

The other passage is his farewell to Octavia (III, vi). Antony resents the usurpations of Caesar, and his cause is at least as good as Caesar's. A quarrel has broken out between them, and Octavia fails in her allegiance to Antony. How much Shakespeare meant to make of this defection one cannot say. He writes out the scene clearly but without implication as to its dramatic significance.

Antony is himself well aware of his own powers in war (III, xi, 35-40):

> He at Philippi kept
> His sword e'en like a dancer; while I struck
> The lean and wrinkled Cassius; and 'twas I
> That the mad Brutus ended: he alone
> Dealt on lieutenantry, and no practice had
> In the brave squares of war; yet now—No matter.

Prowess in war was largely personal prowess, and Antony's dream is that he will get Caesar point to point. Caesar has, however, other ideas (IV, i, 3-6):

> Dares me to personal combat,
> Caesar to Antony: let the old ruffian know
> I have many other ways to die; meantime
> Laugh at his challenge.

The whole play echoes with Antony's martial greatness, and it is on this that his incredible conduct at Actium turns. But Antony has other heroic qualities. He is not only wise and self-restrained in negotiations, displaying prudence, but he is magnanimous and in the Aristotelian sense magnificent. When Enobarbus deserts, Antony sends after him his treasure. His magnanimity breaks the heart of Enobarbus (IV, vi, 30-9):

> I am alone the villain of the earth,
> And feel I am so most. O Antony,
> Thou mine of bounty, how wouldst thou have paid
> My better service, when my turpitude
> Thou dost so crown with gold! This blows my heart:
> If swift thought break it not, a swifter mean
> Shall outstrike the thought: but thought will do't, I feel.
> I fight against thee! No: I will go seek
> Some ditch wherein to die; the foul'st best fits
> My latter part of life.

Where is there to be found a more magnanimous speech than this (IV, v, 16-17)?

> O, my fortunes have
> Corrupted honest men!

The ancient ideal of magnificence is everywhere reflected. Cleopatra's speech (V, ii, 79-92) is the greatest expression of it:

> His face was as the heavens; and therein stuck
> A sun and moon, which kept their course, and lighted
> The little O, the earth. . . .
> His legs bestrid the ocean: his rear'd arm
> Crested the world: his voice was propertied
> As all the tuned spheres, and that to friends;
> But when he meant to quail and shake the orb,
> He was as rattling thunder. For his bounty,
> There was no winter in't; an autumn 'twas
> That grew the more by reaping: his delights
> Were dolphin-like; they show'd his back above
> The element they lived in: in his livery
> Walk'd crowns and crownets; realms and islands were
> As plates dropp'd from his pocket.

What was the tragic guilt of this great hero? The ancient and the modern world had united in the belief that it was the infatuation of love. No man can love and be wise, they said, and Shakespeare gives this idea abundant expression (I, i, 2-10):

> Those his goodly eyes,
> That o'er the files and musters of the war
> Have glow'd like plated Mars, now bend, now turn,
> The office and devotion of their view
> Upon a tawny front: his captain's heart,
> Which in the scuffles of great fights hath burst
> The buckles on his breast, reneges all temper,
> And is become the bellows and the fan
> To cool a gipsy's lust.

Octavius thinks him mad for love, so do all the followers of Antony. His great fault at Actium is thus accounted for. Note the frank words of Enobarbus (III, xiii, 2-12):

> *Cleo.* Is Antony or we in fault for this?
> *Eno.* Antony only, that would make his will
> Lord of his reason.

But Shakespeare is too well versed in human nature to accept completely so simple an explanation. Mainly into the mouth of Enobarbus he has put an explanation which broadens and deepens Antony's error. Enobarbus says that Antony should not have made his will lord of his reason, and he amplifies this idea (III, xiii, 31-7):

> I see men's judgements are
> A parcel of their fortunes; and things outward
> Do draw the inward quality after them,
> To suffer all alike. That he should dream,
> Knowing all measures, the full Caesar will
> Answer his emptiness! Caesar, thou hast subdu'd
> His judgement too.

Enobarbus is not deceived by Antony's parade of boastful, hopeless courage (ll. 195-201):

> Now he'll outstare the lightning. To be furious,
> Is to be frighted out of fear; and in that mood
> The dove will peck the estridge; and I see still,
> A diminution in our captain's brain
> Restores his heart: when valour preys on reason,
> It eats the sword it fights with.

Nor is Enobarbus deceived by the elaborate sentimentality of Antony in the second scene of the fourth act where Antony bids farewell to his servants (ll. 23-4):

> *Cleo.* (*Aside to Eno.*) What does he mean?
> *Eno.* (*Aside to Cleo.*) To make his followers weep.

Antony is a cadent hero dangerous in his downfall, great in his remorse.

> 'Tis better playing with a lion's whelp
> Than with an old one dying

remarks Enobarbus (III, xiii, 94-5), and Antony meets with temporary success by sheer courage (IV, viii, 19-22). Shakespeare nevertheless shows a consciousness of the kind of tragedy he is writing and allows a part for fate to play. There is the strange scene (IV, iii) from Plutarch in which there is "Music of the hautboys as under the stage." The soldiers are puzzled until one of them explains (ll. 16-17):

> 'Tis the god Hercules, whom Antony loved,
> Now leaves him.

And, after all, Antony takes his own life like Cassius because of a false
report (IV, xiv, 34-6, 55-60, 95-101):

> *Ant.*   Dead, then?
> *Mar.*   Dead.
> *Ant.* Unarm, Eros; the long day's task is done,
> And we must sleep. . . .
>   Since Cleopatra died,·
> I have lived in such dishonour, that the gods
> Detest my baseness. I, that with my sword
> Quarter'd the world, and o'er green Neptune's back
> With ships made cities, condemn myself to lack
> The courage of a woman. . . .
>   Thrice-nobler than myself!
> Thou teachest me, O valiant Eros, what
> I should, and thou couldst not. My queen and Eros
> Have by their brave instruction got upon me
> A nobleness in record: but I will be
> A bridegroom in my death, and run into't
> As to a lover's bed.

The tragedy of Cleopatra is very different in its essence from that of
Antony. The doctrine of ultimate self-mastery which controls both Brutus
and Hamlet may also help in the interpretation of the tragedy of Cleopatra. All limitations being duly recognized, the fact remains that Shakespeare presents in her, in her later hours, a tragic greatness comparable
to the finest of his achievements. The vain, selfish, and frivolous woman
rises to a height of magnanimity which, in spite of all the critics have
said, is convincing. It presents the aspect of a movement upward like that
of Brutus and Hamlet, a spiritual triumph, not only in the face of
death, but by the attainment of death, which was normally the Elizabethan symbol of catastrophe (V, ii, 1-6):

> My desolation does begin to make
> A better life. 'Tis paltry to be Caesar;
> Not being Fortune, he's but Fortune's knave,
> A minister of her will: and it is great
> To do that thing that ends all other deeds;
> Which shackles accidents and bolts up change.

And this Roman mind is not of sudden growth. Shakespeare's Cleopatra
is at no time without some evidences of the greatness that Plutarch

attributed to her. She wants Antony for her own, encourages the worst in him, ruins him, and brings about his death; but there is no reason to doubt that she loved him and had a high appreciation of his greatness. The conjecture may be hazarded that, when confronted by the ruin she had wrought, she came to herself, not suddenly or easily and not without perplexities and retrogressions. Perhaps the first evidence of the change is in the thirteenth scene of the third act (ll. 105-58). She has no defense against the angry tirade of Antony: "Good my lord." "O, is't come to this?" "Wherefore this?" "Have you done yet?" "I must stay his time." "Not know me yet?" After the second defection of her fleet, for which there is no evidence that Cleopatra was to blame, Antony denounces her again, threatens her death, and frightens her. Physically a coward, she runs away and out of her poor stock of harlot's devices selects a fatal one. She has him told that she has taken her own life. When Antony dies, Cleopatra confronts her bare existence for the first time; and out of such a mental perturbation, according to Elizabethan psychology and our own, there habitually grow changed characters and new resolutions. Shakespeare marks the point of change in unforgettable words (IV, xv, 72-91):

> No more, but e'en a woman, and commanded
> By such poor passion as the maid that milks
> And does the meanest chares. It were for me
> To throw my sceptre at the injurious gods;
> To tell them that this world did equal theirs
> Till they had stol'n our jewel. All's but naught;
> Patience is sottish, and impatience does
> Become a dog that's mad: then is it sin
> To rush into the secret house of death,
> Ere death dare come to us? . . .
> Our lamp is spent, it's out! Good sirs, take heart:
> We'll bury him; and then, what's brave, what's noble,
> Let's do it after the high Roman fashion,
> And make death proud to take us.

Thus in writing one of the greatest, most mature, and most portentous of all love stories Shakespeare stresses, not the passion of love alone, but the great issues of character and conduct that arise out of the heart. Love makes itself felt as a well-spring of action causing the death of the hero and the regeneration of the heroine.

3. *Coriolanus.*

It is often said that *Coriolanus*, second of the tragedies in the First Folio, has a very bad text, and this is true, but its badness is apparently one of transmission and is to be accounted for largely by the difficulty of the style in which the play is written. Many emendations have been necessary in order to obtain an intelligible modern text; but, if the text is corrupt, the version which it represents was authentic, detailed, and marvelously complete and well thought out. *Coriolanus* seems to have been written at the time of greatest condensation, greatest use of ellipsis, most lightning-like use of imagery in Shakespeare's later style. These "fierce rapidities of speech" produced the difficulties of which editors complain. It would seem as if Shakespeare's disregard of the formalities of the blank verse line by the use of many run-on lines, many double endings, many extra syllables within the line as well as at the end, many light and weak endings may have affected his own manuscript, or a copy of it; for, except in the quarto texts of *King Lear* and *Pericles*, there is no play in which so much re-arrangement of lines is necessary on account of the printing of verse as prose and prose as verse. When, however, the text is ironed out, one sees *Coriolanus* as the end of the series of *King Lear*, *Macbeth*, and *Antony and Cleopatra*, and sees it as most difficult of all in style.

Since there is little external evidence for the dating of *Coriolanus*, critics have taken advantage of the stylistic and metrical situation as a means of telling when it was written. It seems to belong in the series next after *Antony and Cleopatra*, which is dated with some confidence in 1607. *Coriolanus* would therefore belong to 1608 or 1609, probably to the former year. Such external evidence as exists points to that appropriate time. The best piece of such evidence, itself not too convincing, was pointed out by Malone. In the oration of Cominius (II, ii, 105) he says of Marcius, "He lurch'd all swords of th' garland"; that is, robbed all warriors of the victor's wreath. This Ben Jonson seems to parody in *Epicoene* (1609), at the end of Act V: "Well, Dauphine, you have lurch'd your friends of the better half of the garland."

Coriolanus is based immediately and faithfully on the *Life of Caius Martius Coriolanus* in North's Plutarch (1579). Although Shakespeare follows Plutarch very closely, it is impossible not to see that his variations

are dramatically skillful as well as extremely significant in the interpretation of the character and fate of the hero. Shakespeare preserves the
struggle between patricians and plebeians, the siege of Corioli and the
disposition of the battle, the candidacy for the consulship, the banishment with its ungrateful political crookedness, the union with Tullus
Aufidius, the attack on Rome, the embassies of friends and family, the
compromise by which Rome is saved from capture, the treachery of
Aufidius and his conspirators, and the murder of the hero. On the other
hand, Shakespeare reduces the three uprisings to one, although the denial
of the corn and the attack on the institution of the tribunate are both
held as motives against Coriolanus. Also Coriolanus is banished immediately after his ejection from the consulship, to which he had been
legally elected, and not later, as in Plutarch, because of his opposition
to the distribution of corn. The large number of omens and supernatural
visions, so plentifully preserved in *Julius Caesar*, are omitted here, perhaps
because of the more realistic mood of *Coriolanus*. The scene of the conspiracy against Coriolanus is in Corioli instead of in Antium as in Plutarch.
Shakespeare supplies the numerous and often significant speeches of
citizens and officers as well as the dialogue of the servants in the household of Aufidius. These speeches interpret the varying, but not always
unwise or unkindly, mind of the common people. The household scene
of the three ladies is entirely Shakespeare's, as is the third scene of the
fourth act, in which a renegade Roman and a Volscian talk of current
news. It is natural enough that Shakespeare should have invented out-
right the scene of the fourth act in which the family and friends of
Coriolanus persuade him to temporize with his enemies. Menenius
Agrippa is a great and significant creation of Shakespeare's from a hint
in Plutarch where it is said that the senate, being afraid of the secession
of the plebeians to the holy hill, sent to them "certain of the pleasantest
old men and most acceptable to the people" among the senators. The chief
man of these, Menenius Agrippa, told the people an excellent tale of
the rebellion of all the members of man's body against the belly. Of
course the humorous and pitiful rejection of Menenius by Coriolanus is
Shakespeare's own. The "children" of Coriolanus are translated into
the lively young Marcius. One significant change is the subordination of the
gracious Roman lady Valeria to Volumnia, the mother of Coriolanus. It
should, however, be noted that two of the greatest speeches in the play,

namely, that of Aufidius when Coriolanus joins him in Antium and all but the very end of the speech in which Volumnia breaks her son's purpose to destroy Rome, are taken almost word for word from Plutarch. In general it may be said that Shakespeare creates all the minor characters of the play and does so in such a way as to make them reflect the hero. One must discover how that hero in Shakespeare differs from the same hero in Plutarch.

Shakespeare's story is so similar to Plutarch's that one finds it difficult to see, beyond the changes enumerated above, just what Shakespeare did, although in the field of expression the matter is not hard to fathom. North made the French of Amyot into great English just as Amyot had made the Greek of Plutarch into great French, and, in accordance with the theory of translation current in the Renaissance, we may be sure that that is what both authors intended to do. North's Plutarch is a triumph of modernization. It fired Shakespeare's imagination and no doubt served to elevate his style. What Coleridge called "the happy valiancy of style" in *Antony and Cleopatra* carried over into *Coriolanus*, and North had his share in that. But Shakespeare had added qualities of his own, such as complicated, elliptical language and variations in blank verse style. These give *Coriolanus* a special quality, but one may go beyond that. Plutarch's description of his hero does not apply to Shakespeare's Coriolanus in all particulars. Plutarch speaks of him, for example, as "a man too full of passion and choler and too much given to self-will and opinion," who "lacked the gravity and affability that is gotten with judgement of learning and reason," and who had "that wilfulness which the governor of a commonwealth for pleasing should shun," being that which "Plato called solitariness." Plutarch goes on to say that a man that will live in the world must needs have patience. He plainly thinks Coriolanus mad.

> For when sorow (as you would saye) is set a fyre, then it is converted into spite and malice, and driveth awaye for that time all faintnes of harte and natural feare. And this is the cause why the chollericke man is so altered, and mad in his actions, as a man set a fyre with an agewe: for when a mans harte is troubled within, his pulse will beate marvelous strongely. Now that Martius was even in that taking, it appeared true sone after by his doinges.

This is Plutarch's conception and it has colored most of the criticism of Shakespeare's character; yet, although Shakespeare pays some deference to it, it is not his conception. Shakespeare gives another and a more reasonable interpretation of the life of Coriolanus. It is well enough for Plutarch to give us his prudential judgment as to how a man is to get on in the world, but suppose one has to do with a man whose whole being, consistent within itself, refuses to compromise with what he believes to be base, what then? Such a man has a right to a hearing and is indeed of far more heroic mold than is any political compromiser whosoever. Coriolanus is a soldier, an aristocrat, and a man of honor, and yet critic after critic has censured Coriolanus for his lack of sympathy for the common people as if he were a modern republican. Both Plutarch and Shakespeare are perfectly clear in stating that Coriolanus regarded lenity toward the populace as a breeder of disobedience and that the commonality, thus encouraged, would abolish law and bring in all confusion to the state. This was a widely held political opinion among the Elizabethans, indeed may be said to have been the prevalent enlightened view. Shakespeare gives it many expressions, and it was widely held by the court, the universities, and all good citizens. Whether or not Shakespeare dreaded sedition more than he did any other social evil, there is no doubt that he understood fully the aristocratic view of the state. He has made of Coriolanus the complete and uncompromising aristocrat. Perhaps Shakespeare had known such patricians; there were plenty of them to be found; perhaps he realized imaginatively the aristocratic ideal in its completeness and knew that in its pure form it could not enter into compromise; perhaps he believed that aristocracy was right in principle though fraught with danger, and gave us the case of a man whose pure and inherent virtue was his own undoing. Othello suffered tragedy because of his perfect virtue, and a similar explanation would seem to be the best one for Coriolanus.

Certain it is that Coriolanus may be seen as a completely consistent character without the necessity of bringing in so much of the stoical theory of human passions as is often done. As an unswerving aristocrat, Coriolanus is not difficult to understand. Surely, if the plebeians in their fickleness, ignorance, and greed were as dangerous to the state as Plutarch and Shakespeare depict them, and if their leaders were as base in their principles as their words and actions indicate, compromise would have been a crime. On this theory, which is no unknown one, if the plebs refused to occupy their own proper and natural station in society, they should without compunction have been permitted to starve or have been put to the sword. If they had behaved themselves properly, Coriolanus would have been willing to let them eat. But this stern and consistent man never compromises his spirit, and it is not written in the law that he should do so. He was not worse than others; he was much better. He does not wish to seek the consulship in the customary way and, if left to himself, would probably not have done it. He does, however, follow the letter of the law; and, since he has undertaken to stand for the consulship, he has been blamed for not doing it in an approving and politic spirit. He has been called malicious and pettish, but it does not follow that he is so. Shakespeare evidently thought that a dyed-in-the wool aristocrat like Coriolanus would meet the test as he meets it. To have made himself agreeable to the filthy citizens, to have complied with such shameful requirements, either formally or good-naturedly, would have been to endorse them. Plutarch thought he ought to have behaved like a politician; Shakespeare apparently did not.

Coriolanus is not made of steel, but is in his own sphere a compliant and natural person. He yields to the persuasions of his mother and his friends against his better judgment both in the matter of seeking the consulship and in that of attempting to conciliate the popular assembly. He discharges these loathsome duties in his own honest way and performs fairly well; he merely falls victim to the dastardly cunning of the politicians. Are we in ethics obliged to make terms with political bosses? Coriolanus is banished unjustly, ungratefully driven from his country on charges utterly false. He concludes not unnaturally that he has no country. He banishes his oppressors. The patricians, in whose cause he has suffered, go ahead and do business with the plebeians (one may almost conclude that they are having profitable trade with the plebs) and forget him and the principles of noble rectitude for which he has stood. His rejection comes to include his country and with it both patricians and plebeians. It includes his personal friends and former associates. He thought it covered his own flesh and blood, but here he was mistaken. From a strictly idealistic, aristocratic point of view, it is a pity Coriolanus was not a bachelor without relatives. Rome was ripe for destruction. Let it be said that the story of this character is no sermon, no set of maxims about the necessity and beauty of compromise, but an exact application of the principles of justice to human society, with all the consequences. From it one turns to social and family ties almost with reluctance. This sounds severe, but Shakespeare knew and all wise men know that man in the world must be what he is and must accept the purpose of God and the doom assigned. But should we for that reason withhold our admiration from those things which are perfectly, beautifully, although impossibly, right? Shakespeare did not mean to teach us any lesson about the necessity of compromise, still less perhaps about the vintage of the grapes of wrath, but he was disposed to show us that absolute virtue is an heroic and may be a tragic thing. He saw the possibility of dramatizing Plutarch's Coriolanus as a pattern of virtue.

Before we examine the play for evidence for or against this interpretation, let us recall that Shakespeare did not hate the common people, but he did apparently think them unfit to rule the state. His character Coriolanus thought it disastrous that they should bring their fickleness and their proneness to follow demagogues into the business of government. Let us, however, rid ourselves of the idea that Shakespeare thought the common people all fools or all wise men, all just and honest men or all scoundrels. He merely thought of them as people. What they say is always worth attending to. For example, the First Citizen is malicious, but he is no fool. The Second Citizen, who is a just and generous man, says (I, i, 30-9),

> Consider you what services he has done for his country?

The First Citizen replies with a practical interpretation of the character and career of Coriolanus so superficially applicable that, although it is wrong, Shakespeare critics still adhere to it:

> Very well; and could be content to give him good report for't, but that he pays himself with being proud.

It is a quite remarkable statement in and for itself. The First Citizen goes on to amplify this superficial view, and in a shallow sense is right. Coriolanus is not one of those supple patriots who say, "My country wrong or right."

> I say unto you, what he hath done famously, he did it to that end: though soft-conscienced men can be content to say it was for his country, he did it to please his mother, and to be partly proud; which he is, even to the altitude of his virtue.

We shall have to consider this charge of pride, so often repeated, and it may be that we shall conclude that the fundamental quality of Coriolanus is not so much pride as an absolute virtue which embraces his country and transcends it.

In the introductory remarks made before he repeats the famous fable (I, i, 64-77) Menenius says some noteworthy things. He tells the plebeians that

> You may as well
> Strike at the heaven with your staves as lift them
> Against the Roman state.

This is the Roman point of view; it is what Menenius and probably Volumnia believed; perhaps it is the point of view of history. But in any case Coriolanus is as much above the point of view of Roman supremacy as the plebeians are below it. Menenius tells them also that the patricians care for them like fathers. They dispute this and bring somewhat convincing charges against the patricians, but the standing of Menenius and the general theory of the aristocratic state which Shakespeare reflects in this play and elsewhere give substance to the claim that aristocrats do care for common people.

When Caius Marcius enters the scene, his speeches (ll. 116-219) are indeed unlovely, but they are consistent and from his point of view politically sound. If he had any pity for the hunger of the plebeians, it is swallowed up in his indignation at their impudence and their seditiousness. What business had they, after all, to concern themselves with the distribution of the precious corn, the very function of the noble senate? He is still more outraged by the ruinous constitutional provision which has been framed to conciliate them, namely, that they should have five tribunes of their own choice (ll. 221-5). Coriolanus was doomed to defeat, but he at least recognized and openly opposed his enemies, who in his thought and in the thought of many men were also the enemies of order.

There is a simple matter which does much to explain the relation between Coriolanus and Aufidius and indeed runs deeply through all the earlier part of the play. It is the spirit of chivalry, of prowess in battle. Jousts and tournaments, of which one hears so much in the lives of Sidney and Essex, seem to us mere outmoded ceremony; but the Elizabethans took their chivalry very seriously. Chivalric considerations appropriate to romance not only fill the *Faerie Queene*, but are likely to appear in any Shakespearean play. Coriolanus and Aufidius are rival warriors; Coriolanus has had the better of all encounters between them. Aufidius, who is described in North as valiant and chivalrous and a man of great mind, cannot endure a life of defeat; he longs to meet with Coriolanus and have it out (I, ii, 35-6):

> 'Tis sworn between us we shall ever strike
> Till one can do no more.

His resort to any means for victory is intelligible in the light of his desperation.

Volumnia has brought up her son in a highly specialized way. She has quite definitely brought him up to be a soldier, a thing which means in chivalric opinion that he has been reared in pure nobility. She has not brought him up to be a politician. She might have done so, for later in the play she herself acknowledges the necessity of politic action. She chose to breed in him absolute knightliness and pure idealism. Shakespeare does not say except perhaps by remote implication that women should bring up their sons to be discreetly brave and tolerably honest. He merely shows us in the third scene of the first act that this man was brought up a warrior. He does not tell us whether he liked the idea or not. Successful soldiers have to have a measure of ferocity; the other kind do not last. When Valeria describes how "the pretty boy" "mammock'd" the "gilded butterfly," Volumnia remarks complacently (I, iii, 72),

> One on's father's moods.

How absurdly anachronistic and ill-judged it is to demand of Coriolanus that he should combine utter nobility with social compliance! Volumnia explains (III, ii, 129-30):

> Thy valiantness was mine, thou suck'dst it from me,
> But owe thy pride thyself.

What is it she calls "pride"? She cannot mean vanity, inordinate self-esteem, the ruler of the Seven Deadly Sins, or even arrogance and haughtiness (of which qualities Coriolanus has a superabundant store). She must mean stubbornness and intractability, but even these are not Coriolanus' qualities. He has, to quote the dictionary, "a consciousness or feeling of what is befitting or due oneself or one's position, which prevents a person from doing what he considers to be beneath him or unworthy of him." We would not rob him of that quality even though we knew it would be fatal to him.

In the battles before Corioli Marcius is impeccable. To be sure, he curses the cowardly Roman soldiers who have been beaten back to their trenches, and they deserved it. He scorns them for deserting him when he drives through the gates alone, in which action he is not foolhardy but sound in soldiership, as witnessed by his single-handed success. Again when they turned to pillage they merited his contempt. They needed to be shamed and set on fire by his courage. How else are battles to be won? Coriolanus shows while he is assembling troops for his attack on the Antiates (I, vi, 66-85) that he is not unkind to soldiers who do their duty and that he knows how to lead them. It is a crass sort of patriotism which in wartime admires every man who wears a uniform. In these battles too Coriolanus shines by his modesty and his noble personal qualities. If his diffidence seems unnatural to our world, we must not therefore overlook the fact that Shakespeare regarded the modesty of Coriolanus as the finest flower of his exploits. It was and is rather fine for this successful warrior to say (I, ix, 13-19),

> Pray now, no more: my mother,
> Who has a charter to extol her blood,
> When she does praise me grieves me. I have done
> As you have done; that's what I can; induced
> As you have been; that's for my country:
> He that has but effected his good will
> Hath overta'en mine act.

The whole first act is filled with the glory of Coriolanus, and all the envy that exists is in the mind of Aufidius, who indeed is corrupted by it (I, x, 24-7):

> Where I find him, were it
> At home, upon my brother's guard, even there,
> Against the hospitable canon, would I
> Wash my fierce hand in's heart.

The corruption does not rob Aufidius of his knightly honor at once, as we shall see in the fifth act, but this passage is indicative of an ultimate flaw in his chivalry.

When Menenius talks with Sicinius and Brutus at the beginning of the second act one notes a countercharge, probably to be taken seriously, that those who accuse Coriolanus of pride in the evil sense are themselves guilty of that sin (II, i, 31-40). Not one particle of self-interest enters into the noble pride of Coriolanus, whereas the ignoble pride of the tribunes is full of it. That they are scoundrels and conspirators appears whenever they open their mouths to speak (II, i, 260-87):

> *Bru.*   For an end,
> We must suggest the people in what hatred
> He still hath held them; that to's power he would
> Have made them mules, silenc'd their pleaders, and
> Dispropertied their freedoms, holding them,
> In human action and capacity,
> Of no more soul nor fitness for the world
> Than camels in the war, who have their provand
> Only for bearing burdens, and sore blows
> For sinking under them.
> *Sic.*   This, as you say, suggested
> At some time when his soaring insolence
> Shall touch the people—which time shall not want,
> If he be put upon't: and that's as easy
> As to set dogs on sheep—will be his fire
> To kindle their dry stubble; and their blaze
> Shall darken them for ever. . . .
> *Bru.*   Let's to the Capitol;
> And carry with us ears and eyes for the time,
> But hearts for the event.

These men are marked as villains as clearly as Shakespeare knew how to mark them, and the arguments of these crooked politicians should not be used for statements of the faults of Coriolanus. That is often done, and it is no wonder that Shakespeare's hero has suffered derogation since critics have sided with his base enemies. How clearly the distinction between sincerity and plausible defamation is brought out in the dialogue between the First and Second Officers in the second scene of the second act! The Second Officer says quite truly (ll. 11-15),

> Therefore, for Coriolanus neither to care whether they love or hate him manifests the true knowledge he has in their disposition; and out of his noble carelessness lets them plainly see 't.

The false and malevolent reply of the First Citizen is used by so good a critic as Hudson as expressive of the truth about Coriolanus; that is, Hudson thinks Coriolanus capable of the pettiness charged against him in the speech (ll. 18-23):

> If he did not care whether he had their love or no, he waved indifferently 'twixt doing them neither good nor harm: but he seeks their hate with greater devotion than they can render it him; and leaves nothing undone that may fully discover him their opposite.

The rejoinder of the Second Officer (ll. 27-38) is certainly in the voice of Shakespeare and of all just men:

> He hath deserved worthily of his country: and his ascent is not by such easy degrees as those who, having been supple and courteous to the people, bonneted, without any further deed to have them at all into their estimation and report: but he hath so planted his honours in their eyes, and his actions in their hearts, that for their tongues to be silent, and not confess so much, were a kind of ingrateful injury; to report otherwise, were a malice, that, giving itself the lie, would pluck reproof and rebuke from every ear that heard it.

The political incompetency of the people is not a matter of their being unable to understand, but is a matter of their being misled and consequently unreliable in their actions. This idea is repeated so often and so clearly that one wonders that it can be misunderstood. Brutus, perhaps from guile, perhaps from momentary generosity, gives warning (ll. 61-4) that Coriolanus should "remember a kinder value of the people," and Menenius replies quite truly (ll. 68-9),

> He loves your people;
> But tie him not to be their bedfellow.

We may believe that the human rights of the plebs would have been perfectly secure in the hands of Coriolanus had he been permitted to exercise the office of consul, but their social and political equality would certainly have received a check. Surely people familiar with questions of racial discrimination will find no difficulty in understanding this. It is no crime to regard one race as socially and politically superior to another, however much it may be at variance with the principles of democratic constitutions, and Coriolanus meets his greatest tests in this enforced leveling.

Sicinius, an equalitarian (largely for his own profit), insists on the letter of the law (II, ii, 143-5):

> Sir, the people
> Must have their voices; neither will they bate
> One jot of ceremony.

Menenius advises Coriolanus

> Put them not to't:
> Pray you, go fit you to the custom and
> Take to you, as your predecessors have,
> Your honour with your form.

Thus admonished Coriolanus complies well enough, remarking only that he does not like the custom. This is a sore point with Brutus and Sicinius, and they plot to upset the election. Coriolanus, dressed in a gown of humility, goes through the test. He is neither polite nor kind, but he is elected and proclaimed. Sicinius observes that he seems rather pleased at the result (II, iii, 159-60),

> He has it now; and by his looks, methinks,
> 'Tis warm at's heart.

The world has decided with the Third Citizen that Coriolanus mocked the electors, but the First Citizen says rightly that it is not mockery but "his kind of speech." How could a man of the sincerity and of the completely aristocratic principles of Coriolanus have gone further than he did? Who can say that he was not right? Remember the honest thoughts he entertained about the common people. He has been censured and has suffered derogation as a hero and the play itself has been robbed of its power and charm because critics have insisted that Coriolanus ought to have acted like a politician. We have far too many politicians as it is; they may be necessary, but Shakespeare has asked us to contemplate the spectacle of a completely honest and courageous man seeking public office. Most men would have smiled and flattered while they showed their wounds, all for their own advantage; but the law did not require the candidate to smile. In the end of the second act Shakespeare gives us an unforgettable picture of political crookedness. The tribunes lie to the people, tell them what to do, tell them what to say.

In the first scene of the third act, Coriolanus denounces the tribunes, which was and is a gratifying thing to do, but dangerous. He was not discreet; discretion would have been cowardice; he could not have been politic and been himself. He ought to be honored for exposing the scoundrels (ll. 157-71). This is no little group of willful men. The tribunes are unscrupulous bosses bent only on preserving their own privileges, and it is obvious to any right-thinking person that the people would have been better off in the honest hands of Coriolanus than in those of the time-serving politicians. It is true that Coriolanus loses his temper when he is libelously called a traitor, but what would one have? Try it on the greatest aristocrat you know and see how he reacts to insult. Let us be as democratic as we please, but let us not mar Shakespeare's picture of a perfect aristocrat; it is ignorant to do so, and it spoils the tragedy. As if to confirm these views, Shakespeare further on in the scene shows Menenius attempting to reason with the tribunes. Menenius gets nowhere, but he does lay bare the political selfishness of these men. At line 223, when the aediles are about to lay hands upon him, Coriolanus draws his sword and beats the rabble and their leaders in. Is he to be blamed for this? Even had he admitted the authority of such officers, which he did not, the procedure is not according to law; he is resisting a mob. In the next scene arrangements are made for a formal trial, and it was a mistake for his friends to interfere with Coriolanus in the presentation of his case. There might have been bloodshed, but crying injustice and mob tyranny would have been avoided. Volumnia counsels him to policy (ll. 16 ff.), Menenius remonstrates with him, Cominius seeks to get him to "frame his spirit." Coriolanus yields to these persuasions, for he is not a Frankenstein; but, if he is guilty of tragic error, it is in thus ceasing to be himself. Volumnia even urges her son to deceive his enemies in the city as he was wont to deceive his enemies in the field (III, ii, 41-5):

> I have heard you say,
> Honour and policy, like unsever'd friends,
> I' the war do grow together: grant that, and tell me,
> In peace what each of them by the other lose,
> That they combine not there.

Coriolanus' reply is "Tush, tush!" and when she continues the argument, he makes no adequate answer. We may believe that he saw the speciousness of her case, since peace and war differ exactly in this respect, that peace has, or should have, scruples about the use of policy.

Tyrannously banished, Coriolanus makes his famous speech (III, iii, 120-35), and no study of him can afford to disregard it. It expresses his loathing, personal and justifiable, of the populace and its leaders, and cites his reasons for his hatred and contempt. So striking are his words that his "I banish you" is the perfect expression of his new attitude. He despises the citizens for their own sakes; he is superior to the city and the citizens, and he knows it:

> You common cry of curs! whose breath I hate
> As reek o' rotten fens, whose loves I prize
> As the dead carcasses of unburied men
> That do corrupt my air, I banish you;
> And here remain with your uncertainty!
> Let every feeble rumour shake your hearts!
> Your enemies, with nodding of their plumes,
> Fan you into despair! Have the power still
> To banish your defenders; till at length
> Your ignorance, which finds not till it feels,
> Making not reservation of yourselves,
> Still your own foes, deliver you as most
> Abated captives to some nation
> That won you without blows! Despising,
> For you, the city, thus I turn my back:
> There is a world elsewhere.

It is nevertheless interesting to speculate as to what the intentions of Coriolanus were when he departed into banishment. The admirable scene of his leave-taking with his family and his friends gives us but little information. He says (IV, i, 21), one cannot tell how ominously, "I'll do well yet." Later (ll. 51-3) he says, as if he had a plan in his head,

> While I remain above the ground, you shall
> Hear from me still, and never of me aught
> But what is like me formerly.

Plutarch says that outwardly he showed no manner of passion, but that inwardly he was consumed with vehemency of anger and desire of revenge, and adds that Coriolanus spent some time at his houses in the country and then, discouraged at not finding a profitable or honorable cause, joined his country's enemies. Shakespeare seems to follow Plutarch when he has Coriolanus say, as he offers his services to the Volsces (IV, v, 80-4),

> The cruelty and envy of the people,
> Permitted by our dastard nobles, who
> Have all forsook me, hath devour'd the rest;
> And suffer'd me by the voice of slaves to be
> Whoop'd out of Rome.

Perhaps we are to believe that the idea of joining the Volsces was a later thought, but it seems at least possible that the will to destruction sprang forth in full panoply from his head when he denounced his enemies at the time of his banishment. The scene between the Roman renegade and the Volscian (iii) seems, however, to suggest political action in Rome. But in any case it is worthwhile to inquire into the motives of Coriolanus because of A. C. Bradley's widely held interpretation.

Bradley says that Coriolanus was beside himself with passion and had become in mind a complete destroyer. His idea is in line with Plutarch as regards passion, but not as regards the burning of Rome:

> What follows on his exile depends on this self-ignorance. When he bids farewell to his mother and his wife and friends he is still excited and exalted by conflict. He comforts them; he will take no companion; he will be loved when he is lacked, or at least he will be feared; while he remains alive, they shall always hear from him, and never aught but what is like him formerly. But the days go by, and no one, not even his mother, hears a word. When we see him next, he is entering Antium to offer his services against his country. If they are accepted, he knows what he will do: he will burn Rome.
>
> As I have already remarked, Shakespeare does not exhibit the change of mind which issues in this frightful purpose; but from what we see and hear later we can tell how he imagined it; and the key lies in that idea of *burning* Rome. As time passes, and no suggestion of recall reaches Coriolanus, and he learns what it is to be a solitary and homeless exile, his heart hardens, his pride swells to a mountainous bulk, and the wound in it becomes a fire. The fellow-patricians from whom he parted lovingly now appear to him ingrates and dastards, scarcely better than the loathsome mob. Somehow, he knows not how, even his mother and wife have deserted him. He has become nothing to Rome, and Rome shall hear nothing from him. Here in solitude he can find no relief in a storm of words; but gradually the blind intolerable chaos of resentment conceives and gives birth to a vision, not merely of battle and indiscriminate slaughter, but of the whole city in one tower of flame. To see that with his bodily eyes would satisfy his soul; and the way to the sight is through the

Volscians. If he is killed the moment they recognize him, he cares little; better a dead nothing than the living nothing Rome thinks him. But if he lives, she shall know what he is. He bears himself among the Volscians with something that resembles self-control; but what controls him is the vision that never leaves him and never changes, and his eye is red with its glare when he sits in his state before the doomed city.

Eloquent and plausible as this is, it is less than the stature of Coriolanus, who has promised that his friends will never hear aught of him but what is like him formerly. If he is and has always been a flaming fool and a public enemy, he is to that extent an unworthy tragic hero. Very little, if any, evidence supports Bradley's interpretation. There is little or nothing about burning the city, and Bradley himself points out that Plutarch provided only for punishment of the enemies of Coriolanus and for enforcing humiliating terms of peace on Rome. There is evidence in the play that Shakespeare is in this matter following Plutarch's story. Cominius does not say (V, i, 63-5) that Coriolanus will burn Rome. He says only,

> I tell you, he does sit in gold, his eye
> Red as 'twould burn Rome; and his injury
> The gaoler to his pity.

It is no soft peace that he means to enforce, but an affair of "rages and revenges." There would be fire as well as pillage no doubt. Indeed, Volumnia says (V, iii, 181),

> I am hush'd until our city be afire.

But that absolute destruction by fire was not in the plan is borne out by what Coriolanus says to Aufidius (V, iii, 11-17):

> Their latest refuge
> Was to send him; for whose old love I have,
> Though I show'd sourly to him, once more offer'd
> The first conditions, which they did refuse
> And cannot now accept; to grace him only
> That thought he could do more, a very little
> I have yielded to.

This and many other passages make it clear that Coriolanus was a man of very tender feelings, that he is not the man without all compassion or reason, the maniac of revenge, that he is said to be; and yet the main question remains to be answered: Why did he give up his conquest? Rome deserved to be conquered, if not destroyed, at his hands. He certainly showed determination and self-command as well as anger. Over against this we have a certain sweetness and pliability of nature.

Perhaps Shakespeare himself was puzzled, and it is not difficult to imagine that his uncertainty is reflected in the speech of Aufidius (IV, vii, 28-57) more or less intruded into the play. One might ask oneself whether Aufidius speaks the whole truth or merely the truth as he sees it; but the question is worth asking. He begins with an opinion that Coriolanus will be successful in his enterprise against Rome. Then follows a digression on the causes of his overthrow in Rome, then a tribute to his merit (ll. 48-9):

> but he has a merit,
> To choke it in the utterance.

These lines seem to say that whatever faults Coriolanus has or has had are exceeded by his greatness. Aufidius ends with the villain's statement that Coriolanus, once in command of Rome, can again be ruined by a misinterpretation of his virtues, and that Aufidius will then be able to destroy him. Therefore out of this perplexing speech comes merely an acknowledgment on the part of Aufidius of the greatness of Coriolanus and of the tenaciousness of his own envy. The passage (ll. 49 ff.) beginning "So our virtues" seems to point back to the beginning of the speech and to repeat with citation of proverbs the idea that what once happened to Coriolanus will happen to him again. In other words, a man may be as virtuous as he likes, but the success of a life controlled by virtue lies in "interpretation of the time." The passage is so important in the interpretation of the play that one should record it:

> All places yield to him ere he sits down;
> And the nobility of Rome are his:
> The senators and patricians love him too:
> The tribunes are no soldiers; and their people
> Will be as rash in the repeal, as hasty
> To expel him thence. I think he'll be to Rome
> As is the osprey to the fish, who takes it
> By sovereignty of nature. First he was
> A noble servant to them; but he could not
> Carry his honours even: whether 'twas pride,

Which out of daily fortune ever taints
The happy man; whether defect of judgement,
To fail in the disposing of those chances
Which he was lord of; or whether nature,
Not to be other than one thing, not moving
From the casque to the cushion, but commanding peace
Even with the same austerity and garb
As he controll'd the war; but one of these—
As he hath spices of them all, not all,
For I dare so far free him—made him fear'd,
So hated, and so banish'd: but he has a merit,
To choke it in the utterance. So our virtues
Lie in the interpretation of the time:
And power, unto itself most commendable,
Hath not a tomb so evident as a chair
To extol what it hath done.
One fire drives out one fire; one nail, one nail;
Rights by rights falter, strengths by strengths do fail.
Come, let's away. When, Caius, Rome is thine,
Thou art poor'st of all; then shortly art thou mine.

Aufidius in anticipating the conquest of Rome along with his own ultimate triumph was correct up to a certain point. Coriolanus has, however, another quality which Aufidius only vaguely apprehends as "a merit." That merit is his humanity, which is natural as well as acquired. It is moreover a function of his creed to believe that man should be and should act at his best, and that the common domestic virtues are the very bases of the finest aristocracy. Coriolanus embodies the qualities which the Renaissance as well as the ancient world sought to express by the word "magnanimous"—nobility of feeling, superiority to petty resentment or jealousy, generous disregard of injuries. As we contemplate the situation in which Coriolanus stands before Rome, Coriolanus the aristocrat, we realize that he is about to cease to be himself, about to lose his own soul. In working out the salvation of his hero Shakespeare dives deeper into the fundamentals of human existence than he does in perhaps any other place in his dramas.

One doubts if the play of *Coriolanus* can ever come to life again on the strength of its political import, as it did no less than twice in the eighteenth century. Our age has grown too equalitarian even to realize imaginatively the greatness, the essential humanity, of the aristocratic idea. Woodrow

Wilson used to say that the perfect democrat and the perfect aristocrat were almost indistinguishable in their human qualities, but we can no longer see that truth. The play will always be interesting for the picture it gives of Coriolanus himself, of his mother Volumnia, of his wife Virgilia, of Aufidius, of the citizens and servants, and of the genial and shrewd old patrician Menenius. Indeed, there is a witty, lively quality in the whole play that is often overlooked; but the unrecognized greatness of the drama lies in its central issue.

It is ordinarily said that Coriolanus spares Rome and sacrifices himself because as a patriot he realizes that the state is greater than the individual. He has even been put to shame as a grown man and a soldier still tied to his mother's apron strings. A thoughtful consideration of the play as a whole and particularly a careful reading of Volumnia's plea to him to withhold his hand (V, iii, 131-82) will show that these ideas are inadequate. Coriolanus has already rejected all demands and persuasions of the state of Rome. As a political organization and a native country, it has failed to save itself. Volumnia reveals the issue and, wise woman that she is, puts it up to him (ll. 173-82):

> Nay, behold's:
> This boy, that cannot tell what he would have,
> But kneels and holds up hands for fellowship,
> Does reason our petition with more strength
> Than thou hast to deny't. Come, let us go:
> This fellow had a Volscian to his mother;
> His wife is in Corioli, and his child
> Like him by chance. Yet give us our dispatch:
> I am hush'd until our city be afire,
> And then I'll speak a little.

Coriolanus yields not to patriotism as represented by the wretched people and government of Rome, but to patriotism as a force of nature. He cannot repudiate his own flesh and blood, repudiate himself. His motive in yielding to his mother's plea is larger than patriotism; it is the genesis of patriotism; it includes and redefines patriotism in larger terms. The tragedy of Coriolanus lies in the fact that he has been carried by a sort of fate into an impossible conflict with his mother, who is nature and his race. To extricate himself and thus save his soul costs him his life. To conceive of Coriolanus as a mere victim of pride, much less as one crazed by the passions of anger and revenge, is to rob him of his rights as a hero. He has suffered in his popularity because of long and repeated failure to see him as he is, and his play has suffered with him.

If the foregoing interpretation is correct, *Coriolanus* presents us Shakespeare's most advanced political thinking, far in advance of questions at issue between patricians and plebeians—a conception of politics as human life.

CHAPTER XI

Romance or Tragi-Comedy

1. *Pericles.*

THE significance of *Pericles* in the dramatic work of Shakespeare and in the Elizabethan drama lies in its introduction of a new subject matter and a new point of view. *Pericles* gave to romance a dramatic form and to drama a romantic tone. The theme came from a very ancient form of romance—the Greek novel. This was not the first time this element had appeared in Shakespeare, for the Aegeon-Aemilia episode in *The Comedy of Errors* is of exactly the same sort, and that episode itself is a variant of the plot which was to appear in *Pericles*, namely, that of *Apollonius of Tyre*. That romance had lived through the Middle Ages, having achieved a Latin form by the fifth or sixth century. Versions and manuscripts are numerous, and the story of Apollonius of Tyre was translated into all vernacular languages, including Anglo-Saxon. The story appears in the *Gesta Romanorum* and is one of the tales in *Confessio Amantis* of John Gower, who borrowed it from *Pantheon* (c. 1186) by Godfrey of Viterbo. Gower as a chief source "presents" the play of *Pericles*.

The Greek novel dealt extensively in the separation and reunion of families and with capture by pirates, shipwrecks, sensational events and situations, exposure of infants, and disguises such as arise in *The Comedy of Errors, Twelfth Night,* and the minor plot of *The Taming of the Shrew.* Sudden and violent deaths were not unknown. Greek and Latin comedy also employed many of these devices of plot, although of course the range of the Greek novel was far wider than that of Greek and Latin comedy. *Apollonius of Tyre* was made familiar in Shakespeare's *Pericles* and in at least two Elizabethan prose tales. In it Antiochus, King of Syria, because of an incestuous relation to his daughter, endeavors to prevent her marriage and at the same time preserve his dark secret by setting up as a condition of acceptance the answering of a riddle which each suitor on pain of death must attempt to solve. Apollonius of Tyre (Pericles) has gone forth from home and arrived at Antioch. Here he offers himself for the test and solves the riddle. Antiochus nevertheless seeks his life, but Apollonius escapes, visits another kingdom, and marries a princess. He then starts back to Syria to assume his sovereignty, but on the way his ship is smitten with a great storm, and he is separated from his wife and from his daughter (Marina in the play). The story after that concerns itself with the adventures and the ultimate reunion of these three persons. Shakespeare seized on the adventures of the daughter, and nobody doubts that, in the last three acts of the play at least, he worked in a striking and altogether worthy way.

There is every evidence that *Pericles* was a popular play on the Jacobean stage, and it may be inferred that it presented a new and attractive kind of drama. An entry by Edward Blount in the Stationers' Register of May 20, 1608, shows a book called "a booke of Pericles prynce of Tyre." The entry was under the hands of Sir George Buck. In 1609, appeared a quarto version entitled "The Late, And much admired Play, Called Pericles, Prince of Tyre. With the true Relation of the whole Historie, adventures, and fortunes of the said Prince: As also, The no lesse strange, and worthy accidents, in the Birth and Life, of his Daughter Marina. As it hath been diuers and sundry times acted by his Maiesties Servants at the Globe on the Banck-side. By William Shakspeare." This quarto was not published by Edward Blount but by Henry Gosson. The same year appeared another quarto distinguished from the first only by various typographical errors. Other reprints appeared in 1611, 1619, and 1630. There is a mystery in Blount's entry of the play and his failure to publish it. The current explanation is to the effect that Blount, who was apparently a friend of the players, entered *Pericles* in order to prevent the other printer from publishing it. If this is true, his efforts failed. This is to be regretted, since Blount would perhaps have published a better text than that issued by Gosson, which is a poor and probably an unauthorized version.

The entry and publication of a prose version of the story of Pericles concerns us very much, particularly because it pretends to be and is a prose version of the play of *Pericles* and because, although it also makes use of

Shakespeare's source, Laurence Twyne's *The Patterne of Paynful Aduentures* [*of Apollonius of Tyre*] (1576, 1607), this book summarizes, not the play as we have it, but a fuller version of it. It is called *The Painfull Adventures of Pericles Prince of Tyre. Being the true History of the play of Pericles, as it was lately presented by the worthy and ancient Poet Iohn Gower.* The fact that this story of the play was written by a dramatist George Wilkins has served to bring his name into prominence as a possible collaborator with Shakespeare. A great many scholars of importance have seen Wilkins's hand in the play, particularly in the first two acts.

The situation, however, is obvious. *Pericles* is not the result of ordinary collaboration. The text as we have it was printed from the disordered papers of Shakespeare's revision of a play of Pericles of unknown authorship, and Wilkins's novel retells the story of that play. The text of *Pericles,* when its irregularities have been corrected, is excellent, and Wilkins's novel enables us to see how Shakespeare changed his original. Henry Gosson probably got possession of the foul papers of Shakespeare's revision and published them in spite of Edward Blount. *Pericles* does not appear in the First or the Second Folio, but with six other doubtful plays was included in the Third Folio and the Fourth.

As one looks at the play and at the novel based on it, one sees that Gower's story in *Confessio Amantis* is the original source, but one sees also that the play and the prose version made use, both jointly and independently, of Twyne's story of Apollonius of Tyre. It is perhaps significant that Twyne's book was republished in 1607, at the apparent time of the popularity of *Pericles*. Wilkins's novel, although it is clearly based on the play, quotes extensively the actual text of Twyne and retells some episodes of the old story which were apparently never included in the play. On the other hand, it repeatedly paraphrases the play as we have it. For example, we have in *Pericles* (II, iii, 81-5):

> A gentleman of Tyre; my name, Pericles;
> My education been in arts and arms;
> Who, looking for adventures in the world,
> Was by the rough seas reft of ships and men,
> And after shipwreck driven upon this shore.

This appears in Wilkins as follows:

> Pericles . . . thus returneth what he is, that he was a Gentleman of Tyre, his name Pericles, his education been in Artes and Armes,

who looking for adventures in the world, was by the rough and unconstant Seas, most unfortunately bereft both of shippes and men, and after shipwrecke, throwen upon this shoare.

Here and elsewhere Wilkins seems to incorporate phrases from the play.

Not only are there many cases of more or less clear borrowings from the text of *Pericles* as we have it, but Chambers and others would go even further and suspect that there are passages in the prose work which contain "snippets of verse" borrowed from an earlier fuller text than that of the play as preserved, a thing which would indicate that the play of which Wilkins wrote the story was Shakespeare's original version. One can hear the echoes of blank verse in the following passages and others not represented in quarto version of *Pericles*:

> I traytor, quoth the king, that thus disguised, art stolne into my Court, with the witchcraft of thy actions to bewitch, the yeelding spirit of my tender Childe.
> It shall become you still to be even as you are, a peece of goodness, the best wrought uppe, that ever Nature made, and if that any shall inforce you ill, if you but send to me, I am your friend.

We may therefore be certain that the *Pericles* we have is not the original play. Wilkins amplified the story of that play, which was apparently popular in its day, from Twyne's story of Apollonius. He seems to have had no manuscript before him and apparently used notes based on theatrical performances. He repeats the riddles with fair accuracy, but most set speeches, such as Marina's epitaph, are faultily reproduced. He often confuses the narrative and describes gestures and actions he had presumably seen on the stage. There are, however, clear and significant differences between the lost play as Wilkins reports it and *Pericles* as Shakespeare revised it. These appear most clearly in the management of the brothel scenes and in the character and motives of Lysimachus. These are characteristic things for Shakespeare to do. It is also to be noted that there are no indications that *Pericles* was printed from a prompt-copy. Indeed, there is no occasion to make the customary resort to stenography, piracy, memorial reconstruction or other invented causes.

Considering the play of *Pericles* as it has come down to us, one feels that attribution of authorship of various parts is a very uncertain business. Nevertheless there is an opinion pretty firmly fixed in the minds of critics that Shakespeare had a collaborator who was responsible for the first two

acts and that Shakespeare wrote only the last three. This supposition may
be correct, but the evidences are both unreliable and scanty. The confusion
arose because the text has been thought to be bad. Speculation has concerned itself, not only with the division by acts, but with matters of style
and subject matter. Chambers thinks there are unmistakable differences in
style between the first two and the last three acts, but weakens his case by
admitting that one passage in the first act has a Shakespearean ring. There
are a number of such passages. He thinks we have to do with a Jacobean
rehandling of an old dramatic theme, but seems to think it was rewritten
by George Wilkins and Shakespeare jointly. Wilkins as author of the first
two acts of *Pericles* has been a good deal of an obsession with Shakespeare
critics ever since a study by Delius in 1868. Delius was followed by Boyle
and in part by Fleay and by various others down to Deighton and Chambers. Not only is the text of *Pericles* disordered and therefore unreliable
for comparisons, but the parallels are not completely convincing. It is even
a matter of doubt as to whether Wilkins may not have been working over
Pericles about the time that he was writing *The Miseries of Enforced
Marriage.*

Some critics have been unwilling to attribute the brothel scenes (IV, ii,
v, vi) to Shakespeare. These are chiefly in prose and are unpleasantly
realistic in subject and treatment, so that certain critics, having a high
regard for Shakespeare's delicacy of taste, have been unwilling to believe
that he wrote them. If, however, one grants that Shakespeare wrote the
similar scenes in *Measure for Measure,* one need not hesitate to assign
these to him. Indeed, there are those who have looked upon the picture
of the sweetness and innocence of Marina in the midst of sordid and wicked
surroundings as an example of the finest dramatic art. There have also
been objections to Lysimachus, patron of the brothel, as a fit lover for the
gentle Marina. He was such a patron in the older forms of the story, and
he is not entirely exonerated, at least from the charge of keeping bad company, in Shakespeare's play. All that can be said is that the temper of the
times made Shakespeare slightly callous and other dramatists more callous
to the refinements of such thinking. Lysimachus certainly perceives what
Marina is and behaves to her in a noble and upright way.

The prologues and epilogues spoken by Gower and the dumbshows
which accompany them have also been objected to as un-Shakespearean.
As for the dumbshows, they are good enough and may have had some

special interest to the audience at that particular time. They were certainly helpful to the dramatist in the handling of epical material and were no doubt employed for that purpose. But the Gower prologues are often awkward, unmetrical, and false in rhythm. Consider this passage from the prologue to Act I:

> To sing a song that old was sung,
> From ashes ancient Gower is come;
> Assuming man's infirmities,
> To glad your ear, and please your eyes.
> It hath been sung at festivals,
> On ember-eves and holy-ales;
> And lords and ladies in their lives
> Have read it for restoratives:
> The purchase is to make men glorious;
> *Et bonum quo antiquius, eo melius.* . . .
> This king unto him took a fere,
> Who died and left a female heir,
> So buxom, blithe, and full of face,
> As heaven had lent her all his grace;
> With whom the father liking took,
> And her to incest did provoke:
> Bad child; worse father! to entice his own
> To evil should be done by none.

This is obviously an attempt to write in antique style and to imitate the "moral Gower." One sees even Gower's trick of rhyming in an occasional Latin line. In some places the poet presents us with longer but not more skillful or graceful lines (IV, iv):

> Thus time we waste, and longest leagues make short;
> Sail seas in cockles, have an wish but for't;
> Making, to take your imagination,
> From bourn to bourn, region to region.
> But you being pardon'd, we commit no crime
> To use one language in each several clime
> Where our scenes seem to live.

Here and elsewhere one feels the warfare between rhythm and meter that rages in the works of fifteenth-century English poets, even to the habit of rhyming Latin derivatives by their endings. Now, one asks, what was the origin of that unhappy strife? To us Chaucer and for the most part Gower are poets of adequate metrical skill, but they were not so to the

Elizabethans. Chaucer and Gower seemed to be rough in rhythm, uneven in meter, and uncertain in rhyme. The language in which these poets wrote underwent great changes immediately after they had done their work. The pronunciation of final *e* was lost even in the very early manuscripts, so that if one will read either of these poets with a more or less modern pronunciation, one will get an impression of roughness in technique quite unlike the smoother finish of Chaucer and the metrical sufficiency of Gower. The thing then that the author of the Gower prologues and epilogues was trying to do is not so far astray as it seems to be, for, to the Elizabethans, to write as Gower wrote was to write irregularly. It is not improbable that Shakespeare, thus hampered, wrote the prologues and epilogues, which along with their assumed simplicity have a certain directness and poetical excellence. For example, faced with genuine human issues and significant events, Gower as prologue takes on new life at the beginning of the third act:

> Now sleep yslaked hath the rout;
> No din but snores the house about,
> Made louder by the o'er-fed breast
> Of this most pompous marriage-feast.
> The cat, with eyne of burning coal,
> Now crouches fore the mouse's hole;
> And crickets sing at the oven's mouth,
> E'er the blither for their drouth. . . .

And as to the first two acts, are they so different from the last three and so inferior that one must say that they are not the work of Shakespeare? One must bear in mind that the text is in bad condition but that nevertheless the story is well told. It is notable that those who deny that Shakespeare wrote these acts yet find in them certain passages, and not the same ones, which they are tempted to ascribe to Shakespeare. Sir Edmund Chambers regards Act I, scene i, lines 100-2, as possibly Shakespearean:

> The blind mole casts
> Copp'd hills towards heaven, to tell the earth is throng'd
> By man's oppression; and the poor worm doth die for't.

Another critic would accept these lines (II, i, 75-81):

> What I have been I have forgot to know;
> But what I am, want teaches me to think on:
> A man throng'd up with cold: my veins are chill,

And have no more of life than may suffice
To give my tongue that heat to ask your help;
Which if you shall refuse, when I am dead,
For that I am a man, pray see me buried.

This passage certainly suggests the latest manner of Shakespeare, as do other passages in these acts. It is difficult to regard the plain language of the fishermen in the same scene as anything other than Shakespeare's depiction of humorous common men:

Third Fish. Master, I marvel how the fishes live in the sea.
First Fish. Why, as men do a-land; the great ones eat up the little ones.

Exceptions multiply as one proceeds.

The most puzzling thing about the first two acts is the interspersion, without ascertainable purpose, of rhymed couplets. Feminine endings are also fewer than in the last three acts, although they are used in some places in such a way as to suggest *Cymbeline* and *The Winter's Tale.* It has been suggested that there lies back of *Pericles* a very early play, and it would be natural, if Shakespeare were following such a play, for him to keep parts of it in the first two acts where the familiar story of Apollonius of Tyre is being recited. In any case one is indisposed to exclude Shakespeare from the first two acts, which are simple, romantic, usually adequate, and often eloquent. *Pericles* is really a romance like *The Old Wives' Tale* of Peele and seems to be intentionally quaint and archaic, particularly throughout the first three acts. The prologues, epilogues, and dumbshows witness what great pains were taken with the style of the play, which in its present form reminds one of the ruins of a very ornate building under reconstruction. One knows not what archaisms of style Shakespeare may have employed in presenting so carefully and with such a sense of old romance the old story of Apollonius of Tyre. Mixtures of text may account, not only for unexpected rhyme, but also for the inferiorities insisted on by critics in the first two acts. One may at least insist that readers will perceive that the original *Pericles* was a play of the same elaborate workmanship as the other romances.

One may be sure in any case that Shakespeare's imagination was fired by the events recorded in the later acts of the play. These concern the personal misfortunes and ultimate happiness of Pericles and, particularly, the thrilling adventures of his daughter Marina, a young woman in whose very soul was chastity. We know from Helena, Isabella, Imogen, and Perdita that Shakespeare had a poet's interest in chaste and lovely women. Pericles is a philosopher, and Shakespeare was interested in men of the larger view. Pericles bears the buffets of misfortune well and receives his ultimate reward with dignity. Part, however, of the Prospero-like power over circumstances is lodged in Cerimon.

Pericles is at first a sort of fairy tale, but it grows more dramatic as human issues develop. The first act shows Pericles' solution of the riddle of Antiochus and his escape home to Tyre from the wrath of the wicked king. Fearing still, he leaves his kingdom in charge of the faithful Helicanus and sets out on a voyage to Tarsus, none too soon, for Thaliard, assassin from Antioch, arrives only just too late to murder him. Pericles arrives in Tarsus at a moment of great need and saves the famine-stricken people of Tarsus from death by means of the shipload of food which he has brought. All of this is faithfully repeated from the old romance, and narrative and episodic materials from the same source continue in the second act. According to Gower, Pericles again receives warning that Antiochus is on his trail and again sets out on his travels. This time he suffers shipwreck on the coast of Pentapolis. He is alone and destitute. Fishermen tell him of a tournament about to be held in honor of the birthday of Thaisa, a true heroine of romance, daughter of King Simonides of Pentapolis, and very beautiful. Then develops the story of the unknown and unkempt knight. In most miraculous fashion the fishermen draw in with their net a full suit of armor for the use of Pericles in the tournament. The armor is foul but efficacious, and Pericles fights so well that Thaisa falls in love with him. The whole thing is such stuff as Spenser used in the *Faerie Queene* and Sidney in *Arcadia*. Simonides is pleasant to Pericles, but at first does not desire him as a son-in-law. Thaisa, after the fashion of Greene's and Shakespeare's women, vows she will have no one else as husband, and Simonides has to agree to the marriage. So far it is a fine old tale, rather quaintly told, which must have seemed to Shakespeare and his Jacobean audience delightfully old-fashioned.

From this point on the play is different, but not abruptly so. It changes rather gradually into a drama of personal danger and personal passion. That is, it takes on the modern spirit. Faced with genuine human issues, Shakespeare makes his voice distinctly heard. Pericles begins (III, i, 1-6):

Thou god of this great vast, rebuke these surges,
Which wash both heaven and hell; and thou, that hast
Upon the winds command, bind them in brass,
Having call'd them from the deep! O, still
Thy deafening, dreadful thunders; gently quench
Thy nimble sulphurous flashes!

When the nurse, Lychorida, enters bearing a newborn infant, the greatest
of romanticists had a task to tax his powers. The words of Pericles rise to
the occasion (III, i, 27-37). The queen presents the likeness of death and
is coffined and cast into the sea. Pericles orders the ship to put in at Tarsus,
where he may leave the new-born child for careful nursing with Cleon
and his wife, Dionyza. The next scene presents us with a great physician
of romance, one Cerimon, who says of himself (III, ii, 31-42):

'Tis known I ever
Have studied physic, through which secret art,
By turning o'er authorities, I have,
Together with my practice, made familiar
To me and to my aid the blest infusions
That dwell in vegetives, in metals, stones;
And I can speak of the disturbances
That nature works, and of her cures; which doth give me
A more content in course of true delight
Than to be thirsty after tottering honour,
Or tie my treasure up in silken bags,
To please the fool and death.

This speech shows Shakespeare in his latest manner and at a proper poetic
height, and yet Cerimon is the same magical physician that Faustus had
become and that the father of Helena must have been. He has need of
his skill, for at that moment his servants bring Thaisa in her coffin, just
rescued from the sea. We may be sure that nothing less than the skill of
Cerimon could have saved Thaisa's life. She calls upon Diana, goddess
of childbirth, when she awakes; then, believing Pericles dead, she becomes
before the end of the act a votaress in the temple of Diana at Ephesus.
Thus does romance tuck away its unwanted puppets until it is time for
them to play again.

But Pericles has not perished; he has landed safely in Tarsus. There
he leaves his infant daughter in the care of Lychorida, the nurse, under
supervision of his friends. He himself goes again to sea. It will be seen

that his family is now completely separated and will need to be brought together again before the play ends.

The fourth act is not without its perils, and it now serves to make matters worse. Thaisa is in Diana's temple, Pericles is sailing the seas, and, when we see Marina again, she is grown to womanhood. Like Proserpina she is gathering flowers and like Perdita talking sweetly about them (IV, i, 14-18):

> No, I will rob Tellus of her weed,
> To strew thy green with flowers: the yellows, blues,
> The purple violets, and marigolds,
> Shall as a carpet hang upon thy grave,
> While summer-days do last.

She is very beautiful and very well educated by Cleon in music, letters, dancing, and the household arts. She is so enviable indeed that she falls a victim to the jealousy of Dionyza, whose daughter, Philoten, Marina outshines. Nobody is quite safe in romance, and Dionyza, who had seemed a gracious lady and the proper wife of a scholarly gentleman, now takes on the part of a very wicked stepmother. Dionyza bribes Leonine, one of those convenient villains who appear in romances since the time of *Havelok the Dane*, to slay Marina. He is not particularly anxious to do this and is saved the trouble by a band of pirates such as are always ready to descend on any shore in the land of Greek fiction. The pirates carry off Marina, and Leonine reports her dead. Cleon builds a monument to her, and both he and Gower make speeches before it. But, as we know, Marina is not dead. She has been sold by the thrifty pirates to the keepers of a brothel. These keepers are a truly awful lot—a pandar, a bawd, and Boult. The others are commonplace, but Boult has the features, like Pompey in *Measure for Measure*, of an interesting comic villain (IV, vi, 190-211):

> *Mar.*   O, that the gods
> Would safely deliver me from this place!
> Here, here's gold for thee.
> If that thy master would gain by me,
> Proclaim that I can sing, weave, sew, and dance,
> With other virtues, which I'll keep from boast;
> And I will undertake all these to teach.
> I doubt not but this populous city will
> Yield many scholars.
> *Boult.* But can you teach all this you speak of? . . .

Well, I will see what I can do for thee: if I can place thee, I will.

Mar. But amongst honest women.

Boult. 'Faith, my acquaintance lies little amongst them. . . . . Come, I'll do for thee what I can; come your ways.

Marina becomes famous as an embroiderer, a singer, and dancer, and, when the heartbroken Pericles returns to Mytilene, Lysimachus has Marina sing and dance before him. She recalls to Pericles his lost wife, and he recognizes her as his daughter—certainly as fine a piece of old romance as one could desire. Pericles goes to Ephesus to offer sacrifice to Diana. There he tells his story to Thaisa, and they in turn are united. Marina and Lysimachus are married and become rulers of Tyre. On the death of Simonides, Pericles and Thaisa rule in Pentapolis. Marina's purity has been preserved like that of the Lady in *Comus*, or, as Gower puts it, almost Miltonically, at the end,

Virtue preserved from fell destruction's blast,
Led on by heaven, and crown'd with joy at last.

Surely the old complicated story with its many scenes and places, its improbable lapses of time, and its often preposterous events, was never better told, more skilfully and interestingly concluded, or managed with greater skill. Shakespeare seems to have lavished on it the wealth of his theatrical knowledge, and it is a pity that his work has been so unrecognized.

One can see that the play was popular and why it was a new thing. Shakespeare staged the old romance by clever formal devices and gave to the whole an archaic quality and a quality of fairyland in order to render it plausible. These are the ways, he said, that things were done in the good old times. *Pericles* uses masque-like devices and establishes a remote romantic atmosphere later found in *Cymbeline*, *The Winter's Tale*, and *The Tempest* and in *Philaster* and other tragi-comedies by Beaumont and Fletcher. Again we see Shakespeare leading the fashion and molding the future of the drama of his age. As one turns from *Pericles* to *Cymbeline*, *The Winter's Tale*, and *The Tempest*, one sees that Shakespeare has discovered a new species of drama more ornate, more eventful and, above all, more romantic than had yet appeared on the Elizabethan stage. It is perhaps *The Winter's Tale* which best exemplifies the form, but there are, as before stated, parallels in plot, situation, character, and poetic atmosphere among all of them. There is the feature of the reunion of families, the elapse of long periods of time, and some of the wisdom and kindness of age. There is a heightening of the artistic level by the devices of distance in time and space, spectacle, supernaturalism, and poetic tone. As in opera, these qualities serve the cause of plausibility, which, according to Coleridge, is the basis of poetic faith.

2. Cymbeline.

Cymbeline appears last among the tragedies in the First Folio of 1623, and yet there are no grounds for thinking of it as other than a romantic comedy, a comedy, of course, in which the element of danger is more than usually great. It is often spoken of as a tragi-comedy, and in current dramatic classification it may be properly so called. Indeed, of all the later plays of Shakespeare, *Cymbeline* bears greatest resemblance to Jacobean tragi-comedy as written by Beaumont and Fletcher and others. It has remote setting, romantic atmosphere, and a tendency toward the sensational, all of which qualities characterize tragi-comedy. The theory that, when Beaumont and Fletcher captured the public ear with *Philaster*, Shakespeare modified his dramatic form to agree with the dramatic fashion was put forward by A. H. Thorndike in a widely known study called *The Influence of Beaumont and Fletcher in Shakespeare* (1901). His theory, never accepted by many important scholars, is now less confidently held than ever, although there can be no doubt as to the formal similarities to which he called attention.

It is obvious in *Twelfth Night*, *Measure for Measure*, and other plays that Shakespeare built up for himself a standard way of presenting plots and drawing characters. Wendell speaks of it as "recapitulatory" and says that in *Cymbeline* we have "a tissue of motives, situations, and characters which in the earlier work of Shakespeare proved theatrically effective." He is thinking, of course, of the complication in *Cymbeline* arising from a series of not unnatural mistakes and of the results of conflicting motives. Posthumus, the hero, is deceived by Iachimo as Othello is deceived by Iago. Cloten, a new edition of fool and braggart, is a self-deceived and evil creature whose pretenses to the hand of the heroine recall those of Roderigo and other dupes. Like many other heroines Imogen marches forth disguised as a man. Like Juliet she takes a sleeping potion. When she meets her brothers she is drawn to them by mysterious natural forces such as those that appear in *Pericles* and in other accounts of family re-unions. The Queen is a villainess of no special sort but with numerous analogues, being a wicked stepmother who carries out her villainies without much individual motivation. Imogen stands out like half a dozen of Shake-speare's women by her simplicity, wit, faithfulness, and virtue. And Cym-beline himself is not so much created as appointed king by Shakespeare. Deceived like other kings, he plays the tyrant, but his actions are ultimately those befitting a king. His speech and manner are always regal. There are relatively few new elements in *Cymbeline*, and yet every scene is significant and every character individualized. In most cases Shakespeare betters his earlier work, and to the whole bewildering story he gives an atmosphere of unique charm.

One can hardly define this charm except by recalling impressions gained at first acquaintance. In literary kind the play is like a fairy tale, and in general impression like an Indian summer. Certainly Charles and Mary Lamb had no easier task in recounting Shakespeare's plots. The story is as simple as a fairy tale all the way through.

Chambers would date *Cymbeline* in 1609-1610, which is a date satisfac-tory to most scholars. As to the question of its being earlier or later than Beaumont and Fletcher's *Philaster*, which cannot be shown to have been in existence prior to October 8, 1610, Chambers makes no commitment, but like Dowden rejects the theory that Shakespeare was inspired to write *Cymbeline* by the popularity of *Philaster*. Fleay, like many critics since his time, was dissatisfied with the double picture of Cloten, at one time a fool and braggart and at another a wise and patriotic prince speaking well and acting as counselor to the king. Fleay attempted to account for the incon-sistency on the supposition that Shakespeare had embodied the more favor-able view in material dramatized from Holinshed about 1606 and the less favorable view of Cloten as a villain and a ninny at a later time in the intrigue plot derived from Boccaccio. Chambers rejects the idea of a double date. "A brave prince," he says, "may none the less prove a boor in love." This may be true, but the inconsistency in Cloten's character is very great, and the problem remains unsolved. Shakespeare's late style appears in all parts of the play and offers no indication that the composition was at dif-ferent times.

Following the majority of critics, Chambers regards the vision in Act V, scene four as " a spectacular theatrical interpolation." Even Dowden would reject lines 30-92, although he would retain lines 97-126, and possibly lines 93-6, as Shakespeare's. Surely there is something to be said against this rejection, the cause of which is the belief that the vision contains matter beneath the standards of Shakespeare's poetic powers. It is proper enough to use such an argument, but the standards of poetical excellence ought to be, if possible, Elizabethan rather than modern and personal. No one would doubt that the speech uttered by Posthumus before he falls asleep (ll. 3-29) is in every way worthy of Shakespeare. It is rather fine, since it has style and mood, and has about it the impatient realism of Posthumus. One does not know a poet other than Shakespeare to whom it might be attributed. There would be no objection to the dumbshow, the idea of which is pathetic and gratifying. Posthumus has been alone in the world since he drew his first breath. His dead kin were brave, true people and therefore dear to the gods. Why might they not in a romantic play like this look down in consolation and solicitude on their last earthly representative? The vision itself begins with a speech in tumbling measure or doggerel by Sicilius Leonatus, father of Posthumus, a measure which continues to line 92. In spite of " 'Twas the night before Christmas" and many pleasing examples in "Mother Goose" we have lost our taste for doggerel verse, which, however, was not badly thought of in Shakespeare's time. He himself had written a good deal of it, and there is much of it scattered through the poetry of his time. We may believe that it was not painful to the ear as it has grown to be in our age, but was merely old-fashioned. Indeed, there is a certain romantic appropriateness in having these old ghosts speak in an old meter. When we make allowance for the jingle and look at the lines of the vision for ideas and imagery, they turn out not too bad to be assigned to Shakespeare. The epithet "thunder-master" in line 30, is good, and the couplet in which it occurs is strengthened by a parallel with

> As flies to wanton boys, are we to the gods,
> They kill us for their sport

in *King Lear*. And so through the passage the thought and wording are not great but are lively and contrast happily with the ponderous words spoken by Jupiter. One must remember that these are very pitiful ghosts and are timid about rebelling against Jove himself, who tells them in a reproachful way that they are to leave this matter and such matters to

him. It is his business to look after youthful warriors like Posthumus. He
sends them back to "rest upon your never-withering banks of flowers" and
tells (l. 90) these "poor shadows of Elysium,"

> Be not with mortal accidents opprest.

It must have been a theatrical event of importance at the Globe when
Jupiter came down "in thunder and lightning, sitting upon an eagle" and
throwing a thunderbolt. The ghosts are naturally much impressed and
observe (giving rise to more wonder in us),

> His royal bird
> Prunes the immortal wing and cloys his beak,
> As when his god is pleased. . . .
> The marble pavement closes, he is enter'd
> His radiant roof.

The wakening speech of Posthumus is also worthy, and the whole vision
seems to be consistent, skillful, and impressive.

Shakespeare drew together by means of the widely known story of the
wager a considerable body of material collected from several different
places in Holinshed. The chief source of the central episode in *Cymbeline*
is the ninth novel of the second day in the *Decameron* of Boccaccio. Many
critics including Chambers save themselves trouble by declaring that that
novel is Shakespeare's only source, but the matter is not so simple as that.
Boccaccio's novel is a clear account and must be the original source, but
there are features of the story as Shakespeare tells it not to be found in
Boccaccio. The late Professor Thrall brought to the attention of scholars
Frederick of Jennen, an English translation of the German *Historie von
vier Kaufmännern*. This English translation was printed by Vele in 1560.
It must have been popular, for it is one of the items in Captain Cox's
library described by Robert Laneham in his *Letter* about the entertainment
of the Queen at Kenilworth. *Frederick of Jennen* is not put forward as
an immediate source for *Cymbeline*, but is certainly one of the closest
analogues. A version still closer to Shakespeare is *Westward for Smelts* by
"Kitt of Kingston," said by Steevens to have been published in 1603. No
copy of such an edition is known to exist, and since the book was duly
entered in the Stationers' Register in 1620, and an edition appeared that
year, one is forced to conclude that there was no earlier publication and
that *Westward for Smelts* cannot have been known to Shakespeare.

We have to do with a very old story appearing in numerous versions, some of which antedate Boccaccio. Notably there are two French romances and a *miracle de Nôtre Dame*. *Westward for Smelts* is itself a derivative version which had been given a special historical setting during the Wars of the Roses, and it seems probable that it is independent of *Cymbeline*, which in a number of matters it, however, resembles as against Boccaccio. As to the French romances, although they are clearly versions of the story, it seems doubtful if Shakespeare could have known them, but the *miracle de Nôtre Dame* may have been far more accessible than we think. There were probably cycles of the miracles of Our Lady acted in England before the Reformation, and this plot may have been known in that form or preserved as a secular play in England or in France. We should thus have the familiar situation of a lost dramatic source. The dramatic form and a good deal of detail of the French miracle play are repeated in *Cymbeline*, as, for example, the open attempt to seduce the heroine by the slander of her beloved. Even if Shakespeare made use of an old play, it would have been like him to have consulted various available versions.

As to the cave life of Belarius and his foster-sons and the visit of Imogen, the story of Little Snowwhite is an obvious parallel, and other occurrences of this theme have been cited. The sleeping potion is, of course, a device of frequent employment. Finally, an anonymous play called *The Rare Triumphs of Love and Fortune* bears a sort of genetic resemblance to *Cymbeline*. It is an early play acted before the Queen at Christmas 1581 and in February 1582 and published in 1589. It has a first act devoted to conversations between Jupiter and other gods, also a banished courtier who lives and brings up his son in a cave. The son, Hermione, marries the king's daughter, Fidelia, against opposition, fights a duel with a sort of Cloten, and is banished. He summons Fidelia to join him at the cave, and there is an analogue to Pisanio. The play has also some distant resemblances to *The Winter's Tale* and *The Tempest*. *The Rare Triumphs of Love and Fortune* is extremely old-fashioned as compared with Shakespeare's latest plays, but it is made of the same romantic stuff.

These late plays of Shakespeare show a new impulse of genuine vigor. They do not suggest an aged and tired author moved by the contemplation of the world from the safe heights of old age and indifference. They are new and belong to a unique species in the field of drama, full of action, sentiment, and a convincing but not realistic sort of passion. Chambers makes an excellent point to the effect that these plays are consistent with each other and with art and life and present us with "a symbolical and idealized rendering of human life" unbroken by the realities which intruded themselves dangerously into earlier comedies, such as the Proteus episode in *The Two Gentlemen of Verona* and the unpleasant seriousness of *Measure for Measure*. In these late plays, particularly in *Cymbeline*, Shakespeare had undergone "a profound change of spiritual mood" in making his transition from tragedy to romance. It is perhaps unsafe to speculate on Shakespeare's mental state during this period, and it is perhaps sufficient to bear in mind that Shakespeare's art, both dramatic and poetic, had grown freer of conventional restrictions and that he, knowing better than ever the fundamental differences between tragedy and comedy, invented a new species to which his later manner was perfectly adapted. He is ready, however, in any scene and with reference to any character to repeat from new points of view the work of his earlier years.

The principal means by which the level of consistent romance, which may also be described as an avoidance of realism, is achieved is the careful preservation of simplicity. Shakespeare seems to have chosen deliberately to be old-fashioned. However complicated the sentences and however bold and intricate the figures of speech, the plot still proceeds with the utmost naïveté and sincerity. *Cymbeline* begins with the commonplace but still useful device of a dialogue between two gentlemen, the one well informed and the other in need of information, who bring out quickly all the facts necessary for the audience to understand the parting scene between Posthumus and Imogen, including the "dissembling courtesy" of the Queen who has permitted them to say farewell. A plot of this kind requires a token. Imogen gives Posthumus a ring that had been her mother's, and Posthumus puts a bracelet on Imogen's arm. We may believe that these are not ordinary lovers' gifts, but that they will play a part both in complication and denouement. Cymbeline enters quite full of conventional kingly wrath, which we know he has borrowed from the wicked Queen, and Imogen shows us the way by talking back to him, king as he is. The Queen reports indignantly a harmless duel between her beloved Cloten and the banished Posthumus. This introduces Imogen's first reference to her needle, an instrument she evidently knew how to use and does not forget. Knowing how a real fight between Cloten and Posthumus would have ended, she says (I, i, 167-9),

> I would they were in Afric both together;
> Myself by with a needle, that I might prick
> The goer-back.

The next scene presents the duel from the point of view of the foolish, vain, and cowardly Cloten. The Lords to whom he talks make fun of him to his face. The next scene, the third, acquaints us further with the ingenious and fascinating style of Imogen. In her way of speaking she not only ties the knot securely, but stays to arrange the loops (ll. 17-22):

> I would have broke mine eye-strings; crack'd them, but
> To look upon him, till the diminution
> ˙Of space had pointed him sharp as my needle,
> Nay, follow'd him, till he had melted from
> The smallness of a gnat to air, and then
> Have turn'd mine eye and wept.

The speech is brilliant, but the last line makes it Imogen's.

The scene then shifts to Rome, and Shakespeare presents us with the story of the wager. The episode is obnoxious to modern taste. Whether Shakespeare was in any way repelled by it one cannot tell—perhaps no more than was his age and audience, and less than we are. He carries it through with businesslike rapidity. This first act is full of things necessary to the story, and Shakespeare accordingly devotes the fifth scene to the Queen's attempt to obtain from the doctor, Cornelius, a poison which she means for the destruction of Posthumus' faithful servant, Pisanio, on whose superstitious veneration for drugs she relies. Cornelius reassures us by giving her a harmless sleeping potion; it would be unlike this play to have real poison in circulation. So rapidly does the play proceed that in the last scene of the first act we find Iachimo arrived from Rome ready to try his skill in the seduction of Imogen.

When he has seen her he does not think too much of his chances, but lies valiantly in order to win her over, principally by slandering Posthumus; but the sharp mind of Imogen, which might be called the mind of virtuous woman, sees through the baseness of his proposal. Her denunciation (ll. 141-6) is noteworthy as an example of intelligence as well as style:

> If thou wert honourable,
> Thou wouldst have told this tale for virtue, not
> For such an end thou seek'st,—as base as strange.

> Thou wrong'st a gentleman who is as far
> From thy report as thou from honour, and
> Solicit'st here a lady that disdains
> Thee and the devil alike.

Iachimo is a clever deceiver, Italian trained, and in some measure regains her favor by fulsome praises of her beloved Posthumus, so that she is willing to grant him what to us would be a strange request, namely, that he may for safety leave his chest in her bedchamber. Sleeping rooms were the safest places for valuables in those days, as the words "chamber" and "chamberlain" show. His leaving the chest there for safety is the most plausible of all the many devices recorded in sources and analogues.

The second act of *Cymbeline* is also very full of event. Cloten makes his nefarious suit to Imogen and has his folly anatomized by the Lords. He supplies us, however, with the famous song, "Hark, hark! the lark," which he explains, stupidly and mechanically,

> I am advised to give her music o' mornings; they say it will penetrate.

The song is indeed "a very excellent good-conceited thing; after a wonderful sweet air with admirable rich words to it." When he tries "with tongue too," we find that Imogen understands the art of quarreling, as most clever people do, and succeeds in getting under his thick skin so deeply that he begins his grotesque but bloody plotting. His speech (II, iii, 117-28) is a model of malicious and tactless stupidity:

> The contract you pretend with that base wretch,
> One bred of alms and foster'd with cold dishes,
> With scraps o' the court, it is no contract, none:
> And though it be allow'd in meaner parties—
> Yet who than he more mean?—to knit their souls,
> On whom there is no more dependency
> But brats and beggary, in self-figured knot;
> Yet you are curb'd from that enlargement by
> The consequence o' the crown, and must not soil
> The precious note of it with a base slave,
> A hilding for a livery, a squire's cloth,
> A pantler, not so eminent.

These words are vain and foolish, but they are not base in style, so that they may furnish an indication that the clownage of Cloten in certain prose scenes results from an ill-considered revision.

This speech brings upon him words as sharp as a needle, words expertly chosen to offend him by one who knows him well (ll. 130-41):

> Wert thou the son of Jupiter and no more
> But what thou art besides, thou wert too base
> To be his groom: thou wert dignified enough,
> Even to the point of envy, if 'twere made
> Comparative for your virtues, to be styled
> The under-hangman of his kingdom, and hated
> For being preferr'd so well. . . .
> He never can meet more mischance than come
> To be but named of thee. His meanest garment,
> That ever hath but clipp'd his body, is dearer
> In my respect than all the hairs above thee,
> Were they all made such men.

Cloten is proud of his dress, and Imogen's gibe is a masterpiece.

The second scene of this second act offers perhaps the most melodramatic development in Shakespeare, the villain's emergence from the trunk in the heroine's bedchamber. It does not make the scene less sensational to remember that Elizabethans wore no night-clothes. One can but observe how Shakespeare has avoided a too intense realism by putting some very beautiful poetry into the mouth of Iachimo (ll. 11-49):

> The crickets sing, and man's o'er-labour'd sense
> Repairs itself by rest. Our Tarquin thus
> Did softly press the rushes, ere he waken'd
> The chastity he wounded. . . .
>   the flame o' the taper
> Bows toward her, and would under-peep her lids,
> To see the enclosed lights, now canopied
> Under these windows, white and azure laced
> With blue of heaven's own tinct. . . .

The play moves on with the same rapidity, and in the fourth scene we see Iachimo collecting the wager he has won from Posthumus by fraud, Posthumus driven frantic by seeing evidences of his own betrayal. Surely here, if anywhere in the play, we are in danger of being plunged into serious and sober realism. Iachimo deserves punishment, and Posthumus is in a desperate mood. Moreover, some sort of basis must be contrived for the forgiveness of Iachimo, and the fury of Posthumus must be so mixed with heroic action that no shock of tragedy may be left in the play. Mean-

time Iachimo lives on for a season in our contempt, and we leave Posthumus railing at women after the fashion of Shakespeare's tragic heroes
(II, v, 19-35):

> Could I find out
> The woman's part in me! For there's no motion
> That tends to vice in man but I affirm
> It is the woman's part. . . .

The first move of Posthumus is to seek the death of his innocent wife.
He has become a "justicer" like Othello.

The third act opens with historical matters. The placid Cymbeline, in
spite of his having been educated in the Roman court and knighted by
Caesar, is persuaded by the Queen and Cloten to deny to Rome the tribute
agreed to by Cassibelan. In this scene Cloten speaks patriotically and sen-
sibly. His counsel is evil, to be sure, but his words are not the words of a
fool.

Event after event, action after action, have so crowded in that Shakespeare has not had time to introduce a necessary group of characters
engaged in an important subsidiary plot. When he does introduce them,
one might almost say that a new play begins in the middle of this drama
just as in *Pericles* and *The Winter's Tale*. It is an old story of stolen children, and the scene is in the mountainous country of Wales. Belarius with
Guiderius and Arviragus, stolen sons of Cymbeline, are before their cave.
The relation between the old man and his foster sons is very charming,
principally because of an idea from the borders of fairyland that royal
blood will manifest itself in princely behavior even when its possession is
unknown. The youths are impatient for exercise in the court and the battle-
field. Belarius understands how to interpret their spirits (III, iii, 79-86):

> How hard it is to hide the sparks of nature! . . .
> though train'd up thus meanly
> I' the cave wherein they bow, their thoughts do hit
> The roofs of palaces, and nature prompts them
> In simple and low things to prince it much
> Beyond the trick of others.

The fourth scene of the third act is exciting, and might be considered
as a sort of climax to the play if one felt safe in fixing on a turning point
in so mixed a narrative. The honest Pisanio on his way to Milford Haven

with Imogen reveals to her the fact that Posthumus seeks her life. Shake-speare knew that the good are not prone to do or to believe evil, and Pisanio's refusal to commit the crime his master has ordered him to commit is characteristic of him and introduces a situation familiar in romance. Of the same sort is Imogen's faithfulness to Posthumus in spite of his unkindness (ll. 42-98):

> False to his bed! What is it to be false?
> To lie in watch there and to think on him?
> To weep 'twixt clock and clock? if sleep charge nature,
> To break it with a fearful dream of him,
> And cry myself awake? . . .

In the last group of lines one sees in Imogen a strain of a youthful Hermione. Pisanio advises her to seek the Roman camp and for safety to disguise herself in male attire. She will do it (ll. 154-6, 164-6):

> O, for such means!
> Though peril to my modesty, not death on't,
> I would adventure. . . .
>   Nay, be brief:
> I see into thy end, and am almost
> A man already.

Before he leaves her, Pisanio, simply believing that all medicine is good, puts the Queen's box in Imogen's hands.

In the next scene the more rational Cloten emerges into, if not a first-rate, yet a second-rate bullying villain. Surely Cloten is either one of the most complex of characters or is the result of a series of unfortunate mixtures. He will dress himself in the apparel of Posthumus and ravish Imogen.

> She hath despised me rejoicingly, and I'll be merry in my revenge,

he says (l. 150).

The style of Imogen and the unique turn of her mind never shine out more clearly than in the words with which she opens the sixth scene. If the members of her sex ever realize the truth of her statement, it will work a social and domestic revolution:

> I see a man's life is a tedious one.

She is weary and lost, but she is in fairyland, the chief feature of which is coincidence. She actually stands before the cave of her unknown brothers.

Shakespeare does not miss the opportunity for slightly mystical suggestions: Guiderius and Arviragus receive her as a brother, and Imogen
remembers the lost sons of her father.

Cloten arrives at the cave with all his impudence upon him and insists
on fighting with Guiderius, who cuts off his head. As an act of slaughter
this does not matter. To be sure, as Belarius realizes, it is serious to cut
off the head of the Queen's son, but nobody cares. Cloten is disposed of in
the true spirit of the nursery tale. No child is ever distressed at the fact
that the Wolf devours the Grandmother in the tale of Red Ridinghood.
The heroine herself is all that matters. Belarius simply recognizes the deed
of Guiderius as a princely act.

Imogen seems to die from swallowing the sleeping potion, and the
lamentation over her fancied death is of worldwide and perennial significance. Says Arviragus (IV, ii, 197-8),

> The bird is dead
> That we have made so much on.

The brothers repeat the lovely lyric, "Fear no more the heat o' the sun."
The poet Collins, a great lover of Shakespeare, has left us a song for
Guiderius and Arviragus immortal in its beauty:

> To fair Fidele's grassy tomb,
>   Soft maids and village hinds shall bring
> Each opening sweet of earliest bloom,
>   And rifle all the breathing spring.

With rapid action the dramatist shows us Imogen waking to find the head-
less body of Cloten and to mistake it for that of Posthumus, also to be
carried away at once as page to the Roman Lucius.

Further on in the play we have to do with a battle, used with maximum
dramatic skill by Shakespeare in setting his stage and altering his situations,
and with a dénouement than which there is no more triumphant success
in all of Shakespeare. As to the battle, of course the British have to win,
but at the same time the rights of the Roman must be preserved. By means
of it two characters must be restored to heroic standing, namely, Posthumus
and Belarius, and one character, Iachimo, must be given a sort of absolution
on the ground of confession and repentance. The case of Posthumus is
complicated by the circumstance that he is a member of the Roman army.
He cannot fight against his own country and can in his current mood hardly

join the British forces openly. He chooses to fight unknown, renders magnificent service, and then returns and figures as a captive Roman after the battle. He has repented of having caused, as he thinks, the murder of Imogen; he is desperate and desires of life nothing but death. It is the dissipation of his mood of tragic despair which constitutes the chief objective of the dramatist.

As for Belarius, accompanied by his foster sons, the salvation is comparatively easy and extremely interesting as an example of Shakespeare's resourcefulness. He found in Holinshed's *History of Scotland* an account of how a Scottish husbandman named Haie, with two of his sons, had turned the tide of a battle against the Danes by defending a sunken lane and by rallying his own party to his assistance. This event Shakespeare adopted with some particularity for the action of Belarius, Guiderius, and Arviragus in the fictitious battle of the Romans against the British. It is Posthumus who gives the account of the deeds of the heroic three (V, iii, 14 ff.), and the comment of a Lord is a vignette of unforgettable precision and suggestiveness (l. 52):

A narrow lane, an old man, and two boys.

There are some twenty-three points or phases of revelation in the great fifth scene of the fifth act. The scene, a model of dramatic suspense, is managed firmly and naturally, each feature of the whole held back until the time when it will properly fill up its part in the canvas Shakespeare is painting. Excepting the oration of Mark Antony in *Julius Caesar* one would not know where to find such perfect management. To repeat the revelations would be to retell the story of the play of *Cymbeline*. One episode has, however, attracted the notice of critics and has seemed to them indicative of Shakespeare's imitation of Beaumont and Fletcher's *Philaster* and of his indulgence in the melodrama of their tragi-comedy. One need not believe this, but the matter has an interest of its own. It is the crucial moment when Posthumus learns that Imogen still lives, and it is most sensationally presented. Iachimo has made his confession, and Posthumus, who has heard it, comes forward in a mood of melancholic fury. He sees himself as one deceived, as the murderer of innocence, as one who "like to the Egyptian thief at point of death" has killed what he loved. His distress is terrific (ll. 222-7):

> Spit, and throw stones, cast mire upon me, set
> The dogs o' the street to bay me: every villain
> Be call'd Posthumus Leonatus; and
> Be villainy less than 'twas! O Imogen!
> My queen, my life, my wife! O Imogen!
> Imogen, Imogen!

Imogen, no impulsive person, can stand no more and rushes to the succor of her husband, whom she sees undergoing the torments of the damned. She cries

> Peace, my lord; hear, hear—

The bitter Posthumus meets her with

> Shall's have a play of this? Thou scornful page,
> There lie thy part.

And he strikes her down. The action, symbolical perhaps, causes Pisanio to reveal the fact that Imogen herself has suffered in disguise a blow from the hand of Posthumus. It is doubtful if this is pure sensationalism. Beaumont and Fletcher hang on to a situation, alter it, squeeze it until every bit of feeling and excitement has been extracted. It may come to the same thing, but here Shakespeare is merely ingenious, perhaps a bit too ingenious. The scene is full of many fine touches of detail, and in its completeness, in its harmony, in its stylistic beauty serves to finish up as one whole this manifold complexity. *Cymbeline* is great in style, interest, atmosphere.

3. *The Winter's Tale.*

Cymbeline and *The Winter's Tale* are quite alike in poetic style and not widely dissimilar in dramatic effect. One could not tell from tabulations of prose and rhyme, syllabic and pause variation, which is the later of the two, and the romance of the two plays is distinguished mainly by mood. *Cymbeline* is darker, more northern, vaguer, and more mediaeval; *The Winter's Tale* sunnier, more adventurous, more carefully chiseled, and more Greek. There is nothing in *Cymbeline* so light-hearted as the story of Florizel and Perdita, nothing so threatening as the mad and jealous tyranny of Leontes, nothing so moving as the trial of Hermione. Both stories are complicated and both woven together into single narratives; but the plot of *Cymbeline*, more closely knit, is of the two the more difficult to follow. The very splitting of *The Winter's Tale* into two parts makes it easier to follow and, since events and motives are simple, makes its characters stand out more clearly. It is a brighter, more emphatically accentuated drama than is *Cymbeline* in spite of Shakespeare's masterly drawing together of threads in that play. *The Winter's Tale* seems to confirm this difference by its better stage history.

On the stage *The Winter's Tale* is a very charming comedy, not without popularity in our own day. Those who saw the performance of the Stratford Players in the late thirties will recall how lively the play is, how much there is going on before one on the stage. This abundance of life and action would not of itself account for the popularity of the play were it not accompanied by very great clarity and very definite motivation. Again one might say that the poetic beauty of *The Winter's Tale* is comprehensible, great and tangible, not subtle. Perhaps these qualities have combined to give the play a respectable career on the modern stage. No doubt its length still works against it, since the existence of two clearly separable plots increases the difficulty of cutting it down for the modern stage. Until the nineteenth century *The Winter's Tale* was usually acted in some adapted form. The play was presented on May 15, 1611, and in November of the same year and was played before King James I in 1612-13; later at court in 1624 and in 1634. The performance of May 15, 1611 rests on Forman's *Book of Plaies*, about whose authenticity there is in these days considerable doubt, a doubt as yet not fully justified. In the case of *The Winter's Tale*, it makes very little difference since there was a court performance on the 5th of November of the same year, and one may fairly judge that it was one of the latest and most popular of Shakespeare's plays. Its loose structure, indecorous use of kings and clowns, mixture of the comic with the serious, and clear violation of the three unities made it no favorite during the period of the Restoration. It was, however, revived after nearly one hundred years at Goodman's Fields in January 1741, and was repeated at Covent Garden. In 1751, Morgan made a version called *Florizel and Perdita, or the Sheep-Shearing*; but this version was superseded by that of Garrick in 1756, when it was called *A Comedy Altered from Shakespeare*: *The Winter's Tale or Florizel and Perdita*. This kept the stage until near the end of the eighteenth century. The comedy in a form rather more like Shakespeare was played occasionally during the nineteenth century. At Drury Lane in 1802, John

Philip Kemble played Leontes and his sister, Sarah Siddons, made what was considered a magnificent presentation of Hermione in the statue scene. That devoted Shakespearean actor and producer Samuel Phelps put on *The Winter's Tale* at Sadler's Wells in 1845-1846, and in 1856 came the most famous of all performances. Charles Kean put on *The Winter's Tale* at the Princess' Theater with the fullest possible attempt to present it as a Greek play—Greek costumes, Pyrrhic dances, and all possible archeological absurdities. The producers were right in respect to the fact that the play is Greek in setting, but it is not Greek of the classical period. The background of *The Winter's Tale* is ultimately Greek life during the period of the Roman empire, when the Greeks were dispersed in the countries round about the shores of the Mediterranean and were carrying on the world's business for the rather indolent Romans—in other words the same background as that of the Greek novel. In this performance Kean played Leontes, and Ellen Terry, then a child, played Mamillius. In 1906, she was to make a great success with the part of Hermione to the Leontes of Beerbohm Tree. Perhaps the greatest Leontes was that of Forbes-Robertson, who played in a sensational performance of *The Winter's Tale* in 1887, in which the famous Mary Anderson played the parts of both Hermione and Perdita, being adequate both to the matronly beauty and dignity of the one and the girlish loveliness of the other. Many persons saw *The Winter's Tale* for the first time in the Elizabethan performances of Ben Greet about 1910. In those performances Edith Wynne Matthison played the part of Hermione in moving fashion. Besides these there have been many revivals in more recent years, such as that of the Stratford-upon-Avon players and a great performance under the direction of Granville-Barker at the Savoy Theatre in 1912.

One may therefore conclude that *The Winter's Tale* is successful on the stage, and this is what its quality would lead one to expect. It has suspense throughout; its events follow in causal sequence. It is not a mere succession of striking single scenes. Its situations are of the greatest dramatic power; that is, the spectator anticipates and feels their importance. One feature of the plot is unique in Shakespeare: Hermione does not die, as does her prototype, Bellaria, in Greene's *Pandosto*, but is kept concealed, supposedly dead, for sixteen years and finally presented to us as the living statue in the last act as a complete surprise. Nowhere else does Shakespeare mystify his audience. There is no reason why he should not have done so, but, since he does it nowhere else, it may be said to be unlike him to do it. He habitually takes his audience into his confidence. He is the greatest master of dramatic irony, and his spectators always act and feel like God's spies. Of course the motive for the concealment here is obvious, although certain carping critics have censured Hermione for leaving her husband unrelieved in his repentant suffering during all those years. The command of the oracle cannot be fulfilled in any other way except his living without an heir until his lost daughter is found. The puzzling thing is the concealment from the audience.

Since it is puzzling, one has a right to examine *The Winter's Tale* critically to see if the Pygmalion plot is possibly an afterthought. One sees Shakespeare's problem, which is like that he faced in *Measure for Measure*. He must turn a tragic story into a comedy. In the source, Greene's *Pandosto*, Hermione (Bellaria) dies, and Leontes (Pandosto) in seeking another wife finds his own daughter. No word can be found in the play except at the time of the surprise scene itself which even hints at any other situation than that of the source. Shakespeare, it seems, in bringing his play to a conclusion may have hit upon the statue device and made use of it after his play was practically complete. There may be nothing in this idea, but there is one structural indication which seems to give some plausibility to it. In the second scene of the fifth act there is a conversation between certain gentlemen and later with the Shepherd and the Clown in which rather important matters in the plot are given in prose narrative and rather huddled together. There are moreover certain inconsistencies in the plot in this part of the play. According to Shakespeare's usual method there is no particular reason why the audience should not have been led on to anticipate some quite extraordinary dénouement.

The plot of *The Winter's Tale* falls into two separate parts. In its most general aspect it represents "The Triumph of Time," which is the secondary title of Greene's novel *Pandosto* (1588); and, if we may believe the title-page, it was Greene himself who saw "that although by meanes of sinister fortune, Truth may be concealed, yet by Time in spight of fortune it is most manifestly revealed." The adjustments wrought by time are exemplified in a consummate example of the familiar theme of the separation and reunion of the members of a family. What appears to be the complete dispersal and destruction of a family occupies the first three acts and is tragic, even sinister, in its quality. The last two acts treat the theme of the Prince and the Pauper Maid, the love affair between Prince Florizel and the shepherdess Perdita, with a brilliant and unexpected dramatic device by which the first disaster is mainly healed and made happy. Every feature of the play is more or less commonplace Renaissance fiction, and yet no play is seemingly fresher and more plausible. Of course, as in *Cymbeline*, the plausibility is increased by elements of old times and distant lands. Although the first three acts are tragic in tone and consequence and move with the organic rapidity of tragic disaster, the last two are as perfect comedy as *As You Like It* itself. Young love is depicted in as fresh a way as if Shakespeare himself were young. Where is there a lover, except Romeo, whose words are more perfect than those of Florizel (IV, iv, 135-46):

> What you do
> Still betters what is done. When you speak, sweet,
> I'ld have you do it ever: when you sing,
> I'ld have you buy and sell so, so give alms,
> Pray so; and, for the ordering your affairs,
> To sing them too: when you do dance, I wish you
> A wave o' the sea, that you might ever do
> Nothing but that; move still, still so,
> And own no other function: each your doing,
> So singular in each particular,
> Crowns what you are doing in the present deed,
> That all your acts are queens.

In spite of the great gap of time which elapses between the third and fourth acts, the play is a single tale and, in its way, a masterpiece of plot-making. Act I begins with the unprovoked and unmotivated jealousy of Leontes directed against his faithful wife, Hermione, and his friend and guest, Polixenes, King of Sicily. The jealousy of Leontes compares but poorly with that of Othello. After all, Iago was a master of persuasion and does build up a specious but effective case against Cassio and Desdemona. Leontes simply tumbles into jealousy like one possessed. The case in Shakespeare is even worse than that in his source. Greene in *Pandosto* provides a somewhat extensive background of innocent intimacy between Bellaria and her husband's friend and guest which might serve as a means for the kindling of jealousy. For this background of longer experience Shakespeare substitutes a device. Leontes tries to persuade Polixenes to prolong his visit, fails to do so, and demands of Hermione that she add her voice, and she succeeds. This is less plausible than Greene's treatment, and yet Greene's idea that jealousy is "a hellish passion, proof against sensible persuasions and wholesome counsels" is precisely the same as Shakespeare's. About the time that Shakespeare wrote *The Winter's Tale* many books were being issued which taught that reason was dethroned by jealousy and other feral passions and that "unbridled folly was suffused with fury." Greene had learned this in the university, for it was an old theory of the passions, rooted in Galen. The difference in the treatment of the passion of jealousy in *Othello* and *The Winter's Tale* amounts to this: Shakespeare simply accepted his source in both cases. In the one he laid the blame for the madness of his hero upon a persuasive villain, and in the other he followed without question the stoical doctrine of the passions as presented by Greene. The psychology of the passions known to Shakespeare and his age provided not only for obsession but for the obtrusion of all the evil passions. Leontes presents an unpleasant spectacle. He rejects all reasonable persuasion and contemplates the poisoning of Polixenes and the judicial murder of Hermione. He orders Camillo to murder Polixenes, but Camillo, after trying in vain to correct his master's thinking, warns Polixenes, joins him as servant, and escapes with him to Bohemia. It is easy to say that Leontes was made to order to suit this absurd psychology, but the matter is not so easy as that. Every day the press tells us of just such madness, violence, and crime, and just such recoil of reason before it.

After the flight of Polixenes and Camillo, Leontes rages more than ever and turns to wreak his anger on his innocent wife. Shakespeare makes no attempt at this time to save his hero from this manifest disgrace. Probably he thought of Leontes as in the toils of an irresistible force. Later he attempts to set him right with the audience by a sudden and complete return to sanity, by a long and sincere repentance, and by faithfulness to the memory of the wife he thinks he has killed by his tyranny. Hermione's patience in adversity is magnificent, and, except only that of Queen Katharine in *Henry VIII*, there is no such noble behavior anywhere to be found as that of Hermione at her trial. The following passage shows her dignified patience (II, i, 105-22), and a later one (III, ii, 23-125) her intellectual ability and self-command:

> There's some ill planet reigns:
> I must be patient till the heavens look
> With an aspect more favourable. Good my lords,
> I am not prone to weeping, as our sex
> Commonly are; the want of which vain dew
> Perchance shall dry your pities: but I have
> That honourable grief lodged here which burns
> Worse than tears drown: beseech you all, my lords,
> With thoughts so qualified as your charities
> Shall best instruct you, measure me; and so
> The king's will be perform'd! . . .
>   Beseech your highness,
> My women may be with me; for you see
> My plight requires it. Do not weep, good fools;
> There is no cause: when you shall know your mistress
> Has deserved prison, then abound in tears
> As I come out: this action I now go on
> Is for my better grace.

At her trial Hermione's defense is notable, a great oration like those of King Henry V and of Mark Antony. Note the exordium, the clear and logical denial, and the moving peroration:

> Since what I am to say must be but that
> Which contradicts my accusation and
> The testimony on my part no other
> But what comes from myself, it shall scarce boot me
> To say 'not guilty': mine integrity
> Being counted falsehood, shall, as I express it,
> Be so received. . . .
>   For Polixenes,
> With whom I am accused, I do confess
> I loved him as in honour he required,
> With such a kind of love as might become
> A lady like me, with a love even such,
> So and no other, as yourself commanded:
> Which not to have done I think had been in me
> Both disobedience and ingratitude
> To you and toward your friend, whose love had spoke,
> Even since it could speak, from an infant, freely
> That it was yours. Now, for conspiracy,
> I know not how it tastes; though it be dish'd
> For me to try how: all I know of it

Is that Camillo was an honest man;
And why he left your court, the gods themselves,
Wotting no more than I, are ignorant. . . .
　　　　　　　　　　Therefore proceed.
But yet hear this; mistake me not; no life,
I prize it not a straw, but for mine honour,
Which I would free, if I shall be condemn'd
Upon surmises, all proofs sleeping else
But what your jealousies awake, I tell you
'Tis rigour and not law. Your honours all,
I do˙refer me to the oracle:
Apollo be my judge!

Leontes sends to consult the oracle at Delphi. Just why he does so is not very clear, since to all intents and purposes he is still a lunatic. He rejects the Emilia-like remonstrances of Paulina, disowns his own child, and compels Antigonus, the husband of Paulina, to take it to some desert place and abandon it.

The third act is one of the most sensational in Shakespeare. Not only does it present the trial scene of Hermione with her thrice eloquent words, but the messengers sent to Delphi return with the answer of the oracle. The report goes squarely against Leontes:

Hermione is chaste; Polixenes blameless; Camillo a true subject; Leontes a jealous tyrant; his innocent babe truly begotten; and the king shall live without an heir, if that which is lost be not found.

But even this does not break the obstinacy of Leontes, who defies the god. He orders the trial to proceed, but news is brought that his only son, Shakespeare's most charming child, the little prince Mamillius, is dead of grief. There is no improbability in this; children do die of broken hearts. Hermione falls in a deathlike swoon and is borne off the stage. Then at last, feeling the anger of the god, this obdurate man repents. He goes into mourning, a mourning which is to last for sixteen years. Remember too that he is provided with the sharp-tongued Paulina to keep him in mind of his sins.

The third act contains yet another sensational event, the most unexpected thing except one in the whole play: a courtier is eaten by a bear. There was a white bear in *Mucedorus* and two bears in Jonson's masque of *Oberon*. For lack of any other reason one may imagine that Shakespeare makes use of a convenient piece of theatrical property. Antigonus with the infant girl in his charge lands on the seacoast of Bohemia. Bohemia had no seacoast and has not now, but both Greene and Shakespeare evidently thought that it did. Ben Jonson in his *Conversations with Drummond* remembered this error against Shakespeare. But Shakespeare has done worse than this. He has reversed Sicily and Bohemia as they appeared in his source, and this in spite of the fact that Sicily was renowned as a pastoral land. There are several other slips of this kind, and one imagines that, although Shakespeare knew his source well, some of the detail has grown dim in his mind, as if he had no copy of *Pandosto* before him when he wrote. Antigonus is instructed by Hermione in a vision (which seems to indicate that Shakespeare thought of Hermione as dead) to abandon the child in a remote region of Bohemia and to name it Perdita. Out of the freakish anger of the god, Antigonus, because he has had a share in this cruel business, shall never again behold his wife Paulina. Then comes the stage direction, *Exit, pursued by a bear*. Later the Clown gives unpleasant details. As in all well regulated tales of exposed infants, Antigonus has left means of identification, including a gold chain. He leaves also gold, which will play its part in securing the entertainment of the waif. Perdita is found by the Old Shepherd and his son the Clown and carried away to be reared as "the queen of curds and cream." One gets the impression that all this is the business of the god, and that in his unswerving purpose it has been decided that there shall be no witnesses. Accordingly the ship that brought Antigonus to this lonely place is wrecked in the storm and all on board are lost.

Time as chorus speaks eloquently in order to bridge the gap of sixteen years, for eloquence is the material out of which Shakespeare makes this and many other bridges over improbability.

The first news we then hear is that the young prince Florizel, son to Polixenes, is spending much of his time at the cottage of a prosperous shepherd who has a marvelously beautiful daughter. Even the secret courtships of young princes are news of state, and the action of the young prince has been made known to his father. Polixenes goes to a shepherd's fair to investigate. He takes with him Camillo, who has just voiced a deep desire to return to his own land and see his former master, Leontes, now repentant and the model of sweetness and light. In order that these two old gentlemen may succeed in their espionage they assume disguises.

They see Perdita and approve her charms, but refuse her as the prince's bride. Kings are like that, especially in fairy tales. Florizel, enjoying his rôle as fairy prince, makes some condescending speeches out of Greene to the effect that he is like Jupiter who (IV, iv, 27-31)

> Became a bull, and bellow'd; the green Neptune
> A ram, and bleated; and the fire-robed god,
> Golden Apollo, a poor humble swain,
> As I seem now.

Perdita as mistress of the feast is giving satisfaction to everybody but her foster father, the Old Shepherd, who remembers a better hand (ll. 55-64):

> Fie, daughter! when my old wife lived, upon
> This day she was both pantler, butler, cook,
> Both dame and servant; welcomed all, served all;
> Would sing her song and dance her turn; now here,
> At upper end o' the table, now i' the middle;
> On his shoulder, and his; her face o' fire
> With labour and the thing she took to quench it.
> She would to each one sip. You are retired,
> As if you were a feasted one and not
> The hostess of the meeting: pray you, bid
> These unknown friends to's welcome.

Perdita, like Marina and poor Ophelia, deals in flowers and bids the strangers welcome in pretty floral terms (ll. 116-27):

> O Proserpina,
> For the flowers now, that frighted thou let'st fall
> From Dis's waggon! daffodils,
> That come before the swallow dares, and take
> The winds of March with beauty. . . .

The "sweet friend" gives offense, and Polixenes in a great roar of parental sternness lays down the law to Florizel and to Perdita (ll. 444-51):

> And you, enchantment,—
> Worthy enough a herdsman; yea, him too,
> That makes himself, but for our honour therein,
> Unworthy thee,—if ever henceforth thou
> These rural latches to his entrance open,
> Or hoop his body more with thy embraces,
> I will devise a death as cruel for thee
> As thou art tender to't.

Perhaps her reply is to be regarded as royal spirit, but it is notable just as courage (ll. 451-60):

> Even here undone!
> I was not much afeard; for once or twice
> I was about to speak and tell him plainly,
> The selfsame sun that shines upon his court
> Hides not his visage from our cottage but
> Looks on alike.

The famous rogue Autolycus is made to serve a turn in the elopement of Florizel and Perdita somewhat like that of Capnio in the elopement of Dorastus and Fawnia in *Pandosto*, but it is Camillo's defection from his master and his desire to return to Sicily which renders the episode plausible. In general, up to the time of the assembly of characters in Sicily, Shakespeare follows Greene with great fidelity. After that the stories are very different. *Pandosto* seems to be a satisfactory source. The only rival is Francis Sabie's *The Fisherman's Tale*, which tells Greene's story as a sort of romance of chivalry with strongly pastoral content. It is a poem very mythological, very long-winded, but not bad. Sabie inverts the two parts and presents the first as an explanation and solution for the second. There seem to be no grounds for thinking that Shakespeare knew it.

But it is in plot that Shakespeare chiefly follows *Pandosto*. Greene does his characters and their motives well, and he means to be pastoral; but, in point of fact, it is in the pastoral parts that he resorts most to euphuism and formality. One cannot account for the pastoralism of *The Winter's Tale* as an imitation of Greene. The matter is more fundamental. There were two sorts of Greek romance, the one full of adventure, passion, and danger; the other gentle and pastoral. The Greek romance of the second sort had appeared in the Renaissance in *Diana Enamorada* of Montemayor, Sidney's *Arcadia*, and others; and Greene was influenced by Sidney and probably Montemayor, but also knew the Greek romances themselves. *Theagenes and Chariclea* by Heliodorus, a serious romance of action and passion, and *Daphnis and Chloe* by Longus, perhaps the most perfect of all pastoral romances, both appeared in English translation in 1587; and *Pandosto*, like *Arcadia*, seeks to combine the two forms. The first part is, roughly speaking, in the vein of *Theagenes and Chariclea*, and the second part in that of *Daphnis and Chloe*. We have thus the threatening tone in the story of the madness and tyranny of

Leontes and the most perfect piece of gentle and beautiful pastoralism in the story of the young lovers. Shakespeare's pastoral poetry is his own, fresh and natural. There is perhaps in the age no pastoral literature so beautiful as the story of Perdita and Florizel unless it is to be found in the ninth, tenth, and eleventh cantos of the sixth book of the *Faerie Queene*. Greene taints his work with euphuism, and the love-making is stiff, conventional wooing. Fawnia speaks well of the shepherd's life, but too philosophically and mythologically, although, as is usual in Greene's treatment of women, she is a living figure.

Florizel elopes with Perdita in rather expert fashion, and the whole group either pursue or accompany them. When they arrive in Sicily, Shakespeare at least confronts a problem. How is he to save the gracious Hermione, how reward the long penance of Leontes? He must rescue the tale from ultimate sadness, so that it may indeed be "a winter's tale," by saving the life of Hermione. One would wish that he had saved Mamillius, but that lovely child was forgotten or remained, like other lost children, a sad memorial to the errors of his elders (II, i, 21-32).

It is ordinarily said that Shakespeare resorted to the story of Pygmalion, that sculptor king of Cyprus whom Ovid tells about in the *Metamorphoses*, who fell in love with a beautiful statue of a woman he had just made and who prevailed on Aphrodite to make it come alive. No story was more familiar. Marston had written it unpleasantly in *The Metamorphoses of Pygmalion's Image* (1598), and, if it were merely a matter of Shakespeare's having adopted the Ovidian device of a statue come to life, there would be no problem. Unsatisfactory parallels to Shakespeare's version have been cited in the *History of the Tryall of Chevalrie*, an anonymous play published in 1605, and very pertinently in Lope de Vega's *Mármor de Felisardo* and in Lyly's *The Woman in the Moon*; but, as Professor H. C. Lancaster points out, these uses of the original Pygmalion story are not really parallel to the story of Hermione. In that no lifeless stone is metamorphosed into a living woman; Shakespeare's is the tale of a human creature who pretends to be a statue. There are no such cases known in English literature, but Lancaster finds a considerable group of more or less close resemblances in French. They are all later than Shakespeare, but may go back to versions in his time or before.

The statue scene is extremely effective on the stage both to those who know the secret and, we may believe, to those who are still able to be surprised. The actress stands motionless before the audience for a long time while other characters converse. Attention is not too much directed to her, but is sufficient to make the audience more and more aware of impending action. In other words, the scene has a kind of suspense like that of French classical tragedy. Hermione speaks but once, in a speech of great quietude (V, iii, 121-8), like one who has re-entered the world from the shades of death:

> You gods, look down
> And from your sacred vials pour your graces
> Upon my daughter's head!

There is an inescapable parallel on the deepest level between the story of Hermione and the *Alcestis* of Euripides, although there is perhaps not the remotest bond of knowledge connecting them. Admetus receives his life at the expense of his wife, Alcestis, and, like Leontes, sickens of his bargain and repents. Through the favor of the gods both men have their wives restored to them. Both men are allowed to speak, while their wives speak few words or none, and the voices of both men are thin.

About *The Winter's Tale* a good deal remains conjectural, but there is nothing for which probability of greater or less strength may not be stated. It would seem that the copy of *The Winter's Tale* used by the printer of the play in the First Folio of 1623, was prepared by a copyist, probably Ralph Crane, who gave it because of his scribal habits the peculiar features which J. Dover Wilson believes arose from the recomposition of the play by the assembling of players' parts. In date *The Winter's Tale* probably stands between *Cymbeline* and *The Tempest*. No kind of metrical test stands in the way of such a position, and in the handling of the time motive and some other matters *The Tempest* seems the more perfect and mature. The device of the statue was introduced into Greene's story in order to mitigate the tragedy. It may have been introduced into the play during the process of composition, since its effect is that of an afterthought. Here more than anywhere else in his dramas Shakespeare keeps his audience in the dark. The statue episode does away with the tragic event of *Pandosto*, and one must remember also that it does away with all but a trace of the repulsive story of Pandosto's seeking Fawnia for his wife. It is possible, hardly more, that Shakespeare contemplated dramatizing the return of Perdita to her father's court, meant for Autolycus to have some share in it, and later changed his mind in favor of a summary presentation of these events in prose.

As to Autolycus himself, he seems to be a unique creation. His catalogues of goods have been paralleled in *Dives Pragmaticus* by Thomas Newberry (1563), a tract in verse made up of a long and breathless list of wares. Such lists no doubt were commonplace, indeed are found suggested in various comedies. The charm of Autolycus is, after all, not so much in the cleverness of his roguery as in its lack of malice and in its congeniality with poetry. He soliloquizes (IV, iii, 23-31):

> My traffic is sheets; when the kite builds, look to lesser linen. My father named me Autolycus; who being, as I am, litter'd under Mercury, was likewise a snapper-up of unconsidered trifles. With die and drab I purchas'd this caparison, and my revenue is the silly cheat. Gallows and knock are too powerful on the highway: beating and hanging are terrors to me: for the life to come, I sleep out the thought of it.

He carries out on the Clown a conny-catcher's trick which Shakespeare may have learned from Greene, who describes it in the *Second Part of Conny-Catching* (1592). He then leaves the stage with a snatch of a song of the open road which approaches perfection:

> Jog on, jog on, the foot-path way,
>   And merrily hent the stile-a;
> A merry heart goes all the day,
>   Your sad tires in a mile-a.

This scene of Autolycus is, in vaudeville parlance, a perfect act.

Finally, *The Winter's Tale* remains Hermione's play. She and her story make it more deeply serious than is *Cymbeline*, for she has a quality of the deepest tragic suggestiveness, which is never removed. She and Queen Katharine in *Henry VIII* are among Shakespeare's great tragic heroines, and it is merely incidental that Hermione wins and the Queen loses. They are great tragic figures because they represent in single characters perfectly generalized examples of the noblest womanhood under tragic stress.

CHAPTER XII

The Last Comedy and the Last History Play

THE TEMPEST · HENRY VIII

1. *The Tempest.*

THE following paragraph from Richard Garnett has received the approval of George Brandes. Before he quotes it Brandes says, "His [Prospero's] daughter's happiness is the sole thing which greatly interests him now, and he carries his indifference to worldly matters so far that, without any outward compulsion, he breaks his magic wand and casts his book into the sea. Resuming his place among the ranks of ordinary men, he retains nothing but his inalienable treasure of experience and reflection." He then quotes Garnett:

> That this Quixotic height of magnanimity should not surprise, that it should seem quite in keeping with the character, proves how deeply this character has been drawn from Shakespeare's own nature. Prospero is not Shakespeare, but the play is in a certain measure autobiographical. . . . It shows us more than anything else what the discipline of life had made of Shakespeare at fifty—a fruit too fully matured to hang much longer on the tree. Conscious superiority untinged by arrogance, genial scorn for the mean and base, mercifulness into which contempt entered very largely, serenity excluding passionate affection while admitting tenderness, intellect overtopping morality but in no way blighting or perverting it—such are the mental features of him in whose development the man of the world kept pace with the poet, and who now shone as the consummate perfection of both.

One more passage, this time from Dowden, will give us the main features of the accepted criticism of *The Tempest*—criticism largely conjectural, over-idealized, and much too narrow, but no doubt containing much truth:

The tragic gloom and suffering were not, however, to last for ever. The dark cloud lightens and rolls away, the sky appears purer and tenderer than ever. The impression left upon the reader by Shakespeare's last plays is that, whatever his trials and sorrows and errors may have been, he had come forth from them wise, large-hearted, calm-souled. . . . And it will be felt that the name which I have given to this last period—Shakespeare having ascended out of the turmoil and trouble of action, out of the darkness and tragic mystery, the places haunted by terror and crime, and by love contending with these, to a pure and serene elevation—it will be felt that the name, *On the Heights*, is neither inappropriate nor fanciful.

There is no doubt that on a high level of idealism such generalizations as these have not only their appropriateness but their truth. As one comprehends more and more the broader meanings of great literature, one finds new values and new bases of artistic appreciation. But such values are usually not the obvious ones, frequently not those that the author intended or was conscious of, so that these idealistic critical visions sometimes overlook significant things near at hand. Sometimes they do violence to historical and literary truth because, in reading the whole world into the single part and finding it expressed there when it really is not, the critic himself becomes a maker of fiction and not a judge or a mirror whose impressions are controlled by the work itself. There is nothing normally reprehensible about a critic's doing this, and the example before us of the interpretation of Shakespeare in terms of the literary qualities of his latest work is not inherently improbable. But if the idea has truth, it is the truth of a broad symbolism as applied to life and not of fact. We have no knowledge of how Shakespeare felt about his life and his work and know nothing of his state of mind while he was learning his art, writing his comedies and histories and his dark tragedies, and his later, milder romances. The concept of Dowden and others, which has been accepted openly or tacitly by so many scholars and critics, is no doubt probable in the framework of human existence: so we might have felt, and so no doubt Shakespeare felt.

But this attractive hypothesis that the great Prospero is the great Shakespeare, when made the controlling factor of study, the *raison d'être*, of *The Tempest*, fails to do justice to that play as a play and fails to reveal many of its obvious meanings for the age that produced it, for our age, and for all ages; and in failing to allow for such values it does *The Tempest* harm. If serious drama concerns itself with the struggle of the individual man against his environment, one may say in general that where there is no struggle, there is no drama. Timon, as we saw, refuses to participate in the battle of life, does nothing but rail, and loses his vitality as a tragic, or even a dramatic, figure. He does not lose his interest for us as a misanthrope or as a critic of life, but as a dramatic hero he is useless, his story all told as soon as he has been betrayed by his flatterers and parasites. Dramatic character also suffers if, as in the case of the Prospero of the critics, the proponent can do everything, has no opposition, no occasion to struggle. If we think of Hamlet as a typical dramatic figure, we see him poised about halfway between Timon and this Prospero. Prospero has at best too much power for his own good as a dramatic hero. He can do almost everything. It is therefore unfortunate to exalt his virtue to a superhuman eminence at the expense of his dramatic standing, and that is what the hypothesis of Garnett, Brandes, and Dowden tends in some measure to do. One must bear in mind constantly that Prospero has committed error, has suffered wrongs, and has struggled against them, even has some struggles, often overlooked, on the island.

Part of the trouble has arisen from the fact that *The Tempest* is built by and large after the classical and not the romantic pattern. If Shakespeare had written the play, as Dover Wilson thinks he first did, after the pattern of *Pericles*, as a drama which told the full story of Prospero—his reclusive and scholarly habits, the plots against him as Duke of Milan, his banishment, his conquest of the enchanted island by means of his hitherto impractical learning, and the events of the present play—*The Tempest* would be merely a fifth act. Most of the struggles would be over by the time these events happened. Hence the necessity of bearing the full story in mind while the play is being played, so as to give the story of Prospero a weighty classical effect of consummation. To see him only as a magician, philosopher, and superman is to make him very noble but a mere portrait. *The Tempest* is more than the portrait of a man, and it will add to the interest of the play to learn to see it as it was intended to be and actually is. Most modern performances turn out to be series of rather disconnected and vaguely related tableaux illuminated by the eloquence of Prospero and the music of Ariel, with Caliban and the drunkards figuring as an antimasque.

The plot of *The Tempest* is clear-cut and has a certain thematic importance of its own. It is essentially the story of a ruler who, having suffered wrongful banishment from his domain, succeeds in capturing the son of his enemy and in effecting a marriage between that son and his own daughter. The result is that he makes peace with his enemy and regains his state. One very striking analogue to *The Tempest* has been known since the time of Ludwig Tieck. It is *Die schöne Sidea*, a comedy published in 1618, in the *Opus Theatricum* of Jacob Ayrer of Nuremberg, who died in 1605. Ayrer rewrote many English plays, and this fact leads one to suspect that in this case he may have rewritten an English drama now lost. *Die schöne Sidea* cannot be Shakespeare's source, but the parallel is nevertheless striking. Leudolff, prince of Lithuania (or Wiltau) is invaded by Leudegast, also prince of Lithuania, is overthrown in battle, and banished with his infant daughter. Leudolff, who corresponds to Prospero, is a magician and by means of his magic calls into his service an Ariel-like spirit, Runcifall. Leudolff with his daughter Sidea lives in a cabin in the woods. After Sidea has grown to womanhood he captures Engelbrecht, the son of his enemy, who cannot offer resistance because his sword, like that of Ferdinand, is bewitched and sticks in the scabbard. Leudolff compels Engelbrecht to cut wood for him under the at first rather harsh supervision of Sidea. Later without reticence she declares her love for Engelbrecht, who falls in love with her. The lovers exchange vows, elope, and have adventures. Leudegast appears and busies himself about marrying his son off to a Polish princess, but nothing comes of that, and Leudolff and Leudegast are reconciled, Engelbrecht and Sidea are united in matrimony, and Leudolff is restored to his dukedom. One would agree with scholars in the opinion that *Die schöne Sidea* and *The Tempest* probably had a common source.

Another analogue is even more striking in its resemblance to the plot of *The Tempest*, but it also seems not to be a source but to be based on the source. It is to be found in the fourth chapter of a collection of Spanish romances by Antonio de Eslava, *Noches de Invierno*, published in 1609 or 1610. It is also the story of a dethroned ruler, one Dardano, King of Bulgaria. Dardano's enemy is Nicephorus, Emperor of Byzantium. Dardano's daughter, being feminine, cannot inherit his kingdom after him, and Nicephorus tyrannously demands it for his sons. Dardano proposes a marriage between his daughter Seraphina and one of the emperor's sons, but the haughty Nicephorus refuses this compromise and drives Dardano with his daughter from his lands. Dardano knows magic, but has scruples about its use. He does, however, provide himself with a castle under the sea. Seraphina, however, is bored with the quiet life they lead, is interested in love, and knows much about the theories of love. Chance and magic provide her with a husband. Nicephorus disinherits his good son, Valentinian, in favor of his bad son, Julian, and then dies. Dardano, disguising himself as an old seaman, conducts Valentinian to a spot above his residence, and sinks him down to the subterranean palace; then proceeds to arrange for a marriage between Valentinian and Seraphina. Just then a tempest plays a part. Julian has gone to Rome and married the daughter of the Roman emperor. On his way home his fleet passes over the magic palace beneath the sea. Dardano appears above the surface, berates Julian, and wrecks the fleet, and Julian and his bride perish just as they reach the shore. The subjects of the country are struck with this act of apparently divine vengeance and hasten to choose Valentinian as their king. Dardano is restored to his throne, but soon abdicates in favor of his daughter and son-in-law. Thus does Bulgaria peacefully become a part of the Byzantine empire. This Spanish tale in its political intrigue, its adventures, and its use of tempest and sea has much in common with *The.Tempest*.

Finally, Sir Edmund Chambers lays stress on some very close analogues to *The Tempest* to be found in the *scenari* for *commedie dell'arte* "printed by Neri from *Casanatense* MS. 1212 at Rome." Chambers mentions four. "In all of these," he says, "shipwrecked crews land upon an island, and there are love-intrigues between the nobles and the native girls, and comic business in the hunger and greed of the sailors." There is a magician who controls the island. In one of them foreigners are taken for gods as Trinculo is by Caliban. In still another the magician abandons his art in the end. Chambers, following Neri, also calls attention to *Fiammella* (1584), a pastoral comedy by Bartolomeo Rossi, which has the plot of a shipwreck and an enchanter. One cannot tell how old the *commedie dell'arte* are, but they seem to indicate an extensive stage history for a story or stories like that of *The Tempest*.

As to Shakespeare's immediate source, it remains unknown. The current belief is that it must have been an Italian romance or short story. The idea has an interesting history. The unfortunate eighteenth-century poet William Collins was a man of very considerable literary culture, a Greek scholar and well versed in Renaissance literature. Thomas Warton (*His-*

tory of English Poetry, 1824, IV, 309) has the following rather pathetic story that concerns Collins:

> I was informed by the late Mr. Collins of Chichester, that Shakespeare's *Tempest*, for which no origin is yet assigned, was formed on this favorite romance [i.e., Aurelio and Isabella]. But although this information has not proved true on examination, an useful conclusion may be drawn from it, that Shakespeare's story is somewhere to be found in an Italian novel, at least that the story preceded Shakespeare. Mr. Collins had searched this subject with no less fidelity, than judgment and industry: but his memory failing in his last calamitous indisposition, he probably gave me the name of one novel for another. I remember he added a circumstance, which may lead to a discovery, that the principal character of the romance, answering to Shakespeare's Prospero, was a chemical necromancer, who had bound a spirit like Ariel to obey his call and perform his services.

Starting from this idea and equipped with a full knowledge of both Ayrer and Eslava, M. Henri Grégoire in 1940 (*Studies in Philology*, XXXVII, 236-56) discovered, not the Italian short story, but apparently the original source of that story in Bulgaro-Byzantine history. The events concern, in the first instance, Krum of Bulgaria and Nicephorus, the Byzantine emperor, adversary of Krum, whom he at first overthrows and by whom he is immediately defeated and killed. To this story, which furnishes an original for the wrongs of Prospero, there attach themselves certain events concerning one Samuel (980-1014), who like Krum was a champion of Bulgarian independence and seemingly confused with Krum. From the story of Samuel come the essential features of the story in the establishment of his capital by Samuel on the island of Presba, as also this essential plot element: Samuel captures a young prince, son of his enemy, who marries Samuel's daughter. M. Grégoire quotes as follows from the account given in the writings of the Priest of Dioclea:

> Vladimir [the captured prince] in his fetters was fasting and praying. An angel came to fortify him, predict his deliverance, and promise that he should obtain the crown of sanctity. One day the princess Kosara, daughter of Samuel, touched by the Holy Spirit, obtained from her father permission to go with her servants to wash the feet and heads of the prisoners. Seeing Vladimir, and finding that he was good to look at, humble, and sweet, full of reason and divine wisdom, she conversed with him and became enamored of him. She asked her father for the captive as her husband. Samuel agreed to her demand,

and, in presence of all his boyars, granted Vladimir the hand of his daughter and had the wedding celebrated, and restored Vladimir his principality, giving him besides the whole island of Dyrrachium.

We have thus a story of a Bulgarian king defeated by his enemy and retired to an island, who captures the son of his enemy, whom he marries off to his own daughter. It is also to be noted that peace ensues and Bulgaria loses its independence, not by defeat in battle, but by the union of ruling families.

The Latin of the Priest of Dioclea would have made the story accessible to Western readers, and M. Grégoire has so tied the story in with the names of persons and places common to the originals and to Eslava that there can be little doubt that his discovery is valid. The matter is rendered still more plausible by the fact that the whole Bulgarian story appears in the Italian of Abbé Mauro Orbini's *Il Regno degli Slavi* (1601). Orbini's work cannot, however, itself be the common source of the literary versions, since it does not contain certain details present in Eslava, Ayrer, and Shakespeare, such as the carrying of logs by the captured wooer. One point which remains in doubt is the placing of Prospero's prototype on an island. This, according to M. Grégoire, does not occur in Orbini, although it is in the Latin source of Orbini, namely, *Regnum Slavorum* by Diocleas Presbyter. We are thus face to face with the question of whether or not Shakespeare invented the enchanted island. This was the one thing which the older Shakespearean scholars were sure he did do.

There seems always to be an island in the *scenari* of the *commedie dell'arte* mentioned above, and the chances are that Shakespeare did not introduce the island into the story for the first time. It is not an important matter, since the island that Shakespeare uses is so individualized that it may be taken as his creation. Malone read Silvester Jourdain's *A Discovery of the Bermudas, otherwise called the Isle of Divels; by Sir Thomas Gates, Sir George Somers, and Captain Newport, with divers others* (1610) and recognized that he had found an important parallel; for, said he, "the passage in *The Tempest*, in which an account is given of the dispersion of Alonso's fleet, and that the king's ship was, by those who escaped the peril of the storm, supposed to be lost, as well as the peculiar manner in which that ship is said to have been preserved, struck me so forcibly that I thought Shakespeare must have had the incidents attending Somers's voyage immediately in view when he wrote his comedy." In point of fact, there are

considerable numbers of verbal parallels in *The Tempest* not only to
Jourdain but to other accounts of the Gates expedition and the wreck of
a ship on Bermuda. For example, everybody knows Ariel's lines (I, ii,
226-9):

> Safely in harbour
> Is the king's ship; in the deep nook, where once
> Thou call'dst me up at midnight to fetch dew
> From the still-vex'd Bermoothes, there she's hid.

Since Malone's time other accounts of the adventures of Sir Thomas
Gates have been brought into consideration as sources for *The Tempest*,
particularly *A true Repertory of the wrack, and redemption of Sir Thomas
Gates, knight; upon and from the ilands of the Bermudas, his coming to
Virginia, and the estate of that colony* by William Strachey, a letter dated
July 15, 1610, and published in *Purchas his Pilgrims* in 1625. But until
the work of Morton Luce the accounts of Shakespeare's use of these narratives have been confused. There seem to be undoubted parallels in
Shakespeare to only three of the considerable number of writings which
have been brought into consideration, namely, the two mentioned above
and an anonymous pamphlet published by the direction of the Council
of Virginia: *A True Declaration of the estate of the Colonie of Virginia*
(1610). Shakespeare's use of these pamphlets is very vague, merely poetical and suggestive. He has really taken pains to give us an island as fictitious
as Lilliput, without, however, Swift's pretended careful geography.

Shakespeare, as usual, ranged pretty widely in his use of sources for *The
Tempest*. Capell, for example, discovered that he had borrowed as a basis
for Gonzalo's disquisition on the ideal commonwealth (II, i, 147-64) a
passage from Montaigne's *Des Cannibales*. This, together with other
smaller bits from the same essay, Gonzalo renders in the speech beginning:

> I' the commonwealth I would by contraries
> Execute all things.

Steevens found a still more surprising minor source for Prospero, whose
most famous speech (IV, i, 146-63) was apparently suggested by the following lines from Sir William Alexander's *Tragedie of Darius* (1603):

> Let greatnesse of her glascie scepters vaunt;
>   Not scepters, no, but reeds, soone brus'd, soone broken:
> And let this worldlie pomp our wits inchant,

> All fades, and scarcelie leaves behind a token.
> Those golden pallaces, those gorgeous halles,
>   With fourniture superfluouslie faire:
> Those statelie courts, those sky-encountring walles
>   Evanish all like vapours in the aire.

As Shakespeare presents it the thought is appropriate to the scene and marvelously personalized:

> You do look, my son, in a moved sort,
> As if you were dismay'd: be cheerful, sir.
> Our revels now are ended. These our actors,
> As I foretold you, were all spirits, and
> Are melted into air, into thin air:
> And, like the baseless fabric of this vision,
> The cloud-capp'd towers, the gorgeous palaces,
> The solemn temples, the great globe itself,
> Yea, all which it inherit, shall dissolve
> And, like this insubstantial pageant faded,
> Leave not a rack behind. We are such stuff
> As dreams are made on, and our little life
> Is rounded with a sleep.

This passage would not be appropriate to a character who, as critics say, has given over life rather than mastered it.

It is also known that the name Prospero is to be found in Jonson's *Every Man in his Humour*. The names Alonso, Sebastian, Antonio, Ferdinand, and Gonzalo appear in Eden's *History of Travaille* (1577), as also the god Setebos; and Halliwell makes a great point of a character called Prospero in Thomas's *Historye of Italye* (1561). There may be something in it. Thomas says:

> Prospero Adorno was established as the Duke of Millain's lieutenaunt there; but he continued scarcely one yeare, tyl by meane of new practises that he held with Ferdinando, kyng of Naples, he was had in suspicion to the Milanese; who, willynge to depose him, raysed a new commocion of the people, so that where he was before the dukes liuetenaunte, now he was made governoure absolutely of the commonwealth.

Prospero Adorno was, however, deposed and later restored to position.

Ariel (the Lion of God in Hebrew, Isa. xxxix, 1-7) in the Cabbala and in Milton is a prince among the fallen angels. Heywood in his *Hierarchie of the Blessed Angels* calls him "Earth's great Lord" and mentions him as one of four ethereal spirits who control the four elements. In *The Tempest* he is an "airy spirit," and it may be that his special element is air, although he exercises control in the other elements also. In any case Ariel is a superior spirit, one who by the processes of white magic may be brought, in order to work good works, into the services of superior intelligences. Not so Caliban, whose name is apparently a variant of "cannibal." We are told that Caliban's mother was a witch and his father a devil, an evil spirit probably from the elements of earth and water, if one may judge from Caliban's fish-like physique and his groveling behavior. It was certainly a mistake in a recent spectacular performance of *The Tempest* to costume him to resemble an ape, since Caliban is completely pre-Darwinian. Ariel has also minor spirits who serve and assist him. These, we may also believe, are of the better sort and not the evil spirits which are available to the practitioners of black magic. The dividing line among spirits is that which exists between matter and spirit itself, and the law is very general. Anyone who descends in the scale of spiritual being, or who, like savages, has never entered the spiritual domain, anyone who becomes involved in material or sinful action, is thereby subject to fate and not to Providence and is on the level of evil spirits. This is the situation of Stephano and Trinculo, associates of Caliban, and of the base conspirators, Antonio and Sebastian. The good people, including the now repentant Alonso, are not the mere victims of fate, subject to attack, delusion, and torment.

What has been said about sources and backgrounds may serve to indicate the interest and importance of the story that Shakespeare dramatized and the care which he bestowed upon the work.

Prospero is a magician of the noblest order, a Neo-Platonist, who is on his way upward toward equality and union with the gods. Fortunately for the rectification of sundry grievances he has not proceeded all the way. He is still a magician striving to make use of higher powers for good ends. Few thinkers denied that God might grant such powers and privileges to chosen men. But at the end of the play Prospero will cease to practice magic—break his staff and drown his book—not because these instruments have not been good and useful; but because, having set all wrong things right, he will ascend still higher in the scale of spiritual being to the Platonic absolute, the all-embracing unity, in which mundane matters have no part, or rather are controlled without effort by supreme wisdom and supreme goodness. This experience may in its consequences be more practical than it seems. We may very well believe that the returned Prospero will make an excellent duke of Milan as long as he chooses to rule, not by sitting at a desk, holding conferences, inspecting troops, and regulating law enforcement, commerce, and industry, but by merely being Prospero —supremely wise, supremely good, supremely influential. His resumption of his public duties is a practical thing, but not of the sort imagined by critics, who tend to think that, having by too great studiousness lost his dukedom, he will quit studying and attend strictly to business. But the Renaissance put no premium on ignorance.

The Tempest has been particularly liable to allegorical interpretation: many books and articles have been written on the play as an allegory, and the interpretations placed on the character of Prospero are responsible for these allegories. The story of *The Tempest* is typical and widely applicable to affairs and to philosophy. The play is connected with mediaeval and Renaissance culture and folklore. It has many reflections of Shakespeare's work as a whole, seems to present dimly perceived symbols of great but unknown forces, and, finally, has a setting unequaled in romance. Chambers classifies *The Tempest* as a "dramatic spectacle" rather than as a comedy. He even finds it necessary to believe that the play is in some sense an allegory of Shakespeare's life and work. But is it necessary to think of *The Tempest* as a mere pageant? If Prospero is to blame let us examine him more closely.

Prospero is a great character, but his greatness is not primarily his greatness as a magician. The public can think of him as nothing else, and yet we may believe that there were and are plenty of magicians as great as he. Prospero takes pride in his magic and boasts about what he has done, but magic was not his purpose in life. His real objects are more personal and more human. Not only has he the affairs of himself and his daughter to adjust, but he has his own objects to attain. He is a man moving toward the realization of the greatest Renaissance ideal. He has grown on the one side into a competent man of action, and on the other into a man of perfect self-command. He has learned the transitoriness of human existence and the firm foundations of the life of the spirit. It is absurd to see actors who are playing his part moved to tears when he breaks his staff and drowns his book. These things are merely symbols of his growth in competency and are no longer needed. Worldly powers are precisely the things he has learned to control and to assess at their proper values. One group of interpreters have done rather better, indeed wisely, in stressing Prospero's surrender of magical power in return for the chance to live among men. They see that he has learned something about living in the world, and that is exactly what the Renaissance ideal calls for—great power in wise action, great practicality. The men of the age did not think that theory is necessarily at war with practice. However, to their concept of the power of knowledge they add this proviso, that man must not be "lapsed in time and passion" so that he "lets go by the important acting" of a "dread command." Prospero at the end of the play has mastered action and has won his full independence in wisdom and patience. He has learned forgiveness (V, i, 25-30):

> Though with their high wrongs I am struck to the quick,
> Yet with my nobler reason 'gainst my fury
> Do I take part: the rarer action is
> In virtue than in vengeance: they being penitent,
> The sole drift of my purpose doth extend
> Not a frown further.

Prospero is very great, but is he the whole play? Perhaps if in reading and acting *The Tempest* we should put our minds more realistically on the plot, on characters and setting; if we should think of the play as a human story and of Prospero as a man and not a superman, we might be able to rescue the play from its condemnation as a mere dramatic spectacle.

Let us look more simply at the story of Prospero, the banished duke, who has been cruelly treated, betrayed by his brother and his friends. He has not only lost his dukedom, but he has suffered danger and privation. He is shamed in having brought disgrace on learning. There on the lonely island with only his brains and his character to guide him he has mastered a difficult art. It must be remembered that greatness of character was necessary to success in that art. He is eventually able by his superior ability to get his enemies into his power, rectify the wrongs he has suffered, and provide for the happiness and prosperity of his dear daughter. The day of his departure is a different day from that on which the villains hoisted him and his little daughter upon (I, ii, 146-9)

> A rotten carcass of a boat, not rigg'd,
> Nor tackle, sail, nor mast; the very rats
> Instinctively have quit it.

Now, to the Renaissance the loss of a dukedom was no trifling matter, and to suffer wrongs without revenge was an unmanly part. Prospero beats his enemies, and his story cannot have been an insignificant one to the Renaissance. It will be noted that Prospero "requires" his dukedom of Sebastian, accepts it as his right and duty, and will return to Milan to spend his last days. To the Renaissance, rulers did not get worse because they grew older. That *The Tempest* was meant to tell the story of a dukedom lost and recovered is manifest also from the Epilogue:

> Let me not,
> Since I have my dukedom got
> And pardon'd the deceiver, dwell
> In this bare island by your spell;
> But release me from my bands
> With the help of your good hands.

The Tempest has suffered from too much idealization.

The story of the union of Ferdinand and Miranda is linked in Shakespeare and his sources with the story of the captured prince who serves as a means of settlement. It is either a happy invention or a historical actuality by means of which kingdoms were united in peace and amity, and in and for itself it is a love story of great ingenuity and beauty. It will always be so to one who removes his mind from his infatuation with Prospero long enough to contemplate the situation and charm of Ferdinand and Miranda. The felicity of their relations has indeed struck the fancy of the world, even pleased the Restoration; for, when Dryden and D'Avenant prepared their popular version (1670), they went so far as to give Miranda a counterpart, one Hippolyto, a man who had never seen a woman—a truly pitiful principle of symmetry!

Shakespeare does not overtop the modesty of nature, and many critics have written eloquently of Miranda and her lover. Coleridge speaks with his usual insight:

> With love, pure love, there is always an anxiety for the safety of the object, a disinterestedness by which it is distinguished from the counterfeits of its name. Compare *Romeo and Juliet* Act II, Scene ii, with *The Tempest*, III, i. I do not know a more wc_derful instance of Shakespeare's mastery, in playing a distinctly rememberable variation on the same remembered air, than in the transporting love confessions of Romeo and Juliet and Ferdinand and Miranda. There seems more passion in the one, and more dignity in the other; yet

you feel that the sweet, girlish lingering and busy movement of Juliet,
and the calmer and more maidenly fondness of Miranda, might easily
pass into each other.

The love story is an excellent one, and it does not need the supervision of
Prospero to make it so.

An interesting task of interpretation arises in connection with Ariel, who
is an ethereal spirit of very high rank. He is bound to Prospero by a contract which from the human point of view would call for gratitude and
affection. Prospero expects them, and is disappointed when he does not
find them, but there is no emotion in the nature of such spirits. Their one
passion is for freedom. Ariel performs his tasks, evidently enjoys perform-
ing them; but they are irksome and he wishes to be rid of them. The hard
thing to Prospero, who is a mortal, is that Ariel, who is a good spirit, will
leave his service without regret or memory of human bond. Prospero
seems to love him. Prospero's regret is a human regret, and the issue is
between human nature and spirit nature. What a pity it is therefore to
blur this subtle distinction! In a recent performance of *The Tempest* this
elemental spirit, as cool and free as winds and waves, was presented as a
heroine of romantic comedy.

A somewhat similar distinction needs to be made in the interpretation
of the character of Caliban, who has also a mixed nature, evil by tendency;
but he nevertheless has the bad qualities of a demon of earth and water
and not of a degenerate human being. He is keenly conscious of natural
sights and sounds.

> I'll show thee the best springs; I'll pluck thee berries;
> I'll fish for thee and get thee wood enough. . . .
> I prithee, let me bring thee where crabs grow;
> And I with my long nails will dig thee pig-nuts;
> Show thee a jay's nest and instruct thee how
> To snare the nimble marmoset; I'll bring thee
> To clustering filberts and sometimes I'll get thee
> Young scamels from the rock

he says (II, ii, 164-76), and again in a later passage (III, ii, 144-52) of
the most remarkable sensitivity,

> Be not afeard; the isle is full of noises,
> Sounds and sweet airs, that give delight and hurt not.
> Sometimes a thousand twanging instruments

> Will hum about mine ears, and sometime voices
> That, if I then had waked after long sleep,
> Will make me sleep again: and then, in dreaming,
> The clouds methought would open and show riches
> Ready to drop upon me, that, when I waked,
> I cried to sleep again.

As a spirit of lower nature he is born to serve, to hew wood and draw water, and Shakespeare, as well as Bacon, seems to tell us that nature is refractory and has to be forced and compelled to serve man. Caliban is bound to serve, and he is against it. His famous song (II, ii, 184-91) declares a labor strike:

> No more dams I'll make for fish;
>   Nor fetch in firing
>   At requiring;
> Nor scrape trencher, nor wash dish:
>   'Ban, 'Ban, Cacaliban
> Has a new master: get a new man.
> Freedom, hey-day! hey-day, freedom! freedom! hey-day, freedom!

Modern science has changed man's views as to the baseness of matter and its community with evil, but we may believe that the Elizabethans would have understood that all spirits are devoid of human affections and that spirits from the lower elements of earth and water would be by nature evil.

That Shakespeare made up Caliban in part out of bits of travelers' tales about savages, as he seems to have done, is not very significant. All savages, except possibly a few "noble savages," were enmeshed in the natural, elemental universe of fate. Unaffected by Christianity, philosophy, and civic virtue, savages would have been of a lower and evil nature. Caliban is certainly no noble savage, but he is no fool and no degenerate (V, i, 291-7):

> *Pros.*   Go, sirrah, to my cell;
> Take with you your companions; as you look
> To have my pardon, trim it handsomely.
> *Cal.* Ay, that I will; and I'll be wise hereafter
> And seek for grace. What a thrice-double ass
> Was I, to take this drunkard for a god
> And worship this dull fool!

One may take for granted the rapid and skilful management of the drama as drama, as in the scene of the tempest; as also the scheming of Sebastian and Antonio about which Prospero "will tell no tales," the base plots of Stephano, Trinculo, and Caliban, and the charming suggestions of an island in the lonely deep; but one more thing must be mentioned. For some odd reason or perversity certain critics have wished to relieve Shakespeare of what they consider the undesirable responsibility of having written the masque in the fourth act. As masques go, it seems good enough, and in another way it appears indispensable. It offers occasion for two of Prospero's greatest speeches, the one from the fourth act (ll. 146-63) quoted above and the greatest speech of all (V, i, 33-57):

> Ye elves of hills, brooks, standing lakes and groves,
> And ye that on the sands with printless foot
> Do chase the ebbing Neptune and do fly him
> When he comes back; . . .
>   I have bedimm'd
> The noontide sun, call'd forth the mutinous winds,
> And 'twixt the green sea and the azured vault
> Set roaring war: . . .
>   graves at my command
> Have waked their sleepers, oped, and let 'em forth
> By my so potent art. But this rough magic
> I here abjure, and, when I have required
> Some heavenly music, which even now I do,
> To work mine end upon their senses that
> This airy charm is for, I'll break my staff,
> Bury it certain fathoms in the earth,
> And deeper than did ever plummet sound
> I'll drown my book.

There are other elements of dramatic and poetic interest in the play, and one asks if it would do injury even to Prospero to associate with him normal characters and events. There is, for example, something memorable in old Gonzalo, one of those wise and faithful aged counsellors, like Menenius Agrippa, who appear so frequently in Shakespeare's later plays. It is obvious that Prospero would be more fully realized by a fuller recognition of his humanity. One would like to see *The Tempest* read and played with a fairer, broader emphasis on all parts of the play.

2. *Henry VIII.*

When Polonius is recommending the players to Hamlet he declares that they are the best actors in the world for tragedy, comedy, and history; and when Shakespeare's plays were published by his two associates in the King's company, they were divided into "comedies, histories, and tragedies." History plays were certainly a recognized kind of drama. Yet to this day history plays are not fully defined in the minds of critics, who sometimes censure them because they are not tragedies or comedies. History plays may be defined as plays treating historical events, which have no rigid formal structure. If the events treated have a formal structure, history plays will of themselves turn out to be tragedies or comedies. It follows that they may be made up of episodes, even very loosely connected episodes, and that they depict the varied events of an age; and yet they are not entirely free, since they are controlled by the same factors which in the Renaissance were thought to control human events, principally by the belief that God directs happenings in the world and that the fates of men and nations ultimately reveal God's ascertainable purpose. From the events of history might be drawn lessons of the utmost significance, they thought. In other words, historical dramas draw their formal guidance, not from Aristotle and his followers, but from the philosophy of history as then understood. Shakespeare set out in what is probably his last play, *Henry VIII*, to write a history play; and, from the point of view of form, it is one of his greatest achievements. Shakespeare says as much in the Prologue and implies it in the Epilogue. He will present noble scenes "full of state and woe"; he will speak truth:

> think ye see
> The very persons of our noble story
> As they were living; think you see them great,
> And follow'd with the general throng and sweat
> Of thousand friends; then in a moment, see
> How soon this mightiness meets misery.

Henry VIII presents accordingly, not a tragedy, but three tragedies— the ruin of Buckingham, the divorcement and death of Queen Katharine, and the downfall of the great and proud Wolsey. Following these stories, indeed growing out of the midst of them, are the positive justification of a good and great man, Thomas Cranmer, and the vision of a transcendent blessing to England and the world in the birth of Queen Elizabeth. One may well say, as many critics have said, that this ending is not consistent with what precedes, that it does not follow on the premises; but, if Shakespeare replied, "This is what happened, this was the will of God," he would still have the best of the argument and might claim to have presented something interesting, noteworthy, even beautiful.

Henry VIII is written throughout in the latest variety of Shakespeare's late style. It begins in characteristic spirit with a dialogue among nobles which presents the glories and vanities of the Field of the Cloth of Gold. The verdict on the enterprise is unfavorable: the cost of the pageant has ruined many nobles, the meeting of sovereigns has amounted to nothing, and the whole affair has been manipulated for his own ends by the nefarious royal chamberlain and king's favorite, Cardinal Wolsey. Wolsey crosses the stage in his regalia, and he and his bitterest enemy, the Duke of Buckingham, exchange looks of disdain. Buckingham rages against him, his pride, his greed, and his corruption; and the other nobles try to warn the Duke against his danger, to restrain his impulse to follow Wolsey into the King's presence. Their counsel of moderation is ironically wrong. Buckingham's doom is already sealed, and there is enacted before us a cold-blooded judicial murder. In Tudor courts the judge himself acted as prosecuting attorney, and, generally speaking, for a man to be accused meant for him to be convicted. All that was needed in this case were one or two false witnesses, and Wolsey had suborned a group of low-class persons formerly in Buckingham's employment. Only the King's favor could save Buckingham, or any man accused of treason, and the King had said (I, ii, 211-13),

> If he may
> Find mercy in the law, 'tis his; if none,
> Let him not seek't from us.

In the law was neither justice nor mercy, and Buckingham, even at the time of his arrest, bows before his doom (I, i, 202-11):

> Lo, you, my lord,
> The net has fall'n upon me!

When he crosses the stage a condemned man, like his ill-starred father in *Richard III*, his words are among the most telling that Shakespeare ever wrote in all the series of speeches of death-doomed men. Buckingham is personal, penetrating in his pathetic realization that he is treading the same path his father trod before him (II, i, 107-33):

> My noble father, Henry of Buckingham,
> Who first raised head against usurping Richard,
> Flying for succour to his servant Banister,
> Being distress'd, was by that wretch betray'd,
> And without trial fell; God's peace be with him!
> Henry the Seventh succeeding, truly pitying
> My father's loss, like a most royal prince,
> Restored me to my honours, and, out of ruins,
> Made my name once more noble. Now his son,
> Henry the Eighth, life, honour, name, and all
> That made me happy at one stroke has taken
> For ever from the world. I had my trial,
> And must needs say, a noble one; which makes me
> A little happier than my wretched father.

These lines have the simplicities of inescapable doom.

Meantime the second tragic theme has been begun. In the second scene of the first act Queen Katharine has interceded with the King for the subjects of the realm, who, grievously oppressed by Wolsey, have been put under commissions which compel from each the sixth part of his substance (ll. 55-7). She fixes the responsibility on Wolsey, and the King compels him to desist from his exactions. This motive for Wolsey's vindictiveness against the Queen is not stressed, and yet it is taken into account in what follows. Wolsey speaks against the Queen politically (II, ii, 86-98), and yet the King with many oaths seems to clear Wolsey of the charge of having instigated him to divorce his Queen (II, iv, 155-209). Wolsey supported the divorce, or seemed to, but opposed the King's marriage to Anne Bullen; the Queen thinks him guilty, and he probably is so. It must be that we are to believe that the King's conscience, on which he puts such heavy stress, was mainly his passion for Anne, but that he was somehow sincere. The fourth scene of the first act, a brilliant scene at York Place, serves at once to picture the splendor of Cardinal Wolsey and his entrenchment in the King's favor, and Henry's sudden falling in love with Anne. The latter is an event of apparent sincerity, conventionally so in fact; and Shakespeare means to treat Anne well, no doubt as the mother of Queen Elizabeth. To that end he gives us a sort of picture scene between Anne and an Old Lady of the Court (II, iii). Anne is presented as both innocent in herself and reluctant to wrong her mistress.

The Queen at her trial speaks with almost unequaled eloquence (II, iv). She is more passionate and more assertive than is Hermione in the corresponding scene in *The Winter's Tale*, and yet the two women are much alike in their dignity and ability. Katharine verges on a satisfying sort of invective. Her speeches have the same intensely personal quality that characterizes all the eloquence of this play (ll. 13-27, 70-84, 105-21):

> Sir, I desire you do me right and justice;
> And to bestow your pity on me: for
> I am a most poor woman, and a stranger,
> Born out of your dominions; having here
> No judge indifferent, nor no more assurance
> Of equal friendship and proceeding. Alas, sir,
> In what have I offended you? what cause
> Hath my behaviour given to your displeasure,
> That thus you should proceed to put me off,
> And take your good grace from me? Heaven witness,
> I have been to you a true and humble wife,
> At all times to your will conformable;
> Ever in fear to kindle your dislike,
> Yea, subject to your countenance, glad or sorry
> As I saw it inclined. . . .
> *Wol.*   Be patient yet.
> *Q. Kath.* I will, when you are humble; nay, before,
> Or God will punish me. . . .
>   My lord, my lord,
> I am a simple woman, much too weak
> To oppose your cunning. You're meek and humble-mouth'd;
> You sign your place and calling, in full seeming,
> With meekness and humility; but your heart
> Is cramm'd with arrogancy, spleen, and pride.
> You have, by fortune and his highness' favours,
> Gone slightly o'er low steps and now are mounted
> Where powers are your retainers, and your words,
> Domestics to you, serve your will as't please
> Yourself pronounce their office. I must tell you,
> You tender more your person's honour than
> Your high profession spiritual: that again
> I do refuse you for my judge; and here,
> Before you all, appeal unto the pope,
> To bring my whole cause 'fore his holiness,
> And to be judged by him.

The Queen is beaten, the King deserts her for Anne Bullen, and yet twice more we hear her heart-stirring voice—once when in her weakness she is overcome by the cheating churchmen (III, i) and once when she bids farewell (IV, ii). If one understands that the essence of drama is the conflict of wills and motives, one will see that the former of these scenes is very great, comparable to the quarrel between Brutus and Cassius and the interview between Octavius and Cleopatra.

The third of the tragic episodes which compose the body of the play was under way before the defeat of the Queen. Wolsey was marked for destruction. Knowing his pride, his wasteful splendors, his towering selfish ambition, and his unscrupulous civil action, we are in danger of forgetting how great a man Wolsey was. If one has read George Cavendish's *Life of Wolsey* and has studied Wolsey's humanistic activities, such as the founding of Christ Church, Oxford, and of the Ipswich grammar school, one sees that he was not all political but was among the greatest humanists of his day. Shakespeare himself takes a just view of Wolsey. It is embodied in Griffith's speech to the Queen (IV, ii, 48-68):

> This cardinal,
> Though from an humble stock, undoubtedly
> Was fashion'd to much honour from his cradle.
> He was a scholar, and a ripe and good one;
> Exceeding wise, fair-spoken, and persuading:
> Lofty and sour to them that loved him not;
> But to those men that sought him sweet as summer.
> And though he were unsatisfied in getting,
> Which was a sin, yet in bestowing, madam,
> He was most princely: ever witness for him
> Those twins of learning that he raised in you,
> Ipswich and Oxford! one of which fell with him,
> Unwilling to outlive the good that did it;
> The other, though unfinished, yet so famous,
> So excellent in art, and still so rising,
> That Christendom shall ever speak his virtue. . . .

In the fierce partisanship of the court of Henry VIII, Wolsey may have been blackened beyond his deserts. He consented to the dismissal of Katharine, although the King distrusted him in the matter of the divorce (II, iv, 236-41). He opposed the marriage with Anne Bullen, going part of the way with the King; so that Henry called for Cranmer, a man whose political and religious views enabled him to go all the way. Perhaps the historical Wolsey did entertain doubts and scruples as to the King's course of conduct, and perhaps he was religious, rather than moral. He advertises his piety, and it is stressed by others. In any case, he is allowed to repent and die in the odor of sanctity. Perhaps his own comment is adequate (III, ii, 455-7):

> Had I but served my God with half the zeal
> I served my king, he would not in mine age
> Have left me naked to mine enemies.

The fall of Wolsey is brilliantly dramatized. We have seen him in his craft, his tyranny, and his magnificence, and he has had his day. In the second scene of the third act, the earlier part of which is a perfect specimen of Shakespeare's dramatic irony, the King plays with him like a cat with a mouse. As Wolsey squirms and seeks to defend himself, eloquently but in vain, his enemies look on with glee. Later they return to bait him and to rejoice in his arrest. In sheer masculinity the scene is magnificent. Surrey says (ll. 254-6),

> Thy ambition,
> Thou scarlet sin, robb'd this bewailing land
> Of noble Buckingham.

And later he makes the unexplained charge (ll. 294-6):

> I'll startle you
> Worse than the sacring bell, when the brown wench
> Lay kissing in your arms, lord cardinal.

Unexplained, although charges of licentiousness against him were common enough. His rivals are victorious, but Wolsey nevertheless makes a game fight against his tormentors, and to see him thus beset wins back for him the reader's sympathy. When he is left alone he makes his famous speech, one of the best known in all Shakespeare (ll. 351-72):

> Farewell! a long farewell, to all my greatness!
> This is the state of man: to-day he puts forth
> The tender leaves of hopes; to-morrow blossoms,
> And bears his blushing honours thick upon him;
> The third day comes a frost, a killing frost,
> And, when he thinks, good easy man, full surely
> His greatness is a-ripening, nips his root,
> And then he falls, as I do. . . .

This is followed by the no less moving and eloquent speeches to Cromwell (ll. 440-2):

> Cromwell, I charge thee, fling away ambition:
> By that sin fell the angels; how can man, then,
> The image of his Maker, hope to win by it?

The whole Renaissance speaks in those words.

The fourth act has the usual quality of fourth acts in that it deals with consequences. It is made up of two scenes ironically placed side by side— the coronation of Queen Anne and the sad farewell of Queen Katharine. In the latter Shakespeare means to depict the end of a great and good woman and a true Christian. In the former, presented as a procession and by report of the Gentlemen, one can hardly fail to remember a thing of which Shakespeare must have been perfectly conscious although he does not allude to it, namely, the fate in store for the new Queen, a worse fate than that of the old.

In the fifth act the stress is on Cranmer, and those who describe the act as merely a christening might do well to remember this fact. Cranmer stands traditionally as the founder of the order, the religion, and the greatness of Elizabeth's England. He was a forerunner of Parker and even of Burghley, and Henry VIII is given credit for recognizing Cranmer's goodness and greatness and for protecting him against the hostile forces which assailed him. Shakespeare even allows Cranmer to assume the rôle of prophet, and in words more moving, we may believe, to those who heard them than to us, Cranmer lays forth the virtue and the glory of the great Queen.

Modern readers are often surprised to see how well the Elizabethans thought of King Henry VIII. They regarded him as a favorer of learning and a champion of his country against the greed and oppression of Rome. He was the fairy king Oberon to Spenser and perhaps to Shakespeare. He was bluff King Hal, a popular sovereign and one whose heart was tender toward his subjects. The Elizabethans actually knew far less about him than we do, were less offended at his autocracy, and were more willing than we are to condone his immoralities. In modern opinion, on the other hand, Henry's reputation is almost hopeless—despoiler of the church, wasting its wealth and destroying much of its noble architecture; judicial murderer of Buckingham, More, Surrey, and others; husband of a scandalous number of wives, and a Bluebeard. To us he was at best a self-deceiving tyrant; but we are not Elizabethans and, since Shakespeare was, he gives us the picture of a manly man who, when not misled, displayed tenderness of heart, acute insight into affairs and men, and much of the graciousness and magnificence of an ideal king. We find it necessary therefore to build Henry VIII up imaginatively in order to see what he looked like in the eyes of Shakespeare, who evidently thought him sincere (or at least thought that Henry thought himself so), kingly, and even gracious. The play of *Henry VIII* shows no signs of infatuation and no prejudice. Indeed, it seems to say that the most glorious thing about the King's reign was the birth of his daughter Elizabeth, an idea which has a good deal of truth in it to this day.

In the fifth act the King defends Cranmer shrewdly and magnanimously, Cranmer, author of the Book of Common Prayer and in some sense founder of the Church of England, since he established its position and, as was thought, purified its worship. It had not been forgotten that Cranmer was a martyr to his faith, and no part of Foxe's *Book of Martyrs* is more moving than the description of Cranmer's vacillations and his ultimate heroism. There would have been nothing incongruous or inconsistent in Cranmer's assumption of the rôle of prophet. The whole episode of the christening of Elizabeth and of Cranmer's vision can have no purpose other than exalted patriotism. King Henry was probably regarded by Shakespeare as a passionate, erring, inconsistent man who was nevertheless on the side of Cranmer and Elizabeth and therefore on the side of England. Henry impulsively speaks well of the Queen at her trial, and one feels that her dying request in behalf of her daughter and her servants will not remain unheeded (II, iv, 133-43):

> Go thy ways, Kate:
> That man i' the world who shall report he has
> A better wife, let him in nought be trusted,
> For speaking false in that: thou art, alone,
> If thy rare qualities, sweet gentleness,
> Thy meekness saint-like, wife-like government,
> Obeying in commanding, and thy parts
> Sovereign and pious else, could speak thee out,
> The queen of earthly queens: she's noble born;
> And like her true nobility, she has
> Carried herself towards me.

No doubt good words cost little, but in drama words are all we have. Henry VIII at least speaks the right things, for he is represented as a man of easy power and no little danger—reconciling his nobles, dominating his court (V, ii, 25-32):

> Is this the honour they do one another?
> 'Tis well there's one above 'em yet.

Plain-speaking is not without favor in Henry (V, iii, 134-47):

> No, sir, it does not please me.   .
> I had thought I had had men of some understanding
> And wisdom of my council; but I find none.
> Was it discretion, lords, to let this man,
> This good man,—few of you deserve that title,—
> This honest man, wait like a lousy footboy
> At chamber-door?

One feels that a play whose culmination was the birth and christening of the greatest of the Tudors must have had an occasion, and some attempt has been made to find one in the marriage of the Princess Elizabeth to the Elector Palatine on St. Valentine's day in 1613. The newly married couple left England on April 25th in the same year. There were many festivities, and it has been suggested that *Henry VIII* was written to be played during this time; but, even so, it is difficult to see its appropriateness. To be sure, the Princess was the namesake of the great Queen and it is a play of prophecy. James I comes in for a resounding compliment in Cranmer's prophetic speech, but the play glorifies his predecessor, and is in itself serious in tone and rather full of warnings as to the errors and mistakes of royalty.

The date fits well, for through a notorious accident we are able to fix the time of the first performance, or at least an early performance, of *Henry VIII*. It happens that at a performance of this play at the Globe playhouse on June 29, 1613, that famous theater was burnt to the ground. There are many accounts of the fire, and of them Sir Henry Wotton's letter to his nephew Sir Edmund Bacon is most picturesque:

> Now, to let matters of state sleep, I will entertain you at the present with what has happened this week at the Bank's side. The King's players had a new play, called *All is True*, representing some principal pieces of the reign of Henry VIII, which was set forth with many extraordinary circumstances of pomp and majesty, even to the

matting of the stage; the Knights of the Order with their Georges and garters, the Guards with their embroidered coats, and the like: sufficient in truth within a while to make greatness very familiar, if not ridiculous. Now, King Henry making a masque at the Cardinal Wolsey's house, and certain chambers being shot off at his entry, some of the paper, or other stuff, wherewith one of them was stopped, did light on the thatch, where being thought at first but an idle smoke, and their eyes more attentive to the show, it kindled inwardly, and ran round like a train, consuming within less than an hour the whole house to the very grounds. This was the fatal· period of that virtuous fabric, wherein yet nothing did perish but wood and straw, and a few forsaken cloaks; only one man had his breeches set on fire, that would perhaps have broiled him, if he had not by the benefit of a provident wit put it out with a bottle of ale.

It is to be noted that Lorkin and others refer to the play as *Henry VIII;* Wotton calls it *All is True.* This circumstance has caused some question as to whether it was Shakespeare's play that was being performed; but it was Shakespeare's own playhouse, the actors mentioned are King's players, a stage direction after Act I, scene iv, line 49, says plainly, "chambers discharged," and we have *Henry VIII* published as Shakespeare's in the First Folio. It is surely hypercritical to call the matter in question. Wotton speaks of it as a new play, but this does not necessarily refer to a first performance. One concludes that *All is True* must have been a secondary title not reproduced when *The Famous History of the Life of King Henry the Eight* was published in 1623. Some assurance that such was the case comes from the Prologue to *Henry VIII* in which the words "truth" and "true" are repeatedly applied to the play which the audience was about to see. Confirmation may also come from the obvious intention of the author that *All is True* would be appropriate as a secondary title. It would suggest, in the first place, that the play is a faithful representation of history, as it is; Shakespeare nowhere follows his sources more meticulously. The stories of which the play is made up are told in Holinshed's *Chronicle,* which had taken over parts of Cavendish's *Life of Wolsey;* and for the citations about Cranmer, Shakespeare resorts to Foxe's *Acts and Monuments.* The play is to be regarded as a history play, realistic in its presentation, and dealing with true people. Truth and sadness are close together, and the Prologue asks for seriousness (ll. 1-7, 23-30):

I come no more to make you laugh: things now,
That bear a weighty and a serious brow,
Sad, high, and working, full of state and woe,
Such noble scenes as draw the eye to flow,
We now present. Those that can pity, here
May, if they think it well, let fall a tear;
The subject will deserve it. Such as give
Their money out of hope they may believe,
May here find truth too. . . .

As we have tried to show, the play is not planned in haphazard fashion, but carefully; does not break down, as it is often said to do, after the third act. In other words, it is planned as a history play and not as a tragedy or comedy.

The theory that *Henry VIII* was written in part by John Fletcher is an inheritance from the nineteenth century which has been passed down with such authority that it has rarely been called in question. In 1930, however, Peter Alexander presented a careful counter-argument to the effect that the whole play is the work of Shakespeare. There is no external evidence which supports Fletcher's case. Bacon's editor, the great and wise James Spedding, published in *The Gentleman's Magazine* for August 1850, an article entitled "Who Wrote Shakespeare's Henry VIII?" This article advanced the claims of Fletcher as joint author to what is still an almost unshakeable position. Spedding was following a casual observation by the poet Tennyson, recognized as a great metricist, to the effect that many passages in *Henry VIII* were much in the manner of John Fletcher. Fleay, Ingram, Furnivall, the Clarendon Press editors, A. H. Thorndike, and Swinburne himself agreed with Spedding. He had followed a study of double or feminine endings by Hickson, who supported Spedding's contention with further studies. R. Boyle went so far as to remove *Henry VIII* from the Shakespeare canon by argument to the effect that Massinger, and not Shakespeare, was Fletcher's collaborator; but it has been usual to divide the play between Fletcher and Shakespeare, giving Fletcher the lion's share.

A chief difficulty about the partitions of the play between Shakespeare and a fellow dramatist is that they are not consistent with one another. Spedding's division has not been satisfactory to all his followers, who have made changes to conform to their own views. For example, so far as one can see, the latest careful partition, that of Sir Edmund Chambers, achieves a certain consistency by taking all scenes in which the feminine-ending score is below a certain point, and assigning them to Shakespeare, and by assigning the higher scores to Fletcher. There is no sharp dividing line, and one feels that, if Shakespeare were permitted to write more double endings, he would get more and more of the play. This method is actually less satisfactory than that of Spedding, who was guided by what he considered aesthetic considerations, less satisfactory even than the rough-and-ready statement of Dr. Johnson that "the genius of Shakespeare comes in and goes out with Catharine." The present form of the argument is hardly sound. The various scenes of the play range from a considerable number of double endings to a very large number, and it is for one to determine somewhere along the line how many Shakespeare may be allowed to use. Two observations seem worth making: first, double endings are greatest in most, not all, of the lighter scenes and in passages of emotional fervor; and secondly, *Henry VIII* is a consistently planned and well integrated play, following the same sources throughout and obviously bent on reproducing them with the same great degree of fidelity—a circumstance which makes it look like the work of one man.

The scenes reserved for Shakespeare in the mechanical pattern applied are the ones which call for formal, relatively stately, old-fashioned style, and the ones denied him are those of greater emotional appeal. It is even to be noted that in scenes of a more formal and factual quality, when characters grow emotional, they tend to disobey the rules and use many double endings. This is observable in both Buckingham and Katharine in the scenes allowed to Shakespeare. Now, we know that Shakespeare wrote more and more feminine endings as his career progressed. The percentages roughly are these: *Macbeth*, 26; *Antony and Cleopatra*, 27; *Coriolanus*, 28; *Cymbeline*, 31; *The Winter's Tale*, 33; *The Tempest*, 35; *Henry VIII*, 47. Granted a tendency at this time in his career more and more to break down his blank verse style in the direction of prose by an increasing use of double endings and other devices, would he not have been tempted to indulge in his newer manner when he was writing emotionally? After all, *Henry VIII* exceeds *The Tempest* but little more than that play exceeds *Macbeth*. It looks as if we had to do with a habit of Shakespeare's in versification, for excessive double endings do, whenever the situation demands them, creep into the scenes assigned by the critics to him.

Remember that Shakespeare is allowed to inaugurate all themes, but he is not allowed to complete them; and yet, frankly, the voice seems the same and the ideas follow in perfect sequence. He is usually allowed only Act I, scene i (complaints of Buckingham and other nobles against Wolsey); scene ii (Katharine's intercession for the people); Act II, scene iii (Anne Bullen and the Old Lady), scene iv (trial of Katharine); Act III, scene ii as far as line 203 (Wolsey's attempt to ward off the King's anger); Act V, scene i ["altered"] (the King consoles Cranmer). Is it necessary, for example, to believe that Shakespeare wrote the tactful, earnest words of the Queen in behalf of the people in Act I, scene ii, and her defense of herself in Act II, scene iv, and then turned over the pen to his collaborator when he came to her encounter with Wolsey and Campeius (III, ii) and her pathetic farewell to queenship and life at Kimbolton (IV, ii)? How would we have these last two scenes written, since they are the expressions of a heart-broken woman? Indeed, why give Shakespeare the trial scene, for if any passage is entitled to be assigned on stylistic grounds to Fletcher, it is that. Observe this style—

> Sir, I desire you do me right and justice;
> And to bestow your pity on me: for
> I am a most poor woman, and a stranger,
> Born out of your dominions; having here
> No judge indifferent, nor no more assurance
> Of equal friendship and proceeding. Alas, sir,
> In what have I offended you? what cause
> Hath my behaviour given to your displeasure,
> That thus you should proceed to put me off,
> And take your grace from me? Heaven witness, . . .

Here are ten lines with seven double endings and no less than two lingering accents on monosyllables at the ends of lines!

Then again, why allow Shakespeare to write the angry and fearful words of Buckingham and the nobles in Act I, scene i, and deny him Buckingham's farewell, which has no excessive number of double endings? And, finally, shall we allow Shakespeare to write the careful, rather crafty speeches at the climax of the play (III, ii) when Wolsey defends himself and seeks to regain the King's favor, when clarity and convincing argument are all-important, and then call in Fletcher to write the famous speeches which the same character makes in the same scene when he realizes that he has completely lost his hold upon his master and that calamity is upon him? Surely the emotional scenes follow on the others without shock, and the partition would seem to be based on a low estimate of Shakespeare's versatility and a failure to realize the features of his later style. Why, indeed, should the critics assign to Shakespeare the unimportant little scene between Anne and the Old Lady, except that the scene is low (not so very low) in feminine endings? Its verse form is conventional and old-fashioned, probably because Shakespeare is writing a simple dialogue between two very simple people, and his style responds to the situation.

Spedding says,

> In the scene in the council-chamber which follows [Act I, sc. ii], where the characters of Katharine and Wolsey are brought out, I found the same characteristics equally strong [i.e., the qualities of Shakespeare's latest style].
>
> But the instant I entered upon the third scene, in which the Lord Chamberlain, Lord Sands, and Lord Lovel converse, I was conscious of a total change. I felt as if I had passed suddenly out of the language of nature into the language of the stage, or of some conventional mode of conversation. The structure of the verse was quite different and full of mannerism. The expression became suddenly diffuse and languid. The wit wanted mirth and character. And all this was equally true of the supper scene which closes the first act.

What Spedding says is from the point of view of meter entirely true, although he is too severe as regards the wit and liveliness of the little scene, which comes straight out of Holinshed and is one of those static, merely pictorial scenes Shakespeare often uses to enrich background. Henry VIII reproves certain gallants who have brought back with them French fashions in clothing and food and also French vices. The scene is indeed striking in the number of double endings it employs, and one can only suggest that they are there because the scene is light and seems to strive by its mannered style to suggest the quality it satirizes. If there were such contrasts throughout the play, the difference might be more significant; but between these two extremes every possible degree of the employment of double endings is to be found in the play, so that it becomes a question of drawing the line. It seems more probable, since Shakespeare had been displaying more and more fully these very qualities as his work proceeded, that he was merely varying his style to suit his subject. It is rather mechanical thinking to decide that, because in *Henry VIII* there is a considerable increase in the use of feminine endings over *The Winter's Tale* and *The Tempest*, Shakespeare could not have increased still further his use of them.

To do so would be to overlook, on the one side, the many clear indications of Shakespeare's hand in the parts assigned to Fletcher and, on the other, to disregard the vast differences between Shakespeare and Fletcher as dramatic poets. Some of the persons who have entered objections to Fletcher's authorship of parts of this play have said that Fletcher did not anywhere else at any time write anything so excellent as the scenes in *Henry VIII* assigned to him by Spedding and various critics since his time. This is hardly fair. Fletcher was a great poet and dramatist, but his greatness was different from that of Shakespeare, and one finds oneself objecting to the assignment to Fletcher of work of a kind he did not do. Fletcher's normal work is more lyrical, more melodramatic, more sentimental, and in a certain way more skillful than anything in *Henry VIII*. When he treats a situation or issue between characters he holds the development of it back, reveals it bit by bit with dramatic surprise, and sucks the very last bit of sentiment out of every scene.

Fletcher as a writer of blank verse has a style clearly marked and easily recognized. When it is described in metrical terms, the description of it fits in part the style of *The Winter's Tale* and *The Tempest*; but, if the description is carried very far, it breaks down. Fletcher uses double, and even triple and quadruple, endings excessively. Oliphant estimates that Fletcher usually has seventy such endings in every hundred lines. On the other hand, the trick of the multiple ending seems to militate in Fletcher against the run-on line. He is low in this feature, much lower than Shakespeare, and a difference appears in the fact that the so-called Fletcherian parts of *Henry VIII* are far higher in *enjambement* than are plays of undoubted Fletcherian composition. If the question is to rest on metrical grounds, it is difficult to account for this on any theory but Shakespearean authorship. Fletcher is also extremely fond of the trick of stressing an extra accented syllable at the ends of his lines. Such syllables cause a pause in the verse. But Peter Alexander shows that there is an abundance of such cases in Shakespeare's undoubted later plays. Finally, in other tests, such as speeches ending within the line, run-on lines, and number of light and weak endings, *Henry VIII* follows a Shakespearean

pattern, and only in a somewhat excessive use of double endings does
he approach the Fletcherian pattern. One feels like saying something
more in behalf of John Fletcher in this matter. Neither in Shakespeare's
Henry VIII, nor in the work of any other poet, can one find the metrical
movement, the brocaded texture of language, and the response to finer
shades of human feeling that appear freely in all his work. One would be
willing to leave the adjudication of the question of whether or not these
parts of *Henry VIII* were written by Fletcher to a comparison with any
one of scores of passages in Fletcher's work, such as this speech of Bel-
lario's [Euphrasia] in *Philaster*:

> Never was a man,
> Heaved from a sheep-cote to a sceptre, raised
> So high in thoughts as I: you left a kiss
> Upon these lips then, which I mean to keep
> From you for ever: I did hear you talk,
> Far above singing. After you were gone,
> I grew acquainted with my heart, and search'd
> What stirr'd it so: alas, I found it love!
> Yet far from lust; for, could I but have lived
> In presence of you, I had had my end.
> For this I did delude my noble father
> With a feign'd pilgrimage, and dress'd myself
> In habit of a boy. . . .
>   Then sat I by the fount,
> Where first you took me up.

In our judgment, then, *Henry VIII* is a fortunate and beautiful ending
to all that Shakespeare had depicted with reference to the history of his
country and its glory. He had never expected too much of the makers of
history, even kings, and here as before he shows us tragic happenings,
errors, injustices, and occasions for tears. He seems to give final expression
to what he had said in part so often before, namely, that a current of
eternal beauty and goodness runs deep, runs beneath all the ills that
history describes. The Tudor rose blossomed red in the days of Elizabeth.

CHAPTER XIII

Shakespeare as a Citizen of the World

SHAKESPEARE was famous in his own day, popular in the normal sense of that word; but he was not recognized as supreme and probably lacked the suffrages of the weightiest critics of his own day. On the other hand, he was not obscure or neglected by even the greatest critics. For a time, ca. 1597-1600, he was the leading dramatist of the Elizabethan stage. Then he suffered eclipse by Jonson, Chapman, and later Beaumont and Fletcher. Renaissance was giving way to baroque, and his rivals as leaders in a new movement outshone him. Whether they displaced him in popular favor is doubtful. Jonson's gibes seem to indicate that Shakespeare was still close to the hearts of the ordinary people. But, in general, the situation is as suggested by the following words of the dramatist John Webster in the dedication of *The White Devil* (1612):

> Detraction is the sworne friend to ignorance: For mine owne part I have ever truly cherisht my good opinion of other mens worthy Labours, especially of that full and haightned stile of Maister *Chapman*: The labour'd and understanding workes of Maister *Johnson*; The no lesse worthy composures of the both worthily excellent Maister *Beaumont* & Maister *Fletcher*: And lastly (without wrong last to be named), the right happy and copious industry of M. *Shake-speare*, M. *Decker*, & M. *Heywood*, wishing what I write may be read by their light: Protesting, that, in the strength of mine owne judgement, I know them so worthy, that though I rest silent in my owne worke, yet to most of theirs I dare (without flattery) fix that of *Martiall.*—non norunt, Haec monumenta mori.

Webster owed Shakespeare a great debt (his works show it); he means to be generous, but he puts him below the great trio of Jacobean dramatists.

Shakespeare found only one critic in his own age—Ben Jonson—who recognized his genius. But, holding a different theory of drama and being a satirist and a man possibly not devoid of professional jealousy, Jonson condemned Shakespeare on various accounts. Ben Jonson's criticism is none the less valuable and as a whole sound; for Jonson is a genuine critic, and, when all due allowance is made for his philosophy of literature and for the encomiastic situation in which he utters his praises, namely, the publication, as laudatory verses to the First Folio, of his "To the memory of my beloved, the Author Mr. William Shakespeare: and what he hath left us," he does say that Shakespeare was a natural genius possessed of absolute greatness and that he deserved to rank with all "that insolent Greece or haughty Rome sent forth." He says that Shakespeare's works came easily from his pen, a fact attested by Heminges and Condell, who found scarcely "a blot in his papers," and also that Shakespeare labored at his art and was not only a poet born but a poet made. We know that Jonson's praise was a concession on his part, for he made many allusions to Shakespeare of a fault-finding nature. He objected to Shakespeare's lack of classical scholarship, to the wildness of his genius, to his inaccuracy, and to his prolixity. Later in *Timber* and in the "Conversations with Drummond" Jonson is busy justifying himself for his adverse criticism. Hear again his famous protest in *Timber* (after Shakespeare has been in his grave for twenty years):

> I remember, the Players have often mentioned it as an honour to *Shakespeare*, that in his writing, (whatsoever he penn'd) hee never blotted out a line. My answere hath beene, Would he had blotted a thousand. Which they thought a malevolent speech. I had not told posterity this, but for their ignorance, who choose that circumstance to commend their friend by, wherein he most faulted. And to justifie mine owne candor, (for I lov'd the man, and doe honour his memory (on this side Idolatry) as much as any.) Hee was (indeed) honest, and of an open, and free nature: had an excellent *Phantsie*; brave notions, and gentle expressions: wherein he flow'd with that facility, that sometime it was necessary he should be stopp'd.

That is genuine criticism, wrong or right, and we have been almost forced to accept it as the critical view of Jonson's age. It is almost the only considered opinion one finds expressed, and yet there is perceptible even in Jonson another view of Shakespeare which is only partly expressed and largely inferential. Shakespeare was popular in two ways—first in the natural popularity of a dramatist whom the people acclaimed, and not only the people but the literary men also; and, secondly, in personal popularity. There is an immense body of quotations, allusions, and imitations pertaining to Shakespeare in his own and succeeding times. This popular acclaim was not necessarily in Shakespeare's favor with critics then or now; it came from the people themselves. Shakespeare was also personally popular. Shakespeare was a man whom his friends loved. Jonson protests his own affection, and there are other similar cases. The publication of Shakespeare's plays in 1623 and the issue of another possibly larger edition in 1632 are not a bad showing for a dramatist so long dead and already out of style. Drayton, Milton, and many others, contemporaries or close successors of Shakespeare, reflect the opinions (a) that Shakespeare is actually great, (b) that he was popular, (c) that he was lovable, and (d) that he did his work easily. There is the story of the "ever memorable" Mr. John Hales of Eton, who upheld the genius of Shakespeare against the world and said that if Ben Jonson "would produce any topick finely treated by [any of the ancients] he would undertake to shew something upon the same subject at least as well written by Shakespeare." The fashionable Sir John Suckling was a great Shakespeare admirer, borrowed from him profusely, and praised him ardently. Indeed, it may be said that the Caroline poets and dramatists admired and imitated Shakespeare. King Charles I is known to have been a reader of Shakespeare, so that it may be confidently asserted that Shakespeare's fame was growing normally and rapidly when the theaters were closed and the stage and drama put under the ban by the Puritans. Shakespeare offers the most complete expression of the Renaissance spirit and the Renaissance mind, and it is only to be expected that the people, if left to themselves, would discover his importance. England was discovering Shakespeare when in the forties and fifties of the seventeenth century the drama and the stage, even polite literature itself, were overwhelmed by political and religious controversy and by civil war.

But in literature and history, and perhaps in life, admiration always needs a warrant. To admire the wrong thing is vulgar. Those who record their views must always make certain that they are admiring the right things. When critics, who traditionally have the function of recommending books to others, found that it was not proper to admire Shakespeare, his popularity suffered. The natural growth of his influence among people was checked, but never destroyed; for Shakespeare had it and still has it in his power to give pleasure. The things he does and the way he does them give pleasure, and, in the words of Santayana, "whenever the thread of pleasure enters into the web of things our minds are always weaving, a sense of beauty results." But for about one hundred years after the Restoration of King Charles II, the pleasure that Shakespeare gave was not supposed to be a legitimate sort of literary pleasure and was therefore to be deprecated. Shakespeare, however, continued to make friends in spite of his supposed shortcomings, and the great gain that he made in the late eighteenth and early nineteenth centuries was this: critics over all the world became willing to acknowledge that merely to give such pleasure is a justification, and, as is the way of men, proceeded to work out a philosophy which would prove themselves right. All this time Shakespeare had continued to speak to the heart and mind of every man who heard his voice, and that universal appeal of Shakespeare is still his main hope for remaining the foremost literary genius of all the world. Shakespeare still causes the thrill of pleasure to appear in the web of things our minds are always weaving, and the sense of beauty inevitably results.

When the theaters opened again after the restoration of King Charles II, three dramatists emerged. Most of the others were forgotten. One of these was Shakespeare. Ben Jonson was another, and Fletcher (with Beaumont) was the third. The Elizabethan and Jacobean drama had been swept almost away, its traditions almost destroyed; and critically these three dramatists started from scratch. Shakespeare started well, but soon fell behind the other two. The classical theory of drama advocated by Ben Jonson and reinforced enormously by the theories and practices of the French stage now imported by the returning refugees, and indeed holding the general European vogue, militated against Shakespeare. The cliché of Shakespeare as an untutored genius, which has lasted ever since, was almost fatal to him. Nobody had yet had the idea that to give pleasure and satisfaction, merely that, was itself a justification and a passport for the dramatist. That idea had not been discovered and would not be for a hundred years. Drama, the critics taught, was a thing with fixed laws. If a dramatist did not obey these laws he was to that extent deficient and his successes were merely accidental. Dryden was the leading critic of the Restoration, and it was he more than any other man who popularized and enforced these binding restrictions. Dryden admired

Shakespeare and stoutly defended him, but he did so with qualifications, and it is these qualifications which became in the minds of lesser men the things that mattered. Shakespeare, though full of the noblest ideas and equipped with the profoundest genius, was deficient in the matter of compliance with classical rules of drama, derived rather imperfectly from Aristotle. Shakespeare disregarded the unities of time, place, and action. He sinned against the purity of classic tone by the introduction of the comic into his tragedies. He mingled kings and peasants on his stage, and he employed blank verse instead of the newly attested rhymed couplet from France. What Dryden did was to view Shakespeare through a screen of discrimination. Through it he could see Shakespeare's greatness, but his followers, as is the way of small men when they operate by and through a doctrine, could not see Shakespeare at all. They saw only his shortcomings as measured by their standards. The consequence was that Shakespeare criticism and appreciation reached an all-time low about the end of the seventeenth century. This was in the hands of men like Rymer, Gildon, and Dennis. It is, however, evident in the works of persons like Margaret Cavendish, Marchioness of Newcastle, and others that a sound appreciation of Shakespeare lived on among the English people, in spite of all the critics could do.

But there is another side to this picture. The spirit of the age made it inevitable that in due time the age of reason would come to a correct view of Shakespeare. He belonged to the age of art—to the Renaissance. This age was waning in England before he died. Criticism and satire were superseding creation in literature. Rationalism in purpose, variability in form, excessive refinement in method were taking the place of free expression. Neo-stoicism was replacing Neo-Aristotelianism, and what is called the "metaphysical" is evident in Jonson, Middleton, Chapman, Webster, Ford, and Shirley. Shakespeare's productive life coincides in part with that of Bacon, and before Shakespeare ceased to write, the age of science was beginning and the age of art coming to an end.

What was the age of science? It was, first of all, an appeal to reason; and Bacon, Hobbes, Herbert of Cherbury, and other pre-Restoration thinkers were the forerunners of rationalism. Now science and literature are different things, but they are not totally independent. Science affects literature and insists on subjecting it to inquisition. When Shakespeare was thrown up on the shore after the storm of Puritanism, he was taken up slowly but surely by the rationalists of the late seventeenth and the eighteenth centuries, worked on intermittently for more than a hundred years, and finally awarded a just appraisal. To be sure, the men who concerned themselves with Shakespeare were for a long time but feeble scientists—merely literary critics—but they were part and parcel of the age. The phases through which the study of Shakespeare went are precisely the same as those through which the whole world passed. Samuel Johnson, for all his adverse criticism of Shakespeare, is the first who saw that Shakespeare was worth studying, though I have always thought he borrowed something of his attitude from Theobald. Johnson was accompanied and followed by a group of scholars who subjected Shakespeare to genuine study, from which his figure emerged with greater clarity than it had ever possessed before. The great Edmund Malone led this group, but Johnson himself, Capell, Steevens, Reed, Chalmers, and others made notable contributions. Shakespeare had stood the test and now assumed something like his present proportions.

The seventeenth century was a great age in science, and we owe it much in the world. It was an age of measuring and weighing, an age of the adjustment of values. Let us remind ourselves that the seventeenth century invented the telescope, the microscope, the airpump, the thermometer, the barometer, and the pendulum clock. The scientific movement of the seventeenth century began by reviving the ancient doctrine that the universe was built on some sort of fixed plan and that the reason could ascertain the features of that plan. They were at first merely rationalists, but they were soon equipped, not with the ancient tool of rationalism, the syllogism, but with the scientific method of experimentation. At first they said, "According to Aristotle, drama and poetry should conform to these specific rules laid down by the master and practiced successfully by the enlightened French." But later and in due season they looked into the matter more fully and learned that drama and poetry may be excellent and yet not in conformity with the Aristotelian code. No doubt Shakespeare's incurable popularity brought him constantly into the focus of their attention, but, in any case, the eighteenth century came to an end with a mass of information which the scholars had worked out about Shakespeare. They had studied him genetically, critically, and comparatively, and they saw that he was great. They handed this conclusion over to their successors.

Before the end of the eighteenth century rationalism was nodding in its pew. Its day was done. Kant had announced a basis for belief in a set of immaterial values, and Schelling, Fichte, and Hegel were about to reassert and re-explore the kingdom of the transcendental. The Americans and the French were busy overturning the political institutions which rationalism had been so careful to bolster up; or it may be, if you like, that revolution is the inevitable goal of the age of reason. The world was beginning to stir with a new life. The desire to live and not merely to study life was reborn. Burns was singing of the beauty of love. The past, the forgotten, the simple, the rural, and the illogical and unverifiable asserted their claims. Ghosts and spectres came out of their hiding places, chivalry seemed no longer absurd, and man looked about him at green fields and towering mountains. In other words, the Romantic Movement was under way, and Shakespeare was one of the earliest and fullest joys that the romanticists found. That Shakespeare gave pleasure, revealed life, taught wisdom, and manifested beauty had long been known, and latterly admitted. The world now turned to him its full face and by its enthusiasm for him swept him to the topmost height of the world's admiration. The English themselves asserted the greatness of Shakespeare. Scholars like Theobald, Johnson, and Malone did much to establish text and explore background, and Shakespeare enthusiasts like Mackenzie, Morgann, and Richardson introduced Shakespeare idolatry. Goethe, Schlegel, and other Germans came in to assist them. Coleridge, Lamb, and Hazlitt gave full expression to the world's new joy. Shakespeare was, they said, endowed with an insight superhuman in its nature. He was inspired from on high. This they based on a theory of genius which provided for such a thing. Shakespeare revealed an ideal beauty greater than anything to be found on earth. He was wiser than the wisdom of men and more profitable to study than life itself. He was Nature's child. Approached in this reverent and expectant spirit, Shakespeare revealed beauties and excellences undreamed of by earlier students. It was the Romantic critics who gave us the Shakespeare we still enjoy. Hear Coleridge speak of him:

> Make out your amplest catalogue of all the human faculties, as reason or the moral law, the will, the feeling of the coincidence of the two . . . called the conscience, the understanding or prudence, wit, fancy, imagination, judgment—and then of the objects on which these

are to be employed, as the beauties, the terrors, and the seeming caprices of nature, the realities and the capabilities, that is, the actual and the ideal, of the human mind, conceived as an individual or as a social being, as in innocence or in guilt, in a play-paradise, or in a war-field of temptation;—and then compare with Shakespeare under each of these heads all or any of the writers in prose and verse that have ever lived! Who, that is competent to judge, doubts the result?

With the nineteenth century the epitome breaks down by sheer force of numbers. One can only enumerate. On the basis of the revelations of the critics of the earlier part of the century, the nineteenth century with its wonted sincerity devoted itself to the working out in detail of the many virtues claimed by Coleridge and his school. One set of students carried on the traditions of Malone—Collier, Cowden Clarke, Dyce, ten Brink, Halliwell-Phillipps, Furnivall, Daniel, and Sidney Lee. Another pushed Coleridge's study of Shakespeare as critic of life, seer, teacher, and prophet, with all the eminence of art, to its logical conclusions. Here belong Gervinus, Kreyssig, Elze, Dowden, Carlyle, Emerson, Masson, Arnold, Pater, Brandes, Moulton, and A. C. Bradley. On the stage the scholarly exactitude of Coquelin and Sir Henry Irving took the place of the passion of Kean and the rhetoric of Kemble. Late in the century Benson and Ben Greet acted Shakespeare on an Elizabethan stage. Scholars tried to interpret Shakespeare's life in terms of his plays, and speculative scholars constructed a romance about the Dark Lady of the Sonnets. The Baconians and others tried to rob Shakespeare of his honest English renown. The world grew full of Shakespeare dictionaries, concordances, and studies of special subjects, such as Shakespeare's natural history, Shakespeare's flowers, Shakespeare's hermeneutics, Shakespeare's knowledge of history, his heraldry, his language; and, finally and most important, scholars reached an agreement as to the order of his plays and as to his dramatic development. There were great Shakespeare scholars and great appreciative critics in the nineteenth century.

When we come to our own age we reach the period most interesting to us as readers of Shakespeare, and because we are deep in the issues involved, we find ourselves puzzled to define trends and accomplishments. Fortunately the speculations of one intelligent man are about as good as those of another. Perhaps the most striking thing in the Shakespeare scholarship of the twentieth century is the effort made to see Shakespeare as his contemporaries saw him or at least as they understood him. A stubborn and fruitful effort to make vigorous use in the study of Shakespeare of historical imagination has so far marked the century—to find out what Shakespeare said and what he meant when he said it. This impulse has done and is doing much to give Shakespeare a better background, even to realize better than ever before what background is, that is, what part of a man's environment enters into his work. Let me illustrate this idea. We know, for example, that Shakespeare cannot have seen the human mind as John Locke and his followers saw it, that he could not have conceived of the human soul as the behavioristic psychologists conceive of it, that he could not have meant to say anything about the evolutionary hypothesis of Charles Darwin, and that we are doing violence to common sense when we read these things into him. On the other hand, we know that part of his immortality arose from the fact that his interests were largely in that part of the human environment which changes least as the ages roll on. He was interested in love and friendship, in bravery and cowardice, in action and the slothful attitude, in patriotism or the lack of it, in war and peace, in family relations, in the life of taverns, churches, parliaments, and city streets. He was interested in human nature, and his interests have preserved his wisdom for the ages. We know that he practiced a kind of art not even yet recognized as valid by aestheticians. The question which underlies current study is this: Is Shakespeare's own meaning the best possible meaning of his plays? Most competent people believe that it is and that by reading into him ideas derived from later and often less interesting times and situations we are doing him less than justice.

The twentieth century has also given us a group of men, known as the Shakespeare Sceptics, who have questioned Shakespeare's greatness. They have dared to assert that he is not always blameless as an artist or right as a man. Tolstoi assaulted him because he was evidently not a socialist and not on the side of the masses. Bernard Shaw attacked him as a rival playwright and, though he was usually wrong in his indictments, found many flaws in the work of the immortal bard. Robert Bridges and Barrett Wendell showed a disposition to view Shakespeare realistically and critically, and finally L. L. Schücking devoted a volume to Shakespeare's errors and cited the inconsistency of his characters as an evidence of his poor workmanship. E. E. Stoll in this country made bitter attacks on the anachronism of Shakespeare criticism and in a few cases laid rather violent hands on Shakespeare himself. These men and others of the moderns have helped us to realize that Shakespeare was a living man and not an angelic visitant to this planet, and their influence has been salutary.

The technical scholarship of the twentieth century has gone deeper and has developed a new methodology of great promise. A. W. Pollard, W. W. Greg, John Dover Wilson, R. B. McKerrow, and other scholars have thrown great light not only on the text of Shakespeare's plays, but on their composition, their meaning, and the way in which they were performed.

Meantime, perhaps, the man in the street has continued to repeat with satisfaction the dicta of the Romantic Movement. The best-sellers among the recent books on Shakespeare have usually been the most ignorant and the most sentimental. The world has taken Shakespeare to its heart, a particular Shakespeare, which it regards as the only possible one. If, for example, one presents a new interpretation of Hamlet and the audience is popular, one may as well save breath. Nobody will believe that Hamlet is anything but an arch-procrastinator.

What finally can one who is watching the show and keeping up with Shakespeare scholarship and Shakespeare criticism find indicated as to the future? One is not sure that anything can actually be determined, but one might try to say something about this difficult problem.

The critical trend of the age is toward immediacy. Croce is its exponent. His dictum may be said to be that Shakespeare is what you can get out of him, the life in his works you are able to feel, the extent to which he may live again in your mind and heart. This is often (as by Spingarn) taken to mean that scholarship and knowledge have no importance, but this interpretation of Croce is a mistake. Croce begins by assuming a completely informed and completely attuned mind, a mind possessing already all possible and useful knowledge applicable to the matter in hand. To such a mind, we may well believe, the problem is one of complete immediacy, but who possesses such a mind and who can understand without study? In any case, Croce's idea is now the most important idea in the world of criticism. It has also been reinforced by the somewhat kindred philosophy of Dilthey. It is Dilthey and his followers who have insisted that, if we wish to see as past ages saw, we must divest ourselves of our modernity. There is much hope in this point of view now spreading through the present world. As a development perhaps from this current philosophy of criticism there came about after the first World War in Germany a new attitude toward Shakespeare and a new reason for studying him. The disposition is to view Shakespeare as a great guide to life. Friedrich Gundolf's *Shakespeare und der deutsche Geist* is written from this point of view. The most famous chapter in the book is the one entitled "Hamlet ist Deutschland." In it Gundolf finds that Germany failed to act when action was called for, as (according to an antiquated view) Hamlet failed to act when action was due, so that both Hamlet and Germany suffered tragedy. We might deny *in toto* what Gundolf said— that he understands the character of Hamlet or that his country has suffered from hesitation rather than from rash and headlong action—but we might admit that there lies back of his book the thought that Shakespeare has much to teach our world, that Shakespeare is not by any means exhausted, and that each age, as it studies him, interprets him according to its own world pattern, and finds unexhausted riches.

It has been truly said that each age habitually rewrites for itself the history of every other age. They do it largely because they must make a new synthesis of elements. A certain man in a certain age wrote a certain book. He satisfied certain desires of his own, complied with certain restrictions and limitations of his age, and made use of certain liberties then accorded him. This poses the historical problem, which, to put it in Taine's words, is the problem of the man, the age, and the book. We cannot know the book unless we know the factors which produced it. We cannot understand the book unless we know what it means. Much of the detail necessary to make any work of the past intelligible becomes lost in the course of time, but not to know a certain part of that background is merely ignorance. Most of all, we wish to know what the book means to us. We have no interest in it unless it means something to us in our lives in our day. Of course there is the chance that we may discover new and important meanings, that we may hear sweet or significant voices long silent, and give to the forgotten dead a moment of resurrection. This is an attractive aspect, and all true scholars know that the past has much to say that the present ought to hear and would like to hear. But, by and large, we are interested, naturally interested, in our own affairs, and we wish to state what the book means to us. Each age must then make for its own sake a synthesis of a past situation with a present situation. The literature of the dead past thus enters the living present. The making of truer syntheses is the task of the future, a task the future will attend to of itself without prompting; thus the promise of the future with regard to Shakespearean syntheses is that it may make truer and more vital ones than have ever been made.

What then are the things that Shakespeare reveals to all the world? They are elements of feeling and elements of thought. They are the living, speaking phenomena of the earth which we inhabit, particularly those things which our torpid spirits, "lapsed in time and passion," cannot see or hear or feel.

Shakespeare's metaphysical system was not very different from that of the man in the modern street. It sounds complicated, but it was very simple. It had no true metaphysics, no proper dualism. There was a material or perceptible world paralleled by a world of finely attenuated substance, normally imperceptible but likely at any moment to break through into tangibility. This is not unlike the normal consciousness of the modern man. There were two worlds and they had their correspondences. On the more material side were the high heavens, the nine spheres consisting of the fixed stars and the spheres of Saturn, Jupiter, Mars, Venus, Sun, Mercury, Moon—Earth at the center. Earth was made up of the four elements of fire, air, water, and earth. Man on his material side was made up of the four elements; so were the animals, plants, and minerals. Over against this material series there stood a completely correspondent spiritual series made up of the celestial Hierarchy: Seraphim (glory), Cherubim (knowledge), Thrones (power); Dominations, Virtues, Powers; Principalities, Archangels, Angels—each corresponding to one of the spheres. Below them were spirits of fire, air, water, and earth. There were attendant spirits and spirits of the inanimate to the lowest rung of the ladder. Now, a good deal of this was merely a way of talking. The relations of which the men of Shakespeare's time were aware were not essentially different from the relations of which we are aware. And the two ages come together in the statement that man is the bridge between the two worlds.

On two great principles the ages agree. The one is the principle of order, which is heaven's first law, and is obviously the method and architectonic will of God. The material universe is imperfect, dumb, and subject to decay and death; but the correspondence (or similitude or analogy) they believed in was merely a logical form for expressing and rendering effective the other great principle, which is that the spiritual order contains, exemplifies, and expresses complete and perfect truth. These two principles mark pretty closely our limits today. The imaginations of the men of the Renaissance had constructed a world in which truth was vocal. They knew that God had not willed a world in which truth and guidance are denied to man. Theirs therefore was a world that spoke, and Shakespeare, more than any man, became its mouthpiece.

In *Troilus and Cressida* (I, iii, 85 ff.) we hear of order:

> The heavens themselves, the planets and this centre
> Observe degree, priority and place,
> Insisture, course, proportion, season, form,
> Office and custom, in all line of order.

In *The Merchant of Venice* (V, i, 58-65), in their world of astrology, influences, angels, animism, we find them straining their ears, as we do, to hear the cry of the spirit:

> Look how the floor of heaven
> Is thick inlaid with patines of bright gold:
> There's not the smallest orb which thou behold'st
> But in his motion like an angel sings,
> Still quiring to the young-eyed cherubins;
> Such harmony is in immortal souls;
> But whilst this muddy vesture of decay
> Doth grossly close it in, we cannot hear it.

Or hear Pandulph, endowed with the very power of God, using the speaking universe as a weapon against King John (*King John*, III, iv, 149-59):

> This act so evilly born shall cool the hearts
> Of all his people and freeze up their zeal,
> That none so small advantage shall step forth
> To check his reign, but they will cherish it;
> No natural exhalation in the sky,
> No scope of nature, no distemper'd day,
> No common wind, no customed event,
> But they will pluck away his natural cause
> And call them meteors, prodigies and signs,
> Abortives, presages and tongues of heaven,
> Plainly denouncing vengeance upon John.

Hear what Calpurnia says to Julius Caesar (II, ii, 12-26) about the portents in the streets of Rome, or consider the intimacy of the Elizabethan with the skies, when Richard of Gloucester beholds three suns in the heavens (*3 Henry VI*, II, i, 26-32):

> Three glorious suns, each one a perfect sun;
> Not separated with the racking clouds,
> But sever'd in a pale clear-shining sky.
> See, see! they join, embrace, and seem to kiss,
> As if they vow'd some league inviolable:
> Now are they but one lamp, one light, one sun.
> In this the heaven figures some event.

That pulsating world of spirits which Prospero describes (*The Tempest*, V, i, 33-57) is but an analogue to the modern world of chemistry, physics, and biology.

The dividing line between the spiritual and the material we express in our own terms, though Shakespeare's way still seems to us vaguely within the range of possibility. He spoke in terms of spirits, ghosts, fascination, dreams, and curses. John of Gaunt (*Richard II*, II, i, 31 ff.) in the presence of his death says not unintelligibly,

> Methinks I am a prophet new inspired
> And thus expiring do foretell...

There is a thrill of reality in the dream of Clarence (*Richard III*, I, iv, 2 ff.), and Lady Macbeth's sleep-walking is more than somnambulism. Supernatural forces are at work. The ghost of Hamlet the Elder is not mere hocus-pocus, and we might admit him to the modern world, where he would be none the less a ghost, under the shrewd proviso that Hamlet makes (II, ii, 627-32):

> The spirit that I have seen
> May be the devil: and the devil hath power
> To assume a pleasing shape; yea, and perhaps
> Out of my weakness and my melancholy,
> As he is very potent with such spirits,
> Abuses me to damn me.

Is there not still a shiver in the curses of Queen Margaret and in those of Pandulph and of King Lear?

But almost the best illustration of the fact that Shakespeare's world was alive is to be seen in his animism. How he characterizes the dogs he catalogues in *Macbeth* and *King Lear*! Rambures in *Henry V* (III, vii, 150-2) says,

> That island of England breeds very valiant creatures; their mastiffs are of unmatchable courage.

One likes Shylock's phrase "a harmless necessary cat" (*Merchant of Venice*, IV, i, 55). We find in *Venus and Adonis* (l. 1105) "this foul, grim, and urchin-snouted boar"; in *The Rape of Lucrece* it is said "Night-wandering weasels shriek to see him there," and again in the former poem (l. 85):

> Upon this promise did he raise his chin,
> Like a dive-dapper peering through a wave,
> Who, being look'd on, ducks as quickly in.

Note this language (*Henry VIII*, V, iii, 126-7):

> You play the spaniel,
> And think with wagging of your tongue to win me,

and this (*Henry V*, I, ii, 169-72),

> For once the eagle England being in prey,
> To her unguarded nest the weasel Scot
> Comes sneaking and so sucks her princely eggs.

We know "the joiner squirel" in *Romeo and Juliet* (I, v, 69), the "old mole," that "worthy pioner" in *Hamlet* (I, v, 163), the "rugged Russian bear," the "arm'd rhinoceros," and the "Hyrcan tiger" in *Macbeth* (III, iv, 100-1).

In *The Two Gentlemen of Verona* (III, ii, 80-1) we are told of Orpheus' lute which could

> Make tigers tame and huge leviathans
> Forsake unsounded deeps to dance on sands.

We hear of unicorns betrayed with trees, cockatrices with death-darting eyes, and the phoenix, the Arabian bird, the bird of wonder.

Persons are made known in this animated talk of animals. Maria in *Twelfth Night* (III, ii, 70) is described as "the youngest wren of nine"; Rosalind assures Orlando in *As You Like It* (IV, i, 156-7),

I will laugh like a hyen, and that when thou art inclined to sleep.

And in *Much Ado About Nothing* (II, i, 211) Benedick declares that Claudio, like a "poor hurt fowl," will now "creep into sedges." Shakespeare's world of created things tingles with vitality; it has, we say, spirit.

What then is this spirit which is the enduring quality of Shakespeare? To read him well is to learn the answer to this question. He would so expand our minds and hearts that all the world would speak to us and through us. He would, as truly as Shaftesbury, make man a part of nature, so that there would be nothing in the range of God's creation with which we have not brotherhood. Spirit as Shakespeare perceives it is insight, sympathy, and imaginative penetration into the deeper unity and harmony that all the greatest thinkers have sought and found in the created universe.

Shakespeare thus had sensitivity to the world in which he lived and to the world in which we live, a sensitivity rarely found in the modern world except among the greatest poets and the greatest scientists. Not the least of Shakespeare's services to the world is his power to awaken us from our dullness, our insensibility, and our mechanical absorption in ourselves and our affairs. This is to say rather more than that he was one of our greatest poets. Shakespeare was a man of powerful intellect. He is so imaginative, so objective, so dramatic that one tends to forget that he was also a very great thinker, who did actually possess the power of deep, true, coordinated thought. He is actually one of the world's greatest thinkers. The very fact that Shakespeare is so widely quoted over the whole world and that he has entered into all language and into the substance of all modern thought is not solely, or perhaps mainly, due to his artistry, but to the breadth, the perspicacity, and the validity of his thought. One recognizes the greatness of the ideas that are bodied forth in *Hamlet*, *King Lear*, *Macbeth*, and *Antony and Cleopatra*, indeed in all his plays. These are, for the most part, concrete applications of Shakespeare's wisdom to human affairs; but he turns out also to have been a great thinker in the realm of the general and the abstract. He had a great, original mind like Bacon's, and it is not too much to say that Shakespeare had a power of observation of men and things and of clear, cool judgment not inferior to Bacon's. For example, one might pick out and rearrange expressions of Shakespeare's thought about hundreds of subjects important to human life and find consistent wisdom, rich and vast. As Professor George Coffin Taylor has shown, we should find in such a collection of utterances a record of what was perhaps the richest mind of the Renaissance. A prose Shakespeare in essayistic or treatise-like form, and thus in part robbed of its poetic illumination, would have a substantial, intellectual value like that of Montaigne and Bacon. The old saying, that, if the knowledge and wisdom of antiquity were lost, they might be restored from the works of Virgil, might be adapted and applied with equal propriety to Shakespeare and his age, so great is the range of his knowledge and the power of his thought.

In the consideration of Shakespeare as a universal genius and a citizen of the world, many other things might be discussed, but one more in particular needs attention. There is in Shakespeare an unequaled greatness of style. This style is so varied according to character, mood, and situation that his words may not be at first recognized as the utterance of one man; but by long familiarity and repeated comparison with the utterances of other writers, his style reveals itself as the voice of one man, although it seems to be also the voice of every man. It rises in greatest moments to the level of supreme poetic beauty. At those times one perceives a blending of harmony and power which might be described as the music of all the greatest singers. In Shakespeare there is both expression and communication—the expression of feeling and thought of general significance, and with them too always the utterance of ideas applicable to particular people and particular situations. Shakespeare is completely personalized. There is always the flow of event and circumstance and always general human significance. When Richard II and Cardinal Wolsey comment on mutability in human life, when Romeo and Florizel give voice to the raptures of youthful love, when Hamlet, Othello, and Coriolanus utter thoughts of defeat and death, there is perfect dramatic appropriateness in every case, but there is also the general voice of humanity. The general seems to blend with the particular and to reinforce it. In Shakespeare great events and great poetry seem always to go hand in hand. This blending of the individual with the race is seen over and over again in Milton and other great poets. How else could one interpret a sonnet like "On the Late Massacre in Piedmont"?

> Avenge, O Lord, thy slaughtered saints, whose bones
> Lie scattered on the Alpine mountains cold.

Or how else Keats's sonnet "When I Have Fears That I May Cease To Be"?

One kind of style found abundantly in Shakespeare, a style of both general and particular application, has the neat exactitude of Chaucer and Pope. This style is widely scattered in Shakespeare's works and has been culled out for us in the form of an incredibly extensive body of familiar quotations. Our language is studded with Shakespearean gems, neatly turned phrases and expressions, naturalistic or aphoristic passages which have lost their dramatic environment and float about in the common speech of man. Their general use is often inconsistent with their origin. Did Falstaff utter the Platonic commonplace, "The better part of valour is discretion"? And who said, "And hold, as't were, a mirror up to nature"? And who was it, though "to the manner born," held it "a custom more honoured in the breach than in the observance"? How calmly the world quotes maxims from that villain Iago! Shakespearean language is everywhere: "I have not slept one wink." "I am a man more sinn'd against than sinning." "It did me yeoman's service." "Lord, what fools these mortals be!" "The course of true love never did run smooth."

In considering matters of style one needs to remember that the exigencies of Shakespeare's art and the structure of his stage caused him to write prevailingly in the style of oratory. Generally speaking, one might say that situations of conviction or persuasion as well as of exhortation call forth oratorical excellence. One can almost measure the seriousness of a situation in Shakespeare by the length and strength of its speeches, for his drama had mainly this device with which to accomplish its ends. Shakespeare and his age believed in the power of the spoken word, believed that uttered truth was irresistible. It is therefore slightly unfair to use the word "rhetorical" as a deprecatory word, since Shakespeare was compelled by his very artistic medium to be a rhetorician. He wrote as his meticulous age thought writing must be done, and nature and art come together in Shakespeare. William Shakespeare and Alexander Pope differ in a thousand ways, and yet there is no inconsistency in quoting Pope's statement of a fundamental principle of all art:

> Those rules of old discovered, not devised,
> Are Nature still, but Nature methodized;
> Nature, like liberty, is but restrained
> By the same laws which first herself ordained.

There is less justification for Shakespeare in his frequent overuse of current literary clap-trap: mythological allusion, euphuism, stichomythia, oxymoron, far-fetched metaphor, and puns on what seem to us impossible occasions. One can only say that although Shakespeare is often guilty of employing too much literary artifice, he is usually not excessive and rarely loses sight of his dramatic purpose. In general, he is skilful in the employment of the mannered style of the Renaissance. Shakespeare has also the gift of lyrical beauty second to none in that great poetical age. His naturalness, his exalted eloquence, his beauty of language, his perfection of wit, and his charm of humor compel us, in concluding, to agree with Ben Jonson:

> He was not of an age, but for all time!
> And all the Muses still were in their prime,
> When like Apollo he came forth to warme
> Our eares, or like a Mercury to charme!
> Nature her selfe was proud of his designes,
> And ioy'd to weare the dressing of his lines!

Index